Tastes
of the Times

Published by Tyson Foods, Inc.
Springdale, Arkansas

*Investing our experience
in your success.*

Tastes of the Times

Great chicken recipes from foodservice kitchens across America

Tyson®

Publisher: Tyson Foods, Inc., Springdale, Ark.

Agency: Noble & Associates, Springfield, Mo.

Photography: Greg Booth + Associates, Dallas, Tex.

Cover Photography: Stewart Charles Cohen, Dallas, Tex.

Illustrations: Lee Duggan, Alpharetta, Ga.

Paintings of John and Don Tyson: Bernie Fuchs, Westport, Conn.

Lithography: Hanson Graphics, Memphis, Tenn.

Printing: The Wimmer Companies, Memphis, Tenn.

Credits

Jane Adams, Melanie Barnard, Steve Bishop, Jim Burkholder, Dave Carlin,
Ruth Clemmons, Mike Cooper, Diane Cramer, Jim Crowell, Jerry Dowd, Nancy Farthing,
Brian Fewell, Allie Frankfurt, LeAnne Garoutte, Rose Grant, Brian Griffin, Sandi Hagler,
Rebecca Hammond, Paul Hanson, Malissa Hauswirth, Sandy Haymes, Katey Hobbs,
Kat Hughes, Wendy Hughes, Leslie Hutter, Bobbi Hutton, Josh Isenberg, Miles James,
Robin Jensen, Teresa Johnson, Debbie Klein, Florence Kocour, Greg Lee,
Sherry Loumakis, Ben Marshall, Cathy McCue, Mike McNett, Mandy Mitchell,
Darla Moore, Kathy Nehmer, Bob Noble, Barbara Page, Kyle Pertuis, Kristy Pierce,
Steve Popp, Dawn Rhodes, Jeanette Richardson, Cleta Selman, Judy Sipe, Jane Sowell,
Freddie Strange, Katherine Tsolakis, Julie Tumy, Don Tyson, John Tyson,
Diane Westbrooke, Glen Wimmer, Stacey Wingate, Chris Wolf

Special thanks to Oneida Foodservice for providing much of the tableware featured in
the photographs. A complete listing of pages featuring Oneida tableware is on page 238.

Cover and inside cover photographs were taken at James at the Mill, Johnson, Arkansas.

Library of Congress Catalog Card Number: 98-61123

ISBN 0-9665996-0-8

First Edition: November 1998

For information about Tyson products or how to order additional copies of *Tastes of the
Times*, please visit www.tyson.com or call 1-800-24-TYSON, extension 106.

Menu

"There is no substitute for quality."

John Tyson

Tyson's Legacy of Changing with the Times

When my dad, John Tyson, moved our family to Springdale, Arkansas, in 1931, I was just a baby.

We arrived in a beat-up old truck with half a load of hay and a nickel to our name. Dad found work transporting live chickens from growers in northern Arkansas to markets in Kansas City and St. Louis, and during the next 5 years devised ways to carry live birds farther than anyone had previously attempted. As a result, he became one of the area's most successful haulers.

In 1936, Dad heard that chickens were bringing higher prices in Chicago, and so, inspired by opportunity, he decided to test his limits.

With a little help from one of his friends, he bought 500 Arkansas spring chickens, loaded them on his truck, and set out for Chicago, where he sold them for a good profit. When he got home, Dad bought more chickens, then turned around and made the trip again. Within a year, he was delivering chickens to major cities from Houston to Detroit.

It wasn't long before he needed more chickens than his suppliers could provide, so he branched out and built a hatchery, then a feed mill. In time, he also bought broiler farms and began selling chicks to local farmers. When the market declined during the late 1940s, my father guaranteed that farmers who bought Tyson chicks would have customers for their grown birds. It was a promise that kept our family business growing while other businesses were failing. Our growth led to the incorporation of Tyson Feed and Hatchery in 1947.

I joined the company in the early '50s, which turned out to be a very exciting period of growth for us. During the next 15 years we built our first processing plant, established a frozen-distribution system, changed the company's name to Tyson's Foods, and developed new products, such as Cornish hens and roasters. By 1964, half of all our profits came from the sale of products we had developed within the previous 2 years.

Today, I am proud to say that Tyson is over 72,000 members strong, supplies America with more than 41 million chickens each week, and value-adds chicken in most every way imaginable. The company has implemented many changes in the way chicken is grown, transported and prepared since my dad hauled that first load of chickens to Chicago. And I think we have succeeded because our commitment to quality and service has never wavered—just as he would have wanted it.

Don Tyson

Staying in Step with the Tastes of the Times

Tastes of the Times is a collection of over 200 chicken recipes, plus nearly 60 additional recipes for sauces, dressings, and side dishes, intended to help foodservice operators impress today's menu-savvy patrons. It is a tribute to the remarkable versatility and popularity of chicken—once referred to as "the poor man's meat" and now, arguably, the world's most popular source of protein.

Tastes of the Times is a celebration of America's eclectic and sophisticated palate, exemplified by its regional and ethnic variety, and both its refreshingly new and tried-and-true recipes. It salutes the accomplishments of foodservice operators who proudly responded to our recipe search question, "Are you serving the greatest chicken recipes of our times?"

Our mail was flooded with recipe submissions. Each was held up against strict judgment criteria for originality, ease and efficiency of preparation, and trend relevance. Many of the final recipes demonstrate that made-from-scratch flavor, flair, and originality often can be achieved with timesaving ingredients and minimal preparation steps.

Tastes of the Times presents you with chicken dishes to use across the menu—though we're still looking for that great dessert recipe—and every daypart. There are chapters devoted to starters, salads, bowls, handheld meals, one-dish meals, and center-of-plate entrees.

Tyson is proud of the outcome of this year-and-a-half-long project, and looking back, perhaps our greatest challenge was narrowing the field of entries. So to each of those who shared in bringing this collection of recipes together we say, "Thank you for investing your experience in our success."

One day, we may all look back and say, "Menuing chicken sure has changed since then." But for now, we hope you will find *Tastes of the Times* a useful, profitable, and enjoyable source of ideas for making the most of chicken.

Making the Most of Tastes of the Times

Tastes of the Times is a concerted effort to share new ideas and perspectives with operators who want to take advantage of the growing potential in menuing chicken. And Tyson has attempted to structure it in ways that should make the recipes easy to review and implement.

Tastes of the Times recipes came from foodservice operations across America, so they are well suited for today's foodservice kitchen needs. Many of them utilize common back-of-the-house ingredients and laborsaving steps and ingredients.

Each recipe has been kitchen tested and written with an awareness of proper food safety guidelines for handling, preparing, and holding chicken. Within the methods for each recipe, holding temperatures for cold chicken are highlighted in blue, and those for warm holding are highlighted in pink. The recipes do not contain hold and chill times because those may vary from operation to operation; however, we do encourage you to establish and follow safety guidelines.

Recipes are scaled in two quantities—a four-serving quantity suitable for your own sampling and a 24-serving size for full-scale preparation. They have been edited and formatted by foodservice professionals in an effort to make them easy

Bake

 Beat, whisk

 Boil, heat, simmer

 Broil

 Brush

 Char-grill

 Chop, cut, dice, mince, slice, sliver

 Deep-fry

 Grill

 Mix, stir

 Pour

 Process

 Slice pizza

 Toss

to understand and follow. And, although each recipe calls for a specific product, feel free to use your judgment in substituting alternative Tyson products. Each chicken recipe also includes nutritional information to accommodate operators who need it.

Tastes of the Times includes interesting and imaginative culinary hints that range from variations on recipe ingredients to garnish prep techniques. Some recipes are supported with complete complementary recipes to help you bring a whole plate theme to life. There are even historical tidbits and food-related quotes peppered throughout the book to provide entertainment and insight into recipes, Tyson, and chicken in general.

Tastes of the Times includes over a hundred photographs, showcasing plated recipes or recipes as they might appear in a line-service or take-out application. Illustrations throughout the book will help you visualize many of the tips and techniques that are included and will also be useful in reviewing these techniques with your kitchen staff. A complete listing of these illustrations can be found in the index under the heading Illustrations.

A **FAST FACTS VIA FAX**™ Business Tool number is included with each recipe. This allows you to immediately receive an extra kitchen copy of any recipe just by calling our toll-free number and entering the Business Tool number and your fax number. This makes it easy to put the recipe into your reference file and into the hands of the people who are going to prepare it.

Symbols are used to make using *Tastes of the Times* as easy as possible. Recipe methods are illustrated with icons depicting specific preparation steps. They are shown at the left.

Color-coded triangles highlight noteworthy features of each recipe that make it particularly well suited to special foodservice needs or applications. Here is a brief explanation of each one.

Speed-Scratch   *Kid Friendly*   *Lighter Fare*   *Line Service*   *Takeout*

Takeout—Servings from these recipes are particularly suited to being transported and reheated.

Line Service—These recipes can be prepared in sufficient quantities, held, and served in ways that are appropriate for line service operations.

Lighter Fare—These recipes contain approximately 1 gram of fat per ounce of food and will appeal to diet-conscious patrons.

Kid Friendly—These recipes, or an adaptation of them, are great for kids.

Speed-Scratch—Each recipe contains no more than 10 ingredients and utilizes value-added products to replace labor-intensive steps wherever possible. (Garnishes are not included in the 10-or-less-ingredients criteria used to qualify these recipes as speed-scratch.)

Finally, *Tastes of the Times* includes a comprehensive cross-referenced master index that allows you to search the contents of the book by recipe name, chapter, ethnic/regional profile, illustration content, key ingredient, Tyson product, chicken product category, and color-coded triangle (Takeout, Line Service, Lighter Fare, Kid Friendly, and Speed-Scratch).

*"Hunger is the first course
of a good dinner."*

French proverb

Starters

Exploring new beginnings for menus

Greek banquets in Plato's day commenced with little snacks called *tragemata,* which were intended to prime guests' palates for the evening to come. Many of the rich, flavorful foods commonly associated with appetizer menus—pâtés, foie gras, caviar—have been brought to tables for hundreds of years. But when these starter courses were first called "appetizers" is uncertain.

Certainly, chicken's most famous starter application hails from Buffalo, New York, where a resourceful restaurateur whipped up the very first order of Buffalo Wings back in 1964. Wings continue to perform as the second best-selling item on America's appetizer menus, ranking only behind chicken strips.

Today, starters go way beyond the little appetizers that stimulate appetites for the meals to come. Nationwide, the appetizer section is the fastest-growing menu category. In many operations, it has even become a testing ground for new entrees, because customers tend to be more willing to experiment with foods they can sample. Regardless of what they are called—appetizers, tapas, hors d'oeuvres, antipasti, zakuski, or mezes—starters are good for business.

Many of the recipes in this chapter are large enough to share and could easily work as entrees. From the intensely flavorful Chicken and Portobello Strudel to the Tropical Chamorro Chicken, these recipes will help pique patrons' curiosity and appetites with reputation-building success.

Submitted by Stephen Blackler
Century Management Systems
Wilkes-Barre General Hospital
Wilkes-Barre, Pa.

Spicy Chicken Satay

The char-grilled tenderloins in this peppery tongue teaser titillate the taste buds with notes of cayenne pepper, black pepper, and habañero-hot Scotch bonnet chile peppers. Don't be intimidated by the long list of marinade ingredients. The recipe goes together quickly and tastes terrific.

Lighter Fare *Line Service* *Takeout*

INGREDIENT	QUANTITY		METHOD
	4 servings	24 servings	
1 Tyson Ready-to-Cook Flavor-Redi® Savory Tenderloins, frozen	12	72	Place in full-size steam table pans. (Use half-size pan for smaller quantity.)
2 Peanut oil	3 tbsp.	1 cup	Combine in bowl and mix thoroughly. Pour over chicken. Cover and marinate below 40°F for 8 hours.
Sesame oil	⅓ cup	2 cups	
White wine, dry	⅓ cup	2 cups	
Mustard, Dijon	1 tbsp.	⅓ cup	
Sake rice wine	1 tbsp.	⅓ cup	
Rice wine vinegar	1 tbsp.	⅓ cup	
Soy sauce	2 tbsp.	¾ cup	
Worcestershire sauce	½ tbsp.	3 tbsp.	
Cayenne pepper sauce	½ tbsp.	3 tbsp.	
Honey	2 tbsp.	¾ cup	
Green onions, fresh, thinly sliced	1 tbsp.	⅓ cup	
Shallots, fresh, minced	2 tsp.	¼ cup	
Garlic, fresh, minced	1 tsp.	2 tbsp.	
Sesame seeds, whole, toasted	2 tsp.	¼ cup	
Scotch bonnet chiles, fresh, seeded, minced (p. 172)	1 tsp.	2 tbsp.	
Thyme, fresh, minced	1 tsp.	2 tbsp.	
Black pepper, coarse	1 tsp.	2 tbsp.	
Lime juice, fresh	½ tbsp.	3 tbsp.	
Gingerroot, fresh, peeled, grated	1 tsp.	2 tbsp.	
3 Thin wooden skewers, soaked in water	12	72	Remove chicken from marinade and thread each tenderloin on a skewer. Char-grill over high heat for 2 to 3 minutes on each side or until chicken is no longer pink. Remove from grill. Keep warm above 140°F.
4 Mango slices, fresh	8	48	*To assemble single serving:* Arrange 3 skewers on plate. Garnish plate with 2 mango slices, 1 kiwi slice, and 1 strawberry.
Kiwi slices, fresh	4	24	
Strawberries, fresh, whole	4	24	*Serve with peanut sauce.*

Portion: 4 ounces
Nutritional Data/Portion: Calories 160, Protein 26 g, Fat 5 g, Carbohydrate 2 g, Cholesterol 50 mg, Sodium 500 mg

For a **FAST FACTS VIA FAX**™ copy of this recipe, call 1-800-223-3755 and enter Business Tool 2658.

The Scotch bonnet chile is the Jamaican cousin of the habañero chile. This small, irregularly shaped pepper ranges in color from yellow to orange-red and averages between 80,000 and 300,000 Scoville Heat Units compared to the jalapeño, which typically measures between 2,500 and 10,000 SHU.

Habañero chiles may be substituted for the Scotch bonnet chiles.

In 1912, Wilbur Scoville devised the Scoville Organoleptic Test to measure the heat levels of chiles. And even though scientists today use liquid chromatography to determine capsaicin levels, overall heat is still measured in Scoville Heat Units.

This recipe is pictured on the inside cover.

Submitted by Ma. Emelita G. Rudolph
Rudolpho's Restaurant
Saipan, United States Commonwealth
of the Northern Mariana Islands

This recipe works well in a variety of applications— served on a bed of mixed salad greens, stuffed into a raw or roasted chile (poblano or Anaheim), wrapped in a tortilla, or presented in a pineapple half as pictured.

Chamorro food is a mix of Spanish, Filipino, and Pacific influences. On Guam, Chamorro dishes are created with finadene, which is hot sauce made with hot red peppers, soy sauce, lemon juice, and chopped onion. Chamorro cooking is not served widely in foodservice, but it is a customary dish at festivals and private feasts. It is also served year-round at Chamorro Village— a tourist destination—in Agana, Guam.

Tropical Chamorro Chicken

This inviting recipe is based on a classic dish from the Northern Mariana Islands of the Pacific. Every bite of tender grilled chicken bursts with tropical flavor, thanks to a combination of lemon juice, cilantro, crushed red pepper, and shredded coconut.

INGREDIENT	QUANTITY 4 servings	24 servings	METHOD
1 Tyson Fully Cooked Flavor-Redi® Chicken Tenderloins with Grill Marks, frozen	1 lb.	6 lb.	Cover tightly and slack in cooler between 32° and 36°F prior to use.
2 Green onions, fresh, ¼-inch bias-sliced	¾ cup	4½ cups	Combine in bowl. Dice chicken and add to onion mixture. Toss well. Cover and chill below 40°F to hold.
Onions, fresh, minced	¼ cup	1½ cups	
Coconut, frozen, shredded	2 cups	12 cups	
Lemon juice, fresh	⅓ cup	2 cups	
Red pepper, crushed, dried	1½ tsp.	3 tbsp.	
Salt	¾ tsp.	1 tbsp.	
Cilantro, fresh, chopped	¼ cup	1½ cups	
3 Red leaf lettuce leaves, fresh	4	24	*To assemble single serving:* Line plate with 1 lettuce leaf. Top with 1¼ cups chicken mixture. Garnish plate with 2 half slices of orange and 2 starfruit slices.
Orange slices, fresh, cut in half	4	24	
Starfruit slices	8	48	

Serve with warm flour tortillas.

Portion: 7 ounces
Nutritional Data/Portion: Calories 470, Protein 33 g, Fat 20 g, Carbohydrate 43 g, Cholesterol 60 mg, Sodium 1,100 mg

For a **FAST FACTS VIA FAX** copy of this recipe, call 1-800-223-3755 and enter Business Tool 2637.

Submitted by Michael Shane
The Lilac Inn
Brandon, Vt.

Chicken and Portobello Strudel

Here's a beautiful appetizer for banquets or catering. But don't think these strudels are limited to those applications! They are as impressive in a plated presentation as they are on a serving tray. Flaky phyllo pastry encases an herbed filling of savory chicken and portobello mushrooms.

Line Service

INGREDIENT	QUANTITY 24 servings	METHOD
1 Butter, salted	¼ cup	Heat in skillet or braising pan over medium-high heat.
2 Portobello mushrooms, fresh, coarse-chopped	12 cups	Add to butter and sauté for 7 to 9 minutes or until mushrooms are wilted. Remove from heat. Cool and reserve.
Garlic, fresh, minced	1 tsp.	
Salt	1 tsp.	
Black pepper, coarse	½ tsp.	
3 Butter, salted	2 tbsp.	Heat in separate skillet over medium heat.
4 Tyson Fully Cooked Diced White Fryer Meat, ½-inch dice, frozen	2 lb.	Add to butter and sauté for 5 to 6 minutes or until chicken is thoroughly heated. Remove from heat.
Garlic, fresh, minced	½ tsp.	
Rosemary, dried	1 tsp.	
Thyme leaves, dried	1 tsp.	
5 White cheddar cheese, shredded	1 cup	Add to chicken and mix thoroughly. Cover and chill below 40°F to hold.
Lemon juice, fresh	2 tbsp.	
Salt	½ tbsp.	
Black pepper, coarse	1 tsp.	
6 Phyllo dough sheets, 14-inch x 18-inch, commercially prepared	24	*To prepare two strudels:* On parchment-lined work surface, lay down 1 phyllo sheet with 18-inch edge facing you. Brush with butter. Top with second sheet and brush with butter. Repeat until half of phyllo sheets are used.
Butter, salted, melted	as needed	
		Lay half of chicken filling lengthwise across the third of phyllo nearest you, leaving a 2-inch border around front and side edges. Top with half of mushroom filling. Fold front and side borders over filling and roll dough jelly roll style. Place seam side down on half-size sheet pan lined with buttered parchment paper. Brush top with butter. Repeat process to make second strudel.
		Bake in preheated conventional oven[+] at 350°F for 30 to 35 minutes or until golden brown. Remove from oven. Keep warm above 140°F.
7 Pansy flowers, fresh	24	*To assemble single serving:* Cut two ½-inch-thick slices from strudel and shingle on plate. Garnish plate with 1 pansy.

Portion: 3 ounces

Nutritional Data/Portion: Calories 120, Protein 10 g, Fat 6 g, Carbohydrate 6 g, Cholesterol 30 mg, Sodium 450 mg

[+]Convection oven not recommended.

For a **FAST FACTS VIA FAX**™ copy of this recipe, call 1-800-223-3755 and enter Business Tool 2638.

*O*rganization, speed, and practice are the secrets to working with phyllo dough. Because it dries out quickly, have a large work area and all ingredients and utensils ready before rolling it out. Work with one sheet at a time. Keep unused dough completely covered with plastic wrap. Use broad strokes with a pastry brush and butter the sheet from the outside inward. Do not saturate, but lightly brush the butter over the sheet.

*D*ivide this recipe in half for 12 servings.

*T*his recipe can be made into individual triangles, or turnovers, that are held in the cooler and baked as needed.

HOW TO FOLD A PASTRY TRIANGLE

1) *On parchment-lined work surface, lay down 1 phyllo sheet with 18-inch edge facing you. Brush with butter. Repeat process twice, using a total of 3 phyllo sheets. Cut the layered phyllo crosswise into 6 equal strips, 3 inches wide x 14 inches long. Place 1 rounded tablespoon chicken mixture and 1 scant tablespoon mushroom mixture on one end of each strip. Form a triangle with the phyllo strip by folding the right-hand corner to the opposite side.*

2) *Continue folding, as in folding a flag, until the entire strip is used. Transfer to buttered parchment-lined sheet pans and brush tops with butter. Repeat steps until all phyllo sheets are used. (This will yield 48 triangles.) Bake and hold as directed in strudel recipe. Serve 2 triangles per portion.*

Submitted by Frank J. Roudis
Roudigan's
Kingston, N.Y.

The serving size pictured here is intended for sharing. See the recipe for a single-serving suggestion.

Japanese bread crumbs are often called panko *and are extremely light and flaky, with a larger surface area than regular bread crumbs. Imagine tiny, very light and airy cornflake crumbs for a good idea of what* panko *is.*

PINEAPPLE HONEY MUSTARD SAUCE

	4 servings	24 servings
Pineapple preserves	1 cup	5 cups
Mustard, honey	½ cup	2½ cups
Horseradish, prepared	1 tbsp.	⅓ cup
Lime juice, fresh	1 tbsp.	⅓ cup
Cayenne pepper sauce	1 tbsp.	⅓ cup
Salt	½ tsp.	1 tbsp.
Black pepper, fine	½ tsp.	1 tbsp.

Combine in bowl and mix thoroughly. Cover and chill to hold.

Crisp Coconut-Crusted Chicken Tenderloins

These crunchy coconut-coated tenderloins, dipped in pineapple honey mustard sauce spiked with horseradish, are like a taste of a tropical vacation.

Kid Friendly   Line Service   Takeout

INGREDIENT	QUANTITY		METHOD
	4 servings	24 servings	
1 Coconut, frozen, shredded	1½ cups	9 cups	Combine in shallow pan and mix thoroughly.
Japanese bread crumbs, dried	1½ cups	9 cups	
2 Pancake batter mix, commercially prepared	1 cup	6 cups	Combine in bowl and mix thoroughly to make thin batter.
Water	¾ cup	4½ cups	
Cream of coconut, sweetened, canned	¼ cup	1½ cups	
3 Tyson Ready-to-Cook Flavor-Redi® Savory Chicken Tenderloins, frozen	12	72	Dip in batter and drain off excess. Dredge each tenderloin in coconut mixture and shake off excess. Deep-fry at 350°F for 3 to 4 minutes or until golden brown and chicken is no longer pink. Remove from fryer and drain. Keep warm above 140°F.
4 Pineapple Honey Mustard Sauce (see recipe)	1⅓ cups	8 cups	*To assemble single serving:* Arrange 3 chicken tenderloins on plate. Portion ⅓ cup sauce into individual container and place on plate. Garnish plate with 3 kiwi slices and 1 strawberry fan.
Kiwi slices, fresh	12	72	
Strawberry fans, fresh (p. 57)	4	24	

Portion: 7 ounces plus 3 ounces sauce
Nutritional Data/Portion: Calories 580, Protein 31 g, Fat 23 g, Carbohydrate 67 g, Cholesterol 50 mg, Sodium 1,010 mg

For a **FAST FACTS VIA FAX** copy of this recipe, call 1-800-223-3755 and enter Business Tool 2647.

Submitted by Harry Crane
Le Titi De Paris
Arlington Heights, Ill.

Tempura Chicken Strips with Mango Papaya Relish

Exciting flavor and plate presentation go hand-in-hand in this tempura-battered chicken starter. From the colorful mango papaya relish to the artful grid of black bean puree and cilantro oil garnish, patrons are in for a taste and visual treat.

INGREDIENT	QUANTITY		METHOD
	4 servings	24 servings	
1 Tyson Ready-to-Cook Tempura Thigh Strips, frozen	1 lb.	6 lb.	Deep-fry at 350°F for 5 to 5½ minutes or until chicken is no longer pink. Remove from fryer and drain. Keep warm above 140°F.
2 *Mango Papaya Relish*			
Mangoes, fresh, small dice	¼ cup	1½ cups	Combine in bowl and mix thoroughly. Cover and chill to hold.
Papayas, fresh, small dice	¼ cup	1½ cups	
Red bell peppers, fresh, small dice (p. 88)	¼ cup	1½ cups	
Roma tomatoes, fresh, seeded, small dice	¼ cup	1½ cups	
Red onions, fresh, small dice (p. 175)	2 tbsp.	¾ cup	
Jalapeño peppers, fresh, seeded, minced (p. 172)	1 tbsp.	⅓ cup	
Ginger, ground	¼ tsp.	1½ tsp.	
Cilantro, fresh, minced	½ tbsp.	3 tbsp.	
3 Pineapple juice, canned	½ tbsp.	3 tbsp.	One hour before serving, add to mango mixture and toss gently. Cover and allow to come to room temperature before serving.
Lime juice, fresh	¾ tsp.	1½ tbsp.	
Vegetable oil	¼ tsp.	½ tbsp.	
Salt	1/16 tsp.	½ tsp.	
White pepper, fine	1/16 tsp.	½ tsp.	
Rum, light (optional)	½ tsp.	1 tbsp.	
4 Black Bean Puree (see recipe)	as needed	as needed	*To assemble single serving:* Draw a grid of lines on plate with bean puree. Arrange 4 ounces chicken on grid. Portion ¼ cup mango papaya relish at edge of grid and arrange ½ cup baby greens next to relish. Drizzle cilantro oil over plate for garnish.
Mixed baby greens, fresh, commercially prepared	2 cups	12 cups	
Cilantro Oil (see recipe)	as needed	as needed	

Portion: 7 ounces
Nutritional Data/Portion: Calories 320, Protein 14 g, Fat 17 g, Carbohydrate 28 g, Cholesterol 45 mg, Sodium 560 mg

For a **FAST FACTS VIA FAX** copy of this recipe, call 1-800-223-3755 and enter Business Tool 2660.

"How good it is to be well fed,
healthy, and kind all at the same time."
Henry J. Heimlich

BLACK BEAN PUREE

	1 pint
Black beans, canned, rinsed, drained	2 cups
Water	2 cups
Onions, fresh, chopped	½ cup
Garlic, fresh, chopped	2 tsp.
Cilantro sprigs, fresh	6
Salt	1 tsp.

Combine in saucepan and mix thoroughly. Bring to boil over high heat. Reduce heat and simmer for 20 to 30 minutes or until onions are tender and most of liquid has evaporated. Remove from heat and transfer to food processor bowl. Process until pureed. Transfer to squeeze bottle and reserve.

Coriander, the plant whose leaves and stems are commonly referred to as cilantro, first appeared in China around 100 B.C. Today, cilantro is used widely in Asian, Caribbean, and Latin American cooking because its distinctive flavor lends itself to highly spiced foods.

CILANTRO OIL

	1 pint
Water	4 cups
Salt	2 tsp.
Cilantro bunches, fresh	2
Grapeseed oil	2 cups
Salt	¼ tsp.

Bring water and salt to boil in saucepan over high heat.

Dip cilantro in boiling water for 5 seconds. Shock in ice water and drain thoroughly on absorbent towels. Place in food processor bowl.

Add grapeseed oil and salt to cilantro and process until pureed. Transfer to squeeze bottle and reserve.

Submitted by Steven D. Shimmin, CEC
Fine Host Corporation
Albuquerque Convention Center
Albuquerque, N.M.

*Add corn or other small
diced vegetables to
introduce even more color
to the rolls.*⌒

*This versatile recipe can
also work as an entree by
serving it as a wrap.*⌒

Santa Fe Chicken Rolls

This presentation is a work of art. The colorful rolls are filled with char-grilled chicken, spicy
black bean puree, and roasted jalapeño pepper sauce.

INGREDIENT	QUANTITY		METHOD
	4 servings	24 servings	
1 Tyson Ready-to-Cook Tenderpressed™ Savory Chicken Breast Filets, 4-oz., frozen	1	6	Brush each chicken breast filet with butter and sprinkle with seasoning.
Butter, salted, melted	as needed	as needed	Char-grill over medium heat for approximately 4½ minutes on each side or until chicken is no longer pink. Remove from grill. Cool and slice each breast filet into 12 strips. Cover and chill below 40°F to hold
Cajun seasoning, dried	as needed	as needed	
2 *Black Bean Puree*			
Black beans, canned, drained	½ cup	4 cups	Combine in food processor bowl and process until pureed. Remove from processor bowl. Cover and chill to hold.
Jalapeño peppers, fresh, seeded, minced (p. 172)	½ tbsp.	3 tbsp.	
Onions, fresh, minced	½ tsp.	1 tbsp.	
Garlic, fresh, minced	½ tsp.	1 tbsp.	
Cumin, ground	⅛ tsp.	¾ tsp.	
Salt	⅛ tsp.	¾ tsp.	
Black pepper, fine	⅛ tsp.	¾ tsp.	
3 *Roasted Jalapeño Pepper Sauce*			
Spinach leaves, fresh, blanched, refreshed in ice water, drained	1 cup	6 cups	Combine in food processor bowl and process until pureed. Remove from processor bowl. Cover with plastic wrap pressed directly on surface of sauce to preserve color. Chill to hold.
Jalapeño peppers, roasted, peeled, seeded	2	12	
Cilantro, fresh, coarse-chopped	¼ cup	1½ cups	
Garlic, fresh, minced	½ tsp.	1 tbsp.	
Hot chile vinegar, commercially prepared	1 tbsp.	⅓ cup	
Lime juice, fresh	1 tbsp.	⅓ cup	
Orange juice concentrate, frozen	2 tsp.	¼ cup	
Olive oil	¼ cup	1¼ cups	
Salt, kosher	1 tsp.	2 tbsp.	

recipe continued on next page . . .

INGREDIENT	QUANTITY		METHOD
	4 servings	24 servings	
4 Tyson Mexican Original® Herb Garlic Wraps, room temperature	1	6	*To assemble roll:* Place 1 wrap on flat work surface and spread with ½ cup black bean puree. Lay chicken, avocados, and peppers onto bean puree in alternating rows, covering the entire wrap. (Use a total of 36 strips, 12 of each ingredient.) Press to adhere to bean puree. Roll tightly in jelly roll fashion. Repeat process for remaining wraps. Cover and chill below 40°F to hold.
Avocado strips, fresh, tossed in lime juice	12	72	
Red bell pepper strips, fresh	12	72	
5 Jalapeño flowers, fresh	4	24	*To assemble single serving:* Pour 2 tablespoons jalapeño pepper sauce on plate. Slice three ½-inch-thick medallions from chilled chicken roll and arrange on sauce. Garnish plate with 1 jalapeño pepper flower.

Portion: 4 ounces

Nutritional Data/Portion: Calories 300, Protein 10 g, Fat 21 g, Carbohydrate 21 g, Cholesterol 20 mg, Sodium 980 mg

For a *FAST FACTS VIA FAX*™ copy of this recipe, call 1-800-223-3755 and enter Business Tool 2654.

Chicken Mushroom Mousse

After a long absence, savory terrines, mousses, molds, and aspics are back in fashion. Here's a creamy appetizer spread that's great when served with fancy crackers or lavash.

From the Tyson Kitchens

INGREDIENT	QUANTITY		METHOD
	4 servings	24 servings	
1 Cream of mushroom soup, condensed, commercially prepared	½ cup	3 cups	Combine in saucepan and mix thoroughly. Heat over medium-low heat for 8 to 10 minutes, whisking until smooth. (Heat smaller quantity for 4 to 5 minutes.) Remove from heat.
Cream cheese	4 oz.	24 oz.	
Gelatin, unflavored	¾ tsp.	1½ tbsp.	
Water, cold	1½ tbsp.	½ cup	
2 Tyson Fully Cooked Shredded Savory Chicken Breast Meat, frozen	4 oz.	24 oz.	Add to soup mixture and mix thoroughly. Ladle into 24 oiled ½-cup ramekins. (Use 4 ramekins for smaller quantity.) Cover and chill below 40°F until firmly set.
Mayonnaise	½ cup	2 cups	
Celery, fresh, minced	½ cup	3 cups	
Green onions, fresh, thinly sliced	1 tbsp.	⅓ cup	
Garlic, granulated	⅛ tsp.	¾ tsp.	
Salt	⅛ tsp.	¾ tsp.	
Black pepper, fine	⅛ tsp.	¾ tsp.	
3 Celery leaves, fresh	4	24	After mousse is firmly set, garnish top of each ramekin with 1 celery leaf, 1 parsley leaf, and 1 pimiento sliver. Cover and chill below 40°F to hold.
Parsley leaves, flat-leaf, fresh	4	24	
Pimiento slivers, canned, drained	4	24	
4 Black olives, whole, pitted, canned, drained	20	120	*To assemble single serving:* Place 1 ramekin on plate. Garnish plate with 5 olives and 2 green onion spears.
Green onion spears, fresh	8	48	*Serve with assorted crackers.*

Portion: 4 ounces

Nutritional Data/Portion: Calories 340, Protein 11 g, Fat 27 g, Carbohydrate 16 g, Cholesterol 60 mg, Sodium 710 mg

For a *FAST FACTS VIA FAX*™ copy of this recipe, call 1-800-223-3755 and enter Business Tool 2642.

This recipe can be presented in a number of appetizing ways. Simply remove the mousse from the ramekin and serve it on a lettuce leaf for an individual serving, or form the mousse in a large mold for line service. It also works well molded in a terrine to be sliced like pâté.

Spicy Chicken Quesadilla

Quesadilla lovers will fall for this combination of Cajun-spiced chicken, cheese, jalapeños, and fresh tomatoes.

The word quesadilla *refers to any tortilla filled with cheese, specifically a chewy specialty cheese from northern Mexico called "quesadilla."*

This recipe can be made even more kid friendly by using only chicken and cheese inside the tortillas. Or it goes from starter to wonderful entree with the addition of rice and beans, sour cream, and guacamole.

Wearing latex gloves while handling fresh chile peppers can help minimize the risk of burning eyes and hands with pepper oil.

See sidebar on page 19 for how to make a chile pepper flower.

INGREDIENT	QUANTITY		METHOD
	4 servings	24 servings	
Tyson Fully Cooked Flavor-Redi® Chicken Thigh Fajita Strips, frozen	1 lb.	6 lb.	Cover tightly and slack in cooler between 32° and 36°F prior to use.
Monterey Jack and cheddar cheese mix, shredded	2 cups	12 cups	Combine in bowl and mix thoroughly. Cover and chill to hold.
Cajun seasoning, dried	2 tsp.	¼ cup	
Tomatoes, fresh, seeded, diced, drained	1 cup	6 cups	Combine in separate bowl and mix thoroughly. Cover and chill to hold.
Jalapeño peppers, canned, drained, diced	¼ cup	1½ cups	
Green onions, fresh, chopped	¼ cup	1½ cups	
Mexican Original® Flour Tortillas, 7-inch, room temperature	8	48	*To prepare single serving:* Brush 2 tortillas with butter. Place 1 tortilla, buttered side down, on oiled, preheated 350°F flattop griddle.
Butter, salted, melted	as needed	as needed	
Salsa, thick-and-chunky, mild, commercially prepared	1 cup	6 cups	Layer tortilla with 4 ounces chicken, ½ cup cheese mixture, ⅓ cup tomato mixture, and second tortilla, buttered side up.
Chile pepper flowers, fresh	4	24	

Grill for 1 to 3 minutes or until tortilla is golden and crispy. Turn and grill an additional 1 to 3 minutes or until tortilla is golden brown. Remove from griddle. Slice quesadilla into 4 wedges and arrange on plate.

Portion ¼ cup salsa into individual container and place on plate. Garnish plate with 1 chile pepper flower.

Portion: 9 ounces plus 2 ounces salsa
Nutritional Data/Portion: Calories 610, Protein 41 g, Fat 32 g, Carbohydrate 40 g, Cholesterol 165 mg, Sodium 1,830 mg

For a **FAST FACTS VIA FAX** copy of this recipe, call 1-800-223-3755 and enter Business Tool 2367.

Submitted by Robert J. Kurchin
Francis Marion University
Florence, S.C.

Chicken Quesadilla Cordon Bleu

Inspired by a famous French chicken dish, this quesadilla features roasted chicken, smoked ham, and Swiss cheese.

This is one starter that can be equally popular as a lunch offering or a small dinner entree.

INGREDIENT	QUANTITY 4 servings	24 servings	METHOD
1 Tyson Fully Cooked Flavor-Redi® Roasted and Carved Chicken Breast Filets, frozen	1 lb.	6 lb.	Cover tightly and slack in cooler between 32° and 36°F prior to use.
2 Smoked ham, shaved, finely chopped	⅓ cup	2 cups	Combine in bowl. Julienne chicken and add to ham mixture. Mix thoroughly. Cover and chill below 40°F to hold.
Swiss cheese, shredded	2 cups	12 cups	
3 Mixed salad greens, fresh, commercially prepared	8 cups	48 cups	Combine in bowl and toss well. Cover and chill to hold.
Tomatoes, fresh, seeded, diced	½ cup	3 cups	
4 Ranch salad dressing, commercially prepared	1¼ cups	7½ cups	Combine in bowl and mix thoroughly. Cover and chill to hold.
Mustard, Dijon	¼ cup	1½ cups	
5 Tyson Mexican Original® Honey Wheat Wraps, room temperature	4	24	*To prepare single serving:* Brush one side of wrap with butter. Place wrap, buttered side down, on oiled, preheated 350°F flattop griddle. Portion 1½ cups chicken mixture on one half of wrap. Fold other half of wrap over filling.
Butter, salted, melted	as needed	as needed	
Parsley sprigs, fresh	4	24	

Grill for 1 to 2 minutes on each side or until cheese is melted and wrap is crispy. Remove from griddle. Slice into 4 wedges and fan on one side of plate.

Arrange 2 cups salad greens mixture on opposite side of plate and drizzle with 2 tablespoons salad dressing.

Portion ¼ cup additional salad dressing in individual container and place on plate. Garnish plate with 1 parsley sprig.

Portion: 11½ ounces plus 3 ounces dressing
Nutritional Data/Portion: Calories 980, Protein 61 g, Fat 57 g, Carbohydrate 60 g, Cholesterol 160 mg, Sodium 2,390 mg

For a **FAST FACTS VIA FAX**. copy of this recipe, call 1-800-223-3755 and enter Business Tool 2641.

"Man is born to eat."
Craig Claiborne

Recipes on pages 23 and 24.

Submitted by Kirk Brooks
Doubletree Hotel at Reid Park
Tucson, Ariz.

Smoked Chicken and Red Pepper Quesadilla

Roasted red pepper pesto and house-made black bean sauce are the secret ingredients in this full-flavored quesadilla.

INGREDIENT	QUANTITY 4 servings	QUANTITY 24 servings	METHOD
1 Tyson Fully Cooked Flavor-Redi® Smoked Chicken Breast Filets, 2.75-oz., frozen	4	24	Heat in preheated convection oven at 350°F for 10 to 12 minutes. Remove from oven. Keep warm above 140°F.
2 *Red Pepper Pesto*			
Red bell peppers, roasted, canned, drained	½ cup	3 cups	Combine in food processor bowl and process until pureed. Remove from processor bowl. Cover and chill to hold.
Parmesan cheese, grated	⅓ cup	2 cups	
Pine nuts	¼ cup	1½ cups	
Olive oil	2 tbsp.	¾ cup	
3 Tyson Mexican Original® Flour Tortillas, 8-inch, room temperature	4	24	*To prepare single serving:* Brush 1 tortilla with butter. Place tortilla, buttered side down, on oiled, preheated 350°F flattop griddle.
Butter, salted, melted	as needed	as needed	
Monterey Jack cheese, shredded	2 cups	12 cups	Spread with 3 tablespoons red pepper pesto and sprinkle with ½ cup cheese. Place 1 breast filet on one half of tortilla. Fold other half of tortilla over chicken.
			Grill for 1 to 2 minutes on each side or until cheese is melted and tortilla is golden brown. Remove from griddle. Slice quesadilla into thirds and fan on plate.
4 Black Bean Sauce (see recipe)	½ cup	3 cups	Portion 2 tablespoons black bean sauce into individual container and place on plate. Garnish plate with 1 lime wedge and 1 cilantro sprig.
Lime wedges, fresh	4	24	
Cilantro sprigs, fresh	4	24	

Portion: 7 ounces plus 1 ounce sauce
Nutritional Data/Portion: Calories 570, Protein 41 g, Fat 35 g, Carbohydrate 25 g, Cholesterol 105 mg, Sodium 1,060 mg

For a **FAST FACTS VIA FAX**™ copy of this recipe, call 1-800-223-3755 and enter Business Tool 2655.

Increase the spiciness of the black bean sauce by adding crushed red pepper to taste.

BLACK BEAN SAUCE

	4 servings	24 servings
Black beans, canned, undrained	½ cup	3 cups
Chicken broth, canned	2 tbsp.	¾ cup
Thyme, fresh, chopped	½ tsp.	½ tbsp.
Garlic, granulated	⅛ tsp.	¾ tsp.
Salt	⅛ tsp.	¾ tsp.
Black pepper, coarse	⅛ tsp.	¾ tsp.

Combine in food processor bowl and process until pureed. Transfer to saucepan and heat on medium-low heat for 8 to 10 minutes or until flavors are blended. (Heat smaller quantity for 2 to 3 minutes.) Remove from heat and keep warm.

This recipe is pictured on opposite page.

Cilantro-Grilled Chicken Wings with Sweet Chili Dipping Sauce

Cilantro, garlic, and sweet chili sauce coat jumbo wings that will fly off the plate. It's a sweet-and-spicy twist for an old favorite.

INGREDIENT	QUANTITY 4 servings	QUANTITY 24 servings	METHOD
1 Tyson Ready-to-Cook Jumbo Chicken Wings, frozen	20	120	Place in full-size steam table pans.
2 Cilantro, fresh	2 cups	12 cups	Combine in food processor bowl and process until pureed. Remove from processor bowl and rub on chicken. Cover and marinate below 40°F for 24 hours, turning occasionally.
Garlic, fresh, chopped	½ cup	3 cups	
Vegetable oil	¼ cup	1½ cups	
			Char-grill over medium heat for 6 to 8 minutes on each side or until chicken is no longer pink. Remove from grill. Keep warm above 140°F.
3 Sweet chili sauce, commercially prepared	1 cup	4 cups	*To assemble single serving:* Arrange 5 wings on plate. Ladle ¼ cup sauce over wings. Garnish plate with 1 parsley sprig.
Parsley sprigs, fresh	4	24	

Portion: 11½ ounces
Nutritional Data/Portion: Calories 580, Protein 41 g, Fat 37 g, Carbohydrate 23 g, Cholesterol 235 mg, Sodium 1,060 mg

For a **FAST FACTS VIA FAX**™ copy of this recipe, call 1-800-223-3755 and enter Business Tool 2646.

Submitted by Gerald Bonsey, CEC, AAC
The York Harbor Inn
York Harbor, Maine

Commercially prepared sweet chili sauce can be found at many Asian markets.

Chili sauce is made with tomatoes, chiles or chili powder, onions, green peppers, vinegar, sugar, and spices.

This recipe is pictured on opposite page.

Submitted by Jim Lassiter, CCC
Lexington Medical Center
West Columbia, S.C.

Pineapple Chicken Cones with Black Bean Salsa

Pineapple-marinated tenderloins and sweet-and-spicy black bean salsa make these juicy cone-shaped wraps a real delight.

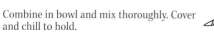

The tomatillo is also known as a Mexican green tomato and jamberry. Like the tomato, it is a member of the nightshade family, but its flavor has hints of lemon, apple, and herbs. Tomatillos should be firm with tight-fitting husks, which should be removed before using.

Canned tomatillos may be substituted for fresh.

This recipe is pictured on page 22.

INGREDIENT	QUANTITY 4 servings	QUANTITY 24 servings	METHOD
1 Tyson Ready-to-Cook Flavor-Redi® Savory Tenderloins, frozen	8	48	Place in full-size steam table pans. (Use half-size pan for smaller quantity.)
2 Pineapple juice, canned	¾ cup	4½ cups	Pour over chicken and toss to coat. Cover tightly and marinate below 40°F for 8 hours.
			Remove from marinade and char-grill over medium heat for 2 to 3 minutes on each side or until chicken is no longer pink. Remove from grill. Keep warm above 140°F.
3 *Black Bean Salsa*			
Black beans, canned, rinsed, drained	1½ cups	9 cups	Combine in bowl and mix thoroughly. Cover and chill to hold.
Tomatoes, fresh, seeded, chopped	1 cup	6 cups	
Green onions, fresh, minced	½ cup	3 cups	
Tomatillos, fresh, chopped	½ cup	3 cups	
Orange juice concentrate, frozen	1 tbsp.	⅓ cup	
Chili powder, light	½ tbsp.	3 tbsp.	
Cumin, ground	½ tbsp.	3 tbsp.	
Cilantro, fresh, chopped	1 tbsp.	⅓ cup	
Honey	2 tbsp.	¾ cup	
Mustard, Dijon	2 tbsp.	¾ cup	
Mayonnaise	2 tbsp.	¾ cup	
Paprika, ground	¼ tsp.	½ tbsp.	
Cayenne pepper sauce	1 tbsp.	⅓ cup	
4 Tyson Mexican Original® Tomato Wraps, room temperature	4	24	*To assemble single serving:* Place 1 wrap on flat work surface and slice into 4 wedges.
Green leaf lettuce, coarse-chopped	2 cups	12 cups	Layer 2 tablespoons lettuce and 2½ tablespoons black bean salsa across center of each wedge from the point to the outside curved edge. Slice 2 chicken tenderloins in half lengthwise and top each wedge with 1 slice.
Club picks	as needed	as needed	
Cayenne pepper sauce	½ cup	3 cups	

Fold 1 straight edge of each wedge over filling and roll into a cone shape. Secure with club picks if necessary and arrange on plate.

Portion 2 tablespoons cayenne pepper sauce into individual container and place on plate.

Portion: 14 ounces plus 1 ounce sauce
Nutritional Data/Portion: Calories 580, Protein 35 g, Fat 14 g, Carbohydrate 82 g, Cholesterol 35 mg, Sodium 1,550 mg

For a **FAST FACTS VIA FAX** copy of this recipe, call 1-800-223-3755 and enter Business Tool 2659.

HOW TO MAKE MINICONES
1) Cut large tortilla into quarters.
2) Add filling and roll into cone shape.
3) Secure with club picks as needed.

Submitted by Edward Carloni
Lebanon Country Club
Myerstown, Pa.

Wild Mushroom and Two-Cheese Chicken Pizza

Savory sautéed portobello, shiitake, and oyster mushrooms blend with creamy Alfredo sauce and Gorgonzola and Romano cheeses to make this chicken pizza a bubbly, golden delight.

	INGREDIENT	QUANTITY 6 servings	METHOD
1	Butter, salted	2 tbsp.	Heat in skillet over medium-high heat.
2	Portobello mushrooms, fresh, diced	¾ cup	Add to butter and sauté for 1 to 2 minutes or until mushrooms are wilted. Remove from heat and reserve.
	Shiitake mushrooms, fresh, diced	⅓ cup	
	Oyster mushrooms, fresh, diced	⅓ cup	
	Thyme leaves, dried	¼ tsp.	
	Rosemary leaves, dried	¼ tsp.	
	Basil leaves, dried	¼ tsp.	
	Oregano leaves, dried	¼ tsp.	
	Parsley leaves, dried	¼ tsp.	
3	Pizza dough, presheeted, 12-inch, unbaked, frozen, slacked according to package directions	1	Place on oiled baking sheet or pizza pan.
4	Alfredo sauce, commercially prepared	⅓ cup	Combine in bowl and mix thoroughly. Spread evenly over crust.
	Romano cheese, grated	2 tbsp.	
5	Tyson Fully Cooked Oven Roasted Julienne Chicken Pizza Toppings, Natural Proportion, frozen	8 oz.	Layer over sauce along with mushroom mixture.
6	Gorgonzola cheese, crumbled	¾ cup	Sprinkle over pizza.
			Bake in preheated conventional oven at 400°F for 18 to 20 minutes or until crust is crisp and golden. Or bake in preheated convection oven at 375°F for 10 to 12 minutes. Remove from oven. Slice into wedges and serve immediately.

Portion: One-sixth of a 12-inch pizza (3⅔ ounces)
Nutritional Data/Portion: Calories 317, Protein 19 g, Fat 15 g, Carbohydrate 26 g, Cholesterol 68 mg, Sodium 635 mg

For a **FAST FACTS VIA FAX** copy of this recipe, call 1-800-223-3755 and enter Business Tool 2652.

Gorgonzola cheese dates back to the 9th century where it was first made in a town outside Milan named, of course, Gorgonzola. It is a rich, creamy blue-veined cow or goat milk cheese, with a pungent flavor that originally came from naturally occurring bacteria found on the stone walls of farm buildings where the cheese was stored.

Any combination of cultivated and wild mushrooms may be substituted.

"Cheese—milk's leap toward immortality."
Clifton Fadiman

Taco Chicken Pizza

Pizza may have originated in Italy, but once it hit these shores, it became fair game for all sorts of American interpretations. Here, it reflects a Tex-Mex influence with salsa, refried beans, and poblano chiles.

Speed-Scratch *Kid Friendly* *Line Service* *Takeout*

INGREDIENT	QUANTITY 6 servings	METHOD
1 Pizza crust, parbaked, 12-inch, commercially prepared	1	Place on oiled baking sheet or pizza pan. Lightly brush top surface with oil.
Olive oil	as needed	
2 Salsa, thick-and-chunky, mild, commercially prepared	⅔ cup	Combine in bowl and mix thoroughly. Spread evenly over crust.
Refried beans, canned	⅔ cup	
Taco seasoning, dried	2 tbsp.	
3 Tyson Fully Cooked Mesquite Chicken Pizza Toppings, Natural Proportion Strips, frozen	6 oz.	Arrange over salsa mixture.
4 Tomatoes, fresh, chopped	½ cup	Layer over chicken.
Pepper Jack cheese, shredded	1½ cups	
5 Poblano chiles, fresh, slivered	¼ cup	Arrange over cheese.
		Bake in preheated conventional oven at 400°F for 18 to 20 minutes or until crust is crisp and golden. Or bake in preheated convection oven at 375°F for 10 to 12 minutes. Remove from oven. Slice into wedges and serve immediately.

Portion: One-sixth of a 12-inch pizza (5⅓ ounces)
Nutritional Data/Portion: Calories 320, Protein 18 g, Fat 16 g, Carbohydrate 26 g, Cholesterol 55 mg, Sodium 850 mg

For a **FAST FACTS VIA FAX** copy of this recipe, call 1-800-223-3755 and enter Business Tool 2369.

Pizza evolved when European explorers returned home from the New World with tomatoes and began adding them, along with cheese, to Neapolitan flat bread.

News of the Italian pizza "pie" came home with soldiers returning from Europe. Today, Americans eat approximately 90 acres of pizza per day.

Poblano peppers look like small green bell peppers, but they are much darker in color. Those that are practically black have the richest flavor. When ripe, poblanos turn reddish-brown and become sweeter. Dried, they are known as ancho chile peppers. Their peak season is summer to early fall.

Fresh green peppers may be substituted for the poblano peppers in this recipe.

Submitted by Greg Babcock
Wildwood Education Center
Hornell, N.Y.

Buffalo Chicken Pizza

Buffalo chicken wings and pizza are two menu favorites, so why not turn them into one over-the-top hit? Spicy Buffalo-style chicken strips are cooled by chunky blue cheese dressing on crispy-chewy pizza crust sprinkled with mozzarella cheese.

Speed-Scratch   Line-Service   Takeout

	INGREDIENT	QUANTITY 6 servings	METHOD
1	Tyson Fully Cooked Buffalo-Style Breast Strips, frozen	1 lb.	Deep-fry at 350°F for 3 to 5 minutes. Remove from fryer and drain. Cut into ½-inch pieces. Keep warm above 140°F.
2	Pizza dough, presheeted, 16-inch, unbaked, frozen, slacked according to package directions	1	Place on oiled baking sheet or pizza pan.
3	Blue cheese salad dressing, chunky, commercially prepared	1 cup	Spread evenly over crust.
4	Pizza sauce, commercially prepared	½ cup	Spread over salad dressing. Top with chicken.
5	Cayenne pepper sauce	½ cup	Combine in bowl and mix thoroughly. Drizzle over chicken.
	Honey	1 tbsp.	
	Butter, salted, melted	1 tbsp.	
6	Mozzarella cheese, shredded	2 cups	Sprinkle over pizza. Bake in preheated conventional oven at 450°F for 10 to 12 minutes or until crust is crisp and golden. Or bake in preheated convection oven at 375°F for 7 to 10 minutes. Remove from oven. Slice into wedges and serve immediately.

Portion: One-sixth of a 16-inch pizza (10⅓ ounces)
Nutritional Data/Portion: Calories 797, Protein 30 g, Fat 43 g, Carbohydrate 75 g, Cholesterol 60 mg, Sodium 2,222 mg

For a **FAST FACTS VIA FAX** copy of this recipe, call 1-800-223-3755 and enter Business Tool 2644.

Tyson Buffalo-flavored Popcorn Chicken Bites™ may be substituted for the breast strips.

Pizza dough performs best when it is allowed to reach at least 65°F.

Make the Taco Chicken Pizza pictured here more kid friendly by omitting the poblano peppers.

Chicken Bruschetta

The term bruschetta comes from the Italian word bruscare, *meaning "to roast over coals."*

Like pizza, bruschetta is now almost an "American" dish after undergoing multiple transformations since it was introduced here. Originally made with toasted bread rubbed with cut garlic cloves, this tasty chicken adaptation builds on the Italian association, with olive oil, fresh basil, balsamic vinegar, roasted red bell peppers, and mozzarella.

Speed-Scratch

INGREDIENT	QUANTITY		METHOD
	4 servings	24 servings	
1 Tyson Fully Cooked Flavor-Redi® Chicken Breast Fajita Strips, frozen	12 oz.	4½ lb.	Place on full-size sheet pans. (Use half-size pan for smaller quantity.)
			Bake in preheated conventional oven at 400°F for 15 to 18 minutes. Or bake in preheated convection oven at 400°F for 4 to 6 minutes. Remove from oven. Keep warm above 140°F.
2 Red bell peppers, roasted, peeled, seeded, diced (p. 66)	⅓ cup	2 cups	Combine in bowl and mix thoroughly. Cover and chill to hold.
Black olives, sliced, canned, drained	3 tbsp.	1 cup	
Balsamic vinegar	1 tbsp.	⅓ cup	
Italian vinaigrette salad dressing, commercially prepared	1 tsp.	2 tbsp.	
3 Basil, fresh, chiffonade	1 tbsp.	⅓ cup	
French bread, sliced diagonally into ½-inch-thick slices	8 slices	48 slices	Brush both sides of bread with oil. Grill on oiled, preheated flattop griddle at 350°F for 1 to 2 minutes on each side or until golden. Remove from griddle.
Olive oil	as needed	as needed	
Garlic cloves, fresh	as needed	as needed	Rub both sides of grilled bread with garlic. Cover and reserve.
4 Mozzarella cheese, shredded	½ cup	3 cups	*To prepare single serving:* Place 2 slices grilled bread on sheet pan. Top each slice with 1½ ounces chicken, 1 tablespoon bell pepper mixture, and 1 tablespoon cheese.
Parsley, fresh, minced (p. 39)	as needed	as needed	
			Broil under salamander for 1 to 2 minutes or until cheese is bubbly. Remove from broiler and arrange on plate. Sprinkle parsley over plate for garnish.

Portion: 6 ounces
Nutritional Data/Portion: Calories 300, Protein 25 g, Fat 9 g, Carbohydrate 31 g, Cholesterol 55 mg, Sodium 950 mg

For a **FAST FACTS VIA FAX**™ copy of this recipe, call 1-800-223-3755 and enter Business Tool 2639.

HOW TO CHIFFONADE
1) Stack washed leaves, then roll tightly like a cigar.
2) Make fine slices across the tightly rolled leaves.

The word marmalade *is Portuguese for "quince jam." Quince is a fruit common to Asia and the Mediterranean and resembles a cross between an apple and a pear. Today, marmalade refers to fruit preserves (generally citrus fruit) that include pieces of the fruit's rind.*

Orange Pepper Glazed Popcorn Chicken

Buffalo-style Popcorn Chicken Bites™ can be menu stars all by themselves, but putting them on a skewer and drizzling them with orange pepper glaze creates a fabulous signature menu item.

Speed Scratch · *Line Service* · *Takeout*

INGREDIENT	QUANTITY		METHOD
	4 servings	24 servings	
1 Tyson Ready-to-Cook Buffalo Popcorn Chicken Bites, frozen	1 lb.	6 lb.	Deep-fry at 350°F for 3 to 3½ minutes or until chicken is no longer pink. Remove from fryer and drain. Keep warm above 140°F.
2 *Orange Pepper Glaze*			
Orange marmalade	¾ cup	4½ cups	Combine in bowl and mix thoroughly. Cover and reserve.
Mustard, spicy brown	2 tbsp.	¾ cup	
Cherry peppers, red, mild, canned, drained, minced	1 tbsp.	⅓ cup	
Apple cider vinegar	1 tbsp.	⅓ cup	
Cayenne pepper sauce	2 tsp.	¼ cup	
Horseradish, prepared	2 tsp.	¼ cup	
3 Thin wooden skewers	8	48	*To assemble single serving:* Thread 4 ounces popcorn chicken on 2 skewers and arrange on plate.
Orange slice twists, fresh	4	24	

Microwave ¼ cup orange pepper glaze on high for 15 to 20 seconds and spoon 1 tablespoon glaze over chicken. Serve remaining glaze in individual container placed on plate. Garnish plate with 1 orange twist.

Portion: 4 ounces plus 2 ounces glaze
Nutritional Data/Portion: Calories 460, Protein 18 g, Fat 18 g, Carbohydrate 61 g, Cholesterol 25 mg, Sodium 1,050 mg

Note: Recipe and nutritionals are based on two skewers per serving.

For a **FAST FACTS VIA FAX™** copy of this recipe, call 1-800-223-3755 and enter Business Tool 2372.

Submitted by Michael A. Pelillo
Cornerstone of Eagle Hill
Sandy Hook, Conn.

These ingredients can also be rolled together in a flour tortilla and served warm or cold for a great-tasting wrap.

This recipe makes a great treat or party snack when cut into bite-size pieces and served cold.

A combination of peanuts, vegetable oil, and salt—better known as peanut butter—was one of 300 uses for peanuts George Washington Carver developed in his lifetime. But the origin of peanut butter is hard to pinpoint. The Incas and some African tribes ate a crude paste of ground peanuts for hundreds of years before Carver's time. A St. Louis doctor named Ambrose Straub is credited with the invention of the first machine to make peanut butter, for which he received a patent in 1903.

A Nutter Chicken Pizza

Children might be the first to ask for this starter pizza, but once their parents take a bite, it will be a fight to the finish. A mixture of creamy peanut butter, honey, and chicken is spread over the crust and topped with dollops of whole-berry cranberry sauce and shredded cheese.

Speed-Scratch   Kid Friendly   Line-Service   Takeout

INGREDIENT	QUANTITY 6 servings	METHOD
1 Pizza dough, presheeted, 16-inch, unbaked, frozen, slacked according to package directions	1	Place on oiled baking sheet or pizza pan.
2 Tyson Fully Cooked Pulled Fryer Leg Meat, frozen	1 lb.	Combine in saucepan and mix thoroughly. Heat over medium heat for 3 to 4 minutes or until peanut butter is melted, stirring frequently. Remove from heat and spread evenly over crust.
Peanut butter, creamy	⅔ cup	
Honey	½ cup	
Salt	2 tsp.	
3 Cranberry sauce, whole-berry, canned	½ cup	Drop by teaspoons over chicken mixture. Do not stir into peanut butter.
4 Mozzarella cheese, shredded	⅔ cup	Sprinkle over pizza.
		Bake in preheated conventional oven at 450°F for 10 to 12 minutes or until crust is crisp and golden. Or bake in preheated convection oven at 375°F for 7 to 10 minutes. Remove from oven. Slice into wedges and serve immediately.

Portion: One-sixth of a 16-inch pizza (9 ounces)
Nutritional Data/Portion: Calories 733, Protein 35 g, Fat 34 g, Carbohydrate 79 g, Cholesterol 103 mg, Sodium 1,308 mg

For a **FAST FACTS VIA FAX** copy of this recipe, call 1-800-223-3755 and enter Business Tool 2635.

"Peanut butter is the pâté of childhood."
Florence Fabricant

Submitted by Thomas Kovacs
Sheraton-Seattle Hotel
Seattle, Wash.

Curried Chicken Bites

Cream cheese is the tie that binds this flavorful chicken spread that's packed with curry seasoning and accented with bites of sweet, juicy peaches.

INGREDIENT	QUANTITY		METHOD
	4 servings	24 servings	
Tyson Fully Cooked Diced Natural-Proportion Chicken Meat, ⅜-inch dice, frozen	8 oz.	3 lb.	Combine in bowl and mix thoroughly. Cover and chill below 40°F to hold.
Cream cheese, room temperature	8 oz.	3 lb.	
Green onions, fresh, minced	1 tbsp.	⅓ cup	
Garlic, fresh, minced	¼ tsp.	½ tbsp.	
Parsley, fresh, minced (p. 39)	1 tbsp.	⅓ cup	
Celery seeds, whole	1 tsp.	2 tbsp.	
Curry powder	½ tsp.	1 tbsp.	
Turmeric, ground	⅛ tsp.	¾ tsp.	
Lemon pepper	⅛ tsp.	¾ tsp.	
Cayenne pepper sauce	⅛ tsp.	¾ tsp.	
Salt	½ tsp.	1 tbsp.	
Pumpernickel bread slices	4	24	*To prepare single serving:* Brush 1 slice bread on one side with butter. Broil under salamander, buttered side up, for 2 to 4 minutes or until toasted. Remove from broiler and spread ½ cup chicken mixture on untoasted side of bread.
Butter, salted, melted	as needed	as needed	
Peach slices, canned, well-drained, sliced in half lengthwise	8	48	Arrange 4 peach slices in pinwheel design over chicken mixture. Lightly brush with butter.
Butter, salted, melted	as needed	as needed	Broil for 3 to 4 minutes or until bubbly. Remove from broiler and slice diagonally into 4 wedges so each wedge is topped with 1 peach slice. Transfer to plate. Garnish plate with 1 grape cluster on 1 lettuce leaf.
Red grape clusters, seedless, fresh	4	24	
Green leaf lettuce leaves, fresh	4	24	

Serve with crunchy carrot and celery sticks.

Portion: 6½ ounces
Nutritional Data/Portion: Calories 470, Protein 25 g, Fat 31 g, Carbohydrate 28 g, Cholesterol 135 mg, Sodium 760

For a **FAST FACTS VIA FAX** copy of this recipe, call 1-800-223-3755 and enter Business Tool 2636.

An Englishman named Sharwood is said to have obtained the secret recipe for Madras curry powder following a banquet with the Maharaja of Madras. He brought the recipe home, and curry has been an integral part of British cuisine ever since.

It is best to keep no more than a 2-month supply of curry powder, as it quickly loses its pungency. Store it in a cool, dark place.

Pear slices may be substituted for peach slices, or use a combination of both fruits.

Submitted by MeLissa Alkinburgh
Marsh Supermarkets
Indianapolis, Ind.

Sun-drying makes tomatoes intensely flavorful, sweet, dark red, and chewy. Dry-packed varieties are best when reconstituted in very hot or boiling water.

Pesto Chicken Pizza

Flavor-packed pesto and sun-dried tomatoes harmonize with zesty Parmesan cheese and Italian chicken breast filets in this easily prepared appetizer pizza.

INGREDIENT	QUANTITY 4 servings	24 servings	METHOD
1. Tyson Fully Cooked Flavor-Redi® Italian Chicken Breast Filets, 3-oz., frozen	4	24	Cover tightly and slack in cooler between 32° and 36°F prior to use.
2. Cheese pizza crusts, prebaked, 8-inch, room temperature	4	24	To prepare single serving: Place 1 crust on baking sheet.
3. Pesto sauce, commercially prepared	½ cup	3 cups	Spread 2 tablespoons evenly over crust.
4. Mozzarella cheese, shredded	2 cups	12 cups	Sprinkle ½ cup over sauce. Julienne 1 breast filet and arrange over cheese.
5. Sun-dried tomatoes, oil-packed, drained, minced	3 tbsp.	1 cup	Top chicken with 2 teaspoons tomatoes, ¼ cup mushrooms, and 1 tablespoon bell peppers.
Button mushrooms, fresh, sliced	1 cup	6 cups	
Green bell peppers, fresh, diced (p. 88)	¼ cup	1½ cups	
6. Parmesan cheese, grated	1½ tbsp.	½ cup	Sprinkle 1 teaspoon over pizza.
			Bake in preheated conventional oven at 350°F for 20 to 22 minutes or until crust is crisp and golden. Or bake in preheated convection oven at 300°F for 7 to 9 minutes. Remove from oven. Slice into wedges and serve immediately.

Portion: 14 ounces
Nutritional Data/Portion: Calories 840, Protein 59 g, Fat 44 g, Carbohydrate 52 g, Cholesterol 150 mg, Sodium 1,560 mg

For a **FAST FACTS VIA FAX™** copy of this recipe, call 1-800-223-3755 and enter Business Tool 2651.

From the Tyson Kitchens

Sprinkle cornmeal on the baking sheet before baking to prevent the crust from sticking.

Kansas City- and Memphis-style barbecue are typically prepared "wet," using a sweet and thick tomato-based sauce. Sweeteners can run the gamut from brown sugar to honey, molasses, and even soda pop.

Kansas City Barbecue Chicken Pizza

Sweet and smoky Kansas City barbecue sauce, tangy pickle relish, and red onions create the perfect complement to chicken on this appetizer pizza.

INGREDIENT	QUANTITY 6 servings	METHOD
1. Pizza crust, parbaked, 12-inch, commercially prepared	1	Place on oiled baking sheet or pizza pan. Lightly brush top surface with oil.
Olive oil	as needed	
2. Tyson Fully Cooked Julienne Fryer Leg Meat, frozen	5½ oz.	Combine in bowl and mix thoroughly. Spread evenly over crust.
Hickory barbecue sauce, commercially prepared	⅔ cup	
Dill pickle relish, commercially prepared	¼ cup	
3. Mozzarella/provolone pizza cheese blend, shredded	1½ cups	Sprinkle over chicken mixture.
4. Red onions, fresh, slivered	½ cup	Arrange over cheese.
		Bake in preheated conventional oven at 400°F for 18 to 20 minutes or until crust is crisp and golden. Or bake in preheated convection oven at 375°F for 10 to 12 minutes. Remove from oven. Slice into wedges and serve immediately.

Portion: One-sixth of a 12-inch pizza (4⅔ ounces)
Nutritional Data/Portion: Calories 300, Protein 17 g, Fat 15 g, Carbohydrate 25 g, Cholesterol 55 mg, Sodium 740 mg

For a **FAST FACTS VIA FAX™** copy of this recipe, call 1-800-223-3755 and enter Business Tool 2362.

The eggs and bread crumbs help bind this innovative spaghetti pizza crust together.—◦

Roasting caramelizes the natural sugars in the tomatoes to produce a wonderful smoky, sweet flavor.—◦

This recipe provides an excellent use for unused portions of cooked spaghetti.—◦

Spaghetti Crust Chicken Pizza

Dazzle patrons with this unique pizza made with spaghetti-Parmesan crust prepared on a griddle, then topped with roasted tomatoes, diced chicken, fresh poblano chiles, and pepper Jack cheese.

INGREDIENT	QUANTITY 4 servings	24 servings	METHOD
1 Tyson Fully Cooked Chicken Salad Chips, frozen	1½ oz.	9 oz.	To prepare crusts, combine in bowl and mix thoroughly. Portion ¾ cup crust mixture onto 1 waxed paper sheet. Top with second sheet and press evenly into a 7-inch circle, leaving no gaps in the crust. Repeat until mixture is used.
Spaghetti, broken into 2-inch lengths, cooked al dente, well-drained	4 oz. (dry)	1½ lb. (dry)	
Eggs, large, whole, well-beaten	1	8	
Bread crumbs, dried, unseasoned	½ cup	3 cups	Grill crusts on oiled, preheated flattop griddle at 350°F for 2 to 3 minutes on each side or until lightly golden. Remove from griddle. Cover and chill below 40°F to hold.
Parmesan cheese, grated	½ cup	3 cups	
Green onions, fresh, minced	¼ cup	1½ cups	
Red bell peppers, fresh, minced	¼ cup	1½ cups	
Garlic, fresh, minced	1 tbsp.	¼ cup	
Oregano leaves, dried	1 tsp.	2 tbsp.	
Salt	¼ tsp.	1½ tsp.	
2 Tomato slices, fresh, ¼-inch thick	12	72	Arrange tomato slices in single layer on oiled sheet pans. Brush tops with oil and sprinkle with seasonings.
Olive oil	as needed	as needed	
Salt	½ tsp.	1 tbsp.	Roast in preheated conventional oven at 425°F for 15 to 20 minutes or until lightly charred. Or roast in preheated convection oven at 375°F for 10 to 12 minutes. Remove from oven. Cover and reserve.
Black pepper, coarse	¼ tsp.	1½ tsp.	
3 Olive oil	4 tsp.	½ cup	*To prepare single serving:* Heat 1 teaspoon oil in small sauté pan over high heat.
Tyson Fully Cooked Diced Chicken Fajita Pizza Toppings, Natural Proportion, ½-inch dice, frozen	8 oz.	3 lb.	When oil is very hot, add 1 pizza crust. Immediately layer crust with 2 ounces chicken, 1 tablespoon chiles, 3 slices tomato, and ½ cup cheese. Immediately place under broiler for 2 to 3 minutes or until cheese is bubbly and golden. Remove from broiler, loosen from pan, and slice into 3 wedges. Arrange on plate.
Poblano chiles, fresh, diced	¼ cup	1½ cups	
Pepper Jack cheese, shredded	2 cups	12 cups	

Portion: 7 ounces
Nutritional Data/Portion: Calories 640, Protein 42 g, Fat 36 g, Carbohydrate 39 g, Cholesterol 165 mg, Sodium 1,480 mg

For a **FAST FACTS VIA FAX**. copy of this recipe, call 1-800-223-3755 and enter Business Tool 2656.

Submitted by Ann Atkins, CHA
Holiday Inn-St. George
St. George, S.C.

𝒟ill is the strongly aromatic cousin of fennel. The Romans used dill to cover the food of gladiators going into the arena because they viewed it as a symbol of good luck. It is known for its strong-flavored seeds and its more delicately flavored leaves.~⌒

Chicken Tropicale

With its delicate flavors and rich, creamy texture, this dreamy chicken salad is as inviting as the tropics.

Lighter Fare   *Line Service*   *Takeout*

INGREDIENT	QUANTITY 4 servings	24 servings	METHOD
1 Tyson Ready-to-Cook Flavor-Redi® Savory Chicken Tenderloins, frozen	12 oz.	4½ lb.	Combine in saucepan or stockpot. Bring to boil over high heat. Reduce heat and simmer for 20 to 25 minutes or until chicken is no longer pink. (Simmer smaller quantity for 13 to 15 minutes.) Remove from heat and drain. Chill below 40°F then coarsely dice. Transfer to bowl.
Chicken broth, canned	½ cup	3 cups	
Chardonnay wine, dry	⅓ cup	2 cups	
Dill sprigs, fresh	1	4	
2 Green grapes, seedless, fresh, halved lengthwise	1 cup	6 cups	Add to chicken.
Celery, fresh, diced (p. 88)	½ cup	3 cups	
Dill, fresh, chopped	½ tbsp.	2 tbsp.	
Salt	½ tsp.	1 tbsp.	
White pepper, fine	¼ tsp.	½ tbsp.	
3 Sour cream	⅓ cup	2 cups	Add to chicken mixture and toss well. Cover and chill below 40°F to hold.
4 Kale leaves, fresh	4	24	*To assemble single serving:* Line plate with 1 kale leaf. Portion ¾ cup chicken mixture on kale. Top with 1 tablespoon coconut. Garnish plate with 1 grape cluster.
Coconut, shredded, toasted	¼ cup	1½ cups	
Green grape clusters, seedless, fresh	4	24	

Portion: 5 ounces
Nutritional Data/Portion: Calories 140, Protein 19 g, Fat 5 g, Carbohydrate 2 g, Cholesterol 45 mg, Sodium 770 mg

For a **FAST FACTS VIA FAX**™ copy of this recipe, call 1-800-223-3755 and enter Business Tool 2662.

Chile Lime Chicken Cocktail

The clever use of pickling spice, lime juice, poblano chiles, and cilantro gives this refreshing "cocktail" a distinctive flavor.

Lighter Fare *Line Service* *Takeout*

INGREDIENT	QUANTITY		METHOD
	4 servings	24 servings	
1 Tyson Fully Cooked Diced Chicken Tenderloins, ¾-inch dice, frozen	12 oz.	4 lb.	Combine in bowl and toss well. Cover and chill below 40°F to hold.
Tomatoes, fresh, seeded, ¼-inch dice	½ cup	3 cups	
Onions, fresh, ¼-inch dice (p. 175)	½ cup	3 cups	
Poblano chiles, fresh, ¼-inch dice	¼ cup	1½ cups	
Garlic, fresh, minced	2 tsp.	¼ cup	
Cilantro leaves, fresh, minced	1 tbsp.	⅓ cup	
2 Water	1 cup	6 cups	Combine in saucepan and bring to boil over high heat. Reduce heat and simmer for 20 to 25 minutes or until flavors are concentrated. (Simmer smaller quantity for 10 to 15 minutes.) Remove from heat and discard cheesecloth bag. Cool, then pour over chicken mixture and toss well. Cover and chill below 40°F for 8 hours before serving.
Lime juice, fresh	½ cup	3 cups	
Pickling spice mix, dried, secured in cheesecloth bag	2 tbsp.	½ cup	
Sugar, granulated	1 tbsp.	⅓ cup	
Red pepper, crushed, dried	¼ tsp.	½ tbsp.	
Olive oil	1 tsp.	2 tbsp.	
Salt	½ tsp.	1 tbsp.	
3 Lime wedges, fresh	4	24	*To assemble single serving:* Drain and portion ¾ cup chicken mixture into stemmed sherbet glass. Garnish with 1 lime wedge and 1 chive sprig.
Chive sprigs, fresh	4	24	
			Serve with melba rounds.

Portion: 4½ ounces
Nutritional Data/Portion: Calories 140, Protein 20 g, Fat 2 g, Carbohydrate 12 g, Cholesterol 45 mg, Sodium 560 mg

For a ***FAST FACTS VIA FAX*** copy of this recipe, call 1-800-223-3755 and enter Business Tool 2663.

There are several creative ways to present this "spa cuisine" dish. The photo includes one alternative to the sherbet glass called for in the recipe. A martini glass is also an attractive option.

Cheesecloth is lightweight, unsized cotton gauze originally used for draining whey in cheese making. Because it is durable and does not affect the flavor of food, it works well in the kitchen for straining liquids, lining molds, and forming seasoning packets to be dropped into soup or stockpots.

To adapt for takeout, place a mound of the spicy chicken mixture in the center of a to-go container and surround it with jicama slices.

Transform this dish from finger food to a handheld meal by simply folding the chicken mixture and chopped jicama into a spicy jalapeño cheese tortilla.

Leftover jicama can be shredded and used in place of cabbage to make an exotic slaw. (See recipe on page 225.)

For a more traditional dish, replace jicama slices with crunchy corn tortilla chips.

FRESH TOMATO SALSA

	4 servings	24 servings
Tomatoes, fresh, seeded, ½-inch dice	1⅓ cups	8 cups
Onions, fresh, ¼-inch dice	⅓ cup	2 cups
Green onions, fresh, bias-sliced	⅓ cup	2 cups
Jalapeño peppers, fresh, seeded, minced	½ tbsp.	3 tbsp.
Cilantro, fresh, chopped	⅓ cup	2 cups
Ice water	1 tbsp.	½ cup
Lime juice, fresh	1 tbsp.	½ cup
Salt	¼ tsp.	2 tsp.

Combine in bowl and mix lightly. Cover and chill for 30 minutes before serving.

Portion: 3 ounces

Spicy Chicken and Jicama Nachos

Here's a fresh idea for fancy nachos. Crispy jicama serves as the carrier for a spicy mixture of chicken, peppers, and salsa con queso.

INGREDIENT	QUANTITY 4 servings	24 servings	METHOD
1 Tyson Fully Cooked Mesquite Chicken Pizza Toppings, Natural Proportion Strips, frozen	8 oz.	3 lb.	Combine in bowl and mix thoroughly. Cover and chill below 40°F to hold.
Green onions, fresh, bias-sliced	¼ cup	1½ cups	
Red bell peppers, fresh, chopped	¼ cup	1½ cups	
Jalapeño peppers, hot, canned, drained, minced	2 tsp.	4½ tbsp.	
Garlic, fresh, minced	½ tsp.	1 tbsp.	
Cilantro leaves, fresh, chopped	1 tbsp.	⅓ cup	
Cumin, ground	1 tsp.	2 tbsp.	
Red pepper, ground	⅛ tsp.	¾ tsp.	
Salt	¼ tsp.	½ tbsp.	
Lime juice, fresh	½ tbsp.	3 tbsp.	
Salsa con queso, commercially prepared	¼ cup	1½ cups	
2 Jicama, fresh, chilled, peeled	1	6	Cut each jicama into quarters. Cut each quarter into ¼-inch-thick slices. Transfer to bowl and toss with lime juice. Cover and chill to hold.
Lime juice, fresh	1 tbsp.	¼ cup	
3 Romaine lettuce leaves, fresh	12	72	*To assemble single serving:* Line plate with 3 lettuce leaves. Arrange 6 jicama slices on leaves. Top each slice with generous ½ tablespoon chicken mixture. Top chicken mixture with ½ teaspoon each of guacamole and sour cream.
Guacamole, commercially prepared	¼ cup	1½ cups	
Sour cream	¼ cup	1½ cups	

Serve with fresh tomato salsa.

Portion: 7½ ounces
Nutritional Data/Portion: Calories 240, Protein 15 g, Fat 12 g, Carbohydrate 20 g, Cholesterol 65 mg, Sodium 590 mg

For a ***FAST FACTS VIA FAX*** copy of this recipe, call 1-800-223-3755 and enter Business Tool 2353.

Submitted by Noah S. Barton
Hyatt Newporter
Newport Beach, Calif.

Pico de Gallo Chicken Pizza

Zesty pico de gallo replaces traditional tomato sauce on this pizza that is topped with chicken tossed in a delicious red onion compote. Sour cream and guacamole help cool the heat.

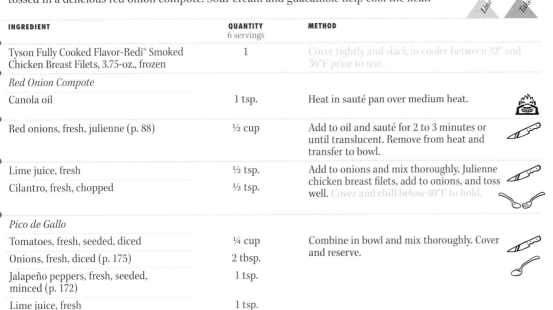

	INGREDIENT	QUANTITY 6 servings	METHOD	
1	Tyson Fully Cooked Flavor-Redi® Smoked Chicken Breast Filets, 3.75-oz., frozen	1	Cover tightly and slack in cooler between 32° and 36°F prior to use.	
2	*Red Onion Compote*			
	Canola oil	1 tsp.	Heat in sauté pan over medium heat.	
3	Red onions, fresh, julienne (p. 88)	½ cup	Add to oil and sauté for 2 to 3 minutes or until translucent. Remove from heat and transfer to bowl.	
4	Lime juice, fresh	½ tsp.	Add to onions and mix thoroughly. Julienne chicken breast filets, add to onions, and toss well. Cover and chill below 40°F to hold.	
	Cilantro, fresh, chopped	½ tsp.		
5	*Pico de Gallo*			
	Tomatoes, fresh, seeded, diced	¼ cup	Combine in bowl and mix thoroughly. Cover and reserve.	
	Onions, fresh, diced (p. 175)	2 tbsp.		
	Jalapeño peppers, fresh, seeded, minced (p. 172)	1 tsp.		
	Lime juice, fresh	1 tsp.		
	Salt	¼ tsp.		
6	Pizza dough, presheeted, 12-inch, unbaked, frozen, slacked according to package directions	1	Place on oiled baking sheet or pizza pan.	
7	Canola oil	½ tbsp.	Combine in bowl and mix thoroughly. Spread evenly over crust. Layer with pico de gallo then red onion compote and chicken mixture.	
	Garlic, fresh, minced	1 tsp.		
	Oregano, fresh, minced	½ tsp.		
8	Mexican cheese blend, shredded	¼ cup	Sprinkle over pizza.	
			Bake in preheated conventional oven at 450°F for 10 to 12 minutes or until crust is crisp and golden. Or bake in preheated convection oven at 375°F for 7 to 10 minutes. Remove from oven.	
9	Sour cream	2 tbsp.	Drop sour cream and guacamole by teaspoon over pizza. Slice into wedges and serve immediately.	
	Guacamole, commercially prepared	2 tbsp.		

Portion: One-sixth of a 12-inch pizza (3⅔ ounces)
Nutritional Data/Portion: Calories 180, Protein 9 g, Fat 6 g, Carbohydrate 23 g, Cholesterol 20 mg, Sodium 480 mg

For a **FAST FACTS VIA FAX**™ copy of this recipe, call 1-800-223-3755 and enter Business Tool 2653.

Pico de gallo, meaning "beak of the rooster," refers to the small cuts of vegetables in the salsa—small enough for a rooster to pick up in its beak.

Canola is the trade name for rapeseed oil, first used by the Chinese in the 14th century. It was renamed canola oil by the Canadian seed-oil industry soon after it was granted GRAS (generally recognized as safe) status by the FDA in the mid-1980s. The rapeseed comes from a member of the mustard family and is most widely produced in Japan and Canada.

Submitted by Cary Neff
Miraval, Life in Balance™ Resort
Catalina, Ariz.

The traditional Napoleon is a creamy layered dessert made with puff pastry and custard.‒◦

A Provençal summer dish, ratatouille is a combination of eggplant, tomatoes, onions, bell peppers, zucchini, garlic, and herbs simmered together. It is excellent served hot, cold, or at room temperature.‒◦

Chicken Tortilla Napoleon with Confetti Ratatouille

This spectacular dish will turn heads when it's brought to the table. Layers of sautéed peppered chicken, crispy flour tortillas, and wonderful black bean sauce are dressed with a colorful "confetti" of eggplant, zucchini, yellow squash, and bell peppers.

	INGREDIENT	QUANTITY		METHOD
		4 servings	24 servings	
1	Tyson Ready-to-Cook Tenderpressed™ Savory Chicken Breast Filets, 4-oz., frozen	4	24	Brush chicken with oil. Grill on oiled, preheated flattop griddle at 350°F for 4½ minutes on each side or until chicken is no longer pink. Remove from griddle.
	Olive oil	as needed	as needed	
2	Parsley, fresh, minced (p. 39)	2 tsp.	¼ cup	Combine in bowl and sprinkle over chicken. Keep warm above 140°F.
	Salt	1 tsp.	2 tbsp.	
3	Black pepper, coarse	¼ tsp.	½ tbsp.	
	Ratatouille of Vegetables			
	Olive oil	1 tbsp.	¼ cup	Heat in skillet or braising pan over medium-high heat.
4	Eggplant, fresh, ⅛-inch dice (p. 88)	½ cup	1¾ cups	Add to oil and mix thoroughly. Sauté for 5 to 6 minutes or until vegetables are tender-crisp. (Sauté smaller quantity for 1 to 2 minutes.)
	Zucchini, fresh, ⅛-inch dice	½ cup	1¾ cups	
	Onions, fresh, ⅛-inch dice (p. 175)	½ cup	1¾ cups	
5	Yellow squash, fresh, ⅛-inch dice	½ cup	1¾ cups	
	Portobello mushrooms, fresh, ⅛-inch dice	¼ cup	1 cup	Add to vegetable mixture and mix thoroughly. Sauté for 2 to 3 minutes or until peppers are tender-crisp. (Sauté smaller quantity for 1 to 2 minutes.)
	Red bell peppers, fresh, ⅛-inch dice	¼ cup	1 cup	
	Yellow bell peppers, fresh, ⅛-inch dice	¼ cup	1 cup	
6	Green bell peppers, fresh, ⅛-inch dice	¼ cup	1 cup	
	Tomatoes, fresh, seeded, ⅛-inch dice	1 cup	3¾ cups	Add to vegetable mixture and mix thoroughly. Bring to boil over medium-high heat. Reduce heat and simmer for 25 to 30 minutes or until liquid has evaporated. (Simmer smaller quantity for 18 to 20 minutes.) Remove from heat and keep warm.
	Garlic, fresh, minced	1 tbsp.	¼ cup	
	Basil, fresh, chopped	½ tbsp.	2 tbsp.	
	Oregano leaves, dried	½ tsp.	½ tbsp.	
	Sherry vinegar	1½ tbsp.	⅓ cup	
	Salt	½ tbsp.	2 tbsp.	
	Black pepper, coarse	1 tsp.	1 tbsp.	

recipe continued on next page . . .

INGREDIENT	QUANTITY		METHOD
	4 servings	24 servings	
7 *Black Bean Sauce*			
Olive oil	¼ tsp.	1 tsp.	Heat in saucepan over medium-high heat.
8 Black beans, canned, rinsed, drained	1½ cups	6½ cups	Add to oil and sauté for 5 to 7 minutes or until onions are translucent. (Sauté smaller quantity for 2 to 3 minutes.)
Onions, fresh, minced	2 tbsp.	½ cup	
Tomatoes, fresh, seeded, minced	2 tbsp.	½ cup	
Garlic, fresh, minced	1 tsp.	1½ tbsp.	
Cilantro, fresh, minced	½ tbsp.	2 tbsp.	
Oregano leaves, dried	1 tsp.	1½ tbsp.	
Serrano chiles, fresh, seeded, minced (p. 172)	½ tsp.	½ tbsp.	
9 Tequila	1 tbsp.	¼ cup	Add to black bean mixture and flambé.
10 Chicken broth, canned	1 cup	4 cups	Add to black bean mixture and mix thoroughly. Bring to boil over high heat. Reduce heat and simmer for 25 to 27 minutes or until liquid is reduced by half. (Simmer smaller quantity for 15 to 20 minutes.) Remove from heat. Transfer to food processor bowl and process until pureed. Remove from processor bowl and strain through fine mesh strainer. Keep warm.
11 Tyson Mexican Original® Flour Tortillas, 7-inch, room temperature, cut into quarters	4	24	Deep-fry at 360°F for 45 to 60 seconds or until brown. Remove from fryer and drain. Keep warm.
12 Cilantro, fresh, minced	¼ cup	1½ cups	*To assemble single serving:* Bias-slice 1 chicken breast filet into 3 pieces. Layer ingredients on plate in the following order to form a stack: 1 tortilla quarter, 1 chicken piece, 1 tablespoon black bean sauce, 1 tablespoon ratatouille. Repeat layers twice, ending with 1 tablespoon ratatouille and 1 tablespoon sauce as final garnish on top. (Total amount to be used for each Napoleon is ¼ cup each of ratatouille and sauce, 1 whole tortilla, and 1 whole chicken breast filet.) Sprinkle entire plate with 1 tablespoon cilantro.

Portion: 8 ounces
Nutritional Data/Portion: Calories 430, Protein 35 g, Fat 13 g, Carbohydrate 44 g, Cholesterol 60 mg, Sodium 2,120 mg

For a **FAST FACTS VIA FAX**™ copy of this recipe, call 1-800-223-3755 and enter Business Tool 2645.

Even though serrano chiles are small, they pack a lot of heat. It is wise to wear latex gloves while handling them.

HOW TO MINCE PARSLEY
1) *Wash parsley in cold water and drain well. Remove sprigs from stems.*
2) *Gripping knife handle in one hand, place other hand on knife tip and hold down on cutting board. Keeping knife tip on board, rock blade up and down while moving it back and forth over parsley.*

Submitted by Glen A. Smith
Nellie's Deli Market & Catering
Sarasota, Fla.

Horseradish is an ancient herb of the mustard family. Although its leaves can be used in salads, it is primarily cultivated for the pungent roots. A well-known catsup maker got its start in 1869 by packing processed horseradish in clear jars.⊸

The recipe describes a single serving, but this dish also works great as a shared starter as pictured.⊸

Trilogy of Chicken Wings

Mountains of wings are waiting to be dipped into a trio of signature-style sauces. It's really three dishes on one plate—a triple play of flavors and colors.

INGREDIENT	QUANTITY 4 servings	24 servings	METHOD
Tyson Fully Cooked Breaded W.W. Flyers® Chicken Wings and Drummies, frozen	32	192	Deep-fry at 350°F for 3½ to 4 minutes. Remove from fryer and drain. Keep warm above 140°F.
Jezebel Sauce			
Orange marmalade	⅔ cup	4 cups	Combine in bowl and mix thoroughly. Cover and chill to hold.
Horseradish, prepared	3 tbsp.	1 cup	
Sour cream	3 tbsp.	1 cup	
Spicy Tomato Salsa			
Tomatoes, fresh, seeded, small dice	1 cup	6 cups	Combine in separate bowl and mix thoroughly. Cover and chill to hold.
Green bell peppers, fresh, small dice (p. 88)	2 tbsp.	¾ cup	
Garlic, fresh, minced	1 tsp.	2 tbsp.	
Red pepper, crushed, dried	¼ tsp.	½ tbsp.	
Lemon juice, fresh	1 tsp.	2 tbsp.	
White wine, dry	1 tsp.	2 tbsp.	
Cilantro, fresh, minced	1 tsp.	2 tbsp.	
Salt	¼ tsp.	½ tbsp.	
Yellow Curry Sauce			
Sour cream	1 cup	6 cups	Combine in separate bowl and whisk thoroughly until smooth. Cover and chill to hold.
Curry powder	½ tbsp.	3 tbsp.	
Paprika	1 tsp.	2 tbsp.	*To assemble single serving:* Arrange 8 wings and drummies on plate. Portion ¼ cup of each dipping sauce into separate containers and serve on the side.
Salt	¼ tsp.	½ tbsp.	
Black pepper, fine	¼ tsp.	½ tbsp.	

Portion: 8 ounces plus 2 ounces each sauce
Nutritional Data/Portion: Calories 800, Protein 33 g, Fat 49 g, Carbohydrate 63 g, Cholesterol 200 mg, Sodium 1,620 mg

For a **FAST FACTS VIA FAX** copy of this recipe, call 1-800-223-3755 and enter Business Tool 2661.

Submitted by Robert Knudson
Casa Mia Restaurants
Olympia, Wash.

Creamy Gorgonzola Chicken Pizza

The ingredients are Italian all the way, but not in the traditional sense. This pizza's Gorgonzola, Parmesan, and roasted-garlic cheese sauce sets it apart from the crowd.

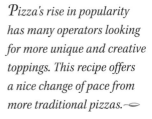

INGREDIENT	QUANTITY 6 servings	METHOD
1 Pizza dough, presheeted, 14-inch, unbaked, frozen, slacked according to package directions	1	Place on oiled baking sheet or pizza pan.
2 *Creamy Gorgonzola Sauce*		
Evaporated milk, canned	¼ cup	Combine in saucepan and mix thoroughly. Heat over medium heat for 3 to 4 minutes, stirring constantly, or until cheese is melted. Remove from heat.
Gorgonzola cheese, crumbled	⅓ cup	
Parmesan cheese, grated	2 tbsp.	
Garlic, roasted, minced	1 tsp.	
Salt	¹⁄₁₆ tsp.	
Black pepper, coarse	¹⁄₁₆ tsp.	
3 Buttermilk, fresh	1½ tbsp.	Add to sauce and mix thoroughly. Spread evenly over crust.
Mayonnaise	1½ tbsp.	
4 Tyson Fully Cooked Diced Italian Chicken Pizza Toppings, ¼-inch dice, frozen	5 oz.	Arrange over sauce.
5 Red onions, fresh, slivered	½ cup	Layer over chicken.
Red bell peppers, roasted, canned, drained, julienne	⅓ cup	
Black olives, sliced, canned, drained	¼ cup	
6 Mozzarella cheese, shredded	1 cup	Sprinkle over pizza.
		Bake in preheated conventional oven at 475°F for 13 to 15 minutes or until crust is crisp and golden. Or bake in preheated convection oven at 425°F for 5 to 7 minutes. Remove from oven.
7 Basil leaves, fresh, minced	1 tbsp.	Sprinkle basil and cheese over pizza. Lightly spray with vinegar. Slice into wedges and serve immediately.
Parmesan cheese, grated	3 tbsp.	
Balsamic vinegar	as needed	

Portion: One-sixth of a 14-inch pizza (6⅔ ounces)
Nutritional Data/Portion: Calories 407, Protein 20 g, Fat 15 g, Carbohydrate 50 g, Cholesterol 51 mg, Sodium 945 mg

For a **FAST FACTS VIA FAX** copy of this recipe, call 1-800-223-3755 and enter Business Tool 2643.

Pizza's rise in popularity has many operators looking for more unique and creative toppings. This recipe offers a nice change of pace from more traditional pizzas.

See sidebar on page 85 for how to roast garlic.

"*Like conversation,
you can put everything into salad
(and the more things the better):
everything depends on the skill of mixing.*"

Charles Dudley Warner

Salads

Tossing salads with fresh ideas

The salad, as we commonly think of it, took root in France during the early 19th century and consisted of greens dressed with oil and vinegar, mashed egg yolk, and a little bit of mustard. In 1861, the author of *The American Practical Cookery-Book* defined the salad's role as part of the second course of a meal, and that is where it was confined for over a century.

Today, menu opportunities abound because people view salads as a healthy connection to everything fresh and wholesome. Salads can be at once adventurous and familiar, exotic and practical. Even side salads can set the stage for a rewarding meal experience with a mélange of exciting greens, crisp vegetables, and specialty dressings.

Adding chicken can help transform the basic salad into a veritable feast, rewarding the diner with indulgent flavors balanced with the satisfaction of eating right. Meal-size signature salads also reward their creators with quicker preparation, reduced food costs, and lower menu prices than most other entrees.

The salad category is a wonderful arena for culinary experimentation and exploration—what grows together, goes together. The combination of acceptable ingredients is limited only by imagination. Served hot or cold, tossed with pasta, or presented as artful palates of colors and shapes, salads can be infused with ethnic flavors from Asian to Mexican.

This chapter contains fresh ideas contributed by operators from Oregon to South Carolina—a sampler of the most popular trends in salads.

Submitted by Edward Carloni
Lebanon Country Club
Myerstown, Pa.

*For a more dramatic plate
presentation, garnish
with fresh shavings of
Parmesan cheese.*

*Legend has it that Alex
Cardini, an Italian Air Force
veteran, invented the
Caesar Salad in 1924 at his
restaurant/hotel in Mexico.
Alex was short on supplies
when a group celebrating the
4th of July holiday arrived.
Using ingredients on hand—
eggs, romaine lettuce,
Parmesan cheese, dried
bread, garlic, olive oil, lemon
juice, and pepper—he
prepared what he first
called Aviator Salad. He
later renamed it after his
brother, Caesar.*

*This salad works well
whether it is served with
warm or chilled chicken.*

Grilled Chicken Caesar Pasta Salad

The popular chicken Caesar salad reaches new heights of flavor with the addition of a few ingredients, including penne pasta, fresh mozzarella cubes, and whole Moroccan olives.

INGREDIENT	QUANTITY		METHOD
	4 servings	24 servings	
1 Tyson Ready-to-Cook Tenderpressed™ Italian Chicken Breast Filets, 5-oz., frozen	4	24	Char-grill over high heat for 5 to 6 minutes on each side or until chicken is no longer pink. Or grill on oiled, preheated flattop griddle at 350°F for 6½ to 7½ minutes on each side. Remove from grill.
2 Caesar salad dressing, commercially prepared	as needed	as needed	Coat both sides of chicken breast filets with dressing. Keep warm above 140°F.
3 Romaine lettuce, fresh, coarse-chopped	12 cups	72 cups	Combine in bowl and toss well. Cover and chill to hold.
Penne pasta, cooked al dente, rinsed, drained, chilled	6 oz. (dry)	2¼ lb. (dry)	
4 Mozzarella cheese, fresh, ½-inch cubes	2 cups	12 cups	*To assemble single serving:* Combine 4 cups salad mixture, ½ cup mozzarella, 2 table-spoons Romano, 5 olives, and ¼ teaspoon pepper in bowl. Slice 1 chicken breast filet into thin strips and add to salad. Toss with ⅓ cup salad dressing and transfer to plate.
Romano cheese, grated	½ cup	3 cups	
Moroccan olives, whole, pitted, oil-cured, drained	20	120	
Black pepper, coarse	1 tsp.	2 tbsp.	
Caesar salad dressing, commercially prepared	1⅓ cups	8 cups	*Serve with herb focaccia bread.*

Portion: 15 ounces
Nutritional Data/Portion: Calories 840, Protein 58 g, Fat 51 g, Carbohydrate 37 g, Cholesterol 195 mg, Sodium 1,640 mg

For a ***FAST FACTS VIA FAX*** copy of this recipe, call 1-800-223-3755 and enter Business Tool 2377.

Submitted by Michael D. Ward
Ochsner Foundation Hospital
New Orleans, La.

Commercially prepared
balsamic vinaigrette or
red wine vinaigrette may
be substituted.

Perfectly ripe honeydews
will have an almost
indistinguishable wrinkling
on the skin's surface, often
detectable only by touch.
Choose melons that are
heavy for their size.
Underripe honeydew
melons can be ripened
at room temperature.

Cantaloupe is a European
melon named for a castle
in Italy. American
cantaloupes are actually
muskmelons. When perfectly
ripe, they have raised
netting on a smooth
grayish-beige skin.

Summer Melon Chicken Salad

Juicy pieces of fresh cantaloupe, honeydew, and grapes are tossed in basil-Dijon balsamic
vinaigrette and topped with a sherry- and garlic-marinated chicken breast filet.

Lighter Fare *Takeout*

INGREDIENT	QUANTITY		METHOD
	4 servings	24 servings	
① Tyson Gourmet Boneless, Skinless Whole Chicken Breast Filets, 7-oz., frozen	4	24	Place in full-size steam table pans. (Use half-size pan for smaller quantity.)
② *Marinade*			
Cooking sherry	⅓ cup	2 cups	Combine in bowl and mix thoroughly. Pour over chicken. Cover and marinate below 40°F for 8 to 10 hours.
Garlic, fresh, minced	1 tbsp.	⅓ cup	
Paprika, ground	¼ tsp.	½ tbsp.	
Salt	1 tsp.	2 tbsp.	
White pepper, fine	¼ tsp.	½ tbsp.	
③ Olive oil	2 tbsp.	¾ cup	Heat in skillet over medium-high heat. Remove chicken from marinade and sauté for 3 to 4 minutes on each side or until chicken is no longer pink. Remove from heat. Keep warm above 140°F.
④ Cantaloupe, fresh, peeled, 1-inch dice	1 cup	6 cups	Combine in bowl and toss well. Cover and chill to hold.
Honeydew melon, fresh, peeled, 1-inch dice	1 cup	6 cups	
Tomatoes, fresh, sliced in wedges	1 cup	6 cups	
Red grapes, seedless, fresh, halved lengthwise	1 cup	6 cups	
⑤ *Basil-Dijon Vinaigrette*			
Red wine vinegar	¼ cup	1¾ cups	Combine in food processor bowl and process until well blended.
Balsamic vinegar	2 tbsp.	1 cup	
Mustard, Dijon	1 tbsp.	⅓ cup	
Sugar, granulated	1 tsp.	3 tbsp.	
Basil leaves, dried	1 tsp.	3 tbsp.	
Salt	½ tsp.	1½ tbsp.	
Black pepper, coarse	½ tsp.	1½ tbsp.	

recipe continued on next page . . .

INGREDIENT	QUANTITY 4 servings	24 servings	METHOD
6 Olive oil	⅓ cup	2½ cups	Gradually add to processor bowl while motor is running and process until emulsified. Remove from processor bowl. Cover and chill to hold.
7 Romaine lettuce, fresh, chopped	12 cups	72 cups	*To assemble single serving:* Combine 3 cups lettuce and 1 cup fruit mixture with ¼ cup vinaigrette in bowl and toss well. Transfer to plate. Slice 1 chicken breast filet into strips and fan over salad. Garnish plate with 1 basil sprig.
Basil sprigs, fresh	4	24	

Serve with crusty French or Italian bread.

This salad works well whether it is served with warm or chilled chicken.

Portion: 16 ounces
Nutritional Data/Portion: Calories 450, Protein 36 g, Fat 23 g, Carbohydrate 23 g, Cholesterol 65 mg, Sodium 550 mg

For a **FAST FACTS VIA FAX** copy of this recipe, call 1-800-223-3755 and enter Business Tool 2381.

Chicken Fajita Salad

The popular Southwestern fajita gains broader operator, daypart, and patron appeal when it moves into the entree salad arena. The spicy fajita dressing and fresh onions, peppers, garlic, and cilantro elevate this salad to a new level of taste.

Submitted by Darren Victory
Willis-Knighton Health System
Shreveport, La.

INGREDIENT	QUANTITY 4 servings	24 servings	METHOD
1 Tyson Fully Cooked Mixed Chicken Fajita Strips, Natural Proportion, frozen	1½ lb.	9 lb.	Cover tightly and slack in cooler between 32° and 36°F prior to use.
2 *Fajita Salad Dressing*			
Italian vinaigrette, fat-free, commercially prepared	1¾ cups	7 cups	Combine in bowl and mix thoroughly. Cover and chill to hold.
Chives, chopped, dried	¼ cup	1 cup	
Parsley flakes, dried	¼ cup	1 cup	
Cumin, ground	1 tbsp.	2 tbsp.	
Chili powder, light	1 tbsp.	2 tbsp.	
Lemon pepper	1 tsp.	2 tsp.	
Garlic, minced, dried	¼ tsp.	1 tsp.	
Greek seasoning, all-purpose, dried	¼ tsp.	1 tsp.	
Creole seasoning, dried	¼ tsp.	1 tsp.	
Red pepper, crushed, dried	⅛ tsp.	½ tsp.	
Salt	¼ tsp.	1 tsp.	
Black pepper, coarse	⅛ tsp.	½ tsp.	
3 Red leaf lettuce leaves, fresh	12	72	*To assemble single serving:* Line plate with 3 lettuce leaves. Arrange 2 cups salad greens on lettuce. Top with 6 ounces chicken. Portion ⅓ cup olives in 12 o'clock position of plate, ¼ cup jalapeños in 3 o'clock position, ⅓ cup cheese in 6 o'clock position, and ¼ cup sour cream in 9 o'clock position. Drizzle ⅓ cup dressing over salad. Portion ⅓ cup pico de gallo into individual container and serve on the side.
Mixed salad greens, fresh, commercially prepared	8 cups	48 cups	
Black olives, sliced, canned, drained	1⅓ cups	8 cups	
Cheddar cheese, sharp, shredded	1⅓ cups	8 cups	
Jalapeño peppers, sliced, canned, drained	1 cup	6 cups	
Sour cream	1 cup	6 cups	
Fiesta Pico de Gallo (see recipe)	1⅓ cups	8 cups	*Serve with warm flour tortillas.*

FIESTA PICO DE GALLO

	4 servings	24 servings
Cherry tomatoes, fresh, diced	⅔ cup	4 cups
Red onions, fresh, diced	⅓ cup	2 cups
Yellow bell peppers, fresh, diced	⅓ cup	2 cups
Garlic, fresh, minced	½ tsp.	1 tbsp.
Jalapeño peppers, fresh, seeded, minced	½ tbsp.	3 tbsp.
Lime juice, fresh	1 tbsp.	⅓ cup
Cilantro, fresh, minced	1 tbsp.	⅓ cup
Sugar, granulated	⅛ tsp.	¾ tsp.
Salt	⅛ tsp.	¾ tsp.
Black pepper, coarse	⅛ tsp.	¾ tsp.

Combine in bowl and mix thoroughly. Cover and chill to hold.

Portion: 16 ounces plus 2 ounces condiment
Nutritional Data/Portion: Calories 600, Protein 38 g, Fat 42 g, Carbohydrate 22 g, Cholesterol 175 mg, Sodium 1,824 mg

For a **FAST FACTS VIA FAX** copy of this recipe, call 1-800-223-3755 and enter Business Tool 2391.

Chicken Niçoise Salad

Inspired by the classic Mediterranean dish served on the French Riviera, the Niçoise Salad is akin to the Cobb Salad in that its ingredients are arranged in groups on the plate.

Niçoise (nee-shwa) is a French term meaning, "as prepared in Nice." Classic salade niçoise includes tomatoes, black olives, garlic, anchovies, French-cut green beans, onions, tuna, hard-cooked eggs, and herbs.

Tarragon is a perennial herb known for its distinctive licoricelike flavor. It is widely used in classic French cooking.

INGREDIENT	QUANTITY 4 servings	24 servings	METHOD
1 Tyson Fully Cooked Flavor-Redi® Roasted and Carved Chicken Breast Filets, frozen	1 lb.	6 lb.	Cover tightly and slack in cooler between 32° and 36°F prior to use.
2 *Niçoise Vinaigrette*			
Tarragon vinegar	⅓ cup	2 cups	Combine in food processor bowl and process until well blended.
Shallots, fresh, chopped	1 tbsp.	⅓ cup	
Mustard, Dijon	1 tbsp.	⅓ cup	
Parsley, fresh, chopped	1 tbsp.	⅓ cup	
Lemon juice, fresh	1 tsp.	2 tbsp.	
Sugar, granulated	⅛ tsp.	¾ tsp.	
Salt	⅛ tsp.	¾ tsp.	
Black pepper, fine	⅛ tsp.	¾ tsp.	
3 Olive oil	1 cup	6 cups	Gradually add to processor bowl while motor is running and process until emulsified. Remove from processor bowl. Cover and chill to hold.
4 New red potatoes, unpeeled, boiled, drained, slightly cooled, sliced	3 cups	18 cups	Combine in bowl with 3 cups vinaigrette and toss well. (Use ½ cup vinaigrette for smaller quantity.) Cover and chill to hold.

recipe continued on next page . . .

INGREDIENT	QUANTITY 4 servings	24 servings	METHOD
⑤ Boston lettuce leaves, fresh	12	72	*To assemble single serving:* Line plate with 3 lettuce leaves. Portion 1 cup torn lettuce in center of plate. Pull 1 chicken breast filet into large pieces and place over torn lettuce. Surround chicken with ⅔ cup potatoes, 10 green beans, 4 egg quarters, 3 tomato halves, and 3 olives. Portion ¼ cup vinaigrette in individual container and place on plate.
Boston lettuce, fresh, torn	4 cups	24 cups	
Green beans, whole, fresh, blanched, drained, chilled	40	240	
Eggs, hard-boiled, quartered	4	24	
Cherry tomato halves, fresh	12	72	
Niçoise olives, whole, canned, drained	12	72	

Serve with warm bread.

Niçoise olives originate in the Provence region of France. They are cured in brine and packed in olive oil. The best niçoise olives have a rich, nutty, mellow flavor.

Portion: 15 ounces plus 2 ounces dressing
Nutritional Data/Portion: Calories 720, Protein 39 g, Fat 49 g, Carbohydrate 35 g, Cholesterol 205 mg, Sodium 900 mg

For a **FAST FACTS VIA FAX** copy of this recipe, call 1-800-223-3755 and enter Business Tool 2398.

Mandarin Chicken Salad

Notes of ginger highlight the low-fat orange yogurt dressing that distinguishes this chicken salad with big flavor and a conservative calorie count.

*Submitted by Lucille Kingsbury, RD
Gerber Memorial Hospital
Fremont, Mich.*

INGREDIENT	QUANTITY 4 servings	24 servings	METHOD
① Tyson Fully Cooked Flavor-Redi® Roasted and Carved Chicken Breast Filets, frozen	1 lb.	6 lb.	Cover tightly and slack in cooler between 32° and 36°F prior to use.
② Mandarin orange segments, canned, drained	1½ cups	9 cups	Combine in bowl. Pull chicken breast filets into large pieces and add to bowl.
Water chestnuts, sliced, canned, drained	½ cup	3 cups	
Green onions, fresh, chopped	¼ cup	1½ cups	
Green bell peppers, fresh, chopped	¼ cup	1½ cups	
③ *Orange-Ginger Dressing*			
Yogurt, orange-flavored, low-fat	½ cup	3 cups	Combine in separate bowl and mix thoroughly until well blended. Add to chicken mixture and toss well. Cover and chill below 40°F to hold.
Salad dressing, mayonnaise-style, low-fat	¼ cup	1½ cups	
Honey	2 tbsp.	¾ cup	
Lemon juice, fresh	1 tbsp.	⅓ cup	
Apple cider vinegar	2 tsp.	¼ cup	
Gingerroot, fresh, peeled, grated	2 tsp.	¼ cup	
④ Endive leaves, curly, fresh	12	72	*To assemble single serving:* Line plate with 3 endive leaves. Portion 1½ cups salad on endive. Top with 3 orange segments and 1 tablespoon almonds.
Mandarin orange segments, canned, drained	12	72	
Almonds, sliced, toasted	¼ cup	1½ cups	*Serve with crunchy breadsticks.*

This salad presents and holds well, making it ideal for buffet lines and catering.

The mandarin orange is a loose-skinned member of the tangerine family. Varieties include clementine, dancy, and satsuma; but the small, seedless Japanese satsuma orange is the most commonly canned mandarin orange.

Portion: 10 ounces
Nutritional Data/Portion: Calories 350, Protein 32 g, Fat 11 g, Carbohydrate 35 g, Cholesterol 80 mg, Sodium 810 mg

For a **FAST FACTS VIA FAX** copy of this recipe, call 1-800-223-3755 and enter Business Tool 2376.

Submitted by Camp Howard
Vanderbilt Dining
Nashville, Tenn.

Mesclun is any mix of small young salad greens that commonly includes arugula, dandelion, frisée, mizuma, oak leaf, mâche, radicchio, and sorrel.

Cubed cornbread makes a wonderful substitute for white bread in the barbecue croutons recipe.

BARBECUE CROUTONS

	4 servings	24 servings
Homestyle white bread, commercially prepared, crusts removed, ½-inch dice	2 cups	12 cups
Barbecue seasoning, dried	1 tbsp.	⅛ cup

Combine in bowl and toss well. Spread on sheet pan and bake in preheated conventional oven at 300°F for 30 to 45 minutes or until crisp and dried. Remove from oven. Cool and store in tightly covered container.

Smoky Mountain Barbecue Chicken Salad

This signature salad is infused with Southern barbecue tradition. It features grilled chicken tenderloins on a bed of romaine lettuce, mesclun greens, and basil leaves tossed with unique barbecue salad dressing and barbecue croutons.

Line Service · Takeout

INGREDIENT	QUANTITY 4 servings	24 servings	METHOD
1 Tyson Fully Cooked Flavor-Redi® Chicken Tenderloins with Grill Marks, frozen	12	72	Cover tightly and slack in cooler between 32° and 36°F prior to use.
2 Roma tomatoes, fresh, diced	1 cup	6 cups	Combine in bowl and mix thoroughly. Cover and chill to hold.
Olive oil	1 tsp.	2 tbsp.	
Black pepper, coarse	1 tsp.	2 tbsp.	
3 Romaine lettuce, fresh, coarse-chopped	12 cups	72 cups	Combine in separate bowl and toss well. Cover and chill to hold.
Mesclun salad greens mix, fresh, commercially prepared	4 cups	24 cups	
Basil, fresh, chiffonade (p. 28)	¼ cup	1½ cups	
4 *Barbecue Salad Dressing*			
Barbecue sauce, commercially prepared	½ cup	3 cups	Combine in bowl and whisk until well blended.
Olive oil	¼ cup	1½ cups	
Balsamic vinegar	2 tbsp.	¾ cup	
5 Red onions, fresh, minced	¼ cup	1½ cups	Add to dressing and mix thoroughly. Cover and chill to hold.
Garlic, fresh, minced	2 tsp.	¼ cup	
Black pepper, coarse	2 tsp.	¼ cup	
6 Barbecue Croutons (see recipe)	1 cup	6 cups	*To assemble single serving:* Combine 4 cups lettuce mixture, ¼ cup salad dressing, 2 tablespoons croutons, and 2 tablespoons cheese in bowl. Toss well and transfer to plate. Top with additional 2 tablespoons cheese and 2 tablespoons croutons. Arrange 3 chicken tenderloins over salad and garnish with ¼ cup tomato mixture.
White cheddar cheese, sharp, shredded	1 cup	6 cups	

Serve with corn muffins.

Portion: 13 ounces
Nutritional Data/Portion: Calories 620, Protein 62 g, Fat 29 g, Carbohydrate 30 g, Cholesterol 140 mg, Sodium 1,660 mg

For a **FAST FACTS VIA FAX**™ copy of this recipe, call 1-800-223-3755 and enter Business Tool 2380.

Submitted by Ella Mae Stutz
Villas of Brookhaven
Brookville, Ohio

Kidney beans are among the most popular beans because of their full-bodied flavor and ready availability dried or canned.‿

For a different presentation, serve this salad in a bread bowl. The bread will soak up the dressing for an added treat.‿

For takeout, package the vinaigrette separately and place the chicken and bean mixture on top of the greens without tossing. The customer should toss the salad when the vinaigrette is added.‿

Tangy Chicken and Bean Salad

Fresh summer garden vegetables and lettuces soak up the tangy dressing—a perfect complement to the char-grilled chicken they're served with.

INGREDIENT	QUANTITY 4 servings	24 servings	METHOD
1 Tyson Ready-to-Cook Tenderpressed™ Savory Chicken Breast Filets, 4.5-oz., frozen	4	24	Char-grill over high heat for 5 to 6 minutes on each side or until chicken is no longer pink. Or grill on oiled, preheated flattop griddle at 350°F for 6½ to 7½ minutes on each side. Remove from grill and slice into thin strips. Cover and chill below 40°F to hold.
2 Kidney beans, canned, rinsed, drained	1½ cups	9 cups	Combine in bowl and add chicken. Toss gently. Cover and chill below 40°F to hold.
Cucumbers, fresh, peeled, halved lengthwise, seeded, sliced	¾ cup	4½ cups	
Celery, fresh, sliced	½ cup	3 cups	
Cheddar cheese, sharp, shredded	½ cup	3 cups	
3 *Spicy Cider Vinaigrette*			
Apple cider vinegar	⅓ cup	2 cups	Combine in food processor bowl and process until sugar is dissolved.
Sugar, granulated	2 tbsp.	¾ cup	
Onions, fresh, grated	½ tbsp.	3 tbsp.	
Dry mustard powder	½ tsp.	1 tbsp.	
Celery seeds, whole	¼ tsp.	½ tbsp.	
Cayenne pepper sauce	¼ tsp.	½ tbsp.	
Paprika, ground	¼ tsp.	½ tbsp.	
Salt	¼ tsp.	½ tbsp.	
4 Vegetable oil	⅔ cup	4 cups	Gradually add to processor bowl while motor is running and process until emulsified. Remove from processor bowl. Cover and chill to hold.
5 Romaine lettuce leaves, fresh	12	72	*To assemble single serving:* Line plate with 3 lettuce leaves. Combine 1½ cups chicken mixture, 1½ cups salad greens, and ¼ cup vinaigrette in bowl and toss well. Arrange salad over lettuce leaves. Garnish plate with 3 tomato wedges.
Mixed salad greens, fresh, commercially prepared	6 cups	36 cups	
Tomato wedges, fresh	12	72	

Serve with crusty whole-wheat rolls.

Portion: 10 ounces
Nutritional Data/Portion: Calories 480, Protein 25 g, Fat 32 g, Carbohydrate 24 g, Cholesterol 55 mg, Sodium 470 mg

For a *FAST FACTS VIA FAX* copy of this recipe, call 1-800-223-3755 and enter Business Tool 2389.

Submitted by Disneyland
Anaheim, Calif.

*Commercially prepared
vinaigrette and fried onion
rings may be substituted.*

*The zesty, tart flavor of
goat cheese is instantly
recognizable. Its texture
ranges from moist and
soft to dry and crumbly,
depending on age. Unlike
most other cheeses, the same
batch of goat cheese may be
eaten at four or five different
stages of ripeness.*

Bronze Chicken Salad

A dish befitting the "Magic Kingdom." Crunchy fresh-fried red onion rings and crumbled goat cheese with juicy slices of roasted spiced chicken breast filets are the secrets to this enchanting salad.

INGREDIENT	QUANTITY 4 servings	24 servings	METHOD
1 Tyson Ready-to-Cook Flavor-Redi® Hot Spiced Chicken Breast Filets, 5-oz., frozen	4	24	Season both sides of chicken breast filets.
2 Cajun seasoning, dried	¼ cup	1½ cups	
Vegetable oil	¼ cup	1½ cups	Heat in skillet or braising pan over medium heat. Add chicken and sauté for 2 to 3 minutes on each side or until golden brown. Transfer to roasting pans.
			Roast in preheated conventional oven at 350°F for 15 to 18 minutes or until chicken is no longer pink. (Roast smaller quantity for 10 to 12 minutes.) Or roast in preheated convection oven at 300°F for 10 to 12 minutes. (Roast smaller quantity for 8 to 10 minutes.) Remove from oven. Keep warm above 140°F.
3 *Spicy Garlic Salad Dressing*			
Garlic, fresh, minced	1 tbsp.	⅓ cup	Combine in bowl and mix thoroughly to form paste.
Romano cheese, grated	2 tsp.	¼ cup	
Mustard, spicy brown	1 tsp.	2 tbsp.	
4 Olive oil	¾ cup	4½ cups	Gradually add to paste, whisking constantly until well blended. Cover and chill to hold.
Lemon juice, fresh	¼ cup	1½ cups	
5 *Crisp Fried Onion Breading*			
Flour, all-purpose	2 cups	12 cups	Combine in bowl and mix thoroughly.
Salt	1½ tbsp.	½ cup	
Garlic, granulated	1 tbsp.	⅓ cup	
Paprika, ground	1 tbsp.	⅓ cup	
Black pepper, fine	1 tbsp.	⅓ cup	
6 Red onions, fresh, thinly sliced, separated into rings	4 cups	24 cups	Dredge in seasoned flour and shake off excess. Deep-fry at 350°F for 1 to 2 minutes or until golden brown, tossing constantly. Remove from fryer. Drain and reserve.

recipe continued on next page . . .

INGREDIENT	QUANTITY		METHOD
	4 servings	24 servings	
7 Mixed baby greens, fresh, commercially prepared	16 cups	96 cups	*To assemble single serving:* Combine 4 cups lettuce mixture and ¼ cup salad
Goat cheese, crumbled	½ cup	3 cups	dressing in bowl and toss well. Add ¾ cup fried onions and toss gently. Slice 1 chicken
Lavash crackers, commercially prepared	12	72	breast filet into strips and fan over salad. Garnish plate with 2 tablespoons cheese and 3 crackers.

Portion: 10 ounces
Nutritional Data/Portion: Calories 1,150, Protein 48 g, Fat 61 g, Carbohydrate 106 g, Cholesterol 85 mg, Sodium 1,770 mg

For a **FAST FACTS VIA FAX**™ copy of this recipe, call 1-800-223-3755 and enter Business Tool 2379.

Lavash is a round, thin, crisp bread that's also known as Armenian cracker bread.

Yin Yang Chicken Salad

This salad is a tantalizing balance of contrasting flavors and textures. It features char-grilled teriyaki chicken, crunchy vegetables, mandarin orange segments, chow mein noodles, roasted cashews, and piquant sweet-and-sour dressing.

Submitted by Bob Wright
Whiskey River
St. Peter, Minn.

INGREDIENT	QUANTITY		METHOD
	4 servings	24 servings	
1 Tyson Ready-to-Cook Tenderpressed™ Teriyaki Chicken Breast Filets, 5-oz., frozen	4	24	Char-grill over high heat for 5 to 6 minutes on each side or until chicken is no longer pink. Or grill on oiled, preheated flattop griddle at 350°F for 6½ to 7½ minutes on each side. Remove from grill. Keep warm above 140°F.
2 *Sweet-and-Sour Salad Dressing*			
Rice wine vinegar	⅓ cup	1¾ cups	Combine in food processor bowl and process until sugar is dissolved.
Sugar, granulated	3 tbsp.	1 cup	
Mustard, Dijon	1 tbsp.	⅓ cup	
Salt	½ tsp.	1 tbsp.	
3 Vegetable oil	⅔ cup	3½ cups	Gradually add to processor bowl while motor is running and process until emulsified. Remove from processor bowl. Cover and chill to hold.
Sesame oil	1 tsp.	2 tbsp.	
4 Napa cabbage leaves, fresh	12	72	*To assemble single serving:* Line plate with 3 cabbage leaves. Portion 2 cups lettuce on cabbage. Layer ¼ cup alfalfa sprouts, 2 tablespoons onions, ¼ cup snow peas, and ¼ cup mandarin oranges over lettuce. Sprinkle with 2 tablespoons cashews and 2 tablespoons chow mein noodles. Julienne 1 chicken breast filet and mound on salad. Drizzle salad with ¼ cup salad dressing. Garnish plate with 1 chile pepper flower.
Romaine lettuce, fresh, chopped	8 cups	48 cups	
Alfalfa sprouts, fresh	1 cup	6 cups	
Red onions, fresh, slivered	½ cup	3 cups	
Snow peas, whole, fresh, blanched	1 cup	6 cups	
Mandarin orange segments, canned, drained	1 cup	6 cups	
Cashew halves, roasted	½ cup	3 cups	
Chow mein noodles, wide-style, commercially prepared	½ cup	3 cups	
Chile pepper flowers, fresh	4	24	*Serve with black pepper crackers.*

Portion: 14 ounces
Nutritional Data/Portion: Calories 720, Protein 38 g, Fat 48 g, Carbohydrate 40 g, Cholesterol 80 mg, Sodium 870 mg

For a **FAST FACTS VIA FAX**™ copy of this recipe, call 1-800-223-3755 and enter Business Tool 2387.

Cashew nuts have a sweet, buttery flavor and should be stored, tightly wrapped, in the refrigerator to protect against rancidity.

Play off of the yin and yang in the name of this salad by garnishing with green and red cabbage.

Commercially prepared sweet-and-sour dressing may be substituted.

See sidebar on page 19 for how to make a chile pepper flower.

Submitted by John B. Franke
Fresh Market–Neiman Marcus
Dallas, Tex.

There are two major types of mustard seed: white (or yellow) and brown (or Asian). White mustard seeds are larger, and brown ones are more pungent. Both types can be stored, tightly covered, up to a year in a dry, dark place.

Creole mustard is a specialty of Louisiana's German Creoles that is made with brown mustard seeds and horseradish.

Mustard Roasted Chicken Salad with White Beans and Summer Vegetables

This dish epitomizes Neiman Marcus quality. It's a medley of summertime flavors, featuring roasted, mustard-marinated chicken breast filets placed on a bed of chilled vegetables, white beans, and mixed greens.

Lighter Fare
Takeout

INGREDIENT	QUANTITY 4 servings	24 servings	METHOD
1 Tyson Gourmet Boneless Whole Chicken Breast Filets, 8-oz., frozen	4	24	Place in full-size steam table pans. (Use half-size pan for smaller quantity.)
2 *Marinade*			
Shallots, fresh, minced	¾ cup	4½ cups	Combine in bowl and mix thoroughly. Brush on chicken. Cover and marinate below 40°F for 24 hours.
Garlic, fresh, minced	¼ cup	1½ cups	
Mustard, Dijon	½ cup	3 cups	
Mustard, Creole	¼ cup	1½ cups	
Salt	½ tsp.	1 tbsp.	
Black pepper, coarse	1 tsp.	2 tbsp.	
3 Olive oil	2 tbsp.	¾ cup	Heat in skillet or braising pan over medium heat. Remove chicken from marinade and sauté for 3 to 3½ minutes on each side or until golden brown. Transfer to roasting pans.
			Roast in preheated conventional oven at 350°F for 10 to 12 minutes or until chicken is no longer pink. (Roast smaller quantity for 7 to 8 minutes.) Or roast in preheated convection oven at 300°F for 6 to 7 minutes. (Roast smaller quantity for 4 to 5 minutes.) Remove from oven and cool. Remove skin and cut each breast filet into 2 pieces. Cover and chill below 40°F to hold.
4 *Mustard Seed Vinaigrette*			
Red wine vinegar	¼ cup	1¾ cups	Combine in bowl. Cover and soak overnight in cooler.
5 Mustard seeds, whole, dried	2 tbsp.	¾ cup	
Shallots, fresh, minced	¼ cup	1½ cups	Combine in bowl and add vinegar/mustard seed mixture.
Lemon juice, fresh	⅓ cup	2⅓ cups	
Lemon zest, fresh	½ tbsp.	3 tbsp.	

recipe continued on next page . . .

	INGREDIENT	QUANTITY		METHOD
		4 servings	24 servings	
6	Olive oil	¾ cup	4¾ cups	Combine and gradually add to shallot mixture, whisking constantly. Cover and chill to hold.
	Salt	¾ tsp.	2 tbsp.	
	Black pepper, coarse	½ tsp.	1 tbsp.	
7	*White Bean and Summer Vegetable Salad*			
	Great Northern beans, canned, rinsed, drained	3 cups	18 cups	Combine in bowl and mix thoroughly.
	Garlic, fresh, minced	2 tsp.	¼ cup	
8	Bay leaves, ground	⅛ tsp.	¾ tsp.	
	Water, boiling	to cover	to cover	Combine vegetables and blanch in boiling water for 2 to 2½ minutes. (Blanch smaller quantity for 30 to 60 seconds.) Drain and shock in ice water. Drain again thoroughly. Add to bean mixture.
	Onions, fresh, small dice (p. 175)	¼ cup	1 cup	
	Carrots, fresh, small dice (p. 88)	¼ cup	1 cup	
	Zucchini, fresh, small dice	¼ cup	1 cup	
	Yellow squash, fresh, small dice	¼ cup	1 cup	
	Celery, fresh, small dice	¼ cup	1 cup	
9	Red bell peppers, roasted, small dice (p. 66)	¼ cup	1 cup	Add to bean mixture. Add 4 cups vinaigrette and toss well. (Add ⅔ cup vinaigrette to smaller quantity.) Cover and chill to hold.
	Yellow bell peppers, roasted, small dice	¼ cup	1 cup	
	Lemon juice, fresh	1 tbsp.	⅓ cup	
10	Salt	¼ tsp.	½ tbsp.	
	Mixed salad greens, fresh, commercially prepared	16 cups	96 cups	*To assemble single serving:* Combine 4 cups salad greens in bowl with 3 tablespoons vinaigrette and toss well. Transfer to plate. Top with 1 cup white bean and vegetable mixture. Shingle 2 chicken pieces over beans and drizzle with additional 1 tablespoon vinaigrette. Garnish salad with sprinkling of ¼ teaspoon pepper.
	Black pepper, coarse	1 tsp.	2 tbsp.	

Serve with crusty French bread.

Portion: 20 ounces
Nutritional Data/Portion: Calories 760, Protein 69 g, Fat 26 g, Carbohydrate 66 g, Cholesterol 85 mg, Sodium 1,600 mg

For a **FAST FACTS VIA FAX**™ copy of this recipe, call 1-800-223-3755 and enter Business Tool 2378.

Great Northern beans are large white beans with a delicate, distinctive flavor. They can be used in almost any recipe that calls for white beans.

Italian Colors Chicken Pasta Salad

This savory pasta salad shows its true Italian colors with tender white chicken, pasta, and green and red bell pepper.

Speed-Scratch *Kid Friendly* *Line Service* *Takeout*

Submitted by Bill Kellermeyer Community Northview Care Center Anderson, Ind.

	INGREDIENT	QUANTITY		METHOD
		4 servings	24 servings	
1	Tyson Fully Cooked Diced White Fryer Meat, ¾-inch dice, frozen	1 lb.	6 lb.	Cover tightly and slack in cooler between 32° and 36°F prior to use.
2	Penne pasta, cooked al dente, rinsed, drained	6 oz. (dry)	2¼ lb. (dry)	Combine in bowl and add chicken.
	Red bell peppers, fresh, julienne (p. 88)	⅔ cup	4 cups	
	Green bell peppers, fresh, julienne	⅔ cup	4 cups	
	Red onions, fresh, slivered	¼ cup	1½ cups	
3	Italian vinaigrette, commercially prepared	1 cup	6 cups	Pour over chicken mixture and toss well. Cover and chill below 40°F to hold.
4	Red leaf lettuce leaves, fresh	8	48	*To assemble single serving:* Line plate with 2 lettuce leaves. Combine 2 cups salad and 2 tablespoons vinaigrette in bowl. Toss well and arrange on lettuce. Sprinkle with 2 tablespoons cheese. Garnish plate with 1 cherry tomato.
	Italian vinaigrette, commercially prepared	½ cup	3 cups	
	Parmesan cheese, grated	½ cup	3 cups	
	Cherry tomatoes, fresh	4	24	*Serve with breadsticks.*

Portion: 11 ounces
Nutritional Data/Portion: Calories 750, Protein 39 g, Fat 52 g, Carbohydrate 48 g, Cholesterol 90 mg, Sodium 750 mg

For a **FAST FACTS VIA FAX**™ copy of this recipe, call 1-800-223-3755 and enter Business Tool 2392.

Vary this recipe with any short pastas, such as rotini, shells, or radiatore.

This recipe is ideal for line service, buffets, and catering.

CHICKEN
WALDORF SALAD

CHICKEN
ORECCHIETTE SALAD

TERIYAKI CHICKEN
AND FRUIT SALAD

Recipes on pages 57 to 59.

Submitted by Sherri Driscoll
Dakota Heartland Health System
Fargo, N.D.

Teriyaki Chicken and Fruit Salad

A strawberry fan, mandarin orange segments, and fresh fried wontons crown this jewel of a salad, featuring teriyaki chicken, crisp bacon, and water chestnuts.

INGREDIENT	QUANTITY 4 servings	24 servings	METHOD
1 Tyson Ready-to-Cook Tenderpressed™ Teriyaki Chicken Breast Filets, 5-oz., frozen	4	24	Char-grill over high heat for 5 to 6 minutes on each side or until chicken is no longer pink. Or grill on oiled, preheated flattop griddle at 350°F for 6½ to 7½ minutes on each side, or roast on foil-lined baking sheet in preheated convection oven at 350°F for 17 to 19 minutes. Remove from heat. Keep warm above 140°F.
2 Romaine lettuce, fresh, chopped	4 cups	24 cups	Combine in bowl and toss well. Cover and chill to hold.
Spinach, fresh, stemmed, torn	4 cups	24 cups	
Water chestnuts, sliced, canned, drained	1⅓ cups	8 cups	
Celery, fresh, chopped	1 cup	6 cups	
3 Wonton wrappers, commercially prepared	4	24	Cut into ½-inch-wide strips. Deep-fry at 350°F for 30 to 45 seconds or until golden brown. Remove from fryer and drain. Keep warm.
4 Mandarin orange segments, canned, drained	1 cup	6 cups	*To assemble single serving:* Portion 2½ cups lettuce mixture in bowl. Add ¼ cup mandarin oranges, 2 tablespoons bacon crumbles, 2 tablespoons almonds, and ⅓ cup dressing. Toss well and transfer to plate. Slice 1 chicken breast filet into strips and arrange over salad. Garnish salad with 2 orange segments, 1 strawberry fan, and 7 wonton strips.
Bacon, crisp, crumbled	½ cup	3 cups	
Almonds, sliced, toasted	½ cup	3 cups	
Poppy seed salad dressing, commercially prepared	1⅓ cups	8 cups	
Mandarin orange segments, canned, drained	8	48	
Strawberry fans, fresh	4	24	*Serve with poppy seed roll.*

Portion: 14 ounces
Nutritional Data/Portion: Calories 940, Protein 44 g, Fat 66 g, Carbohydrate 50 g, Cholesterol 80 mg, Sodium 808 mg

For a ***Fast Facts Via Fax***™ copy of this recipe, call 1-800-223-3755 and enter Business Tool 2375.

Commercially prepared chow mein noodles may be substituted for the wonton strips.

There are approximately 900,000 poppy seeds per pound.

The almond is a kind of fruit called a drupe, as are cherries, plums, and peaches.

This recipe is pictured on opposite page.

HOW TO MAKE A STRAWBERRY FAN

1) Choose a large strawberry with a green leaf stem. Slice into thin slivers starting at the tip and working to within ⅛ inch of the stem.

2) Fan slivers out and place on the salad.

Submitted by
Bennie E. Dewberry, Jr., CEC
Atria Courtyard at San Marcos
Retirement Community
San Marcos, Calif.

The Waldorf Salad was
created in 1893 by Swiss chef
Oscar Tschirky, the newly
hired maitre d' of New York's
Waldorf-Astoria Hotel. The
original Waldorf Salad was
made with bits of apple,
lettuce, and mayonnaise.

This recipe is pictured
on page 56.

Chicken Waldorf Salad

The savory-sweet flavor of teriyaki chicken adds a new dimension to this classic salad of apples, carrots, English walnuts, raisins, and mayonnaise.

Speed-Scratch   Line Service   Takeout

INGREDIENT	QUANTITY 4 servings	24 servings	METHOD
1 Tyson Ready-to-Cook Flavor-Redi® Teriyaki Chicken Breast Filets, 4-oz., frozen	4	24	Char-grill over high heat for 5 to 6 minutes on each side or until chicken is no longer pink. Or grill on oiled, preheated flattop griddle at 350°F for 6 to 7 minutes on each side. Remove from grill. Cover and chill below 40°F, then cut into 1-inch dice.
2 Red Delicious apples, fresh, unpeeled, cored, ½-inch dice, tossed in lemon juice	5 cups	30 cups	Combine in bowl and add chicken.
Celery, fresh, chopped	1 cup	6 cups	
Carrots, fresh, shredded	½ cup	3 cups	
English walnuts, chopped	½ cup	3 cups	
3 Raisins, dark	½ cup	3 cups	
Mayonnaise	½ cup	3 cups	Combine in separate bowl and mix thoroughly. Add to chicken mixture and toss well. Cover and chill below 40°F to hold.
Sugar, granulated	¼ cup	1½ cups	
4 Salt	¼ tsp.	½ tbsp.	
Red romaine lettuce leaves, fresh	8	48	*To assemble single serving:* Line plate with 2 lettuce leaves. Portion 2 cups salad on lettuce. Garnish plate with 1 celery fan.
Celery fans, fresh	4	24	*Serve with poppy seed rolls.*

Portion: 12 ounces
Nutritional Data/Portion: Calories 530, Protein 27 g, Fat 22 g, Carbohydrate 64 g, Cholesterol 75 mg, Sodium 780 mg

For a **FAST FACTS VIA FAX** copy of this recipe, call 1-800-223-3755 and enter Business Tool 2394.

HOW TO MAKE A CELERY FAN

1) Slice thin stalks of celery into 4-inch lengths. Celery must not be too wide.

2) Make a number of long, thin slits at both ends, cutting to within ½ inch of the center of the stalk. For a smaller fan, cut celery into shorter lengths and slit only one end.

3) Place in ice water to open the slits.

Chicken Orecchiette Salad

This *primavera*, or "spring-style," orecchiette pasta salad features pieces of chicken tossed with fresh vegetables, black olives, grated Parmesan cheese, and fragrant basil mayonnaise.

INGREDIENT	QUANTITY		METHOD
	4 servings	24 servings	
① Tyson Fully Cooked Diced White Fryer Meat, 1-inch dice, frozen	12 oz.	4½ lb.	Cover tightly and slack in cooler between 32° and 36°F prior to use.
② Orecchiette pasta, cooked al dente, rinsed, drained	6 oz. (dry)	2¼ lb. (dry)	Combine in bowl and add chicken.
Broccoli florets, fresh, blanched	2 cups	12 cups	
Yellow squash, fresh, halved lengthwise, seeded, ¼-inch slice	1½ cups	9 cups	
Zucchini, fresh, halved lengthwise, seeded, ¼-inch slice	1½ cups	9 cups	
Red bell peppers, fresh, julienne (p. 88)	1 cup	6 cups	
Green onions, fresh, ½-inch slice	¼ cup	1½ cups	
Black olives, whole, pitted, canned, drained	⅔ cup	4 cups	
③ *Basil Mayonnaise Salad Dressing*			
Mayonnaise	1 cup	6 cups	Combine in separate bowl and mix thoroughly. Fold into chicken mixture.
Sour cream	¼ cup	1½ cups	Cover and chill below 40°F to hold.
Parmesan cheese, grated	⅓ cup	2 cups	
Basil, fresh, minced	¼ cup	1½ cups	
Garlic, fresh, minced	1 tsp.	2 tbsp.	
Dry mustard powder	½ tsp.	1 tbsp.	
Tarragon vinegar	1 tbsp.	⅓ cup	
Lemon juice, fresh	½ tsp.	1 tbsp.	
Salt	¾ tsp.	1½ tbsp.	
Black pepper, fine	⅛ tsp.	¾ tsp.	
④ Red romaine lettuce leaves, fresh	8	48	*To assemble single serving:* Line plate with 2 lettuce leaves. Portion 3 cups salad on lettuce. Sprinkle with 2 tablespoons cheese. Garnish plate with 1 basil sprig.
Parmesan cheese, grated	½ cup	3 cups	
Basil sprigs, fresh	4	24	

Serve with focaccia bread.

Portion: 14 ounces
Nutritional Data/Portion: Calories 630, Protein 37 g, Fat 28 g, Carbohydrate 60 g, Cholesterol 90 mg, Sodium 1,290 mg

For a **FAST FACTS VIA FAX**™ copy of this recipe, call 1-800-223-3755 and enter Business Tool 2396.

Orecchiette is a traditional pasta from Italy's "deep south" Apulia and is generally hand made. The Italian translation of orecchiette is "little ears," which this small disk-shaped pasta resembles. If orecchiette cannot be found, use small pasta shells instead.

The common name for basil, basileus, is Greek for "king." But because it was found scattered on graves in ancient Persia and Malaysia, sweet basil was thought by the Greeks to bode misfortune. In Crete it symbolized "love washed with tears."

This recipe is pictured on page 56.

"Salad is not a meal. It is a style."
Fran Lebowitz

Submitted by Gail Cunningham
Greenhouse Market
Springfield, Mo.

This salad is an example of "fusion cuisine." North American wild rice, Southwest-flavored chicken, and Asian-seasoned rice, served with Italian bread.◦

When French explorer Jacques Marquette discovered the headwaters of the Mississippi River in 1673, he also discovered and wrote about a grain he called fausse avoine, *or "false oat," known today as wild rice.*◦

Asian Chicken Wild Rice Salad

This chilled Asian feast is a colorful combination of chicken, rice, and vegetables infused with classic Oriental flavorings such as soy sauce, sesame oil, and rice wine vinegar.

Lighter Fare *Line Service* *Takeout*

INGREDIENT	QUANTITY		METHOD
	4 servings	24 servings	
Tyson Fully Cooked Flavor-Redi® Chicken Breast Fajita Strips, frozen	12 oz.	4½ lb.	Cover tightly and slack in cooler between 32° and 36°F prior to use.
Long-grain and wild rice blend, commercially prepared, cooked without enclosed seasoning packet, chilled	3 cups	18 cups	Combine in bowl. Add chicken and toss well.
Green onions, fresh, 1-inch bias-sliced	⅔ cup	4 cups	
Green bell peppers, fresh, julienne (p. 88)	½ cup	3 cups	
Red bell peppers, fresh, julienne	½ cup	3 cups	
Almonds, slivered, toasted	2 tbsp.	¾ cup	
Parsley, fresh, minced (p. 39)	1 tbsp.	⅓ cup	
Soy sauce	¼ cup	1½ cups	Combine in separate bowl and mix thoroughly. Pour over chicken mixture and toss well. Cover and chill below 40°F to hold.
Rice wine vinegar	¼ cup	1½ cups	
Sesame oil	3 tbsp.	1 cup	
Red pepper, crushed, dried	⅛ tsp.	¾ tsp.	
Baby field greens salad mix, fresh, commercially prepared	8 cups	48 cups	*To assemble single serving:* Portion 2 cups salad greens on plate. Top with 1½ cups chicken mixture. Garnish plate with 1 green onion brush.
Green onion brushes, fresh (p. 125)	4	24	*Serve with thin-sliced toasted garlic bread and chilled fruit.*

Portion: 11 ounces
Nutritional Data/Portion: Calories 400, Protein 26 g, Fat 16 g, Carbohydrate 42 g, Cholesterol 45 mg, Sodium 1,590 mg

For a *FAST FACTS VIA FAX*™ copy of this recipe, call 1-800-223-3755 and enter Business Tool 2395.

Submitted by Edward Carloni
Lebanon Country Club
Myerstown, Pa.

Grilled Cajun Tenderloins on Spinach and Mixed Greens

A sophisticated dish that is simple to prepare. Cajun-spiced tenderloins top balsamic vinaigrette-dressed greens, finished off with fresh grated Romano cheese.

INGREDIENT	QUANTITY 4 servings	QUANTITY 24 servings	METHOD
1 Tyson Ready-to-Cook Flavor-Redi® Savory Chicken Tenderloins, frozen	12	72	Place in full-size steam table pans. (Use half-size pan for smaller quantity.)
2 Marinade			
Olive oil	½ cup	3 cups	Combine in bowl and mix thoroughly. Pour over chicken. Cover and marinate below 40°F for 8 to 10 hours .
Cajun seasoning, dried	2 tbsp.	¾ cup	
			Remove chicken from marinade. Char-grill over medium heat for 2 to 3 minutes on each side or until chicken is no longer pink. Remove from grill. Keep warm above 140°F.
3 Mixed salad greens, fresh, commercially prepared	12 cups	72 cups	*To assemble single serving:* Combine 3 cups salad greens, 1 cup spinach, and 2 tablespoons vinaigrette in bowl. Toss well and transfer to plate. Arrange 3 chicken tenderloins over greens and sprinkle with 1 tablespoon cheese.
Spinach, fresh, stemmed, torn	4 cups	24 cups	
Balsamic vinaigrette, commercially prepared	½ cup	3 cups	
Romano cheese, grated	¼ cup	1½ cups	*Serve with warm Italian bread.*

Portion: 8 ounces
Nutritional Data/Portion: Calories 360, Protein 31 g, Fat 25 g, Carbohydrate 11 g, Cholesterol 30 mg, Sodium 1,460 mg

For a **FAST FACTS VIA FAX**™ copy of this recipe, call 1-800-223-3755 and enter Business Tool 2386.

When the British expelled the last French settlers, Acadians, from the Nova Scotia peninsula in 1755, over 1,600 of them joined others who had resettled in Louisiana (another French territory at the time). Their cooking experience melded with that of earlier Acadian settlers to establish Cajun cookery.

This recipe is pictured on the back cover.

Lemon Herb Chicken Salad

This colorful combination of mixed greens and mixed vegetables, tossed with lemon herb dressing, is topped with slices of roasted lemon herb chicken that has a distinctive crumb coating.

INGREDIENT	QUANTITY 4 servings	QUANTITY 24 servings	METHOD
1 Tyson Ready-to-Cook Homestyle Crusted Chicken Breast Filets, 4-oz., frozen	4	24	Place on foil-lined sheet pans. Roast in preheated conventional oven at 400°F for 20 to 23 minutes or until chicken is no longer pink. For extra crispiness, broil for 2 to 3 minutes or until golden brown. Or roast in preheated convection oven at 350°F for 15 to 18 minutes. Remove from oven. Keep warm above 140°F.
2 Caesar salad dressing, commercially prepared	1 cup	6 cups	Combine in bowl and whisk well. Cover and chill.
Lemon herb seasoning, dried	1 tsp.	2 tbsp.	
3 Mixed salad greens, fresh, commercially prepared	8 cups	48 cups	*To assemble single serving:* Combine 2 cups salad greens, ¼ cup vegetables, and ¼ cup dressing in bowl. Toss well and transfer to plate. Slice 1 chicken breast filet into strips and arrange over salad. Top chicken with 2 tablespoons tomatoes, ¼ cup croutons, and 1½ tablespoons cheese. Garnish plate with 1 lemon twist.
Premixed vegetables, fresh, commercially prepared (cauliflower florets, broccoli florets, and sliced carrots), cut into bite-size pieces	1 cup	6 cups	
Tomatoes, fresh, seeded, diced	¾ cup	4½ cups	
Salad croutons, commercially prepared	1 cup	6 cups	
Romano cheese, grated	½ cup	3 cups	
Lemon slice twists, fresh	4	24	*Serve with crusty French bread.*

Portion: 12 ounces
Nutritional Data/Portion: Calories 770, Protein 38 g, Fat 56 g, Carbohydrate 31 g, Cholesterol 140 mg, Sodium 2,360 mg

For a **FAST FACTS VIA FAX**™ copy of this recipe, call 1-800-223-3755 and enter Business Tool 2384.

Submitted by Michael J. Monti
Shaw Enlisted Club
Shaw Air Force Base, S.C.

In 1626, Sir Francis Bacon experimented with the idea of freezing chickens by stuffing them with snow. He caught pneumonia and died April 9 at age 65.

This recipe is pictured on the inside cover.

Old-Fashioned Chicken Salad

This salad works wherever it is placed—on a roll, between slices of soft bread, stuffed in a ripe tomato or melon half, in a pita or wrap, or atop a bed of greens or cold pasta. Use what is in season or on hand.

For a variation, try adding any one, or more, of these: peeled cucumber chunks, capers, diced melon, chopped pineapple, crisp red or green grape halves, julienne strips of red bell pepper, pecan halves or chopped English walnuts, spring green peas, crunchy water chestnuts, or fresh tarragon.

Looking for a traditional chicken salad recipe? This is it. Generous portions of chicken and fresh celery are folded into a rich dressing of heavy whipped cream and mayonnaise, then topped with almond slivers.

INGREDIENT	QUANTITY 4 servings	24 servings	METHOD
1 Tyson Fully Cooked Pulled White Fryer Meat, frozen	1½ lb.	9 lb.	Cover tightly and slack in cooler between 32° and 36°F prior to use.
2 Celery, fresh, bias-sliced	1 cup	6 cups	Combine in bowl and add chicken.
Mayonnaise	1 cup	6 cups	
Black pepper, fine	½ tsp.	1 tbsp.	
Salt, kosher	¼ tsp.	½ tbsp.	
3 Heavy cream, whipped	½ cup	3 cups	Fold into chicken mixture. Cover and chill below 40°F to hold.
4 Red leaf lettuce leaves, fresh	4	24	*To assemble single serving:* Line plate with 1 lettuce leaf. Top with 1¼ cups salad and sprinkle with 1 tablespoon almonds. Garnish plate with 1 red and 1 green grape cluster.
Almonds, sliced, toasted	¼ cup	1½ cups	
Red grape clusters, seedless, fresh	4	24	
Green grape clusters, seedless, fresh	4	24	

Portion: 9 ounces
Nutritional Data/Portion: Calories 711, Protein 51 g, Fat 56 g, Carbohydrate 5 g, Cholesterol 184 mg, Sodium 564 mg

For a **FAST FACTS VIA FAX** copy of this recipe, call 1-800-223-3755 and enter Business Tool 2354.

Curried Chicken Salad

*Submitted by Prescott Slee
Herman Miller, Inc.
Zeeland, Mich.*

For a signature sandwich, stuff the salad into a lettuce-lined pita pocket.

Here is a variation on the classic, bringing exotic color and flavor to a favorite American salad.

INGREDIENT	QUANTITY 4 servings	24 servings	METHOD
1 Tyson Fully Cooked Diced Chicken Tenderloins, ¾-inch dice, frozen	1½ lb.	8 lb.	Cover tightly and slack in cooler between 32° and 36°F prior to use.
2 Red grapes, seedless, fresh, halved lengthwise	½ cup	3 cups	Combine in bowl and add chicken.
Celery, fresh, ¼-inch dice (p. 88)	½ cup	3 cups	
Onions, fresh, ¼-inch dice (p. 175)	⅓ cup	2 cups	
Almonds, sliced, toasted	2 tbsp.	1 cup	
3 Mayonnaise	½ cup	3 cups	Combine in separate bowl and mix thoroughly. Pour over chicken mixture and toss gently. Cover and chill below 40°F to hold.
Mustard, yellow	½ tsp.	1 tbsp.	
Curry powder	½ tsp.	1 tbsp.	
Sugar, granulated	½ tsp.	1 tbsp.	
Black pepper, fine	¼ tsp.	½ tbsp.	
4 Red leaf lettuce leaves, fresh	4	24	*To assemble single serving:* Line plate with 1 lettuce leaf. Top with 1½ cups chicken salad. *Serve with coconut, raisins, and chutney.*

Portion: 8 ounces
Nutritional Data/Portion: Calories 330, Protein 39 g, Fat 14 g, Carbohydrate 15 g, Cholesterol 100 mg, Sodium 760 mg

For a **FAST FACTS VIA FAX** copy of this recipe, call 1-800-223-3755 and enter Business Tool 2385.

Wilted Cobb Salad

Replacing the original French dressing with hot bacon dressing gives this famous salad a whole new wrinkle. Like the original, this meal-size salad is made with rows of olives, tomato, avocado, chicken, bacon, and eggs atop a bed of fresh greens.

Line Service *Takeout*

INGREDIENT	QUANTITY		METHOD
	4 servings	24 servings	
Tyson Fully Cooked Diced White Fryer Meat, ½-inch dice, frozen	12 oz.	4½ lb.	Cover tightly and slack in cooler between 32° and 36°F prior to use.
Green leaf lettuce, fresh, torn	4 cups	24 cups	Combine in bowl and toss well. Cover and chill to hold.
Spinach, fresh, stemmed, torn	4 cups	24 cups	
Black olives, sliced, canned, drained	½ cup	3 cups	*To assemble single serving:* Arrange 2 cups lettuce mixture on platter. From left to right, arrange ingredients in rows over lettuce from top to bottom in the following order: 2 tablespoons black olives, 2 tablespoons tomatoes, 2 tablespoons avocado, ½ cup diced chicken, 2 tablespoons bacon, 2 tablespoons eggs, 2 tablespoons green onions.
Tomatoes, fresh, seeded, chopped	½ cup	3 cups	
Avocados, fresh, chopped, tossed in lime juice	½ cup	3 cups	
Bacon, crisp, crumbled	½ cup	3 cups	
Eggs, hard-boiled, diced	½ cup	3 cups	
Green onions, fresh, bias-sliced	½ cup	3 cups	Arrange ¼ cup cheese in a perpendicular row across center of platter. Portion ¼ cup dressing in separate container and serve on the side. Garnish platter with 1 tomato rose.
Blue cheese crumbles	1 cup	6 cups	
Bacon dressing, commercially prepared, heated	1 cup	6 cups	
Tomato roses, fresh	4	24	*Serve with crusty sourdough rolls.*

Portion: 10 ounces plus 2 ounces dressing
Nutritional Data/Portion: Calories 667, Protein 41 g, Fat 50 g, Carbohydrate 13 g, Cholesterol 182 mg, Sodium 1,820 mg

For a **FAST FACTS VIA FAX** copy of this recipe, call 1-800-223-3755 and enter Business Tool 2350.

From inside an L.A. restaurant shaped to resemble a large hat came an American favorite— the Cobb Salad, named for Brown Derby restaurant owner Bob Cobb. The restaurant itself was named for the hat.

Add drama to the presentation by tossing and wilting this classic tableside.

HOW TO MAKE A TOMATO ROSE

1) *Begin by cutting a ½-inch strip of skin around the tomato's stem. There should be some flesh attached to the skin, but do not cut deep enough to expose seeds. Continue peeling the entire tomato in one long, continous ribbon.*
2) *Lay the ribbon flat, skin side down, on a work surface. The ribbon will naturally form an "S" shape.*
3) *Gently roll the ribbon into a rose shape.*

Commercially prepared creamy Italian or ranch-style salad dressing may be substituted for the yogurt-mint dressing.

Porcini mushrooms that are tan to pale brown in color have the best flavor. The robust, woodsy flavor of dried porcini emerges with rehydration.

Substitute any of the following fresh mushrooms for dried porcini: cremini, button, shiitake, or oyster. All varieties offer an attractive earthy flavor.

Warm Chicken and Artichoke Pizza Salad

Salad becomes a finger food when fresh mixed salad greens are layered on warm pizza dough spread with yogurt-mint dressing, then topped with sautéed strips of chicken, artichokes, porcini mushrooms, and tomatoes.

INGREDIENT	QUANTITY 4 servings	24 servings	METHOD
1 Olive oil	2 tbsp.	¼ cup	Heat in skillet or braising pan over medium-high heat.
2 Tyson Fully Cooked Flavor-Redi® Chicken Breast Fajita Strips, frozen	8 oz.	3 lb.	Add to oil and sauté for 4 to 6 minutes or until vegetables are tender-crisp. (Sauté smaller quantity for 3 to 4 minutes.)
Onions, fresh, slivered	1 cup	3 cups	
Celery, fresh, bias-sliced	1 cup	3 cups	
Porcini mushrooms, dried, rehydrated according to package directions, chopped	1 tbsp.	¼ cup	
Garlic, fresh, minced	1 tbsp.	¼ cup	
Basil leaves, dried	2 tsp.	2 tbsp.	
Fennel seeds, whole	1 tsp.	1 tbsp.	
Thyme leaves, dried	1 tsp.	1 tbsp.	
3 Artichoke hearts, canned, drained, quartered	1 cup	6 cups	Add to chicken mixture and sauté for 5 to 10 minutes or until mixture is thoroughly heated and most of liquid has evaporated. (Sauté smaller quantity for 2 to 3 minutes.) Remove from heat. Keep warm above 140°F.
Tomatoes, diced, canned, drained	¼ cup	1½ cups	
Lemon juice, fresh	1 tbsp.	3 tbsp.	
Salt	½ tsp.	1 tsp.	
Black pepper, coarse	¼ tsp.	1 tsp.	
4 *Yogurt-Mint Salad Dressing*			
Yogurt, plain	1 cup	6 cups	Combine in bowl and mix thoroughly. Cover and chill to hold.
Olive oil	¼ cup	1½ cups	
Sour cream	2 tbsp.	¾ cup	
Garlic, fresh, minced	2 tsp.	¼ cup	
Mint, fresh, minced	2 tsp.	¼ cup	
Salt	1 tsp.	1½ tbsp.	
Black pepper, fine	½ tsp.	1 tbsp.	

recipe continued on next page . . .

INGREDIENT	QUANTITY		METHOD
	4 servings	24 servings	
5 Pizza crusts, thin, 7-inch, prebaked, heated	4	24	*To assemble single serving:* Place one pizza crust on flat work surface. Spread 2 tablespoons salad dressing evenly over crust. Portion ½ cup salad greens over dressing. Layer ½ cup chicken mixture over greens and drizzle with additional 2 tablespoons dressing. Sprinkle with 1 tablespoon cheese. Slice into wedges and arrange on plate.
Mixed salad greens, fresh, commercially prepared	2 cups	12 cups	
Feta cheese crumbles	¼ cup	1½ cups	

Portion: 12 ounces
Nutritional Data/Portion: Calories 481, Protein 21 g, Fat 28 g, Carbohydrate 38 g, Cholesterol 49 mg, Sodium 1,867 mg

For a **FAST FACTS VIA FAX** copy of this recipe, call 1-800-223-3755 and enter Business Tool 2351.

Serve with a simple soup that will complement the robust flavors of this premium salad.

Bombay Chicken and Fruit Salad with Honey-Lime Dressing

Exotic honey-lime dressing and toasted sesame seeds distinguish this medley of tempura-battered chicken and five fruits, served over fresh kale leaves.

*Submitted by Eric C. Nielsen, CFM
Wyndham Northwest Chicago Hotel
Itasca, Ill.*

INGREDIENT	QUANTITY		METHOD
	4 servings	24 servings	
1 Tyson Ready-to-Cook Tempura Thigh Strips, frozen	1½ lb.	9 lb.	Deep-fry at 350°F for 5 to 5½ minutes or until chicken is no longer pink. Remove from fryer and drain. Spread in single layer on sheet pans. Chill uncovered below 40°F to hold.
2 Honeydew melon, fresh, peeled, ¾-inch dice	2 cups	14 cups	Combine in bowl and toss gently. Cover and chill to hold.
Cantaloupe, fresh, peeled, ¾-inch dice	2 cups	14 cups	
Pineapple, fresh, peeled, ¾-inch dice	2 cups	14 cups	
Red grapes, seedless, fresh, whole	1 cup	6 cups	
Strawberries, fresh, quartered	1 cup	6 cups	
Sesame seeds, lightly toasted	1 tbsp.	⅓ cup	
3 *Honey-Lime Salad Dressing*			
Peanut oil	2 tbsp.	¾ cup	Combine in food processor bowl and process until well blended. Remove from processor bowl. Cover and chill to hold.
Lime juice, fresh	2 tbsp.	¾ cup	
Honey	¼ cup	1 cup	
Sesame oil	½ tsp.	1 tbsp.	
Cayenne pepper, ground	½ tsp.	1 tbsp.	
Coriander, ground	½ tsp.	1 tbsp.	
Sesame seeds, lightly toasted	¼ tsp.	½ tbsp.	
Salt	½ tsp.	1 tbsp.	
Cumin, ground	½ tsp.	1 tbsp.	
4 Kale leaves, fresh	8	48	*To assemble single serving:* Line plate with 2 kale leaves. Combine 2 cups fruit mixture, 6 ounces chicken, and 2 tablespoons dressing in bowl. Toss gently and transfer to plate.

Portion: 16 ounces
Nutritional Data/Portion: Calories 800, Protein 21 g, Fat 45 g, Carbohydrate 85 g, Cholesterol 90 mg, Sodium 1,090 mg

For a **FAST FACTS VIA FAX** copy of this recipe, call 1-800-223-3755 and enter Business Tool 2383.

When preparing this dish for takeout, put chicken, fruit, and dressing in separate containers.

Toast sesame seeds over low heat to avoid burning.

Coriander seeds have been discovered in Egyptian tombs dating back as early as 960 B.C. A member of the parsley family, coriander is also grown for its aromatic leaves, which are commonly called cilantro.

Submitted by Joseph A. Kunst
Catering to You Culinary Services
New York, N.Y.

*Watercress is a member
of the mustard family and
can often be found in the
wild near streams and
brooks. The small, crisp,
dark-green leaves have a
pungent, slightly bitter
and peppery flavor.*⌐

*Jicama has a sweet, nutty
flavor and crisp texture, and
it can be served both raw
and cooked.*⌐

Grilled Chicken on Watercress and Sweet Pepper Jicama Slaw

Thin strips of citrus-marinated char-grilled chicken top this mouthwatering and colorful salad. It is built on a mound of crunchy jicama and sweet pepper slaw tossed with tangy citrus vinaigrette. Fresh watercress leaves add a pungent bite to this salad.

INGREDIENT	QUANTITY		METHOD
	4 servings	24 servings	
1 Tyson Ready-to-Cook Tenderpressed™ Southwest Citrus Chicken Breast Filets, 4-oz., frozen	4	24	Char-grill over high heat for 5 to 6 minutes on each side or until chicken is no longer pink. Or grill on oiled, preheated flattop griddle at 350°F for 6 to 7 minutes on each side. Remove from grill. Keep warm above 140°F.
2 *Sweet Pepper Jicama Slaw*			
Red bell peppers, roasted, julienne	2 cups	12 cups	Combine in bowl and mix thoroughly. Cover and chill to hold.
Yellow bell peppers, roasted, julienne	2 cups	12 cups	
Jicama, fresh, peeled, julienne (p. 88)	2 cups	12 cups	
Red onions, fresh, shredded	1 cup	6 cups	
Salt	1 tsp.	2 tbsp.	
Black pepper, coarse	½ tsp.	1 tbsp.	
3 *Citrus Vinaigrette*			
Orange juice concentrate, frozen	¼ cup	1½ cups	Combine in food processor bowl and process until sugar is dissolved.
Lime juice, fresh	¼ cup	1½ cups	
Sugar, granulated	1 tbsp.	⅓ cup	
4 Olive oil	½ cup	3 cups	Gradually add to processor bowl while motor is running and process until emulsified.
5 Jalapeño peppers, fresh, seeded, minced (p. 172)	2 tsp.	¼ cup	Add to citrus vinaigrette and pulse until blended. Remove from processor bowl. Cover and chill to hold.
Cilantro, fresh, minced	½ cup	3 cups	
Oregano, fresh, minced	¼ cup	1½ cups	
Basil, fresh, minced	¼ cup	1½ cups	
Orange zest, fresh	2 tsp.	¼ cup	
Salt	½ tsp.	1 tbsp.	
Black pepper, coarse	¼ tsp.	½ tbsp.	
6 Watercress, fresh, stemmed	4 cups	24 cups	*To assemble single serving:* Combine 1 cup slaw mixture and 3 tablespoons vinaigrette in bowl and toss well. Mound slaw in center of plate. Arrange 1 cup watercress around upper half of slaw. Cut 1 chicken breast filet into 5 slices and fan around base of slaw. Drizzle 1 tablespoon dressing over chicken.

Serve with hot cornbread sticks.

Portion: 14 ounces
Nutritional Data/Portion: Calories 380, Protein 25 g, Fat 21 g, Carbohydrate 24 g, Cholesterol 60 mg, Sodium 1,210 mg

For a **FAST FACTS VIA FAX** copy of this recipe, call 1-800-223-3755 and enter Business Tool 2399.

 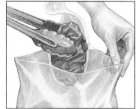 

HOW TO ROAST BELL PEPPERS

1) Quickly char pepper skins over a high open flame or under a broiler until evenly blackened.

2) Transfer peppers to a plastic bag for approximately 10 minutes.

3) Remove peppers from the bag. Peel, seed, and slice each pepper according to the recipe.

Chicken Spinach Salad with Chili Ranch Dressing

The dramatic presentation of this dish alone will make it an instant favorite. The ever-popular flavor of Buffalo wings comes through in the Strips of Fire that grace a bed of spinach greens, laced with creamy ranch dressing spiked with chili powder and cumin.

INGREDIENT	QUANTITY 4 servings	24 servings	METHOD
① Tyson Ready-to-Cook Strips of Fire™ Breaded Chicken Breast Strips, frozen	12	72	Deep-fry at 360°F for 3½ to 4½ minutes or until chicken is no longer pink. Remove from fryer and drain. Keep warm above 140°F.
② *Chili Ranch Salad Dressing*			
Ranch salad dressing, commercially prepared	1 cup	6 cups	Combine in large bowl and whisk thoroughly until well blended. Cover and chill to hold.
Chili powder, dark	2 tsp.	¼ cup	
Cumin, ground	1 tsp.	2 tbsp.	
③ Spinach, fresh, stemmed, lightly packed	8 cups	48 cups	Combine in separate bowl and toss well. Cover and chill to hold.
Red bell peppers, fresh, slivered	2 cups	12 cups	
Button mushrooms, fresh, sliced	2 cups	12 cups	
Water chestnuts, sliced, canned, drained	1 cup	6 cups	
Green onions, fresh, sliced	1 cup	6 cups	
Black olives, sliced, canned, drained	½ cup	3 cups	
④ Blue cheese crumbles	½ cup	3 cups	*To assemble single serving:* Portion 3½ cups lightly packed spinach mixture on plate. Top with 3 chicken strips. Drizzle ¼ cup salad dressing over salad. Sprinkle 2 tablespoons cheese over top for garnish.

Serve with sesame rolls or breadsticks.

Portion: 13 ounces
Nutritional Data/Portion: Calories 780, Protein 32 g, Fat 52 g, Carbohydrate 47 g, Cholesterol 70 mg, Sodium 1,980 mg

For a **FAST FACTS VIA FAX**® copy of this recipe, call 1-800-223-3755 and enter Business Tool 2368.

Commercially prepared fat-free ranch salad dressing may be substituted in the Chili Ranch Dressing.

Sliced fresh jicama is a flavorful substitute for canned water chestnuts.

Food and religion have been closely related in Chinese cooking for centuries. Taoists searched for nourishment and longevity through food. Confucianists, on the other hand, were more interested in taste, texture, and appearance. This dish should appeal to both groups.

Water chestnuts are the edible tubers of a water plant. Unpeeled, they resemble a chestnut. While readily available canned, fresh water chestnuts have superior flavor and texture.

If fresh snow peas are unavailable, substitute frozen ones.

Chicken Wonton Salad

The bold hoisin sesame salad dressing, with its notes of garlic and ginger, brings this sweet-and-spicy salad to life. It features julienned strips of teriyaki chicken, shredded cabbage and romaine lettuce, snow peas, carrots, green onions, and cucumbers, and is topped with deep-fried wonton strips.

INGREDIENT	QUANTITY 4 servings	24 servings	METHOD
1 Tyson Ready-to-Cook Flavor-Redi® Teriyaki Chicken Breast Filets, 5-oz., frozen	4	24	Char-grill over medium heat for 6 to 7 minutes on each side or until chicken is no longer pink. Or grill on oiled, preheated flattop griddle at 350°F for 6 to 7 minutes on each side. Remove from grill. Cover and chill below 40°F to hold.
2 Napa cabbage, fresh, shredded	6 cups	36 cups	Combine in bowl and toss well. Cover and chill to hold.
Romaine lettuce, fresh, shredded	6 cups	36 cups	
Snow peas, fresh, blanched, ½-inch bias-sliced	1 cup	6 cups	
Cucumbers, fresh, halved lengthwise, seeded, ¼-inch bias-sliced	1 cup	6 cups	
Carrots, fresh, halved lengthwise, ¼-inch bias-sliced	1 cup	6 cups	
Green onions, fresh, ½-inch bias-sliced	½ cup	3 cups	
Water chestnuts, sliced, canned, drained, julienne	½ cup	3 cups	
Cilantro, fresh, chopped	½ cup	3 cups	
3 *Hoisin Sesame Salad Dressing*			
Hoisin sauce, commercially prepared	⅔ cup	4 cups	Combine in separate bowl and whisk together until well blended. Cover and chill to hold.
Sesame oil	¼ cup	1½ cups	
Rice wine vinegar	2 tbsp.	¾ cup	
Soy sauce	1 tbsp.	⅓ cup	
Garlic, fresh, minced	1 tsp.	2 tbsp.	
Gingerroot, fresh, peeled, grated	1 tsp.	2 tbsp.	

recipe continued on next page . . .

INGREDIENT	QUANTITY		METHOD
	4 servings	24 servings	
4 Wonton wrappers, commercially prepared	8	48	Cut into ¼-inch-wide strips. Deep-fry at 350°F for 30 to 60 seconds or until golden. Remove from fryer. Drain and reserve.
5 Sesame seeds, toasted	1½ tbsp.	½ cup	*To assemble single serving:* Combine 4 cups salad mixture, 1 teaspoon sesame seeds, and ¼ cup salad dressing in bowl. Toss well and arrange on plate. Julienne 1 chicken breast filet and arrange over top. Garnish salad with 20 wonton strips. *Serve with sesame seed crackers or wonton chips.*

Portion: 17 ounces
Nutritional Data/Portion: Calories 810, Protein 48 g, Fat 46 g, Carbohydrate 52 g, Cholesterol 85 mg, Sodium 1,410 mg

For a **FAST FACTS VIA FAX**™ copy of this recipe, call 1-800-223-3755 and enter Business Tool 2397.

The Chinese have long appreciated the medicinal values of the foods they eat. Ginger, for instance, is used as a cold remedy and to settle upset stomachs.

Santa Fe Chicken Pasta Salad

Here is a colorful fajita pasta salad that goes "crunch" and treats the taste buds to a snappy combination of hot salsa and cool creamy ranch dressing.

*Submitted by Sue Brinkhaus
Mount Olivet Retreat Center
Farmington, Minn.*

INGREDIENT	QUANTITY		METHOD
	4 servings	24 servings	
1 Tyson Fully Cooked Flavor-Redi® Mixed Fajita Strips, Natural Proportion, frozen	14 oz.	5 lb.	Cover tightly and slack in cooler between 32° and 36°F prior to use.
2 Penne pasta, cooked al dente, rinsed, drained	3 oz. (dry)	1¼ lb. (dry)	Combine in bowl and add chicken.
Roma tomatoes, fresh, seeded, julienne	⅔ cup	4 cups	
Green bell peppers, fresh, julienne (p. 88)	⅓ cup	2 cups	
Red onions, fresh, slivered	3 tbsp.	1 cup	
Black olives, whole, pitted, canned, drained	⅓ cup	3 cups	
Pepper Jack cheese, shredded	¼ cup	1½ cups	
Cheddar cheese, sharp, shredded	¼ cup	1½ cups	
3 Ranch salad dressing, commercially prepared	1 cup	6 cups	Combine in separate bowl and mix thoroughly. Add to chicken mixture and toss well. Cover and chill below 40°F to hold.
Salsa, thick-and-chunky, hot, commercially prepared	½ cup	3 cups	
Ranch salad dressing mix, dry	1 tsp.	2 tbsp.	
Garlic salt	⅛ tsp.	¾ tsp.	
4 Green leaf lettuce leaves, fresh	8	48	*To assemble single serving:* Line plate with 2 lettuce leaves. Toss ½ cup crushed tortilla chips with 1⅔ cups salad. Arrange on lettuce. *Serve with cornbread sticks or multicolored tortilla chips.*
Corn tortilla chips, crushed	2 cups	12 cups	

Portion: 12 ounces
Nutritional Data/Portion: Calories 600, Protein 29 g, Fat 41 g, Carbohydrate 32 g, Cholesterol 130 mg, Sodium 1,140 mg

For a **FAST FACTS VIA FAX**™ copy of this recipe, call 1-800-223-3755 and enter Business Tool 2374.

Create variations with ziti, rotini, or another short pasta in place of the penne.

Make this dish kid-friendly by removing the red onions and black olives.

According to research, eating pasta releases serotonin, a chemical in the brain that makes a person feel relaxed and calm.

Submitted by Anthony Danna, CEC
Kernville Steak & Seafood
Lincoln City, Ore.

Store whole cucumbers, unwashed, in a plastic bag in the cooler for up to 7 days. Sliced cucumbers can be refrigerated, tightly wrapped, for up to 5 days.

Cucumbers are an ancient part of man's diet in literature. The Gilgamesh, the first known written legend, lists wild cucumbers as part of the Sumerian diet in 3000 B.C.

Greek Chicken Salad

This medley of Mediterranean flavors, including feta cheese, kalamata olives, pine nuts, and sun-dried tomatoes, showcases slices of garlic-marinated grilled chicken breast filet on a bed of mesclun salad greens.

INGREDIENT	QUANTITY 4 servings	24 servings	METHOD
1 Tyson Ready-to-Cook Gourmet Boneless, Skinless Whole Chicken Breast Filets, 6-oz., frozen	4	24	Place in full-size steam table pans. (Use half-size pan for smaller quantity.)
2 *Marinade*			
Olive oil	½ cup	3 cups	Combine in bowl and mix thoroughly. Pour over chicken. Cover and marinate below 40°F for 8 to 10 hours.
Garlic, fresh, chopped	2 tsp.	¼ cup	
Black pepper, coarse	1 tsp.	1 tbsp.	Remove chicken from marinade. Grill on oiled, preheated flattop griddle at 350°F for 2 to 4 minutes on each side or until chicken is no longer pink. Remove from griddle. Keep warm above 140°F.
3 *Greek Salad Dressing*			
Red wine vinegar	⅓ cup	1 cup	Combine in food processor bowl and process until well blended.
Mustard, Dijon	2 tbsp.	¼ cup	
Garlic, fresh, chopped	2 tsp.	2 tbsp.	
Oregano, fresh, chopped	2 tsp.	2 tbsp.	
4 Olive oil	1 cup	5 cups	Gradually add to processor bowl while motor is running and process until emulsified. Remove from processor bowl. Cover and chill to hold.
5 Mesclun salad greens mix, fresh, commercially prepared	8 cups	48 cups	*To assemble single serving:* Portion 2 cups salad greens on plate. Top with 4 tomato wedges and 4 cucumber slices. Sprinkle with 2 tablespoons feta cheese. Slice 1 chicken breast filet and fan over salad. Garnish salad with 1 rounded tablespoon sun-dried tomatoes, 1 tablespoon pine nuts, and 4 olives. Portion ¼ cup salad dressing into individual container and place on plate.
Tomato wedges, fresh	16	96	
Cucumber slices, fresh	16	96	
Feta cheese crumbles	½ cup	3 cups	
Sun-dried tomatoes, packed in oil, drained, julienne	⅓ cup	2 cups	
Pine nuts, whole, toasted	¼ cup	1½ cups	
Kalamata olives, whole, canned, drained	16	96	*Serve with pita crisps.*

Portion: 14 ounces plus 2 ounces dressing
Nutritional Data/Portion: Calories 760, Protein 48 g, Fat 57 g, Carbohydrate 19 g, Cholesterol 80 mg, Sodium 730 mg

For a **FAST FACTS VIA FAX** copy of this recipe, call 1-800-223-3755 and enter Business Tool 2382.

"Garlic is the catsup of intellectuals."
Anonymous

Submitted by Steven D. Shimmin, CEC
Fine Host Corporation
Albuquerque Convention Center
Albuquerque, N.M.

Asiago Chicken Roulade Salad with Asparagus Spears and Spicy Pecans

Create a new signature dish with this gourmet Asiago and spinach-stuffed roulade atop a sophisticated salad of mixed greens and asparagus spears, sprinkled with irresistible spicy caramelized pecans.

INGREDIENT	QUANTITY 4 servings	24 servings	METHOD
1 Tyson Signature Specialties™ Asiago Roulade, frozen	1	3	Brush chicken with oil and place on parchment-lined sheet pans.
Vegetable oil	as needed	as needed	Roast in preheated conventional oven at 350°F for 65 to 75 minutes. Or roast in preheated convection oven at 325°F for 55 to 65 minutes. Remove from oven. Remove and discard netting. Cover and chill below 40°F overnight.
			Slice into 1½-ounce slices. Cover and chill below 40°F to hold.
2 *Spicy Pecan Mix*			
Butter, salted	1 tbsp.	⅓ cup	Melt in skillet over medium heat.
3 Brown sugar, golden	2 tbsp.	¾ cup	Add to butter and stir until sugar is dissolved. Remove from heat.
Cayenne pepper, ground	⅛ tsp.	¾ tsp.	
Chili powder, light	⅛ tsp.	¾ tsp.	
Red pepper, crushed, dried	⅛ tsp.	¾ tsp.	
4 Pecans, coarsely chopped	¼ cup	1½ cups	Add to brown sugar mixture and stir well to coat with butter mixture. Spread on half-size sheet pan in single layer.
			Toast in preheated conventional oven at 350°F for 10 to 15 minutes or until sugar caramelizes. Or toast in preheated convection oven at 300°F for 8 to 10 minutes. Remove from oven. Cool and break into small pieces. Cover and reserve.
5 *Orange Vinaigrette*			
Sugar, granulated	3 tbsp.	1 cup	Combine in food processor bowl and process until sugar is dissolved.
Apple cider vinegar	3 tbsp.	1 cup	
Orange juice concentrate, frozen	3 tbsp.	1 cup	
Onions, fresh, minced	½ tbsp.	3 tbsp.	
Dry mustard powder	¾ tsp.	1½ tbsp.	
Poppy seeds, whole	¾ tsp.	1½ tbsp.	
Paprika, ground	½ tsp.	1 tbsp.	
6 Vegetable oil	½ cup	3 cups	Gradually add to processor bowl while motor is running and process until emulsified. Remove from processor bowl. Cover and chill to hold.
7 Spring greens salad mix, fresh, commercially prepared	16 cups	96 cups	*To assemble single serving:* Portion 4 cups salad greens on plate. Fan 3 slices chicken over greens. Arrange 5 cucumber slices, 3 asparagus spears, 3 orange segments, and 4 tomato halves over salad. Sprinkle salad with 2 tablespoons pecans and ¼ cup vinaigrette. Garnish plate with 3 olives and 1 carrot flower.
Cucumber slices, fresh	20	120	
Asparagus spears, fresh, blanched	12	72	
Mandarin orange segments, canned, drained	12	72	
Cherry tomato halves, fresh	16	96	
Black olives, whole, pitted, canned, drained	12	72	
Carrot flowers, fresh, blanched	4	24	*Serve with minicroissants.*

Portion: 11 ounces
Nutritional Data/Portion: Calories 740, Protein 41 g, Fat 46 g, Carbohydrate 47 g, Cholesterol 105 mg, Sodium 500 mg

For a **FAST FACTS VIA FAX** copy of this recipe, call 1-800-223-3755 and enter Business Tool 2390.

Commercially prepared spiced nuts and citrus vinaigrette dressing may be substituted.

The first known recipe using asparagus was written by Marcus Apicius, a Roman gastronome, who authored the first book of recipes in A.D. 14. Some Romans of that period thought so highly of this vegetable that they considered a dinner unimportant if it did not have an appetizer of asparagus.

Native to America, the pecan is a member of the hickory family and has the highest fat content of all nuts.

Submitted by Audrey Mitchell
Taco Hut
Joplin, Mo.

Aztec Cheekon Taco Salad

Flavorful slices of mesquite-flavored chicken distinguish this from the typical chicken taco salad.

For an optional presentation style, or to adapt this salad to line service, serve it surrounded by tortilla chips. For added variety and color, use blue or red corn chips.

INGREDIENT	QUANTITY 4 servings	24 servings	METHOD
1 Tyson Fully Cooked Flavor-Redi® Smoked Chicken Breast Filets, 3.75-oz., frozen	4	24	Cover tightly and slack in cooler between 32° and 36°F prior to use.
2 Taco shell bowls, 6¼-inch, commercially prepared	4	24	*To assemble single serving:* Spread 1½ cups lettuce in bottom of taco bowl. Slice 1 chicken breast filet into strips and mound on lettuce. Top with ½ cup additional lettuce, sprinkle with ¼ cup cheese, and arrange 4 tomato quarters over cheese. Drizzle ¼ cup picante sauce over salad. Garnish salad with 1 tablespoon sour cream and 1 tablespoon guacamole.
Iceberg lettuce, fresh, finely shredded	8 cups	48 cups	
Cheddar cheese, sharp, shredded	1 cup	6 cups	
Tomato slices, fresh, ½-inch-thick, cut into quarters	4	24	
Picante sauce, mild, commercially prepared	1 cup	6 cups	
Sour cream	¼ cup	1½ cups	
Guacamole, commercially prepared	¼ cup	1½ cups	

Portion: 14 ounces
Nutritional Data/Portion: Calories 440, Protein 35 g, Fat 24 g, Carbohydrate 23 g, Cholesterol 100 mg, Sodium 1,260 mg

For a **FAST FACTS VIA FAX** copy of this recipe, call 1-800-223-3755 and enter Business Tool 2388.

Southwest Chicken Salad

From the Tyson Kitchens

Tender pulled chicken, black beans, corn, bell pepper, and cilantro give this dish a distinct yet familiar appeal.

Maximize the health benefits of these great ingredients by using low-fat or fat-free vinaigrette.

Research shows that beans actually work against the development of cancer-causing compounds in the human body and are capable of lowering blood cholesterol. They are also recommended by the American Diabetic Association because they help stabilize blood glucose.

INGREDIENT	QUANTITY 4 servings	24 servings	METHOD
1 Tyson Fully Cooked Pulled White Fryer Meat, frozen	14 oz.	5¼ lb.	Cover tightly and slack in cooler between 32° and 36°F prior to use.
2 Black beans, canned, rinsed, drained	3 cups	16 cups	Combine in bowl and add chicken. Toss well.
Corn/onion/bell pepper mix, commercially prepared, frozen, thawed, drained	2 cups	12 cups	
3 Green onions, fresh, sliced	½ cup	3 cups	
Italian vinaigrette, commercially prepared	¾ cup	4½ cups	Combine in separate bowl and mix thoroughly. Pour over chicken mixture and toss well. Cover and chill below 40°F to hold.
Apple cider vinegar	1½ tbsp.	½ cup	
Sugar, granulated	1½ tbsp.	½ cup	
Cilantro, fresh, minced	3 tbsp.	1 cup	
4 Salad savoy leaves, fresh	4	24	*To assemble single serving:* Line plate with 1 savoy leaf. Top with 1¾ cups salad. Garnish plate with 2 tomatoes and 1 cilantro sprig. *Serve with fried tortilla chips.*
Cherry tomatoes, whole, fresh	8	48	
Cilantro sprigs, fresh	4	24	

Portion: 13 ounces
Nutritional Data/Portion: Calories 560, Protein 41 g, Fat 27 g, Carbohydrate 48 g, Cholesterol 80 mg, Sodium 400 mg

For a **FAST FACTS VIA FAX** copy of this recipe, call 1-800-223-3755 and enter Business Tool 2366.

Submitted by
A. William Allen, CEC, DTR
Capitol Cafeteria
Charleston, W. Va.

Americans eat more than 30 pounds of lettuce every year, which is about five times more than they ate in the early 1900s. ⌐

For an alternate presentation, drizzle a small amount of ranch dressing over the salad and serve remaining dressing as pictured. ⌐

Buffalo Icy Hot Chicken Salad

This salad really lives up to its name. It contrasts spicy Buffalo flavor Popcorn Chicken Bites with a chilled salad mixture of greens, carrots, yellow bell pepper, and cucumber slices, all topped with blue cheese crumbles and creamy ranch dressing.

Speed-Scratch

INGREDIENT	QUANTITY 4 servings	24 servings	METHOD
Tyson Buffalo Popcorn Chicken Bites™, frozen	1 lb.	6 lb.	Deep-fry at 350°F for 3 to 3½ minutes or until chicken is no longer pink. Remove from fryer and drain. Keep warm above 140°F.
Mixed salad greens, fresh, commercially prepared	8 cups	48 cups	Combine in bowl and toss well. Cover and chill to hold.
Carrots, fresh, shredded	½ cup	3 cups	
Yellow bell peppers, fresh, diced (p.88)	½ cup	3 cups	
Cucumber slices, fresh	16	96	*To assemble single serving:* Portion 2 cups salad mixture on plate. Arrange 4 cucumber slices over greens and sprinkle with 2 tablespoons cheese. Top with 4 ounces chicken, then drizzle with ¼ cup salad dressing. Portion ¼ cup sauce into individual container and serve on the side. Garnish plate with 2 tomato halves.
Blue cheese crumbles	½ cup	3 cups	
Ranch salad dressing, commercially prepared	1 cup	6 cups	
Buffalo wing sauce, commercially prepared	1 cup	6 cups	
Cherry tomato halves, fresh	8	48	*Serve with corn muffins.*

Portion: 12 ounces plus 2 ounces sauce
Nutritional Data/Portion: Calories 620, Protein 26 g, Fat 45 g, Carbohydrate 31 g, Cholesterol 60 mg, Sodium 1,790 mg

For a **FAST FACTS VIA FAX**₋ copy of this recipe, call 1-800-223-3755 and enter Business Tool 2393.

"Part of the secret of success in life is to eat what you like and let the food fight it out inside." ⌐

Mark Twain

*"Only the pure of heart
can make a good soup."*

Ludwig van Beethoven

Bowls

*P*utting stock into your menu

Soup is important in virtually every culture, but its name is derived from the French word *souppe*, which comes from "sip" or "sop"—the sound made while eating it. In 1765, a French tavern keeper transformed his establishment into the first public restaurant, following a court battle in which he won the right to keep serving a soup he claimed to be restorative *(restorante)*. Soup thus became the first official menu item. Over 200 years later, it is still a healthful, hearty, and comforting part of the menu.

Chicken is a traditional part of soup making. The proverbial chicken soup was first prescribed as a remedy for fevers and coughs by the philosopher/physician Maimonides during the 12th century. And while its medicinal value has been subject to debate ever since, its popularity has not. Today, chicken soup tops the foodservice "leading sellers" list in the soup category.

Bowls is dedicated to foods prepared in a single pot—soup, chili, chowder, gumbo, jambalaya, and stew—and served in a bowl. Some recipes provide familiar connections with home and family, others serve as savory melting pots of ethnic flavor and variety, while some reach new levels of culinary ingenuity and artistry.

Recipes in this chapter deliver high flavor and convenience with relatively low food costs and great labor efficiency. Many can be made ahead of the rush, refrigerated, reheated with ease, and even held over heat with flavor-enhancing results. Therefore, they are excellent means of managing labor and getting great food to the table fast.

This chapter is an appetizing array of contributions from diverse operations across the country. Steeped in imagination, each recipe satisfies the growing love of flavorful chicken dishes served in bowls.

Submitted by Jane Schimpf
Bowling Green State University
Auxiliary Services
Bowling Green, Ohio

Chicken Oriental Soup

Tender chicken chunks and crunchy vegetables get a lift from an irresistible broth steeped in roasted sesame oil, tangy soy, and fresh ginger.

Lighter Fare *Line Service* *Takeout*

For takeout, package rice noodles in separate container.

INGREDIENT	QUANTITY		METHOD
	4 servings	24 servings	
1 White rice, raw	3 tbsp.	1 cup	Combine in saucepan and bring to boil over high heat. Cover and reduce heat. Simmer for 15 to 20 minutes or until rice is tender. Remove from heat and reserve.
Water, cold	⅓ cup	2 cups	
2 Lemon juice, fresh	1 tsp.	2 tbsp.	
Tyson Fully Cooked Pulled Natural Proportion Fryer Meat, frozen	6 oz.	2¼ lb.	Combine in saucepan or stockpot and mix thoroughly. Bring to boil over high heat. Reduce heat and simmer for 15 to 17 minutes or until carrots are tender, stirring frequently. (Simmer smaller quantity for 10 to 12 minutes.)
Chicken broth, canned	3½ cups	19 cups	
Celery, fresh, ¼-inch bias-sliced	⅔ cup	4 cups	
3 Carrots, fresh, julienne (p. 88)	⅓ cup	2 cups	
Snow peas, fresh, ½-inch bias-sliced	½ cup	3 cups	Add to chicken mixture. Add rice and mix thoroughly.
Green onions, fresh, ¼-inch bias-sliced	3 tbsp.	1 cup	
4 Red bell peppers, fresh, julienne	2 tbsp.	¾ cup	
Soy sauce	1 tbsp.	⅓ cup	Combine in small bowl and mix until smooth. Gradually stir into soup and simmer for 2 to 5 minutes or until soup becomes clear and slightly thickened. Remove from heat.
Sherry, dry	1 tbsp.	⅓ cup	
Gingerroot, fresh, peeled, grated	1 tsp.	2 tbsp.	
Cornstarch	¾ tsp.	2 tbsp.	
5 Sesame oil	½ tsp.	½ tbsp.	Add to soup and mix thoroughly. Keep warm above 140°F.
6 Green onions, fresh, minced	2 tbsp.	¾ cup	*To assemble single serving:* Ladle 1¼ cups soup into bowl. Garnish with ½ tablespoon green onions and 1 tablespoon noodles.
Crispy rice noodles, commercially prepared	¼ cup	1½ cups	

Serve with steamed Chinese buns.

Portion: 10 ounces
Nutritional Data/Portion: Calories 190, Protein 17 g, Fat 4 g, Carbohydrate 19 g, Cholesterol 40 mg, Sodium 950 mg

For a **FAST FACTS VIA FAX** copy of this recipe, call 1-800-223-3755 and enter Business Tool 2527.

Rice noodles are extremely thin Chinese noodles that explode into a tangle of airy, crunchy strands when deep-fried. This traditional ingredient in Chinese chicken salad can also be presoaked and used in soups and stir-fries.

Submitted by Marlin Freyholtz, Jr.
Jake's Supper Club
Menomonie, Wis.

For variety, add sliced fresh mushrooms. For heartier soup, add more chicken.⌐

A long-grain and wild rice blend may be substituted.⌐

The thickness of this soup lends itself to being served in a bread bowl as pictured.⌐

Creamy Chicken Wild Rice Soup

No one will guess they're eating sensibly when they dive into this flavor-rich and creamy chicken soup, whose complex character is defined by sherry and garlic.

INGREDIENT	QUANTITY		METHOD
	4 servings	24 servings	
1 Water, cold	1 cup	6 cups	Combine in saucepan or stockpot and bring to boil over high heat. Reduce heat and simmer for 9 to 10 minutes or until vegetables are tender-crisp. (Simmer smaller quantity for 5 to 7 minutes.)
Chicken base concentrate**	1 tbsp.	⅓ cup	
Carrots, fresh, diced (p. 88)	½ cup	3 cups	
Celery, fresh, diced	½ cup	3 cups	
Onions, fresh, diced (p. 175)	½ cup	3 cups	
Garlic, fresh, minced	½ tbsp.	3 tbsp.	
2 Tyson Fully Cooked Shredded Savory Chicken Breast Meat, frozen	8 oz.	3 lb.	Add to vegetable mixture and return to boil over high heat. Reduce heat and simmer for 10 to 12 minutes or until chicken is thoroughly heated, stirring frequently. (Simmer smaller quantity for 4 to 5 minutes.)
3 Wild rice, cooked according to package directions, drained	1 cup	4 cups	Add to chicken mixture and mix thoroughly. Return to simmer.
Milk, whole	2 cups	10 cups	
Sherry, dry	¼ cup	1 cup	
4 Flour, all-purpose	1 tbsp.	⅓ cup	Combine in small bowl and mix until smooth. Gradually stir into soup. Simmer for 2 to 5 minutes or until soup thickens. Remove from heat. Keep warm above 140°F.
Water, cold	1½ tbsp.	½ cup	

To assemble single serving: Ladle 1¼ cups soup into bowl.

Serve with carrot and celery sticks.

Portion: 10 ounces
Nutritional Data/Portion: Calories 230, Protein 19 g, Fat 7 g, Carbohydrate 22 g, Cholesterol 50 mg, Sodium 600 mg

**This recipe uses a base with the reconstitution ratio of 1 teaspoon per cup.

For a ***FAST FACTS VIA FAX*** copy of this recipe, call 1-800-223-3755 and enter Business Tool 2530.

Submitted by Lee Valentine, Jr.
Chesapeake Golf Club
Chesapeake, Va.

Chicken and Wild Rice Soup

White chicken chunks and fiber-rich rice make this soup appealing to health-minded patrons who demand full flavor and a satisfying bite. White pepper adds a subtle but definite kick.

INGREDIENT	QUANTITY		METHOD
	4 servings	24 servings	
1 Wild rice, raw	¼ cup	1⅔ cups	Prepare according to package directions. Drain and reserve.
2 Vegetable oil	1 tsp.	¼ cup	Heat in saucepan or stockpot over medium heat.
3 Onions, fresh, minced	½ cup	3 cups	Add to oil and sauté for 3 to 4 minutes or until onions are translucent but not brown. (Sauté smaller quantity for 1 to 2 minutes.)
Celery, fresh, minced	¼ cup	1½ cups	
4 Tyson Fully Cooked Diced White Fryer Meat, ¾-inch dice, frozen	3 oz.	1 lb.	Add to vegetable mixture and mix thoroughly. Add wild rice and bring to boil over high heat. Reduce heat and simmer for 6 to 8 minutes or until chicken is thoroughly heated, stirring frequently. (Simmer smaller quantity for 1 to 2 minutes.)
Chicken broth, canned	4 cups	20 cups	
Salt	¼ tsp.	½ tsp.	
White pepper, fine	⅛ tsp.	¼ tsp.	
5 Cornstarch	1 tbsp.	¼ cup	Combine in small bowl and mix until smooth. Gradually stir into soup. Simmer for 2 to 5 minutes or until soup is slightly thickened. Remove from heat. Keep warm above 140°F.
Water, cold	1 tbsp.	¼ cup	
6 Parsley, fresh, minced (p. 39)	1½ tbsp.	½ cup	*To assemble single serving:* Ladle 1 cup soup into bowl. Garnish with 1 teaspoon parsley.
			Serve with whole-wheat rolls.

Portion: 9 ounces
Nutritional Data/Portion: Calories 130, Protein 13 g, Fat 3 g, Carbohydrate 13 g, Cholesterol 15 mg, Sodium 940 mg

For a **FAST FACTS VIA FAX** copy of this recipe, call 1-800-223-3755 and enter Business Tool 2536.

Fresh or reconstituted diced dry mushrooms (button, portobello, shiitake, or oyster) may be added to this soup for extra flavor.

Wild rice, sometimes referred to as Indian rice, is actually a long-grain marsh grass indigenous to the lakes and marshes around the upper Mississippi River valley. It was a substantial part of the Native American (Chippewa and Sioux) diet, especially through the winter months.

"I wish that there would not be a peasant so poor in all my realm who would not have a chicken in his pot every Sunday."
Henry IV

The word "chowder"
originates from the French
word chaudiére, *which was*
a cauldron where French
fishermen made their stews
from the day's catch. Today,
chowder can refer to any
rich, thick, chunky soup.

Offer this hearty bowl of
soup as part of a soup and
salad meal.

Chicken and Three Pepper Corn Chowder

Corn chowder can be a tasty starter or a serious meal in a bowl. Colorful bell peppers, large pieces of chicken, cheese, and cilantro add the personality to make this creamy soup a menu staple.

Speed-Scratch   Line Service   Takeout

INGREDIENT	QUANTITY		METHOD
	4 servings	24 servings	
1 Butter, salted	2 tbsp.	¾ cup	Heat in saucepan or stockpot over medium-high heat.
2 Corn/onion/bell pepper mix, frozen	3 cups	18 cups	Add to butter and sauté for 8 to 10 minutes or until vegetables are tender. (Sauté smaller quantity for 2 to 3 minutes.)
Garlic, minced, commercially prepared	½ tbsp.	3 tbsp.	
Cayenne pepper, ground	⅛ tsp.	¾ tsp.	
3 Tyson Fully Cooked Pulled White Fryer Meat, frozen	8 oz.	3 lb.	Add to vegetable mixture and bring to boil over high heat. Reduce heat and simmer for 15 to 20 minutes or until chicken is thoroughly heated, stirring frequently. (Simmer smaller quantity for 8 to 10 minutes.)
Chicken broth, canned	2 cups	12 cups	
4 Pasteurized process cheese food, shredded	2 cups	12 cups	Add to chicken mixture and mix thoroughly. Simmer an additional 5 to 10 minutes or until flavors are blended, stirring frequently. (Simmer smaller quantity for 4 to 5 minutes.) Remove from heat. Keep warm above 140°F.
Heavy cream	½ cup	3 cups	
Cilantro, fresh, minced	1 tbsp.	⅓ cup	
5 Cilantro sprigs, fresh	4	24	*To assemble single serving:* Ladle 1½ cups soup into bowl. Garnish with 1 cilantro sprig. *Serve with crusty sourdough rolls.*

Portion: 12 ounces

Nutritional Data/Portion: Calories 540, Protein 35 g, Fat 37 g, Carbohydrate 21 g, Cholesterol 155 mg, Sodium 1,300 mg

For a *FAST FACTS VIA FAX* copy of this recipe, call 1-800-223-3755 and enter Business Tool 2364.

Pollo Con Calabacita

Calabacita is Spanish for "zucchini," but spicy Southwest flavors make this colorful, chunky chicken "stew" a dish that will satisfy in any language.

Lighter Fare   Line Service   Takeout

Submitted by Brenda McGahagin, RD
Texas Department of Mental Health, Mental Retardation
Austin, Tex.

	INGREDIENT	QUANTITY 4 servings	24 servings	METHOD
1	Tyson Fully Cooked Flavor-Redi® Mixed Fajita Strips, Natural Proportion, frozen	1 lb.	6 lb.	Combine in saucepan or stockpot and mix thoroughly. Bring to boil over high heat. Cover and reduce heat. Simmer for 12 to 15 minutes or until vegetables are tender, stirring frequently. (Simmer smaller quantity for 4 to 5 minutes.)
	Onions, fresh, diced (p. 175)	½ cup	3 cups	
	Celery, fresh, diced (p. 88)	½ cup	3 cups	
	Green bell peppers, fresh, diced	½ cup	3 cups	
	Chicken broth, canned	⅓ cup	2 cups	
	Cumin, ground	¾ tsp.	1½ tbsp.	
	Garlic powder	¼ tsp.	½ tbsp.	
	Black pepper, coarse	¼ tsp.	½ tbsp.	
2	Tomatoes, diced, canned, undrained	½ cup	3 cups	Add to chicken mixture and mix thoroughly. Return to simmer, then remove from heat. Keep warm above 140°F.
	Tomato paste, canned	1½ tbsp.	½ cup	
	Zucchini, fresh, halved lengthwise, seeded, diced	3 cups	18 cups	
	Yellow corn, whole kernel, frozen	½ cup	3 cups	
3	Parsley sprigs, fresh	4	24	*To assemble single serving:* Ladle 1⅓ cups stew into bowl. Garnish with 1 parsley sprig. *Serve with warm flour tortillas.*

Portion: 11 ounces
Nutritional Data/Portion: Calories 270, Protein 26 g, Fat 10 g, Carbohydrate 21 g, Cholesterol 105 mg, Sodium 630 mg

For a **FAST FACTS VIA FAX**® copy of this recipe, call 1-800-223-3755 and enter Business Tool 2528.

Cave dwellers in the Tamaulipas Mountains of Mexico began domesticating plants sometime between 7000 and 5000 B.C. These original garden plants were summer squashes, corn, and beans, which were grown together and usually eaten together. ‑☞

Add a measure of beans to this recipe for variety and a truly Old-World style. ‑☞

Quick Chicken Tortilla Soup

Here's a basic tortilla soup that's a snap to make, and customers will be quick to say how good it tastes.

Speed-Scratch   Kid Friendly   Line Service   Takeout

Submitted by Brian Martin
Lambrusco'z To-Go Deli and Catering Market
Tulsa, Okla.

	INGREDIENT	QUANTITY 4 servings	24 servings	METHOD
1	Tyson Fully Cooked Pulled Natural Proportion Fryer Meat, frozen	8 oz.	3 lb.	Combine in saucepan or stockpot and mix thoroughly. Bring to boil over high heat. Reduce heat and simmer for 10 to 15 minutes or until chicken is thoroughly heated, stirring frequently. (Simmer smaller quantity for 6 to 8 minutes.)
	Water, cold	1½ cups	9 cups	
	Chicken broth, canned	1½ cups	9 cups	
	Chili powder, light	2 tsp.	¼ cup	
2	Yellow corn, whole kernel, frozen	1¼ cups	7½ cups	Add to chicken mixture and mix thoroughly. Return to simmer, then remove from heat. Keep warm above 140°F.
	Salsa, thick-and-chunky, mild, commercially prepared	1 cup	6 cups	
3	Cheddar cheese, sharp, shredded	1 cup	6 cups	*To assemble single serving:* Ladle 1¼ cups soup into bowl. Top with ¼ cup cheese, 1 tablespoon guacamole, and 8 tortilla chips. *Serve with cheese and green chile quesadillas.*
	Guacamole, commercially prepared	¼ cup	1½ cups	
	Tortilla chips, commercially prepared	32	192	

Portion: 12 ounces
Nutritional Data/Portion: Calories 390, Protein 28 g, Fat 20 g, Carbohydrate 29 g, Cholesterol 85 mg, Sodium 820 mg

For a **FAST FACTS VIA FAX**® copy of this recipe, call 1-800-223-3755 and enter Business Tool 2531.

For a lower-fat garnish, top the soup with baked tortilla chips. ‑☞

Tortillas are the daily bread of Mexico. Depending upon the region of the country, they are made from corn or wheat flour, then cooked on a griddle. In Spain, a tortilla is a thin omelet. ‑☞

Add visual appeal by frying multicolored flour tortilla strips.

Some things do get better with age. Day-old tortillas are fantastic fried.

For a colorful garnish, add fresh-sliced avocado and olives to the side of the plate.

Chicken Tortilla Soup

Thin strips of crispy fried corn tortillas, shredded cheese, and a fresh cilantro sprig make a great first impression atop this chunky chicken soup. Garlic and cumin give the broth great character.

INGREDIENT	QUANTITY		METHOD
	4 servings	24 servings	
1 Butter, salted	¼ cup	1 cup	Heat in saucepan or stockpot over medium-high heat.
2 Onions, fresh, chopped (p. 175)	½ cup	3 cups	Add to butter and sauté for 2 to 3 minutes or until onions are tender. (Sauté smaller quantity for 1 to 2 minutes.)
Garlic, fresh, minced	1 tbsp.	⅓ cup	
Red pepper, crushed, dried	1 tsp.	2 tbsp.	
Cumin, ground	1 tsp.	2 tbsp.	
3 Tyson Fully Cooked Pulled White Fryer Meat, frozen	8 oz.	3 lb.	Add to onion mixture and mix thoroughly. Bring to boil over high heat. Reduce heat and simmer for 30 to 45 minutes or until flavors are concentrated, stirring frequently. (Simmer smaller quantity for 15 to 18 minutes.) Remove from heat. Keep warm above 140°F.
Tomatoes, diced, canned, drained	½ cup	3 cups	
Chicken broth, canned	7 cups	42 cups	
Cilantro leaves, dried	2 tsp.	¼ cup	
4 Tyson Mexican Original® Yellow Corn Tortillas, 6-inch, room temperature	8	48	Cut into ¼-inch-wide strips. Deep-fry at 350°F for 1 minute or until crispy. Remove from fryer and drain. Reserve.
5 Cheddar and Monterey Jack cheese blend, finely shredded	1⅓ cups	8 cups	*To assemble single serving:* Ladle 1½ cups soup into bowl. Top with 1 cup tortilla strips and ⅓ cup cheese. Garnish with 1 cilantro sprig.
Cilantro sprigs, fresh	4	24	*Serve with chilled pinto bean salad.*

Portion: 15 ounces
Nutritional Data/Portion: Calories 412, Protein 24 g, Fat 29 g, Carbohydrate 16 g, Cholesterol 73 mg, Sodium 1,218 mg

For a **FAST FACTS VIA FAX** copy of this recipe, call 1-800-223-3755 and enter Business Tool 2358.

"Etiquette is the noise you don't make while having soup."

Anonymous

Submitted by Susan Dearborn
Baldwin-Wallace College
Berea, Ohio

Mexican Chicken Black Bean Soup

Chicken fajita strips are the perfect choice for this spicier version of black bean soup. The blending of picante sauce, chili powder, and cumin flavors adds a Mexican twist to a traditionally Cuban black bean soup.

Lighter Fare   Line Service   Takeout

INGREDIENT	QUANTITY		METHOD
	4 servings	24 servings	
1 Olive oil spray	as needed	as needed	Spray saucepan or stockpot with oil.
2 Red onions, fresh, diced (p. 175)	½ cup	3 cups	Add to oil and sauté over medium heat for 2 to 4 minutes or until vegetables are tender-crisp. (Sauté smaller quantity for 1 to 2 minutes.)
Green bell peppers, fresh, diced (p. 88)	½ cup	3 cups	
3 Tyson Fully Cooked Flavor-Redi® Chicken Thigh Fajita Strips, frozen	8 oz.	3 lb.	Add to vegetable mixture and mix thoroughly. Bring to boil over high heat. Reduce heat and simmer for 30 to 45 minutes or until flavors are concentrated, stirring frequently. (Simmer smaller quantity for 12 to 15 minutes.)
Chicken broth, canned	2 cups	12 cups	
Black beans, canned, undrained	1½ cups	9 cups	
Tomatoes, diced, canned, undrained	1 cup	6 cups	
Tomato juice, canned	½ cup	3 cups	
Picante sauce, mild, commercially prepared	¼ cup	1½ cups	
Chili powder, light	2 tsp.	2 tbsp.	
Cajun seasoning, dried	½ tsp.	1 tbsp.	
Cumin, ground	½ tsp.	1 tbsp.	
Garlic powder	⅛ tsp.	1 tsp.	
Salt	¼ tsp.	½ tbsp.	
Black pepper, coarse	¼ tsp.	½ tbsp.	
4 Yellow corn, whole kernel, frozen	¼ cup	1½ cups	Add to chicken mixture and mix thoroughly. Return to simmer, then remove from heat. Keep warm above 140°F.
5 Sour cream	½ cup	3 cups	*To assemble single serving:* Ladle 1½ cups soup into bowl. Top with 2 tablespoons sour cream, 1 tablespoon cheese, and ½ tablespoon green onions.
Cheddar cheese, mild, shredded	¼ cup	1½ cups	
Green onions, fresh, chopped	2 tbsp.	¾ cup	

Serve with cheddar cheese cornbread.

Portion: 14 ounces
Nutritional Data/Portion: Calories 330, Protein 22 g, Fat 15 g, Carbohydrate 28 g, Cholesterol 75 mg, Sodium 2,200 mg

For a ***Fast Facts Via Fax*** copy of this recipe, call 1-800-223-3755 and enter Business Tool 2537.

To adjust the heat level in this tangy soup, use medium or hot picante sauce instead of mild.

Low-fat sour cream and cheddar cheese may be substituted to achieve a reduced-fat version.

Black beans, also known as turtle beans, have only recently become widely available in the U.S. They have long been used in Mexican, South American, and Caribbean cooking.

USE YOUR NOODLE

Surprisingly, Asian noodles are relatively inexpensive. They can be seasoned and mixed with chopped vegetables for a dish that's flavorful and easy to prepare.

Cellophane
Made from the starch of green mung beans, these translucent threadlike noodles are also called "bean threads." Serve in salads, stir-fries, or soups as shown here. They also make a nice presentation when formed into nests and deep-fried.

Soba
Japanese noodles made from buckwheat flour; brownish in color, nutty in flavor. Serve with a dipping sauce or in bowls of steaming broth.

Udon
Round or flat wheat noodles that vary in size. They are typically white, but some are made with eggs, which make them yellow. They are great for hearty soups and stews.

Rice-flour
Extremely long, thin, and translucent Chinese noodles that are used for delicate stir-fries, soups, and salads.

Ramen
Japanese deep-fried noodles that are usually served in broth with vegetables.

Wrappers
Typically thin and round, wrappers are technically noodles and are used to make steamed dumplings. Thicker versions are deep-fried.

Add some snap to this dish by adding crushed red pepper.

See sidebar on page 19 for how to make a chile pepper flower.

Chicken and Bean Thread Noodle Bowl

Asian noodle shops are sprouting all over the country because they offer quick, flavorful, inexpensive meals. But patrons don't have to search the inner cities to taste this delectable dinner bowl. Stir-fried strips of chicken share the stage with shiitake mushrooms, napa cabbage, snow peas, and garlic in a savory chicken stock over bean thread noodles.

Speed-Scratch Lighter Fare Line Service Takeout

INGREDIENT	QUANTITY 4 servings	24 servings	METHOD
1 Peanut oil	1 tbsp.	⅓ cup	Heat in saucepan or stockpot over medium-high heat.
2 Napa cabbage, fresh, shredded	¼ cup	1½ cups	Add to oil and stir-fry for 5 to 8 minutes or until vegetables are wilted. (Stir-fry smaller quantity for 1 to 2 minutes.)
Snow peas, fresh, julienne	¼ cup	1½ cups	
Shiitake mushrooms, fresh, chopped	¼ cup	1½ cups	
Garlic, minced, commercially prepared	1 tbsp.	⅓ cup	
3 Tyson Fully Cooked Pulled Fryer Leg Meat, frozen	12 oz.	4½ lb.	Add to vegetable mixture and bring to boil over high heat. Reduce heat and simmer for 15 to 20 minutes or until chicken is thoroughly heated, stirring frequently. (Simmer smaller quantity for 4 to 5 minutes.) Remove from heat.
Chicken broth, canned	2 cups	12 cups	
Soy sauce	1½ tbsp.	½ cup	
4 Sesame oil	1 tbsp.	¼ cup	Add to chicken mixture and mix thoroughly. Keep warm above 140°F.
Green onions, fresh, ¼-inch bias-sliced	¼ cup	1½ cups	
5 Bean thread noodles, soaked in warm water according to package directions	4 oz. (dry)	24 oz. (dry)	*To assemble single serving:* Portion 1 cup noodles into bowl. Ladle 1 cup soup over noodles. Garnish with 1 chile pepper flower.
Chile pepper flowers, fresh	4	24	*Serve with crispy sesame crackers.*

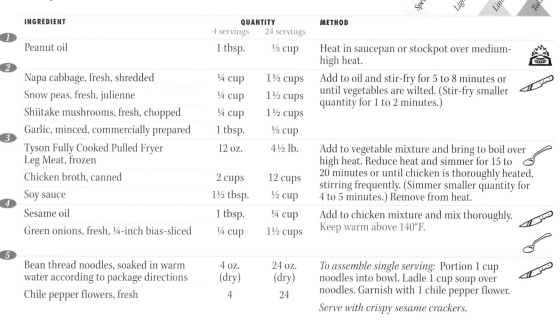

Portion: 12 ounces
Nutritional Data/Portion: Calories 330, Protein 24 g, Fat 13 g, Carbohydrate 28 g, Cholesterol 105 mg, Sodium 640 mg

For a **FAST FACTS VIA FAX** copy of this recipe, call 1-800-223-3755 and enter Business Tool 2361.

Submitted by Edward Carloni
Lebanon Country Club
Myerstown, Pa.

Chicken, Potato, and Roasted Garlic Soup

Tender bites of chicken and the robust flavor of roasted garlic show that a simple potato soup can be much finer than peasant fare.

INGREDIENT	QUANTITY		METHOD
	4 servings	24 servings	
1 Chicken broth, canned	2 cups	10 cups	Combine in saucepan or stockpot and mix thoroughly. Bring to boil over high heat.
Red potatoes, fresh, peeled, sliced	14 oz.	4½ lb.	
Garlic, fresh, roasted, minced	2 tbsp.	¾ cup	
2 Heavy cream	1 cup	5 cups	Add to broth mixture and mix thoroughly. Reduce heat and simmer for 10 to 12 minutes or until potatoes are tender, stirring frequently. (Simmer smaller quantity for 8 to 10 minutes.) Remove from heat and cool slightly. Transfer to food processor bowl and process until pureed. Return to saucepan or stockpot.
White wine, dry	2 tbsp.	¾ cup	
Salt	¼ tsp.	2½ tsp.	
White pepper, fine	⅛ tsp.	¾ tsp.	
3 Tyson Fully Cooked Diced White Fryer Meat, ½-inch dice, frozen	10 oz.	3½ lb.	Add to potato mixture and return to boil over medium heat. Reduce heat and simmer for 4 to 5 minutes or until chicken is thoroughly heated, stirring frequently. (Simmer smaller quantity for 1 to 2 minutes.) Remove from heat. Keep warm above 140°F.
4 Chive spears, fresh	12	72	*To assemble single serving:* Ladle 1¼ cups soup into bowl. Garnish with 3 chive spears.
			Serve with crusty sourdough rolls and a salad of mixed field greens.

Portion: 10 ounces
Nutritional Data/Portion: Calories 440, Protein 29 g, Fat 25 g, Carbohydrate 24 g, Cholesterol 140 mg, Sodium 990 mg

For a **FAST FACTS VIA FAX** copy of this recipe, call 1-800-223-3755 and enter Business Tool 2526.

Any waxy potato, such as long, round white potatoes or golden potatoes may be substituted for the red potatoes.

Potatoes were first introduced to Spain in 1539 by conquistadors who discovered South American natives eating them in 1530. Sir Francis Drake tasted them in Chile for the first time in 1580. He carried them back to England as a New World curiosity in 1586. By some accounts, potatoes arrived in Ireland when wreckage from the Spanish Armada washed ashore there in 1588.

To roast garlic, slice the top off of a whole garlic head, exposing the individual cloves. Place in a roasting pan and drizzle with oil. Then, cover and roast in a preheated conventional oven at 350°F for 30 to 35 minutes or until the garlic is tender. Finally, remove from the oven and cool.

Packaging the Chicken and Bean Thread Noodle Bowl broth separately helps preserve the fresh-served taste customers experience when they dine in.

Leaving the seeds and ribs in chiles, as this recipe calls for, increases the heat level because they are the most concentrated source of capsaicin, which is the oil that produces the heat in peppers.➝

Spicy Chicken Chili

Chicken fajita strips, simmered with onions, garlic, and jalapeño peppers, set the flavor tone for this robust chili.

Lighter Fare   Line Service   Takeout

INGREDIENT	QUANTITY 4 servings	QUANTITY 24 servings	METHOD
1 Vegetable oil	2 tbsp.	¼ cup	Heat in saucepan or stockpot over medium heat.
2 Onions, fresh, chopped (p. 175)	1 cup	6 cups	Add to oil and sauté for 3 to 5 minutes or until onions are tender. (Sauté smaller quantity for 2 to 3 minutes.)
Garlic, fresh, minced	2 tsp.	¼ cup	
Jalapeño peppers, fresh, with seeds, minced	1 tsp.	2 tbsp.	
3 Tyson Fully Cooked Flavor-Redi® Chicken Breast Fajita Strips, frozen	12 oz.	4½ lb.	Add to onion mixture and mix thoroughly. Bring to boil over high heat. Reduce heat and simmer for 30 to 40 minutes or until flavors are concentrated, stirring frequently. (Simmer smaller quantity for 15 to 20 minutes.) Remove from heat.
Chicken broth, canned	3 cups	16 cups	
Great Northern beans, canned, undrained	1½ cups	9 cups	
Tomatoes, diced, canned, drained	½ cup	2 cups	
Green chiles, chopped, canned	½ cup	2 cups	
Cumin, ground	1 tsp.	2 tbsp.	
Chili powder, dark	½ tsp.	1 tbsp.	
4 Cilantro leaves, fresh, minced	1 tbsp.	⅓ cup	Add to chicken mixture and mix thoroughly. Keep warm above 140°F.
5 Salsa, thick-and-chunky, mild, commercially prepared	¼ cup	1½ cups	*To assemble single serving:* Ladle 1½ cups chili into bowl. Top with 1 tablespoon each of salsa, sour cream, avocado, and cheese.
Sour cream	¼ cup	1½ cups	
Avocado, fresh, diced, tossed in lime juice	¼ cup	1½ cups	
Monterey Jack cheese, finely shredded	¼ cup	1½ cups	*Serve with corn muffins or cornbread.*

Portion: 14 ounces
Nutritional Data/Portion: Calories 420, Protein 32 g, Fat 18 g, Carbohydrate 33 g, Cholesterol 55 mg, Sodium 1,400 mg

For a ***FAST FACTS VIA FAX*** copy of this recipe, call 1-800-223-3755 and enter Business Tool 2532.

Submitted by Doug Hammond
Bar H BBQ
Antioch, Tenn.

Chicken Chili Verde

Texans normally ask for a "bowl of red" when they want chili, but now people looking for a change of pace can ask for a "bowl of green." Green chiles, garlic, and cloves make this dish stand out proudly from the crowd.

INGREDIENT	QUANTITY		METHOD
	4 servings	24 servings	
1 Vegetable oil	½ tbsp.	3 tbsp.	Heat in saucepan or stockpot over medium heat.
2 Onions, fresh, chopped (p. 175)	2 cups	10 cups	Add to oil and sauté for 10 to 12 minutes or until onions are tender. (Sauté smaller quantity for 5 to 10 minutes.)
Garlic, fresh, minced	1 tsp.	2 tbsp.	
3 Tyson Fully Cooked Diced White Fryer Meat, ¾-inch dice, frozen	8 oz.	3 lb.	Add to onion mixture and bring to boil over high heat. Reduce heat and simmer for 30 to 40 minutes or until thickened, stirring frequently. (Simmer smaller quantity for 20 to 30 minutes.)
Chicken broth, canned	3 cups	14 cups	
Green chiles, chopped, canned	½ cup	3 cups	
Cumin, ground	2 tsp.	¼ cup	
Oregano leaves, dried	½ tbsp.	3 tbsp.	
Cayenne pepper, ground	½ tsp.	1 tbsp.	
Cloves, ground	¼ tsp.	½ tbsp.	
4 Great Northern beans, canned, undrained	2 cups	10 cups	Add to chicken mixture and simmer for 3 to 5 minutes or until beans are thoroughly heated, stirring frequently. Remove from heat. Keep warm above 140°F.
5 Monterey Jack cheese, shredded	½ cup	3 cups	*To assemble single serving:* Ladle 1½ cups chili into bowl. Top with 2 tablespoons each of cheese, salsa, and sour cream.
Salsa, thick-and-chunky, mild, commercially prepared	½ cup	3 cups	
Sour cream	½ cup	3 cups	*Serve with cornbread sticks.*

Portion: 14½ ounces
Nutritional Data/Portion: Calories 440, Protein 35 g, Fat 16 g, Carbohydrate 41 g, Cholesterol 70 mg, Sodium 1,000 mg

For a **FAST FACTS VIA FAX**. copy of this recipe, call 1-800-223-3755 and enter Business Tool 2548.

There are over 200 varieties of chiles in the genus Capsicum, of which over half are indigenous to Mexico. Capsaicin, the substance that gives chiles their heat, is recognized for its decongestant qualities and also stimulates the brain to produce endorphins.

"Legumes are truly a culinary treasure."
Jimmy Schmidt

Submitted by Todd Adelman
Brooklyn School for Special Children
Brooklyn, N.Y.

Teriyaki Chicken and Rice Soup

Teriyaki-marinated chicken is the base for this amazingly easy soup. It might also be called "Asian gumbo."

Please sophisticated palates by adding more ginger.

To shorten the fresh-ingredient list, garnish with chopped leeks instead of green onions.

Teriyaki flavoring is a mix of soy sauce, sake (or sherry), sugar, ginger, and other seasonings.

INGREDIENT	QUANTITY 4 servings	24 servings	METHOD
1 Tyson Ready-to-Cook Flavor-Redi® Teriyaki Chicken Breast Filets, 5-oz., frozen	2	12	Slack in cooler between 32° and 36°F prior to use.
2 Chicken broth, canned	4 cups	24 cups	Combine in saucepan or stockpot and mix thoroughly. Bring to boil over high heat. Slice chicken into julienne strips and add to broth. Reduce heat and simmer for 15 to 20 minutes or until chicken is no longer pink, stirring frequently. (Simmer smaller quantity for 4 to 5 minutes.)
Ginger, ground	¼ tsp.	½ tbsp.	
Dry mustard powder	¼ tsp.	½ tbsp.	
3 Olive oil	1 tbsp.	⅓ cup	Heat in skillet over medium-high heat.
4 Carrots, fresh, julienne	½ cup	3 cups	Add to oil and stir-fry for 5 to 7 minutes or until vegetables are tender-crisp. (Stir-fry smaller quantity for 2 to 3 minutes.) Remove from heat. Add to chicken mixture and simmer for 4 to 5 minutes or until flavors are blended, stirring frequently. (Simmer smaller quantity for 2 to 3 minutes.) Remove from heat. Keep warm above 140°F.
Leeks, fresh, thinly sliced (p. 189)	⅓ cup	2 cups	
5 White rice, steamed	1 cup	6 cups	*To assemble single serving:* Portion ¼ cup rice into bowl. Ladle 1¼ cups soup over rice. Garnish with 1 tablespoon green onions.
Green onions, fresh, chopped	¼ cup	1½ cups	

Serve with crisp cucumber salad with sesame dressing, and rice crackers.

Portion: 11½ ounces
Nutritional Data/Portion: Calories 250, Protein 27 g, Fat 7 g, Carbohydrate 17 g, Cholesterol 45 mg, Sodium 1,820 mg

For a **FAST FACTS VIA FAX** copy of this recipe, call 1-800-223-3755 and enter Business Tool 2534.

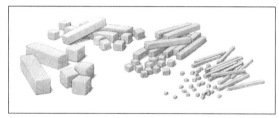

HOW TO MAKE JULIENNE, BATONNET, AND DICE CUTS OF VEGETABLES

1) *Trim peeled vegetable to length appropriate for desired cut. Length for julienne should be 1 to 2 inches; length for batonnet should be 2 to 2½ inches. Once trimmed, cut into even slices. Julienne should be ⅛ inch thick, and batonnet should be ¼ inch thick.*

2) *Stack slices and again cut evenly into strips of same thickness.*

3) *To dice vegetables, make perpendicular cuts along strips, producing cubes. Brunoise is ⅛-inch cube from julienne plank; small dice is ¼-inch cube from batonnet plank; medium dice is ⅜-inch cube; large dice is ⅝-inch cube.*

Chicken Neapolitan Soup

Neapolitan soup comes not from Naples but from Harvey House, a famed restaurant chain on the Atchison, Topeka & Santa Fe railroad line that offered railroad travelers a decent and delicious place to eat from the 1880s until the 1960s. The legend lives on with this revived classic.

Kid Friendly   *Lighter Fare*   *Line Service*   *Takeout*

INGREDIENT	QUANTITY		METHOD
	4 servings	24 servings	
1 Butter, salted	1 tbsp.	⅓ cup	Heat in saucepan or stockpot over medium-high heat.
2 Onions, fresh, chopped (p. 175)	¾ cup	4½ cups	Add to butter and sauté for 8 to 10 minutes or until vegetables are tender. (Sauté smaller quantity for 4 to 5 minutes.)
Carrots, fresh, chopped	⅓ cup	2 cups	
Green bell peppers, fresh, chopped	⅓ cup	2 cups	
Smoked ham, ¼-inch dice	⅓ cup	2 cups	
3 Tyson Fully Cooked Diced White Fryer Meat, ¾-inch dice, frozen	8 oz.	3 lb.	Add to vegetable mixture and mix thoroughly.
Cream of chicken soup, concentrated, commercially prepared	1¼ cups	7½ cups	
Milk, whole	1¼ cups	7½ cups	
Chicken broth, canned	¾ cup	4½ cups	
Tomatoes, diced, canned, undrained	½ cup	3 cups	
4 Elbow macaroni, small, cooked al dente, drained	1 cup	6 cups	Add to chicken mixture and mix thoroughly. Heat over low heat for 8 to 10 minutes or until chicken is thoroughly heated, stirring frequently. DO NOT ALLOW TO SIMMER. (Heat smaller quantity for 4 to 5 minutes.) Remove from heat. Keep warm above 140°F.
White rice, steamed	½ cup	3 cups	
Half-and-half	¾ cup	4½ cups	
Salt	¼ tsp.	½ tbsp.	
White pepper, fine	⅛ tsp.	¾ tsp.	
5 Parsley, fresh, minced (p. 39)	1½ tbsp.	½ cup	*To assemble single serving:* Ladle 1⅔ cups soup into bowl. Garnish with 1 teaspoon parsley. *Serve with mixed green salad and crusty Italian bread.*

Portion: 14 ounces
Nutritional Data/Portion: Calories 430, Protein 31 g, Fat 19 g, Carbohydrate 33 g, Cholesterol 100 mg, Sodium 1,330 mg

For a ***FAST FACTS VIA FAX*** copy of this recipe, call 1-800-223-3755 and enter Business Tool 2543.

Frederick Henry Harvey was an English immigrant who built a network of acclaimed restaurants, dining cars, and hotels along the Atchison, Topeka & Santa Fe railroad route. They all served good food on Irish linens with Sheffield silverware.

Macaroni is one of America's most dearly loved pastas. Legend has it that upon being served elbow pasta, an Italian sovereign exclaimed, "Ma caroni!" which means "how very dear." Rigatoni, ziti, penne, mostaccioli, and elbow are among the best known forms of this semolina-and-water pasta.

Submitted by John Randolph
Wal-Mart Cafeteria
Bentonville, Ark.

The first jambalaya, cooked up by a group of French immigrant women living on the Gulf Coast, was a mixture of meat, rice, tomatoes, peppers, and onions.⌒

For a more traditional presentation, cooked rice may be substituted for the fried potatoes.⌒

Chicken Jambalaya

Jambalaya is a famous Creole dish whose name is derived from the French *jambon*, or "ham"; but don't believe there is only one way to make it, as ingredients vary widely from chef to chef.

INGREDIENT	QUANTITY		METHOD
	4 servings	24 servings	
1 Chicken broth, canned	1½ cups	9 cups	Combine in saucepan or stockpot and mix thoroughly. Bring to boil over high heat. Reduce heat and simmer for 45 to 50 minutes or until flavors are concentrated, stirring frequently. (Simmer smaller quantity for 20 to 25 minutes.)
Picante sauce, mild, commercially prepared	1½ cups	9 cups	
Picante sauce, hot, commercially prepared	½ cup	3 cups	
Tomato paste, canned	3 tbsp.	1 cup	
Liquid smoke, hickory	½ tsp.	1 tbsp.	
Garlic powder	½ tsp.	1 tbsp.	
Thyme leaves, dried	½ tsp.	1 tbsp.	
Oregano leaves, dried	½ tsp.	1 tbsp.	
Bay leaves, whole, dried	1	6	
2 Vegetable oil	½ tbsp.	3 tbsp.	Heat in skillet over medium-high heat.
3 Andouille sausage, ¼-inch dice	½ cup	3 cups	Add to oil and sauté for 5 to 6 minutes or until meat is brown. (Sauté smaller quantity for 2 to 3 minutes.) Add to broth mixture.
Smoked ham, ¼-inch dice	½ cup	3 cups	
Celery, fresh, sliced	½ cup	3 cups	
4 Tyson Fully Cooked Shredded Savory Chicken Breast Meat, frozen	1½ lb.	9 lb.	Add to broth mixture and mix thoroughly. Simmer for 10 to 15 minutes or until chicken is thoroughly heated, stirring frequently. (Simmer smaller quantity for 5 to 6 minutes.) Remove from heat and discard bay leaves. Keep warm above 140°F.
5 Green onions, fresh, chopped	¼ cup	1½ cups	*To assemble single serving:* Ladle 1½ cups jambalaya into bowl. Garnish with 1 tablespoon green onions.
			Serve with fried potatoes.

Portion: 12 ounces
Nutritional Data/Portion: Calories 550, Protein 51 g, Fat 26 g, Carbohydrate 28 g, Cholesterol 140 mg, Sodium 2,500 mg

For a **FAST FACTS VIA FAX** copy of this recipe, call 1-800-223-3755 and enter Business Tool 2525.

Submitted by Thomas Kovacs
Sheraton-Seattle Hotel
Seattle, Wash.

Chicken Gumbo

Gumbo is the signature soup of New Orleans, its name coming from the African word for okra, which is the ingredient used for flavor and thickening in gumbo recipes. This version uses filé powder to thicken the hearty Creole broth just prior to serving.

Step	INGREDIENT	QUANTITY 4 servings	24 servings	METHOD
1	Vegetable oil	1 tsp.	2 tbsp.	Heat in skillet over medium-high heat.
2	Andouille sausage, ¼-inch dice	½ cup	3 cups	Add to oil and sauté for 4 to 5 minutes or until brown. (Sauté smaller quantity for 2 to 3 minutes.) Remove from skillet. Drain and reserve.
	Hot link sausage, fully cooked, ¼-inch dice	½ cup	3 cups	
3	Vegetable oil	3 tbsp.	1 cup	Combine in heavy skillet over medium-low heat. SLOWLY cook roux to deep, dark reddish brown, stirring constantly. (This process may take 15 to 30 minutes.) DO NOT BURN ROUX.
	Flour, all-purpose	3 tbsp.	1 cup	
4	Onions, fresh, chopped (p. 175)	3 cups	18 cups	Immediately add to roux, stirring constantly. Sauté for 10 to 15 minutes or until vegetables are tender. (Sauté smaller quantity for 5 to 8 minutes.) Remove from heat and transfer to saucepan or stockpot.
	Green bell peppers, fresh, chopped	¾ cup	4½ cups	
	Celery, fresh, chopped	½ cup	3 cups	
5	Chicken broth, canned	3 cups	18 cups	Add to vegetable mixture and bring to boil over high heat. Reduce heat and simmer for 55 to 60 minutes or until flavors are concentrated, stirring frequently. (Simmer smaller quantity for 25 to 30 minutes.)
	Garlic, fresh, minced	1 tbsp.	⅓ cup	
	Thyme leaves, dried	¼ tsp.	½ tbsp.	
	Basil leaves, dried	¼ tsp.	½ tbsp.	
	Allspice, ground	⅛ tsp.	¾ tsp.	
	Cayenne pepper, ground	⅛ tsp.	¾ tsp.	
	Black pepper, coarse	⅛ tsp.	¾ tsp.	
	Bay leaves, whole, dried	1	6	
6	Tyson Fully Cooked Pulled Natural Proportion Chicken Meat, frozen	1 lb.	6 lb.	Add to vegetable mixture. Add sausage and mix thoroughly. Simmer for 25 to 30 minutes or until chicken is thoroughly heated, stirring frequently. (Simmer smaller quantity for 10 to 15 minutes.) Remove from heat and discard bay leaves.
7	Green onions, fresh, chopped	¼ cup	1½ cups	Add to chicken mixture and mix thoroughly. Keep warm above 140°F.
8	White rice, steamed	2 cups	12 cups	*To assemble single serving:* Mound ½ cup rice into center of bowl. Surround with 1¾ cups gumbo and sprinkle with ⅛ teaspoon filé powder.
	Gumbo filé powder	½ tsp.	1 tbsp.	

Portion: 17 ounces
Nutritional Data/Portion: Calories 700, Protein 50 g, Fat 36 g, Carbohydrate 43 g, Cholesterol 160 mg, Sodium 1,380 mg

For a **FAST FACTS VIA FAX**™ copy of this recipe, call 1-800-223-3755 and enter Business Tool 2542.

Twenty-five young French women in search of husbands arrived in Mobile in 1704. Arriving with cassettes, "small trunks," filled with their dowries, the Cassette girls, as they were known, borrowed ingredients from Congolese slaves and Choctaw Indians and developed creations including gumbo, jambalaya, and crawfish pie. Their assimilation of French and local cooking methods marked the beginning of Creole cuisine.

Filé powder is made from crushed dried sassafras leaves and has a woodsy flavor reminiscent of root beer. It can get tough and stringy if cooked too long.

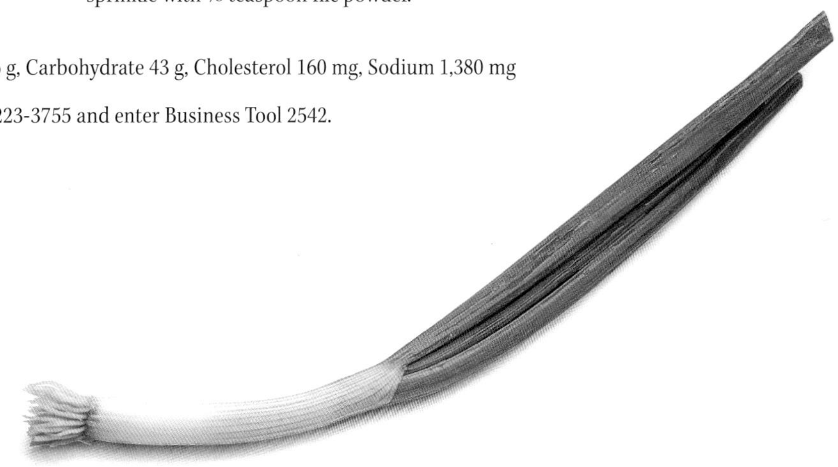

Brunswick Stew is a tasty part of Virginia folklore dating back to 1828 when Andrew Jackson visited Brunswick County during his presidential campaign. The host of the gathering asked one of his hunting buddies to prepare the squirrel-meat stew he often made on camping trips, but instead of using squirrel he used 210 pounds of chicken. The rally was a success, Andrew Jackson won the election, and the popularity of Chicken Brunswick Stew spread far and wide.

Chicken Brunswick Stew

Garlic mashed potatoes are piped around this hearty country stew of tomatoes, lima beans, chicken, and ham for a stick-to-your-ribs kind of meal. While Virginia and North Carolina lay claim to the origin of this symbol of neighborly hospitality, it will serve as a satisfying welcome to patrons everywhere.

Lighter Fare   *Line Service*   *Takeout*

INGREDIENT	QUANTITY 4 servings	24 servings	METHOD
1 Butter, salted	2 tbsp.	¾ cup	Heat in saucepan or stockpot over medium-high heat.
2 Onions, fresh, chopped (p. 175)	1 cup	6 cups	Add to butter and sauté for 7 to 8 minutes or until vegetables are tender. (Sauté smaller quantity for 3 to 4 minutes.)
Celery, fresh, chopped	1 cup	6 cups	
Green bell peppers, fresh, chopped	½ cup	3 cups	
Garlic, fresh, minced	½ tsp.	1 tbsp.	
3 Tyson Fully Cooked Pulled Natural Proportion Chicken Meat, frozen	1 lb.	6 lb.	Add to vegetable mixture and mix thoroughly. Bring to boil over high heat. Cover and reduce heat. Simmer for 15 to 20 minutes or until chicken is thoroughly heated, stirring frequently. (Simmer smaller quantity for 10 to 15 minutes.)
Tomatoes, crushed, in purée, canned	1½ cups	9 cups	
Baby lima beans, frozen	1 cup	6 cups	
Smoked ham, ¼-inch dice	1 cup	6 cups	
Barbecue sauce, smoky, commercially prepared	½ cup	3 cups	
Worcestershire sauce	½ tbsp.	3 tbsp.	
Red pepper, crushed, dried	¼ tsp.	½ tbsp.	
Black pepper, coarse	⅛ tsp.	¾ tsp.	
4 Yellow corn, whole kernel, frozen	1 cup	6 cups	Add to stew mixture and mix thoroughly. Return to simmer, then remove from heat. Keep warm above 140°F.
5 *Garlic Mashed Potatoes*			
Milk, whole	1⅓ cups	7 cups	Combine in saucepan or stockpot and heat over medium heat for 6 to 7 minutes or until milk is steaming. (Heat smaller quantity for 1 to 2 minutes.)
Butter, salted	2 tbsp.	¾ cup	
Garlic, minced, commercially prepared	½ tsp.	1 tbsp.	
Salt	¼ tsp.	1 tsp.	
White pepper, fine	⅛ tsp.	½ tsp.	

recipe continued on next page . . .

INGREDIENT	QUANTITY 4 servings	24 servings	METHOD
6 Mashed potatoes, frozen, commercially prepared	2⅔ cups	16 cups	Add to milk and mix thoroughly. Cook over medium heat for 7 to 8 minutes, stirring constantly to avoid scorching. (Cook smaller quantity for 3 to 4 minutes.) Remove from heat and keep warm.
7 Parsley, fresh, minced (p. 39)	1½ tbsp.	½ cup	*To assemble single serving:* Ladle 1⅔ cups stew into bowl. Pipe ½ cup potatoes around edge of stew and garnish with 1 teaspoon parsley.

Portion: 18 ounces

Nutritional Data/Portion: Calories 1,040, Protein 58 g, Fat 24 g, Carbohydrate 152 g, Cholesterol 170 mg, Sodium 1,260 mg

For a **FAST FACTS VIA FAX** copy of this recipe, call 1-800-223-3755 and enter Business Tool 2544.

Fresh or dehydrated potatoes may be substituted for frozen mashed potatoes.

Chicken Florentine Soup

Italians may not have invented this dish, but savvy patrons will recognize "Florentine" as a menu code for dishes that typically include spinach. With chicken and cheese, this is a richly satisfying main course soup.

Submitted by Nancy Joseph
Bowling Green State University
Bowling Green, Ohio

INGREDIENT	QUANTITY 4 servings	24 servings	METHOD
1 Butter, salted	¼ cup	1½ cups	Heat in saucepan or stockpot over medium-high heat.
2 Button mushrooms, fresh, sliced	1 cup	6 cups	Add to butter and sauté for 4 to 5 minutes or until vegetables are tender-crisp. (Sauté smaller quantity for 1 to 2 minutes.)
Celery, fresh, chopped	½ cup	3 cups	
Onions, fresh, chopped (p. 175)	⅓ cup	2 cups	
Carrots, fresh, julienne (p. 88)	⅓ cup	2 cups	
3 Flour, all-purpose	¼ cup	1½ cups	Add to vegetable mixture and mix thoroughly. Stir over low heat for 8 to 10 minutes or until flour is cooked but not brown. (Stir smaller quantity for 2 to 3 minutes.)
Seasoned salt	½ tbsp.	3 tbsp.	
White pepper, fine	¼ tsp.	½ tbsp.	
4 Milk, whole	4 cups	24 cups	Add to vegetable mixture and mix thoroughly. Bring to simmer over low heat and simmer for 20 to 30 minutes or until mixture thickens, stirring frequently. (Simmer smaller quantity for 10 to 12 minutes.)
Water, cold	¾ cup	4 cups	
Chicken base concentrate**	2 tsp.	¼ cup	
5 Tyson Fully Cooked Diced Natural Proportion Chicken Meat, ½-inch dice, frozen	8 oz.	3 lb.	Add to vegetable mixture and mix thoroughly. Return to simmer over low heat and simmer for 4 to 5 minutes or until chicken is thoroughly heated, stirring frequently. (Simmer smaller quantity for 1 to 2 minutes.) Remove from heat. Keep warm above 140°F.
Spinach, fresh, stemmed, coarse-chopped	4 cups	24 cups	
Pasteurized process cheese sauce	¼ cup	1½ cups	
Pimientos, sliced, canned, drained	2 tbsp.	¾ cup	
6 Parsley, fresh, chopped	1½ tbsp.	½ cup	*To assemble single serving:* Ladle 1½ cups soup into bowl. Garnish with 1 teaspoon parsley. *Serve with Italian breadsticks.*

Portion: 12 ounces

Nutritional Data/Portion: Calories 420, Protein 28 g, Fat 24 g, Carbohydrate 26 g, Cholesterol 125 mg, Sodium 1,090 mg

**This recipe uses a base with the reconstitution ratio of 1 teaspoon per cup.

For a **FAST FACTS VIA FAX** copy of this recipe, call 1-800-223-3755 and enter Business Tool 2540.

Spinach has been part of Italian cooking since the 9th century, when it was brought to Sicily by North African invaders who discovered the plant in Persia.

Submitted by Cristo Christu
Pinellas County School Food Service
Largo, Fla.

Greek Chicken Soup

A rich chicken, lemon, and egg soup inspired by Greece's own *soupa avgolemono.*

This soup should be made to order in small batches and held for only a short time.

Fresh lemon juice is essential for the recipe.

INGREDIENT	QUANTITY		METHOD
	4 servings	24 servings	
1			
Chicken broth, canned	6 cups	32 cups	Combine in saucepan or stockpot and bring to boil over high heat. Cover and reduce heat. Simmer for 15 to 20 minutes or until rice is tender.
White rice, raw	⅔ cup	4 cups	
2			
Tyson Fully Cooked Diced White Fryer Meat, ½-inch dice, frozen	6 oz.	2 lb.	Add to broth mixture. Return to boil, then remove from heat.
3			
Eggs, large, whole	2	10	Combine in mixer bowl and beat on high speed until frothy. Reduce speed and gradually add 3 to 4 cups hot chicken broth from stockpot, mixing slowly. (Add 1 to 2 cups chicken broth for smaller quantity.) Return egg and broth mixture to chicken mixture in saucepan or stockpot and mix thoroughly. Keep warm above 140°F.
Lemon juice, fresh	2 tbsp.	⅓ cup	
Lemon zest, fresh	½ tsp.	2 tsp.	
Salt	¼ tsp.	1 tsp.	
Black pepper, fine	⅛ tsp.	¾ tsp.	
4			
Lemon slices, fresh	4	24	*To assemble single serving:* Ladle 1½ cups soup into bowl. Garnish with 1 lemon slice and 3 chive spears.
Chive spears, fresh	12	72	

Serve with Greek salad and olive bread.

Portion: 12 ounces
Nutritional Data/Portion: Calories 270, Protein 33 g, Fat 7 g, Carbohydrate 17 g, Cholesterol 130 mg, Sodium 2,040 mg

For a **FAST FACTS VIA FAX** copy of this recipe, call 1-800-223-3755 and enter Business Tool 2538.

Soupa avgolemono is a classic Greek soup made with rice, chicken broth, whole eggs or egg yolks, and lemon juice.

Chicken Noodle Soup

Elegant but simple to prepare, this recipe is a welcome update to an all-time favorite. The large pulled pieces of chicken, along with the tangy hint of green onion in the rich broth, make it a memorable dish.

Speed-Scratch *Kid Friendly* *Lighter Fare* *Line Service* *Takeout*

INGREDIENT	QUANTITY		METHOD
	4 servings	24 servings	
Chicken broth, canned	7 cups	42 cups	Combine in saucepan or stockpot and bring to boil over high heat.
Butter, salted	¼ cup	1 cup	
Black pepper, coarse	½ tsp.	1 tbsp.	
Tyson Fully Cooked Pulled White Fryer Meat, frozen	8 oz.	3 lb.	Add to broth mixture and mix thoroughly. Return to boil. Reduce heat and simmer for 50 to 60 minutes or until flavors are concentrated, stirring frequently. (Simmer smaller quantity for 15 to 18 minutes.)
Egg noodles, frozen, commercially prepared	10 oz.	3¾ lb.	
Green onions, fresh, bias-sliced	¼ cup	1½ cups	Add to chicken mixture and mix thoroughly. Remove from heat. Keep warm above 140°F.

To assemble single serving: Ladle 1⅔ cups soup into bowl.

Serve with crusty French baguettes.

Portion: 14 ounces
Nutritional Data/Portion: Calories 301, Protein 21 g, Fat 11 g, Carbohydrate 27 g, Cholesterol 70 mg, Sodium 1,114 mg

For a **FAST FACTS VIA FAX** copy of this recipe, call 1-800-223-3755 and enter Business Tool 2349.

Increase the appetite appeal of this soup by adding a few drops of yellow food coloring to the broth before boiling.

Researchers at Florida's Mount Sinai Medical Center have determined that chicken noodle soup's vapors open clogged nasal passages. Although it's not a cure, it seems there is proof that chicken noodle soup is indeed good for what ails us.

For easy portioning in take-out containers, substitute diced chicken for pulled fryer meat.

Submitted by Helen Doherty, RD
Massachusetts General Hospital
Boston, Mass.

This stew can be made ahead and refrigerated, but keep peas separate until it's time to reheat and serve.

For take-out applications, it is best to package the couscous separately.

In some areas, garbanzo beans are called chickpeas.

Couscous, along with macaroni, was one of 12 foods and medicines recommended for seamen in a document written in 1607 by an Englishman named Sir Hugh Plat.

Moroccan Chicken Stew

Take an excursion to Marrakesh with this aromatic stew ladled around couscous.
Garbanzo beans and butternut squash add to the character of this dish, which patrons
will find exotic and irresistible.

Lighter Fare   *Line Service*   *Takeout*

INGREDIENT	QUANTITY 4 servings	24 servings	METHOD
1 Tyson Fully Cooked Pulled Natural Proportion Fryer Meat, frozen	12 oz.	4½ lb.	Combine in saucepan or stockpot and mix thoroughly. Bring to boil over high heat.
Tomatoes, diced, canned, drained	1¾ cups	10 cups	Reduce heat and simmer for 15 to 20 minutes or until squash is tender, stirring frequently.
Chicken broth, canned	1¾ cups	10 cups	(Simmer smaller quantity for 10 to 15 minutes.)
Butternut squash, fresh, ½-inch dice (p. 88)	1¾ cups	10 cups	
Garbanzo beans, canned, drained	1½ cups	9 cups	
Onions, fresh, slivered	¼ cup	1½ cups	
Garlic cloves, fresh, cut in half	2	12	
Cumin, ground	1 tsp.	2 tbsp.	
Cinnamon, ground	½ tsp.	1 tbsp.	
Salt	½ tsp.	1 tbsp.	
Black pepper, coarse	⅛ tsp.	¾ tsp.	
2 Green peas, frozen	½ cup	3 cups	Add to chicken mixture and mix thoroughly. Return to simmer, then remove from heat. Keep warm above 140°F.
3 Couscous, prepared according to package directions	2 cups	12 cups	*To assemble single serving:* Portion ½ cup couscous into bowl. Ladle 1½ cups stew around couscous. *Serve with a fruit plate.*

Portion: 17 ounces
Nutritional Data/Portion: Calories 380, Protein 36 g, Fat 6 g, Carbohydrate 46 g, Cholesterol 85 mg, Sodium 1,020 mg

For a **FAST FACTS VIA FAX** copy of this recipe, call 1-800-223-3755 and enter Business Tool 2541.

Submitted by John R. Gorman
Catering by John
Redmond, Wash.

"Texas Truffle" Chicken Chili

Traditional Texas-style chili may not have beans, but this earthy chicken chili has appeal in the Lone Star state since it's laced with black Texas truffles (a.k.a. black beans). Patrons are sure to like it, even if they are not from Texas.

INGREDIENT	QUANTITY		METHOD
	4 servings	24 servings	
1 Olive oil	½ tbsp.	⅓ cup	Heat in saucepan or stockpot over medium heat.
2 Onions, fresh, chopped (p. 175)	¾ cup	4½ cups	Add to oil and sauté for 8 to 10 minutes or until onions are translucent. (Sauté smaller quantity for 4 to 5 minutes.)
Garlic, fresh, minced	½ tbsp.	3 tbsp.	
3 Tyson Fully Cooked Diced Fryer Leg Meat, ½-inch dice, frozen	1 lb.	6 lb.	Add to onion mixture and mix thoroughly. Bring to boil over high heat. Reduce heat and simmer for 25 to 30 minutes or until flavors are concentrated, stirring frequently. (Simmer smaller quantity for 15 to 20 minutes.) Remove from heat. Keep warm above 140°F.
Tomato sauce, canned	1 cup	6½ cups	
Black beans, canned, rinsed, drained	1 cup	6 cups	
Beer	¾ cup	4½ cups	
Chicken base concentrate**	½ tbsp.	3 tbsp.	
Chili powder, light	½ tbsp.	3 tbsp.	
Cumin, ground	½ tbsp.	3 tbsp.	
Oregano leaves, dried	½ tsp.	1 tbsp.	
Soy sauce	½ tsp.	1 tbsp.	
Worcestershire sauce	½ tsp.	1 tbsp.	
Cayenne pepper, ground	¼ tsp.	½ tbsp.	
Turmeric, ground	⅛ tsp.	1 tsp.	
Sage, ground	⅛ tsp.	1 tsp.	
Thyme leaves, dried	⅛ tsp.	1 tsp.	
Dry mustard powder	⅛ tsp.	1 tsp.	
4 Sage sprigs, fresh	4	24	*To assemble single serving:* Ladle 1¼ cups chili into bowl. Garnish with 1 sage sprig. *Serve with jalapeño cornbread.*

Portion: 10 ounces
Nutritional Data/Portion: Calories 320, Protein 33 g, Fat 10 g, Carbohydrate 21 g, Cholesterol 140 mg, Sodium 840 mg

**This recipe uses a base with the reconstitution ratio of 1 teaspoon per cup.

For a **FAST FACTS VIA FAX** copy of this recipe, call 1-800-223-3755 and enter Business Tool 2535.

Chili con carne, *or "chiles with meat," dates back to the early 1800s when Texas was still a Mexican territory. In order to extend the meat they had for their tables, people would cut it into small pieces, then stew it with a nearly equal amount of chiles. Sometime around 1835, English settlers devised an easier way to season their chili when they developed the first chili powder.*

The First Annual World *Championship Chili Cook-off was held in Terlingua, Texas, in 1967.*

"Real chili—chili Texas style—will make a poet sing of rhapsodious harmony in thunder . . . it is a panacea to man in want or woe."
Joe Cooper

Submitted by Ralph Binder
Mill Way Fish & Lobster Market
Barnstable, Mass.

Chicken and Rice Minestrone

Minestrone is a term Italians use to describe thick vegetable soup that is hearty enough to be considered a complete meal. Along with the traditional kidney beans and vegetables, this American interpretation includes rice instead of pasta. In Italy, minestrone is usually topped with grated Parmesan cheese.

Minestrone has been part of Italian cookery for hundreds of years. It is recorded as part of a lavish meal served by the Spanish ambassador to Rome on November 30, 1638.

Minestra *is Italian for* "soup." Minestrina *is* "little soup" *with thin broth, while* minestrone *is* "big soup" *with thicker broth that can be prepared with meat, vegetables, and pasta. Some minestrones also contain peas or beans.*

This recipe is pictured on the inside cover.

INGREDIENT	QUANTITY 4 servings	24 servings	METHOD
1 Olive oil	1 tbsp.	⅓ cup	Heat in saucepan or stockpot over medium heat.
2 Bacon, chopped	⅓ cup	1 cup	Add to oil and sauté for 4 to 5 minutes or until bacon is translucent but not brown. (Sauté smaller quantity for 2 to 3 minutes.)
3 Leeks, fresh, diced (p. 189)	¾ cup	3 cups	Add to bacon and mix thoroughly. Sauté for 5 to 6 minutes or until vegetables are tender. (Sauté smaller quantity for 4 to 5 minutes.)
Onions, fresh, diced (p. 175)	½ cup	2 cups	
Celery, fresh, diced (p. 88)	½ cup	2 cups	
Garlic, fresh, minced	1 tbsp.	¼ cup	
4 Tyson Fully Cooked Diced Natural Proportion Chicken Meat, ½-inch dice, frozen	4 oz.	1½ lb.	Add to vegetable mixture and mix thoroughly. Bring to boil over high heat. Reduce heat and simmer for 15 to 20 minutes or until rice is tender, stirring frequently. Remove from heat and discard bay leaves. Keep warm above 140°F.
Chicken broth, canned	5 cups	24 cups	
Tomatoes, diced, canned, drained	1 cup	4 cups	
Kidney beans, canned, rinsed, drained	½ cup	2 cups	
Tomato paste, canned	1 tbsp.	⅓ cup	
White rice, raw	2 tbsp.	1 cup	
Rosemary leaves, dried	½ tsp.	1 tbsp.	
Thyme leaves, dried	½ tsp.	1 tbsp.	
Bay leaves, whole, dried	1	3	
Salt	½ tsp.	1 tbsp.	
Black pepper, coarse	⅛ tsp.	¾ tsp.	
5 Basil pesto, commercially prepared	2 tbsp.	¾ cup	*To assemble single serving:* Ladle 1½ cups soup into bowl. Garnish with ½ tablespoon pesto. *Serve with soft garlic breadsticks.*

Portion: 12 ounces
Nutritional Data/Portion: Calories 310, Protein 23 g, Fat 12 g, Carbohydrate 26 g, Cholesterol 30 mg, Sodium 1,630 mg

For a **FAST FACTS VIA FAX** copy of this recipe, call 1-800-223-3755 and enter Business Tool 2533.

"I live on good soup, not on fine words."
Molière

Submitted by Charles Carter
San Juan Regional Medical Center
Farmington, N.M.

Chicken Posole

Distinguished by hominy, red bell peppers, and olives, this soup is traditionally served at Christmastime in Mexico. But patrons will enjoy it throughout the fall and winter months.

INGREDIENT	QUANTITY		METHOD
	4 servings	24 servings	
1 Olive oil spray	as needed	as needed	Spray saucepan or stockpot with oil.
2 Onions, fresh, chopped (p. 175)	1 cup	6 cups	Add to oil and sauté over medium heat for 10 to 12 minutes or until onions are translucent. (Sauté smaller quantity for 3 to 4 minutes.)
Garlic, fresh, minced	1 tsp.	2 tbsp.	
Cumin, ground	1 tsp.	2 tbsp.	
Oregano leaves, dried	1 tsp.	2 tbsp.	
Salt	½ tsp.	1 tbsp.	
3 Tyson Fully Cooked Diced White Fryer Meat, ½-inch dice, frozen	1 lb.	6 lb.	Add to onion mixture and mix thoroughly. Bring to boil over high heat. Reduce heat and simmer for 25 to 30 minutes or until flavors are concentrated, stirring frequently. (Simmer smaller quantity for 10 to 15 minutes.)
Chicken broth, canned	3½ cups	12 cups	
Yellow hominy, canned, rinsed, drained	2 cups	12 cups	
Picante sauce, mild, commercially prepared	¾ cup	4½ cups	
4 Red bell peppers, fresh, chopped	1 cup	6 cups	Add to chicken mixture and mix thoroughly. Simmer for 4 to 5 minutes or until peppers are tender-crisp. (Simmer smaller quantity for 1 to 2 minutes.)
5 Flour, all-purpose	1 tbsp.	⅓ cup	Combine in small bowl and mix until smooth. Gradually stir into soup. Simmer for 2 to 5 minutes or until soup thickens.
Water, cold	2 tbsp.	½ cup	
6 Black olives, sliced, canned, drained	½ cup	3 cups	Add to soup and mix thoroughly. Remove from heat. Keep warm above 140°F.
7 Picante sauce, mild, commercially prepared	¼ cup	1½ cups	*To assemble single serving:* Ladle 1⅔ cups soup into bowl. Garnish with 1 tablespoon picante sauce and 1 cilantro sprig.
Cilantro sprigs, fresh	4	24	*Serve with crusty French bread.*

Portion: 14 ounces
Nutritional Data/Portion: Calories 330, Protein 36 g, Fat 9 g, Carbohydrate 26 g, Cholesterol 70 mg, Sodium 2,000 mg

For a **FAST FACTS VIA FAX** copy of this recipe, call 1-800-223-3755 and enter Business Tool 2529.

In the early 1600s, English colonists encountered native Americans boiling the coarse parts of corn for hours to make a potage that the new Americans would call hominy. Today, hominy is dried white or yellow corn kernels whose hulls and germs have been removed mechanically, or chemically by soaking the corn in slaked lime or lye.

To adjust the heat level, substitute medium or hot picante sauce for mild.

For a different color combination, use white hominy and green bell peppers.

The dry ingredients may be easily replaced with self-rising flour. Substitute ¾ cup flour for the 4-serving quantity, or 4 cups flour for the 24-serving quantity. ⌐

Add texture and heat to the dumplings with a drizzle of cornmeal and a dash of cayenne. ⌐

Chopped chives, finely grated lemon zest, or saffron can also transform traditional dumplings into a contemporary classic. ⌐

Chicken and Dumplings

This updated version of an American classic has old-fashioned appeal. Flecks of parsley in the dumplings make them as lovely and new as they are delicious.

Kid Friendly   Lighter Fare   Line Service   Takeout

INGREDIENT	QUANTITY 4 servings	24 servings	METHOD
1			
Butter, salted	1 tbsp.	½ cup	Heat in stockpot or full-size, 4-inch-deep steam table pan over medium heat.
2			
Carrots, fresh, bias-sliced	½ cup	3 cups	Add to butter and sauté for 5 to 10 minutes or until vegetables are tender-crisp. (Sauté smaller quantity for 3 to 5 minutes.)
Celery, fresh, bias-sliced	½ cup	3 cups	
Onions, fresh, slivered	½ cup	3 cups	
Poultry seasoning, dried	⅛ tsp.	½ tsp.	
Bay leaves, whole, dried	1	2	
3			
Tyson Fully Cooked Flavor-Redi® Roasted and Carved Chicken Breast Filets, frozen	2	12	Add to vegetable mixture and mix thoroughly. Bring to boil over medium-high heat. Reduce heat and simmer for 15 to 20 minutes or until chicken is thoroughly heated. Stir frequently to separate chicken into large pieces. (Simmer smaller quantity for 12 to 15 minutes.)
Chicken broth, canned	6 cups	24 cups	
Heavy cream	⅓ cup	2 cups	
4			
Dumplings (p. 101)			
Flour, all-purpose	¾ cup	4 cups	Sift together in bowl.
Baking powder, double-acting	½ tbsp.	8 tsp.	
Salt	¼ tsp.	1 tsp.	
Poultry seasoning, dried	¼ tsp.	1 tsp.	
5			
Eggs, large, whole	1	3	Combine in separate bowl. Beat well and stir into flour mixture. Lower dumpling mixture by heaping teaspoon into gently simmering broth mixture. (Make 72 dumplings for large quantity; 12 dumplings for smaller quantity.) Cover and gently simmer for 8 to 10 minutes or until dumplings are fluffy and tender. Remove from heat and discard bay leaves. Keep warm above 140°F.
Milk, whole	2 tbsp.	1 cup	
Parsley, fresh, minced (p. 39)	1 tbsp.	½ cup	
6			
Parsley, fresh, minced	2 tbsp.	¾ cup	*To assemble single serving:* Ladle 1⅔ cups chicken mixture into bowl. (This should include 3 dumplings.) Garnish with ½ tablespoon parsley.

Portion: 14 ounces
Nutritional Data/Portion: Calories 275, Protein 20 g, Fat 12 g, Carbohydrate 20 g, Cholesterol 101 mg, Sodium 1,451 mg

For a **FAST FACTS VIA FAX**™ copy of this recipe, call 1-800-223-3755 and enter Business Tool 2356.

Chicken Egg Drop Soup

Traditionally a popular starter in Chinese restaurants, egg drop soup gets a fresh start for broader menu appeal.

INGREDIENT	QUANTITY 4 servings	24 servings	METHOD
1 Tyson Fully Cooked Diced White Fryer Meat, ½-inch dice, frozen	4 oz.	1½ lb.	Combine in saucepan or stockpot and mix thoroughly. Bring to boil over high heat. Reduce heat and simmer for 2 to 3 minutes or until chicken is thoroughly heated. (Simmer smaller quantity for 1 to 2 minutes.) Remove from heat.
Chicken broth, canned	4 cups	26 cups	
Soy sauce	2 tsp.	⅓ cup	
2 Eggs, large, whole, well-beaten	1	6	Combine in bowl and mix thoroughly. Gradually add to soup in thin stream, stirring constantly until eggs form long threads. Keep warm above 140°F.
Sesame oil	½ tsp.	1 tbsp.	
3 Spinach leaves, fresh, chiffonade (p. 28)	½ cup	3 cups	*To assemble single serving:* Ladle 1¼ cups soup into bowl. Garnish with 2 tablespoons spinach chiffonade.

Portion: 10 ounces
Nutritional Data/Portion: Calories 140, Protein 21 g, Fat 5 g, Carbohydrate 2 g, Cholesterol 70 mg, Sodium 1,750 mg

For a **FAST FACTS VIA FAX** copy of this recipe, call 1-800-223-3755 and enter Business Tool 2545.

The secret to making egg drop soup is stirring it in a figure-8 pattern while adding the eggs, to break them into threads.

Literally, the French word chiffonade *means "made of rags." As it applies to cooking, chiffonade refers to vegetables that have been torn into thin strips and either sautéed or used raw to garnish soups.*

"A wise man does not trust all his eggs to one basket."

Cervantes

HOW TO POACH DUMPLINGS
Using two teaspoons, gently lower dumplings into simmering liquid.

Submitted by Cary Neff
Miraval, Life in Balance Resort™
Catalina, Ariz.

Chicken and Ginger Stew in a Kabocha Squash

Here's a satisfying soup that's really worth the effort. Patrons will rave over the spaetzle-style spinach noodles, as well as the tender chicken pieces in smoked ginger broth—but only after they've talked about the kabocha squash bowl it's presented in.

Lighter Fare

INGREDIENT	QUANTITY		METHOD
	4 servings	24 servings	
1 Kabocha squashes, fresh	4	24	Cut in crown pattern around top third of each squash. Remove all seeds and spray cavities with olive oil.
Olive oil spray	as needed	as needed	
2 Salt	1 tsp.	2 tbsp.	Season each cavity with ¼ teaspoon salt and ¼ teaspoon pepper. Place ½ tablespoon crushed garlic, 2 thyme sprigs, and 2 oregano sprigs in each cavity. Replace top of each squash and transfer to oiled full-size sheet pans.
Black pepper, coarse	1 tsp.	2 tbsp.	
Garlic, fresh, crushed	2 tbsp.	¾ cup	
Thyme sprigs, fresh, 2-inch lengths	8	48	
Oregano sprigs, fresh, 2-inch lengths	8	48	Bake in preheated conventional oven at 350°F for 40 to 50 minutes or until tender. Or bake in preheated convection oven at 300°F for 25 to 30 minutes. Remove from oven and discard herbs. Keep warm.
3 *Smoked Ginger Broth*			
4 Olive oil spray	as needed	as needed	Spray shallow metal pan with oil.
Gingerroot, fresh, unpeeled, ¼-inch dice	½ cup	3 cups	Spread in pan and place on preheated medium-hot char-grill. Cover with metal bowl to catch the smoke. Smoke over medium heat for 5 to 7 minutes. Remove from grill.
5 Lemon grass, fresh, chopped	½ cup	3 cups	Combine in saucepan or stockpot and add smoked ginger. Cover and sweat over medium heat for 10 to 12 minutes or until onions are tender, stirring occasionally. (Sweat smaller quantity for 4 to 5 minutes.)
Gingerroot, fresh, unpeeled, ¼-inch dice	½ cup	3 cups	
Onions, fresh, chopped (p. 175)	¼ cup	1½ cups	
Garlic, fresh, minced	2 tsp.	¼ cup	
Thyme sprigs, fresh, 2-inch lengths	3	18	
Cilantro, fresh, whole leaves	¼ cup	1½ cups	
6 White wine, dry	½ cup	3 cups	Add to vegetable mixture and bring to boil over high heat. Reduce heat and simmer for 14 to 15 minutes or until almost evaporated, stirring frequently. (Simmer smaller quantity for 5 to 7 minutes.)
7 Chicken broth, canned	6 cups	36 cups	Add to vegetable mixture and mix thoroughly. Bring to boil over high heat. Reduce heat and simmer for 25 to 30 minutes or until flavors are concentrated, stirring frequently. (Simmer smaller quantity for 15 to 20 minutes.) Remove from heat. Strain and press through fine mesh strainer. Reserve.
Red pepper, crushed, dried	½ tsp.	1 tbsp.	
Sea salt	1 tbsp.	¼ cup	
8 *Barley and Spinach Spaetzle Noodles (p. 104)*			
Pearled barley, dry	3 tbsp.	1 cup	Toast in dry sauté pan over medium-high heat for 7 to 8 minutes or until lightly golden. (Toast smaller quantity for 2 to 4 minutes.) Remove from heat and transfer to saucepan.
9 Vegetable broth, canned	½ cup	3 cups	Add to barley and bring to boil over high heat. Reduce heat and simmer for 20 to 25 minutes or until barley is tender and all liquid is absorbed. (Simmer smaller quantity for 10 to 12 minutes.) Spread on sheet pan to cool. Transfer to food processor bowl and process until coarsely chopped. Remove from processor bowl and reserve.

recipe continued on next page . . .

Although the usual shape of kabocha squashes makes them more suitable as bowls, acorn squashes or sugar pumpkins can be used successfully.

The kabocha is a winter squash with a beautiful dark green rind with celadon (grayish yellow-green) streaks. Its pale orange flesh is tender-smooth and sweet when cooked. Choose a squash that is heavy for its size. The rind should be dull and firm, with no soft spots.

This recipe is pictured on opposite page.

Al dente, *which means "to the tooth" in Italian, is frequently used to describe pasta or other foods that offer a slight resistance when bitten.*

INGREDIENT	QUANTITY 4 servings	24 servings	METHOD
10 11 Olive oil spray	as needed	as needed	Spray skillet with oil.
Onions, fresh, minced	1 tbsp.	⅓ cup	Add to oil and sauté over medium heat for 1 to 3 minutes or until onions are translucent.
12 Spinach, fresh, lightly packed	6 cups	36 cups	Add to onions and sauté for 3 to 4 minutes or until spinach is thoroughly wilted. (Sauté smaller quantity for 1 to 2 minutes.)
Garlic, fresh, minced	½ tsp.	1 tbsp.	
Thyme, fresh, chopped	¼ tsp.	½ tbsp.	
13 Nutmeg, ground	⅛ tsp.	¾ tsp.	
Vegetable broth, canned	¼ cup	1⅓ cups	Add to onion mixture and mix thoroughly. Transfer to food processor bowl and process until mixture becomes smooth paste. Remove from processor bowl and reserve.
14 Pastry flour, whole-wheat, sifted	1 cup	6 cups	Combine in bowl. Add spinach paste and barley and mix thoroughly.
Egg whites, lightly beaten but not frothy	2 tbsp.	¾ cup	
Salt	1 tsp.	2 tbsp.	
15 Black pepper, coarse	1 tsp.	2 tbsp.	
Water, boiling	as needed	as needed	Press noodle mixture through spaetzle maker or perforated pan into boiling salted water. Stir noodles and simmer for 2 to 3 minutes or until al dente.
Salt	as needed	as needed	
16 Ice water bath	as needed	as needed	Skim noodles from water and immediately plunge into ice water to stop cooking process. Drain and lightly toss with oil to prevent sticking. Repeat cooking process as needed. Cover and reserve.
Olive oil	as needed	as needed	
17 Olive oil spray	as needed	as needed	*To prepare single serving:* Spray sauté pan with oil. Add 4 ounces chicken and sauté over medium heat for 2 to 3 minutes or until lightly browned and thoroughly heated.
Tyson Fully Cooked Diced White Fryer Meat, 1-inch dice, frozen	1 lb.	6 lb.	
18 Red bell peppers, fresh, batonnet (p. 88)	1⅓ cups	8 cups	Add 1 cup smoked ginger broth, ⅓ cup red bell peppers, ¼ cup parsnips, ¼ cup carrots, ¼ cup turnips, and ¼ cup green onions. Simmer for 1 to 2 minutes or until vegetables are tender-crisp. Skim vegetables from broth and spoon into bottom half of 1 squash, leaving broth and chicken in sauté pan.
Parsnips, fresh, batonnet	1 cup	6 cups	
Carrots, fresh, batonnet	1 cup	6 cups	
Turnips, fresh, batonnet	1 cup	6 cups	
Green onions, fresh, 2-inch lengths	1 cup	6 cups	
			Add ½ cup noodles to broth remaining in sauté pan. Simmer for 2 to 3 minutes or until thoroughly heated. Pour noodles, broth, and chicken over vegetables in squash. Place squash in large pasta bowl and garnish with squash lid.

Portion: 20 ounces (54 ounces including squash bowl)
Nutritional Data/Portion: Calories 530, Protein 52 g, Fat 6 g, Carbohydrate 66 g, Cholesterol 90 mg, Sodium 3,816 mg

For a ***FAST FACTS VIA FAX*** copy of this recipe, call 1-800-223-3755 and enter Business Tool 2539.

HOW TO MAKE SPAETZLE NOODLES
Press noodle mixture through spaetzle maker or perforated pan into boiling salted water. The result should be short textured noodles of varying shapes and lengths. Tend with care; if overcooked, the noodles can become tough.

Submitted by John Gonzales
Colonial Williamsburg
Williamsburg, Va.

Colonial Peanut Chicken Chili

Like roasted garlic, the peanuts in this dish become tender and mild, picking up the cumin, chili powder, and garlic flavors. Tortilla chips mixed in also become soft and help thicken the chili while maintaining their delicious corn flavor.

Line Service *Takeout*

INGREDIENT	QUANTITY 4 servings	24 servings	METHOD
1 Chicken broth, canned	3 cups	18 cups	Combine in saucepan or stockpot and mix thoroughly. Bring to boil over high heat. Reduce heat and cover. Gently simmer for 4 hours or until peanuts are tender, stirring occasionally.
Water, cold	1⅓ cups	8 cups	
Peanuts, shelled, raw	1 cup	6 cups	
2 Tyson Fully Cooked Diced Chicken Tenderloins, ¾-inch dice, frozen	12 oz.	4½ lb.	Add to peanuts and mix thoroughly.
Cumin, ground	1 tsp.	2 tbsp.	
Chili powder, dark	½ tsp.	1 tbsp.	
Oregano leaves, dried	½ tsp.	1 tbsp.	
Garlic, granulated	½ tsp.	1 tbsp.	
Salt	½ tsp.	1 tbsp.	
Cayenne pepper sauce	½ tsp.	1 tbsp.	
3 Olive oil	2 tbsp.	¾ cup	Heat in skillet over medium heat.
4 Onions, fresh, diced (p. 175)	½ cup	3 cups	Add to oil and sauté for 5 to 6 minutes or until vegetables are tender. (Sauté smaller quantity for 3 to 4 minutes.) Remove from heat, add to peanuts, and mix thoroughly. Simmer, uncovered, for an additional 55 to 60 minutes or until flavors are concentrated, stirring frequently. (Simmer smaller quantity for 40 to 45 minutes.)
Green bell peppers, fresh, diced (p. 88)	½ cup	3 cups	
Celery, fresh, diced	⅓ cup	2 cups	
5 Tortilla chips, salt-free, ground fine	½ cup	3 cups	Add to chili and mix thoroughly. Remove from heat. Keep warm above 140°F.
6 Tomatoes, fresh, seeded, diced	½ cup	3 cups	*To assemble single serving:* Ladle 1½ cups chili into bowl. Top with 2 tablespoons tomatoes, 1 tablespoon cilantro, and a dash of pepper sauce.
Cilantro, fresh, chopped	¼ cup	1½ cups	
Green jalapeño pepper sauce, commercially prepared	as needed	as needed	*Serve with cornbread sticks.*

Portion: 13 ounces
Nutritional Data/Portion: Calories 510, Protein 34 g, Fat 31 g, Carbohydrate 26 g, Cholesterol 45 mg, Sodium 1,170 mg

For a **FAST FACTS VIA FAX** copy of this recipe, call 1-800-223-3755 and enter Business Tool 2546.

While peanuts are considered common today, the ancient Peruvians regarded them so highly that they buried their dead with enough peanuts to nourish them as they made their journeys into the afterlife.

"I hate television. I hate it as much as peanuts. But I can't stop eating peanuts."
Orson Welles

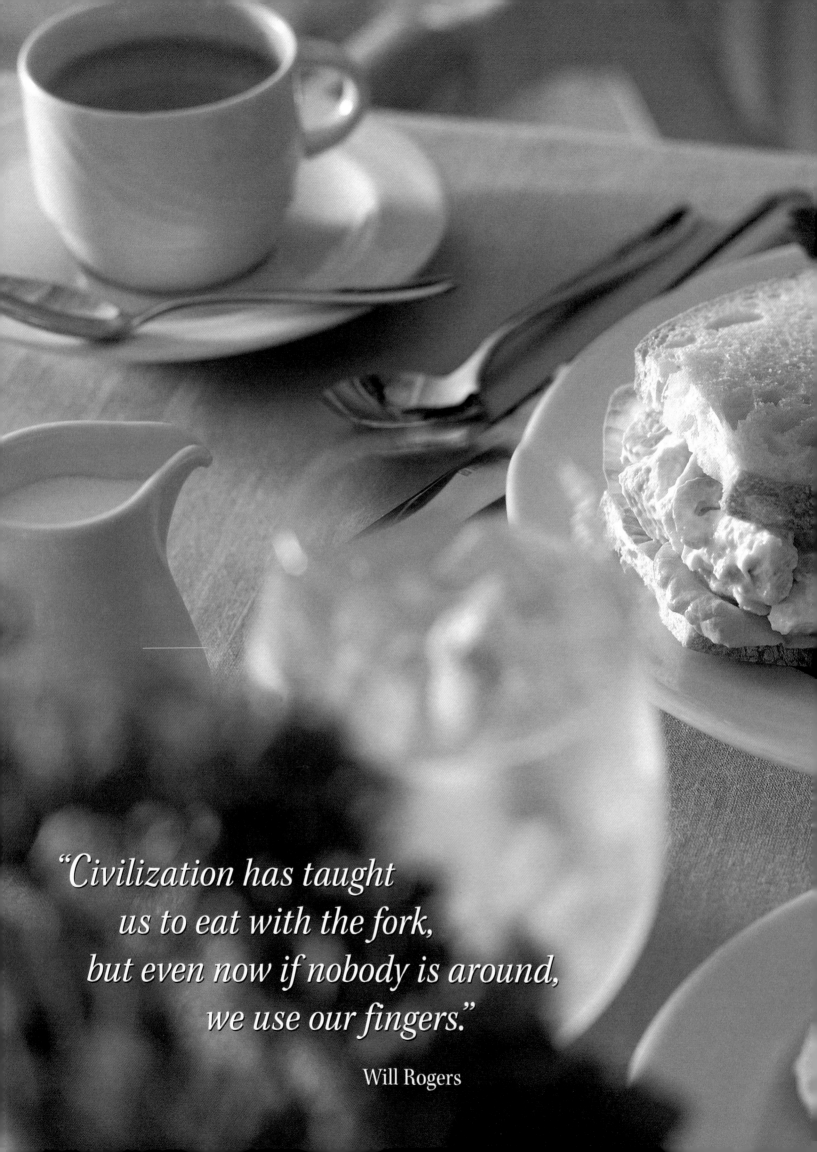

"*Civilization has taught
us to eat with the fork,
but even now if nobody is around,
we use our fingers.*"

Will Rogers

Handheld Meals

*G*rabbing hold of menu opportunity

The handheld class of meals is often attributed to John Montagu, the fourth earl of Sandwich, who ordered "some beef or fowl and slices of bread" after spending 24 hours at a gaming table. He stuffed the meat between the bread slices and ate without interrupting his play. Though the earl may be credited with the sandwich, there has always been something comforting and convenient about eating with our hands. Indeed, the fork remained more novelty than necessity until the late 19th century.

Whether today's diners choose handheld meals for comfort or convenience, chances are they want to dine well. The sandwich category has thus evolved to include hoagies, subs, melts, wraps, and burritos. Bread choices have gone way beyond plain white to include ethnic and regional favorites such as focaccia, pitas, tortillas, and bagels. Interesting condiments and enhancements range from a world of cheeses to dozens of mustards and all sorts of crisp exotic lettuces.

The handheld menu category has benefited greatly from advancements in poultry processing. Deboning, sizing, marinating, breading, and a litany of other processes make it possible for diners to enjoy chicken in forms that are as fast and mobile as their lifestyles. From the sophisticated Chicken Cordon Bleu Sandwich to the contemporary Chicken Caesar Salad Wrap, here are over 30 new ways to satisfy America's penchant to eat chicken hands-on.

Submitted by William Cordo
Gourmet Pizza & Things
Hicksville, N.Y.

Chicken Provolone Hero

Depending on the area of the country, this sandwich might be called a sub, grinder, hoagie or po' boy, but it's universally loved for its heroic proportions. Spaghetti sauce, salami, olives, and provolone cheese give it an unmistakable Italian flavor, and the melted cheese with the pepper chicken tenderloins makes it really stand out.

INGREDIENT	QUANTITY 4 servings	24 servings	METHOD
1 Tyson Ready-to-Cook Marinated Breaded Homestyle Pepper Chicken Tenderloins, frozen	12	72	Deep-fry at 350°F for 3 to 5 minutes or until chicken is no longer pink. Remove from fryer and drain. Keep warm above 140°F.
2 Olive oil	1 tbsp.	⅓ cup	Heat in skillet or braising pan over high heat.
3 Button mushrooms, fresh, sliced	1½ cups	9 cups	Add to oil and sauté for 6 to 8 minutes or until wilted. (Sauté smaller quantity for 2 to 3 minutes.) Remove from heat. Cover and reserve.
4 French rolls, 6-inch long, sliced horizontally for sandwich, grilled	4	24	*To prepare single serving:* Place 1 roll on flat work surface, grilled sides up.
Salami slices, thin	12	72	Layer ingredients on bottom half of roll in the following order: 3 salami slices, 3 chicken tenderloins, 2 tablespoons mushrooms, 1 tablespoon black olives, ⅓ cup spaghetti sauce, and 2 cheese halves. Close sandwich with top half of roll.
Black olives, sliced, canned, drained	¼ cup	1½ cups	
Spaghetti sauce, chunky, commercially prepared	1⅓ cups	8 cups	
Provolone cheese slices, cut in half	4	24	
5 Basil sprigs, fresh	4	24	Bake in preheated conventional oven† at 350°F for 3 to 5 minutes or until cheese is melted. Remove from oven, slice in half diagonally, and arrange on plate. Garnish plate with 1 basil sprig.

Serve with battered onion rings.

Portion: 11 ounces
Nutritional Data/Portion: Calories 710, Protein 39 g, Fat 39 g, Carbohydrate 51 g, Cholesterol 75 mg, Sodium 2,310 mg

†Convection oven not recommended.

For a **FAST FACTS VIA FAX**™ copy of this recipe, call 1-800-223-3755 and enter Business Tool 2504.

Provolone, a cow's milk cheese originally from southern Italy, is now manufactured in the United States. Most provolones for sandwiches are aged between 2 months and 1 year, until they are firm but sliceable and have a mild, smoky flavor. Provolones aged longer are stronger in flavor and can be grated, much like Parmesan cheese.

Package the spaghetti sauce separately for takeout.

*By some accounts, the club
sandwich originated near
the turn of the century at the
Saratoga Club in Saratoga
Springs, New York. Others
believe it was first made in
the club car of a passenger
train. Either way, it's an all-
American sandwich.*

*New, different types of chips
help keep plate presentation
on-trend and unexpected
as pictured.*

California Chicken Club

These days, just about anything can go in club sandwiches. This version includes chicken
with the customary bacon, cheese, lettuce, and tomato, and makes a California statement
with creamy guacamole spread on each layer.

Speed-Scratch *Take-out*

INGREDIENT	QUANTITY		METHOD
	4 servings	24 servings	
Tyson Ready-to-Cook Tenderpressed™ Savory Chicken Breast Filets, 4.5-oz., frozen	4	24	Char-grill over high heat for 8 to 10 minutes on each side or until chicken is no longer pink. Or grill on oiled, preheated flattop griddle at 350°F for 7 to 9 minutes on each side. Remove from grill. Keep warm above 140°F.
Homestyle white sandwich slices, toasted	12	72	*To assemble single serving:* Place 3 toasted bread slices on flat work surface. Spread each slice with ½ tablespoon guacamole.
Guacamole, commercially prepared	6 tbsp.	2¼ cups	
Green leaf lettuce leaves, fresh	4	24	Layer on bottom slice of bread in the following order: 1 lettuce leaf, 3 tomato slices, 2 bacon slices, 1 bread slice, 1 chicken breast filet, and 1 cheese slice.
Tomato slices, thin, fresh	12	72	
Bacon slices, crisp	8	48	
Swiss cheese slices	4	24	
Club picks	16	96	Close sandwich with third slice of bread and slice diagonally into quarters. Secure each quarter with 1 club pick and arrange on plate.

Serve with colorful vegetable chips.

Portion: 8 ounces
Nutritional Data/Portion: Calories 540, Protein 41 g, Fat 21 g, Carbohydrate 48 g, Cholesterol 95 mg, Sodium 1,390 mg

For a **FAST FACTS VIA FAX** copy of this recipe, call 1-800-223-3755 and enter Business Tool 2506.

Submitted by Ann Atkins, CHA
Holiday Inn–St. George
St. George, S.C.

Grilled Chicken and Brandied Mustard Sandwich

Bringing two French staples—Dijon mustard and brandy—together gives this grilled chicken sandwich its extraordinary sophisticated flavor.

Speed-Scratch   Line-Service   Takeout

INGREDIENT	QUANTITY 4 servings	24 servings	METHOD
1 Tyson Fully Cooked Flavor-Redi® Natural Grill Chicken Breast Filets, 4.5-oz., frozen	4	24	Place on foil-lined sheet pans. Heat in pre-heated conventional oven at 400°F for 17 to 22 minutes. Or heat in preheated convection oven at 375°F for 10 to 12 minutes. Remove from oven. Keep warm above 140°F. 
2 *Brandied Mustard Sauce*			
Mustard, honey-Dijon	¼ cup	1½ cups	Combine in bowl and mix thoroughly. Cover and chill to hold.
Sour cream	¼ cup	1½ cups	
Brandy	2 tsp.	¼ cup	
Parsley, fresh, minced (p. 39)	1 tsp.	2 tbsp.	
3 Club picks	4	24	To prepare mini fruit kabobs for garnish, spear 1 orange wedge, 1 strawberry, and 1 melon ball on each pick. Cover and chill to hold.
Orange wedges, seedless, unpeeled, fresh	4	24	
Strawberries, whole, fresh	4	24	
Cantaloupe melon balls, fresh	4	24	
4 Kaiser rolls, sliced horizontally for sandwich, grilled	4	24	*To assemble single serving:* Place 1 roll on flat work surface, grilled sides up. Spread each side with 1 tablespoon brandied mustard sauce. Layer 1 lettuce leaf and 1 tomato slice on bottom half of roll. Top with 1 chicken breast filet. Close sandwich with top half of roll and slice in half. Arrange on plate. Garnish plate with 1 fruit kabob.
Green leaf lettuce leaves, fresh	4	24	
Tomato slices, fresh	4	24	

Serve with new potato salad.

Portion: 10 ounces
Nutritional Data/Portion: Calories 510, Protein 35 g, Fat 20 g, Carbohydrate 49 g, Cholesterol 90 mg, Sodium 1,000 mg

For a **FAST FACTS VIA FAX**™ copy of this recipe, call 1-800-223-3755 and enter Business Tool 2517.

This sandwich translates easily to party platters. Just cut it into quarters.

For thousands of years, mustard has been important in food history. The city of Dijon has been home to fine examples since the 13th century. And yellow mustard has been an American icon since it was first introduced during the 1904 World's Fair. But today, mustard is more popular than ever. There is even a mustard museum in Mount Horeb, Wisconsin, that proudly displays over 1,500 varieties!

For a savory twist, add a slice of smoked provolone cheese and a thin slice of red onion to the sandwich.

Blackened Chicken Sandwich

Cajun seasonings and a hot iron skillet are the basics of great blackened chicken. Cayenne pepper sauce gilds the finished sandwich.

Speed-Scratch   Lighter Fare   Takeout

Submitted by Francisco Lira
94th Aero Squadron Restaurant
San Diego, Calif.

INGREDIENT	QUANTITY 4 servings	24 servings	METHOD
1 Tyson Ready-to-Cook Tenderpressed™ Savory Chicken Breast Filets, 4.75-oz., frozen	4	24	Cover tightly and slack in cooler between 32° and 36°F prior to use.
2 Butter, salted, melted	as needed	as needed	*To prepare single serving:* Brush 1 chicken breast filet with butter. Dredge in seasoning and shake off excess.
Cajun seasoning, dried	as needed	as needed	
			Heat small heavy iron skillet over medium-high heat for 6 to 8 minutes. Add chicken to hot, dry skillet and blacken for 2 to 2½ minutes on each side or until chicken is no longer pink. Remove from heat. 
3 Wheat sub rolls, sliced horizontally for sandwich, grilled	4	24	Place 1 roll on flat work surface, grilled sides up. Spread ½ tablespoon mayonnaise on each half. Layer bottom half of roll with 1 lettuce leaf, 2 onion slices, and chicken breast filet. Drizzle ½ teaspoon cayenne pepper sauce over top.
Mayonnaise	¼ cup	1½ cups	
Red leaf lettuce leaves, fresh	4	24	
Red onion slices, thin, fresh	8	48	Close sandwich with top half of roll and slice in half diagonally. Arrange on plate.
Cayenne pepper sauce	2 tsp.	¼ cup	

Serve with chilled slices of mango, pineapple, and kiwi.

Portion: 9 ounces
Nutritional Data/Portion: Calories 310, Protein 28 g, Fat 12 g, Carbohydrate 26 g, Cholesterol 85 mg, Sodium 680 mg

For a **FAST FACTS VIA FAX**™ copy of this recipe, call 1-800-223-3755 and enter Business Tool 2502.

While it is recommended to cook from frozen in most cases, blackening works best when chicken is prepared from a thawed state.

Blackening started at Paul Prudhomme's K-Paul Louisiana Kitchen in 1979. The now-famous cooking method occurred somewhat by accident according to Prudhomme, when one of his cooks scorched a fish over a fire that was too hot.

Submitted by Barbara Ball
225 Cafe
Chicago, Ill.

Focaccia is yeast dough that is shaped into a large, flat round or rectangle. The dough is then dappled with fingertip depressions, brushed with olive oil, sprinkled with coarse salt, and allowed to rise before baking. Herbs, especially rosemary, can also season the focaccia.

The classic Genovese pesto is an uncooked sauce made with pureed fresh basil, garlic, pine nuts, Parmesan or pecorino cheese, and olive oil.

Chicken Caprese Focaccia

Traditionally eaten as a snack or with soups and salads, Italian focaccia has been adopted into the American sandwich family. Another Italian favorite, *caprese*, which is a simple dish made of slices of tomato, basil, and vinaigrette, is the inspiration for this elegant sandwich.

	INGREDIENT	QUANTITY		METHOD
		4 servings	24 servings	
1	Tyson Ready-to-Cook Boneless, Skinless Chicken Thigh Filets, 3.5-oz., frozen	8	48	Place in full-size steam table pans. (Use half-size pan for smaller quantity.)
2	Italian vinaigrette salad dressing, commercially prepared	¼ cup	2 cups	Pour over chicken.
				Roast in preheated conventional oven at 425°F for 18 to 22 minutes or until chicken is no longer pink. (Roast smaller quantity for 12 to 15 minutes.) Or roast in preheated convection oven at 375°F for 10 to 12 minutes. (Roast smaller quantity for 6 to 8 minutes.) Remove from oven. Keep warm above 140°F.
3	Focaccia bread rounds, 8-inch, sliced in half vertically, then sliced horizontally for sandwich	2	12	*To prepare single serving:* Place 1 top and bottom half-round piece of focaccia on flat work surface, cut sides up. (Reserve other half for another sandwich.) Spread bottom half with 1 tablespoon mayonnaise.
	Mayonnaise	¼ cup	1½ cups	
	Tomato slices, fresh	8	48	Top with 2 chicken thigh filets and spoon ½ teaspoon pan sauce over each filet. Layer 1 tomato slice and 1 cheese slice over each filet. Spread top half of focaccia with 1 tablespoon pesto and close sandwich.
	Mozzarella cheese slices	8	48	
	Basil pesto, commercially prepared	¼ cup	1½ cups	
	Basil sprigs, fresh	4	24	
				Transfer to sheet pan and bake in preheated conventional oven† at 250°F for 12 to 15 minutes or until cheese is melted and sandwich is thoroughly heated. Remove from oven. Slice in half and arrange on plate. Garnish plate with 1 basil sprig.
				Serve with pasta salad.

Portion: 14 ounces
Nutritional Data/Portion: Calories 800, Protein 48 g, Fat 48 g, Carbohydrate 47 g, Cholesterol 170 mg, Sodium 1,090 mg

†Convection oven not recommended.

For a **FAST FACTS VIA FAX**™ copy of this recipe, call 1-800-223-3755 and enter Business Tool 2510.

"The creation of bread has to rank right up there as significant to man as the invention of the spoon."
Herald-Palladium

Focaccia Chicken Grill

This sophisticated and flavorful sandwich is made with grilled chicken, portobello mushrooms, and tapenade, and served with an equally unusual sweet-and-sour baked potato salad.

Takeout

INGREDIENT	QUANTITY		METHOD
	4 servings	24 servings	
1 Tyson Fully Cooked Flavor-Redi® Natural Grill Chicken Breast Filets, 4.5-oz., frozen	4	24	Place on foil-lined sheet pans. Heat in preheated conventional oven at 400°F for 17 to 22 minutes. Or heat in preheated convection oven at 375°F for 10 to 12 minutes. Remove from oven. Keep warm above 140°F.
2 Tomato slices, ¼-inch-thick, fresh	24	144	Arrange tomato slices in single layer on oiled sheet pans. Brush tops with oil and sprinkle with sugar and seasonings.
Olive oil	as needed	as needed	
Salt	¾ tsp.	1½ tbsp.	Roast in preheated conventional oven at 425°F for 15 to 20 minutes or until lightly charred. Or roast in preheated convection oven at 375°F for 10 to 12 minutes. Remove from oven. Cover and reserve.
Sugar, granulated	½ tsp.	1 tbsp.	
Black pepper, coarse	¼ tsp.	½ tbsp.	
3 Portobello mushrooms, whole, fresh	4	24	Combine in bowl and toss well. Cover and marinate for 30 minutes. Drain, then char-grill over medium heat for 3 to 4 minutes on each side or until tender. Remove from grill. Cover and reserve.
Italian vinaigrette salad dressing, commercially prepared	½ cup	3 cups	
4 *Tapenade*			
Black olives, sliced, canned, drained	⅓ cup	2 cups	Combine in food processor bowl and pulse until finely chopped. Remove from processor bowl. Cover and chill to hold.
Green olives, sliced, canned, drained	⅓ cup	2 cups	
Olive oil	1 tbsp.	⅓ cup	
Capers, rinsed, drained	½ tbsp.	3 tbsp.	
Mustard, Dijon	1 tsp.	2 tbsp.	
Anchovy paste	½ tsp.	1 tbsp.	
5 Focaccia bread, sliced into 4½-inch squares, then sliced horizontally for sandwich	4	24	*To prepare single serving:* Place bottom half of 1 focaccia square on flat work surface, cut side up.
Provolone cheese slices, smoked	4	24	Layer on bottom half of bread in the following order: 1 cheese slice, 3 tomato slices, 1 whole mushroom, 1 chicken breast filet, 3 tomato slices, 2 tablespoons tapenade. Close sandwich with top half of bread.
Olive oil	as needed	as needed	
Basil sprigs, fresh	4	24	Brush oil on outside surfaces of focaccia. Grill on oiled, preheated flattop griddle at 350°F for 4 to 5 minutes on each side or until cheese is melted and bread is golden brown. Remove from griddle. Slice in half diagonally and arrange on plate. Garnish plate with 1 basil sprig.

Serve with sweet-and-sour baked potato salad.

Portion: 11½ ounces
Nutritional Data/Portion: Calories 510, Protein 39 g, Fat 29 g, Carbohydrate 25 g, Cholesterol 105 mg, Sodium 1,800 mg

For a **FAST FACTS VIA FAX**™ copy of this recipe, call 1-800-223-3755 and enter Business Tool 2513.

SWEET-AND-SOUR BAKED POTATO SALAD

	4 servings	24 servings
Baked potatoes, skin-on, chilled, ½-inch dice	3 cups	18 cups
Red onions, fresh, slivered	½ cup	3 cups
Celery, fresh, ¼-inch dice	¼ cup	1½ cups
Red bell peppers, fresh, ¼-inch dice	2 tbsp.	1 cup
Sweet pickles, chopped	2 tbsp.	1 cup
Salt	¼ tsp.	2 tsp.
Red wine vinegar	¼ cup	¾ cup
Olive oil	¼ cup	¾ cup
Mustard, Dijon	2 tbsp.	⅓ cup
Parsley, fresh, minced	1 tbsp.	3 tbsp.
Dill weed, dried	1 tsp.	1 tbsp.
Radicchio leaves, fresh	4	24

Combine first six ingredients in bowl.

Combine next five ingredients in separate bowl and whisk until well blended. Pour over potato mixture and toss well. Cover and chill to hold.

Portion ¾ cup potato salad on radicchio leaf and serve with each sandwich.

Portion: 5 ounces

Submitted by
D.L. Webster and Staff
Payless Foods, Inc.
Freeland, Wash.

Eight strombolis will fit on one full-size sheet pan.

Commercially prepared sour cream, which contains from 18 to 20 percent fat, is treated with a lactic acid culture that gives sour cream its characteristic tang. Light sour cream contains about 40 percent less fat because it's made from half-and-half. They are generally interchangeable.

This dish is particularly attractive when sliced into wedges and plated in a wheel with tomato wedges placed between the slices.

An alternate Tyson product, ¼-inch diced leg meat, may be substituted for the breast filet.

Hot Pepper Chicken Ranch Stromboli

Creamy hot pepper cheese and cool ranch dressing give a Southwestern twist to this Italian chicken stromboli.

INGREDIENT	QUANTITY 4 servings	24 servings	METHOD
1 Tyson Fully Cooked Flavor-Redi® Italian Chicken Breast Filets, 3-oz., frozen	4	24	Cover tightly and slack in cooler between 32° and 36°F prior to use.
2 Sour cream	1 cup	6 cups	Combine in bowl. Cut chicken into 1-inch dice and add to bowl. Mix thoroughly. Cover and chill below 40°F to hold.
Imitation sour cream	1 cup	6 cups	
Red onions, fresh, diced (p. 175)	½ cup	3 cups	
Red bell peppers, roasted, chopped (p. 66)	¼ cup	1½ cups	
Green bell peppers, fresh, diced (p. 88)	¼ cup	1½ cups	
Jalapeño peppers, fresh, seeded, minced (p. 172)	2 tbsp.	¾ cup	
Ranch salad dressing mix, dried, commercially prepared	1 tbsp.	⅓ cup	
Hot pepper cheese, shredded	¼ cup	1½ cups	
3 Pizza dough, presheeted, 7-inch, unbaked, frozen, slacked according to package directions	4	24	*To prepare stromboli:* Place pizza rounds on floured work surface. Stretch dough to approximately 8-inch diameter. Portion 1 cup chicken mixture into center of each round. Bring dough together over center of filling and pinch edges together securely. Repeat process for each round. Transfer to oiled sheet pans and cut 2 vents in each stromboli. Cover lightly and let rise at 140°F for 30 minutes or until dough has doubled.
			Bake in preheated conventional oven at 350°F for 35 to 40 minutes or until golden brown. (Bake smaller quantity for 20 to 30 minutes.) Or bake in preheated convection oven at 300°F for 16 to 18 minutes. (Bake smaller quantity for 10 to 15 minutes.) Remove from oven.
4 Ranch salad dressing, commercially prepared	as needed	as needed	Immediately brush on each stromboli. Keep warm above 140°F.
5 Parsley, fresh, minced (p. 39)	3 tbsp.	1 cup	*To assemble single serving:* Place 1 stromboli on plate and sprinkle with 2 teaspoons parsley. Garnish plate with 1 parsley sprig.
Parsley sprigs, fresh	4	24	

Serve with Caesar salad.

Portion: 12 ounces
Nutritional Data/Portion: Calories 530, Protein 27 g, Fat 37 g, Carbohydrate 25 g, Cholesterol 100 mg, Sodium 590 mg

For a ***Fast Facts Via Fax*** copy of this recipe, call 1-800-223-3755 and enter Business Tool 2522.

Submitted by Lillian Walsh
Lillian's Pan Pizza
Perdido Key, Fla.

Three-Cheese Chicken Pesto Calzone

The calzone, essentially a pizza turnover, is a truly portable, handheld dish that has huge menu potential. This recipe will create an instant following.

Kid Friendly *Line Service* *Takeout*

INGREDIENT	QUANTITY 4 servings	24 servings	METHOD
Tyson Fully Cooked Flavor-Redi® Fajita Chicken Breast Strips, frozen	8 oz.	3 lb.	Cover tightly and slack in cooler between 32° and 36°F prior to use.
Ricotta cheese	⅔ cup	4 cups	Combine in bowl and mix thoroughly.
Parmesan cheese, grated	⅔ cup	4 cups	
Pizza dough, presheeted, 7-inch, unbaked, frozen, slacked according to package directions	4	24	*To prepare calzones:* Place pizza rounds on floured work surface.
Basil pesto, commercially prepared	½ cup	3 cups	Spread ingredients over half of each round in the following order, leaving a border around outside edges: ¼ cup ricotta mixture, 2 tablespoons pesto, 2 ounces chicken, 3 tablespoons tomatoes, ¼ cup mushrooms, ¼ cup mozzarella cheese.
Roma tomatoes, fresh, diced	¾ cup	4½ cups	
Button mushrooms, fresh, diced	1 cup	6 cups	
Mozzarella cheese, shredded	1 cup	6 cups	Fold dough over filling to form half rounds and crimp edges to seal securely. Transfer to oiled sheet pans and cut 5 vents in top of each calzone.
			Bake in preheated conventional oven at 475°F for 15 to 20 minutes or until golden brown. (Bake smaller quantity for 12 to 15 minutes.) Or bake in preheated convection oven at 425°F for 8 to 10 minutes. (Bake smaller quantity for 7 to 9 minutes.) Remove from oven. Keep warm above 140°F.
Butter, melted	as needed	as needed	*To assemble single serving:* Brush 1 calzone with butter, then slice in half diagonally. Sprinkle with 2 teaspoons cheese and arrange on plate.
Parmesan cheese, grated	3 tbsp.	1¼ cups	
Marinara sauce, commercially prepared, hot	1 cup	6 cups	Portion ¼ cup sauce into individual container and place on plate. Garnish plate with 1 basil sprig.
Basil sprigs, fresh	4	24	

Portion: 13 ounces plus 2 ounces sauce
Nutritional Data/Portion: Calories 840, Protein 48 g, Fat 41 g, Carbohydrate 74 g, Cholesterol 100 mg, Sodium 2,120 mg

For a **FAST FACTS VIA FAX**™ copy of this recipe, call 1-800-223-3755 and enter Business Tool 2507.

The calzone is a pizza turnover from Naples, Italy, and is customarily intended as a single serving. Calzones can be stuffed with a variety of meats, vegetables, and cheeses. They are sometimes deep-fried, but are usually brushed with olive oil and baked.

The cheese mixture in this recipe adds more than just great flavor. It gives the calzone a firm consistency and keeps it from being runny.

In its native Italy, ricotta, which means "recooked," is made from the whey left over from processing cheeses such as mozzarella and provolone.

Submitted by Rob S. Enniss
Robby's Goods To Go
Pawley's Island, S.C.

Spicy Chicken Whiskey Po' Boy

South Carolina is famous for its pulled barbecue sandwiches stuffed with slaw. Here's a great
variation that's been spiked with unique whiskey barbecue sauce.

INGREDIENT	QUANTITY 4 servings	24 servings	METHOD
1 *Whiskey Barbecue Sauce*			
Catsup	¾ cup	4½ cups	Combine in saucepan and mix thoroughly. Bring to boil over medium-high heat. Reduce heat and simmer for 35 to 45 minutes or until flavors are concentrated. (Simmer smaller quantity for 6 to 8 minutes.) Remove from heat.
Apple cider vinegar	¾ cup	4½ cups	
Cola soft drink	2 tbsp.	¾ cup	
Mustard, Dijon	1 tbsp.	⅓ cup	
Chili powder, dark	¾ tsp.	1½ tbsp.	
Garlic, granulated	¼ tsp.	½ tbsp.	
Onion powder	¼ tsp.	½ tbsp.	
Lemon juice, fresh	¼ tsp.	½ tbsp.	
Black pepper, fine	¼ tsp.	½ tbsp.	
White pepper, fine	⅛ tsp.	¾ tsp.	
Habeñero pepper sauce, commercially prepared	¾ tsp.	1½ tbsp.	
Salt	⅛ tsp.	¾ tsp.	
2 Sour mash whiskey	2 tsp.	¼ cup	Add to catsup mixture and mix thoroughly. Cover and chill to hold.
3 *Two-Cabbage Slaw*			
Green cabbage, fresh, shredded	4 cups	24 cups	Combine in bowl and toss well.
Red cabbage, fresh, shredded	1 cup	6 cups	
Carrots, fresh, shredded	½ cup	3 cups	
4 Mayonnaise	1 cup	6 cups	Combine in food processor bowl and process until well blended. Pour over cabbage mixture and toss well. Cover and chill to hold.
Red wine vinegar	1½ tbsp.	½ cup	
Brown sugar, golden	1 tbsp.	⅓ cup	
Onions, fresh, minced	½ tbsp.	3 tbsp.	
Mustard, Dijon	½ tsp.	1 tbsp.	
Salt	¼ tsp.	½ tbsp.	
Black pepper, fine	¼ tsp.	½ tbsp.	
5 Olive oil	2 tbsp.	½ cup	Heat in skillet or braising pan over medium-high heat.
6 Tyson Ready-to-Cook Flavor-Redi® Savory Chicken Tenderloins, frozen	12	72	Add to oil and sauté for 3 to 4 minutes on each side or until lightly browned.
			Add barbecue sauce and mix thoroughly. Bring to boil over high heat. Reduce heat and simmer for 7 to 8 minutes or until sauce thickens and chicken is no longer pink. (Simmer smaller quantity for 5 to 6 minutes.) Remove from heat. Keep warm above 140°F.
7 Sourdough hoagie buns, grilled	4	24	*To assemble single serving:* Place 1 bun on flat work surface, grilled sides up.
Parsley sprigs, fresh	4	24	
			Portion 1 cup slaw on bottom half of bun. Top with 3 chicken tenderloins and ¼ cup sauce from pan.
			Close sandwich with top half of bun and slice in half diagonally. Arrange on plate. Garnish plate with 1 parsley sprig.
			Serve with french-fried potatoes.

Portion: 15 ounces
Nutritional Data/Portion: Calories 900, Protein 41 g, Fat 32 g, Carbohydrate 114 g, Cholesterol 70 mg, Sodium 1,992 mg

For a **FAST FACTS VIA FAX** copy of this recipe, call 1-800-223-3755 and enter Business Tool 2521.

Submitted by
Andina Cafe & Coffee Roastery
Little Rock, Ark.

One 4-ounce or 5-ounce Tenderpressed™ breast filet may be substituted for the double-lobe breast. Choose the size that best satisfies portion-control needs.⌐

Char-Grilled Kickin' Chicken Sandwich

Sharp cheddar cheese and a spicy marinade with hints of espresso transform this chicken breast filet into a macho sandwich with spicy-hot kick.

Line Service   Takeout

INGREDIENT	QUANTITY		METHOD
	4 servings	24 servings	
① Tyson Ready-to-Cook Gourmet Boneless, Skinless Whole Chicken Breast Filets, 6-oz., frozen	4	24	Place in full-size steam table pans. (Use half-size pan for smaller quantity.)
② *Marinade*			
Vegetable oil	¾ cup	4 cups	Combine in bowl and mix thoroughly. Pour over chicken. Cover and marinate below 40°F for 24 hours.
Espresso coffee, brewed	2 tsp.	¼ cup	
Red pepper, crushed, dried	½ tsp.	1 tbsp.	
Garlic powder	½ tsp.	1 tbsp.	Remove chicken from marinade and char-grill over high heat for 5 to 6 minutes on each side or until chicken is no longer pink. Or grill on oiled, preheated flattop griddle at 350°F for 5 to 8 minutes on each side. Remove from grill. Keep warm above 140°F.
Onion powder	½ tsp.	1 tbsp.	
Southwestern seasoning, dried	½ tsp.	1 tbsp.	
Cajun seasoning, dried	½ tsp.	1 tbsp.	
Cumin, ground	½ tsp.	1 tbsp.	
Cilantro, fresh, minced	½ tsp.	1 tbsp.	
Garlic, fresh, minced	⅛ tsp.	¾ tsp.	
Salt	¼ tsp.	½ tbsp.	
Black pepper, coarse	¼ tsp.	½ tbsp.	
③ Multigrain sandwich buns, grilled	4	24	*To assemble single serving:* Place 1 bun on flat work surface, grilled sides up. Spread ½ tablespoon mustard on each half.
Mustard, Dijon	¼ cup	1½ cups	
Green leaf lettuce leaves, fresh	4	24	Layer on bottom half of bun in the following order: 1 lettuce leaf, 1 tomato slice, 1 chicken breast filet, 1 cheese slice, 2 onion rings.
Tomato slices, fresh	4	24	
Cheddar cheese slices, sharp	4	24	
Red onion rings, fresh	8	48	Close sandwich with top half of bun and place on plate.

Serve with fried potatoes and pickle spear.

Portion: 10 ounces
Nutritional Data/Portion: Calories 650, Protein 50 g, Fat 37 g, Carbohydrate 31 g, Cholesterol 120 mg, Sodium 760 mg

For a **FAST FACTS VIA FAX** copy of this recipe, call 1-800-223-3755 and enter Business Tool 2503.

Chicken Soft Taco

Flour tortillas and fresh cilantro offer patrons a taqueria-style alternative to the more common American-style traditional crunchy corn-tortilla tacos.

Taquerias are counter-service businesses that offer corn-tortilla tacos and flour-tortilla burritos with taste-tempting fillings such as grilled and broiled chicken, beef, pork, and fish, with ingredients such as black beans, cilantro, onions, tomatoes, hot sauce, and green peppers.

The typical American version of a taco—meat, cheese, lettuce, and tomato—barely resembles its Mexican namesake. Tacos in Mexico include corn (most commonly) or flour tortillas that are usually fried, although they may also be served steamed or soft. They are filled with thick meat stews, grilled or hard meats, or potatoes and eggs. They are often sold by vendors in the streets of Mexico either folded, rolled, or wrapped.

El Cholo, a Los Angeles restaurant, may have established the basis of the modern Mexican American restaurant menu in 1931. The restaurant served enchiladas, burritos, chimichangas, tacos, chiles rellenos, and tamales. A few years later, they added margaritas to the menu.

INGREDIENT	QUANTITY 4 servings	QUANTITY 24 servings	METHOD
1 Olive oil	¼ cup	½ cup	Heat in skillet or braising pan over medium-high heat.
2 Tyson Fully Cooked Flavor-Redi® Chicken Breast Fajita Strips, frozen	1½ lb.	9 lb.	Add to oil and sauté for 20 to 30 minutes or until most of liquid has evaporated. (Sauté smaller quantity for 5 to 8 minutes.) Remove from heat.
Onions, fresh, chopped (p. 175)	2 cups	10 cups	
Tomatoes, diced, canned, drained	2 cups	10 cups	
Garlic, fresh, minced	2 tsp.	¼ cup	
Cumin, ground	2 tsp.	¼ cup	
Red pepper, crushed, dried	1 tsp.	2 tbsp.	
Chili powder, dark	1 tsp.	2 tbsp.	
Oregano leaves, dried	1 tsp.	2 tbsp.	
Salt	½ tsp.	1 tbsp.	
3 Cilantro, fresh, minced	1 cup	3 cups	Add to chicken mixture and mix thoroughly. Keep warm above 140°F.
4 Tyson Mexican Original® Flour Tortillas, 7-inch, warm	8	48	*To assemble single serving:* Place 2 tortillas on flat work surface.
Iceberg lettuce, fresh, shredded	4 cups	24 cups	Portion a generous ½ cup chicken mixture across center of each tortilla. Fold lower half of tortillas over filling and arrange on plate.
Tomatoes, fresh, seeded, diced	1 cup	6 cups	
Black olives, sliced, canned, drained	¼ cup	1½ cups	Layer "salad" alongside tacos in the following order: 1 cup lettuce, ¼ cup tomatoes, 1 tablespoon black olives, 1 tablespoon guacamole, 1 tablespoon sour cream. Garnish plate with 1 jalapeño and 1 lime wedge.
Guacamole, commercially prepared	¼ cup	1½ cups	
Sour cream	¼ cup	1½ cups	
Jalapeño peppers, red, fresh	4	24	
Lime wedges, fresh	4	24	

Portion: 15 ounces
Nutritional Data/Portion: Calories 690, Protein 45 g, Fat 30 g, Carbohydrate 63 g, Cholesterol 95 mg, Sodium 1,744 mg

For a **FAST FACTS VIA FAX** copy of this recipe, call 1-800-223-3755 and enter Business Tool 2360.

Submitted by Tom Vissers
Sodexho Marriott Services
The New York Law School
New York, N.Y.

Tijuana Yard Bird Stroller

Move over ordinary fajitas. This variation is bound for stardom with its extra notes of lime, cilantro, and cumin. Assemble the plate back-of-house or let your patrons do it fajita-style.

INGREDIENT	QUANTITY 4 servings	24 servings	METHOD
1 Tyson Gourmet Boneless, Skinless Chicken Breast Filets, 4-oz., frozen	4	24	Place in full-size steam table pans. (Use half-size pan for smaller quantity.)
2 Olive oil	1 cup	6 cups	Combine in bowl and whisk together until well blended. Pour half of marinade over chicken. Cover and marinate below 40°F for 6 to 8 hours.
Lime juice, fresh	¾ cup	4½ cups	
Cilantro, fresh, chopped	1½ tbsp.	½ cup	
Jalapeño peppers, fresh, seeded, minced (p. 172)	2 tbsp.	¾ cup	
Chili powder, dark	2 tbsp.	¾ cup	
Cumin, ground	2 tsp.	¼ cup	
3 Red bell peppers, fresh, seeded	1	6	Slice each pepper into 8 strips. Combine in separate bowl and pour remaining marinade over peppers. Cover and marinate for 6 to 8 hours.
Green bell peppers, fresh, seeded	1	6	
4 Salt	1 tsp.	2 tbsp.	Remove chicken from marinade. Grill on oiled, preheated flattop griddle at 350°F for 5 to 6 minutes on each side or until chicken is no longer pink. Remove from griddle and season with salt and pepper. Slice each breast filet into 4 strips. Keep warm above 140°F.
Black pepper, coarse	½ tsp.	1 tbsp.	
5 Salt	1 tsp.	2 tbsp.	Remove peppers from marinade. Grill on oiled, preheated flattop griddle at 350°F for 6 to 7 minutes or until tender-crisp. Remove from griddle and season with salt and pepper. Keep warm.
Black pepper, coarse	½ tsp.	1 tbsp.	
6 Tyson Mexican Original® Cheese Jalapeño Wraps, room temperature (p. 121)	4	24	*To assemble single serving:* Place 1 wrap on flat work surface. Spread with ¼ cup guacamole.
Guacamole, commercially prepared	1 cup	6 cups	Layer ingredients across center of wrap in the following order: 2 tablespoons red onions, ¼ cup cheese, 4 chicken strips, 2 red bell pepper strips, 2 green bell pepper strips, 1½ tablespoons cilantro, 1 teaspoon lime zest, 1 cup lettuce, ¼ cup tomatoes.
Red onions, fresh, small dice (p. 175)	½ cup	4½ cups	
Monterey Jack cheese, shredded	1 cup	6 cups	
Cilantro, fresh, chopped	6 tbsp.	2¼ cups	
Lime zest, fresh	1½ tbsp.	½ cup	
Iceberg lettuce, fresh, chopped	4 cups	24 cups	Fold both sides of wrap over filling. Then fold lower end of wrap over filling and roll closed, keeping ingredients tightly packed. Slice in half diagonally and arrange on plate.
Tomatoes, fresh, seeded, chopped	1 cup	6 cups	
Guacamole, commercially prepared	1 cup	6 cups	
Sour cream	1 cup	6 cups	Portion ¼ cup each of guacamole and sour cream into individual containers and arrange on plate. Garnish plate with 1 lime twist.
Lime slice twists, fresh	4	24	

Portion: 16 ounces
Nutritional Data/Portion: Calories 760, Protein 46 g, Fat 41 g, Carbohydrate 58 g, Cholesterol 120 mg, Sodium 1,832 mg

For a **FAST FACTS VIA FAX** copy of this recipe, call 1-800-223-3755 and enter Business Tool 2523.

Lime juice is an excellent source of vitamin C. Persian limes are most readily found in the U.S., followed by Florida's Key limes. Key limes are smaller, rounder, and more yellow than green.

Avocados, also known as alligator pears, were first grown in America by horticulturist Henry Perine near Miami, Florida, in 1833. Although Mexican Americans used them to make breads and guacamole, avocados were not grown commercially in America until the turn of the 20th century.

This chicken salad recipe works great on or off bread. Use it as a lunch entree on a bed of lettuce or to accompany a fruit plate.

Neiman Marcus Chicken Salad Sandwich

Inspired by the original recipe created by Neiman Marcus's own Helen Corbitt back in 1955, this elegant though incredibly simple recipe continues to be the benchmark for chicken salad. The secret to its richness is the heavy cream.

Speed-Scratch   *Kid Friendly*   *Line Service*   *Takeout*

	INGREDIENT	QUANTITY		METHOD
		4 servings	24 servings	
1	Tyson Fully Cooked Diced White Fryer Meat, 1-inch dice, frozen	1 lb.	6 lb.	Cover tightly and slack in cooler between 32° and 36°F prior to use.
2	Apple cider vinegar	1 tbsp.	⅓ cup	Place chicken in bowl. Sprinkle over chicken and toss well.
3	Celery, fresh, diced (p. 88)	⅓ cup	2 cups	Add to chicken.
4	Mayonnaise	⅔ cup	4 cups	Combine in separate bowl and mix thoroughly. Pour over chicken mixture and toss well. Cover and chill below 40°F to hold.
	Heavy cream	3 tbsp.	1 cup	
	White pepper, fine	⅛ tsp.	¾ tsp.	
5	Sourdough bread slices	8	48	*To assemble single serving:* Place 1 slice of bread on flat work surface. Top with 1 lettuce leaf and ¾ cup chicken salad. Close sandwich with second slice of bread and cut in half diagonally. Arrange on plate. Garnish plate with 1 grape cluster and 1 strawberry.
	Boston lettuce leaves, fresh	4	24	
	Red grape clusters, seedless, fresh	4	24	
	Strawberries, whole, fresh	4	24	

Portion: 8 ounces
Nutritional Data/Portion: Calories 460, Protein 37 g, Fat 19 g, Carbohydrate 36 g, Cholesterol 110 mg, Sodium 650 mg

For a *FAST FACTS VIA FAX* copy of this recipe, call 1-800-223-3755 and enter Business Tool 2518.

Submitted by George Upton
Motorola Hospitality Group
Schaumburg, Ill.

Char-Grilled Chicken Wrap with Black Bean Relish

Smoky chipotle peppers make the signature black bean relish a great match for char-grilled chicken breast filets.

INGREDIENT	QUANTITY 4 servings	24 servings	METHOD
1 Tyson Ready-to-Cook Tenderpressed™ Savory Chicken Breast Filets, 3-oz., frozen	4	24	Char-grill over high heat for 4 to 6 minutes on each side or until chicken is no longer pink. Remove from grill. Keep warm above 140°F.
2 *Black Bean Relish*			
Black beans, canned, drained	1½ cups	9 cups	Place 3 cups black beans in food processor bowl and process until pureed. (Process ½ cup black beans for smaller quantity.) Combine remaining ingredients in separate bowl. Add bean puree and mix thoroughly. Cover and chill to hold.
Tomatoes, fresh, diced	½ cup	3 cups	
Green chiles, chopped, canned	2½ tbsp.	1 cup	
Chipotle peppers, dried, reconstituted in boiling water, chopped	1½ tsp.	3 tbsp.	
Cumin, ground	¾ tsp.	1½ tbsp.	
Chili powder, light	¾ tsp.	1½ tbsp.	
Sour cream	2 tbsp.	¾ cup	
Salt	½ tsp.	1 tbsp.	
3 Tyson Mexican Original® Honey Wheat Wraps, room temperature	4	24	*To assemble single serving:* Place 1 wrap on flat work surface. Spread with ½ cup black bean relish.
Green leaf lettuce, fresh, shredded	4 cups	24 cups	Layer 1 cup lettuce, 3 tomato slices, and ¼ cup onions across center of wrap. Slice 1 chicken breast filet into thin strips and arrange over top.
Tomato slices, thin, fresh	12	72	
Red onions, fresh, slivered	1 cup	6 cups	Fold both sides of wrap over filling. Then fold lower end of wrap over filling and roll closed, keeping ingredients tightly packed. Slice in half diagonally and arrange on plate.
Salsa, thick-and-chunky, mild, commercially prepared	1 cup	6 cups	
Sour cream	¼ cup	1½ cups	Portion ¼ cup salsa into individual container. Top with 1 tablespoon sour cream and place on plate. Garnish plate with 1 parsley sprig.
Parsley sprigs, fresh	4	24	

Serve with freshly fried plantain chips.

Portion: 14 ounces plus 2 ounces sauce
Nutritional Data/Portion, Calories 550, Protein 34 g, Fat 14 g, Carbohydrate 75 g, Cholesterol 40 mg, Sodium 1,400 mg

For a **FAST FACTS VIA FAX**™ copy of this recipe, call 1-800-223-3755 and enter Business Tool 2514.

Chipotle peppers are dried, smoked jalapeño peppers with wrinkled dark-brown skin and a smoky, sweet flavor. Chipotles are packed dried, pickled, and canned. Most are used as ingredients in cooking, but pickled chipotles are sometimes eaten as appetizers.

Remove the stems from chipotle peppers before reconstituting, and make sure the peppers are soft before using them.

The black bean relish used in this sandwich also makes an excellent dip for tortilla chips.

A signature black bean recipe may be substituted for canned black beans in the relish.

HOW TO FOLD A WRAP
1) Layer ingredients across the center of the wrap.
2) Fold in both sides of the wrap.
3) Roll the wrap from the bottom to the top, keeping the ingredients tightly packed.

Submitted by Bonnie B. Severance
North Loup Scotia Schools
North Loup, Neb.

Honey Chicken Rollup

Back-of-the-house staff will smile at the simplicity of this recipe, but patrons of all ages will smile while they order this fun wrap that appeals to the kid in everyone.

For an upscale variation of this recipe, use half of a 4-ounce Tyson Homestyle Crusted Breast Filet in place of a tenderloin.

Honey should be stored in a tightly sealed container and will keep in a cool, dry place for up to a year. It crystallizes when refrigerated, but can easily be reliquefied by microwaving at 100 percent power for about 30 seconds.

INGREDIENT	QUANTITY 4 servings	24 servings	METHOD
1 Tyson Ready-to-Cook Original Breaded Chicken Tenderloins, frozen	8	48	Deep-fry at 350°F for 2½ minutes or until chicken is no longer pink. Remove from fryer and drain. Keep warm above 140°F.
2 Tyson Mexican Original® Flour Tortillas, 6-inch, warm	8	48	*To assemble single serving:* Place 2 tortillas on flat work surface and brush with honey.
Honey	as needed	as needed	Place 1 chicken tenderloin vertically in center of each tortilla. Fold lower end of tortillas up over tenderloins. Then fold sides over tenderloins, leaving top open with part of tenderloins visible. Place on plate, folded side up.
Honey-Dijon salad dressing, commercially prepared	½ cup	3 cups	
Barbecue sauce, smoky, commercially prepared	½ cup	3 cups	
Parsley sprigs, fresh	4	24	Portion 2 tablespoons of each dipping sauce into individual containers and place on plate. Garnish plate with 1 parsley sprig.

Portion: 5 ounces plus 1 ounce each sauce
Nutritional Data/Portion: Calories 330, Protein 16 g, Fat 8 g, Carbohydrate 48 g, Cholesterol 25 mg, Sodium 1,010 mg

For a **FAST FACTS VIA FAX** copy of this recipe, call 1-800-223-3755 and enter Business Tool 2511.

Garden Chicken Sandwich

Veggie lovers will love this! Layers of fresh tomatoes, roasted red bell peppers, red onions, and grilled eggplant accompany a juicy grilled chicken breast filet, all between slices of crunchy Italian ciabatta.

Submitted by MeLissa Alkinburgh
Marsh Supermarkets
Indianapolis, Ind.

A crusty Italian loaf may be substituted for the ciabatta.

Ciabatta is a traditional flat bread from Italy's Lake Como region. This short, stubby bread has a crusty exterior and a porous, chewy interior that resembles Swiss cheese in appearance. The word ciabatta *means "slipper."*

This sandwich may also be grilled in a skillet or on a sandwich grill.

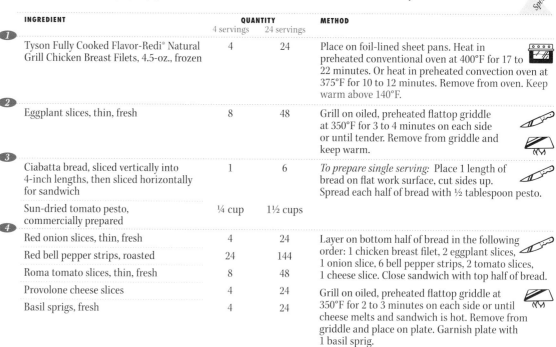

INGREDIENT	QUANTITY 4 servings	24 servings	METHOD
1 Tyson Fully Cooked Flavor-Redi® Natural Grill Chicken Breast Filets, 4.5-oz., frozen	4	24	Place on foil-lined sheet pans. Heat in preheated conventional oven at 400°F for 17 to 22 minutes. Or heat in preheated convection oven at 375°F for 10 to 12 minutes. Remove from oven. Keep warm above 140°F.
2 Eggplant slices, thin, fresh	8	48	Grill on oiled, preheated flattop griddle at 350°F for 3 to 4 minutes on each side or until tender. Remove from griddle and keep warm.
3 Ciabatta bread, sliced vertically into 4-inch lengths, then sliced horizontally for sandwich	1	6	*To prepare single serving:* Place 1 length of bread on flat work surface, cut sides up. Spread each half of bread with ½ tablespoon pesto.
Sun-dried tomato pesto, commercially prepared	¼ cup	1½ cups	
4 Red onion slices, thin, fresh	4	24	Layer on bottom half of bread in the following order: 1 chicken breast filet, 2 eggplant slices, 1 onion slice, 6 bell pepper strips, 2 tomato slices, 1 cheese slice. Close sandwich with top half of bread.
Red bell pepper strips, roasted	24	144	
Roma tomato slices, thin, fresh	8	48	
Provolone cheese slices	4	24	Grill on oiled, preheated flattop griddle at 350°F for 2 to 3 minutes on each side or until cheese melts and sandwich is hot. Remove from griddle and place on plate. Garnish plate with 1 basil sprig.
Basil sprigs, fresh	4	24	

Serve with chilled pasta salad.

Portion: 14 ounces
Nutritional Data/Portion: Calories 550, Protein 38 g, Fat 21 g, Carbohydrate 52 g, Cholesterol 80 mg, Sodium 1,050 mg

For a **FAST FACTS VIA FAX** copy of this recipe, call 1-800-223-3755 and enter Business Tool 2550.

Chicken Muffaletta

The muffaletta is a hero-style specialty deli meat sandwich that was invented in 1906 at the Central Grocery in New Orleans. The secret of its flavor and long-standing popularity lies in the "olive salad" relish. This interpretation features a crispy beer-battered chicken breast filet served on a kaiser roll, with olive relish of course.

An alternate way to prepare this sandwich is shown in the photo. Use muffaletta rounds and several chicken breasts to make one large sandwich. Slice in wedges, and wrap for customers to grab and go.

INGREDIENT	QUANTITY		METHOD
	4 servings	24 servings	
Tyson Ready-to-Cook Breaded Original Natural Chicken Breast Filets, 4-oz., frozen	4	24	Deep-fry at 350°F for 3½ to 4 minutes or until chicken is no longer pink. Remove from fryer and drain. Keep warm above 140°F.
Olive Relish			
Green salad olives, canned, drained	1 cup	6 cups	Combine in food processor bowl and pulse until coarsely chopped. Remove from processor bowl.
Black olives, sliced, canned, drained	½ cup	3 cups	
Garlic, minced, commercially prepared	2 tsp.	¼ cup	
Oregano leaves, dried	1 tsp.	1½ tbsp.	
Mayonnaise	3 tbsp.	1 cup	Add to olive mixture and mix thoroughly. Cover and chill to hold.
Kaiser rolls, sliced horizontally for sandwich, grilled	4	24	*To assemble single serving:* Place 1 roll on flat work surface, grilled sides up. Layer bottom half of roll with 1 cheese slice and 1 chicken breast filet. Top with ¼ cup olive relish.
Provolone cheese slices	4	24	
Oregano sprigs, fresh	4	24	Close sandwich with top half of roll and slice in half. Arrange on plate. Garnish plate with 1 oregano sprig.
			Serve with spicy battered onion rings.

Portion: 9 ounces
Nutritional Data/Portion: Calories 380, Protein 23 g, Fat 15 g, Carbohydrate 41 g, Cholesterol 50 mg, Sodium 1,790 mg

For a **FAST FACTS VIA FAX** copy of this recipe, call 1-800-223-3755 and enter Business Tool 2370.

Sushi rice is a sticky short-grained rice that is slightly harder in texture than rice used in other dishes.

Cabbage, first mentioned in Chinese literature around 500 B.C., is a wide and varied food family that includes Brussels sprouts, broccoli, cauliflower, and kale.

Napa cabbage has many names, including Chinese cabbage, hakusai, celery cabbage, wong bok, and Peking cabbage.

Asian Chicken Cone

The Pacific Rim gets hold of the tortilla wrap and turns it into a sushi-style cone filled with thin slices of grilled chicken mixed with sweet rice, cabbage, carrots, and celery. The house stir-fry sauce will round out this Asian-style wrap.

INGREDIENT	QUANTITY 4 servings	24 servings	METHOD
1 Tyson Fully Cooked Flavor-Redi® Natural Grill Chicken Breast Filets, 3-oz., frozen	4	24	Cover tightly and slack in cooler between 32° and 36°F prior to use.
2 Napa cabbage, fresh, shredded	2 cups	12 cups	Combine in bowl and mix thoroughly. Cover and chill to hold.
Carrots, fresh, julienne (p. 88)	1 cup	6 cups	
Celery, fresh, julienne	1 cup	6 cups	
Green onions, fresh, chopped	½ cup	3 cups	
3 Sweet or sushi rice, cooked	2 cups	12 cups	Combine in separate bowl. Julienne chicken and add to rice. Mix thoroughly. Cover and chill below 40°F to hold.
Stir-fry sauce, commercially prepared	¾ cup	4½ cups	
4 Tyson Mexican Original® Asian Ginger Wraps, room temperature	4	24	*To prepare single serving:* Place 1 wrap on flat work surface and slice in half. Roll half into cone shape measuring 2½ to 3 inches in diameter across the opening.
Carrot curls, fresh	4	24	
Green onion brushes, fresh (p. 125)	4	24	

Holding cone with point down, portion ¼ cup cabbage mixture into cone. Top with ½ cup chicken mixture and an additional ¼ cup cabbage mixture. Place cone, seam side down, on plate. Repeat process for remaining half of wrap.

Microwave on high for 25 to 35 seconds or until thoroughly heated. Garnish plate with 1 carrot curl and 1 green onion brush.

Serve with chilled gingered peaches.

Portion: 14 ounces
Nutritional Data/Portion: Calories 600, Protein 32 g, Fat 13 g, Carbohydrate 87 g, Cholesterol 50 mg, Sodium 640 mg

For a *FAST FACTS VIA FAX*™ copy of this recipe, call 1-800-223-3755 and enter Business Tool 2500.

Submitted by Cristo Christu
Pinellas County School Food Service
Largo, Fla.

Grilled Chicken Gyro

The classic gyro might be considered the original wrap. It is a Greek specialty of seasoned minced lamb shaped around a vertical spit, then grilled, sliced thin, and served in a piece of pita bread with onions and cucumber-yogurt sauce. The concept translates beautifully with chicken.

INGREDIENT	QUANTITY 4 servings	24 servings	METHOD
1 Tyson Ready-to-Cook Tenderpressed™ Lemon Herb Chicken Breast Filets, 5-oz., frozen	4	24	Char-grill over high heat for 5 to 6 minutes on each side or until chicken is no longer pink. Or grill on oiled, preheated flattop griddle at 350°F for 6½ to 7½ minutes on each side. Remove from grill and slice each breast filet into 6 strips. Keep warm above 140°F.
2 *Cucumber-Yogurt Sauce*			
Yogurt, plain, drained	½ cup	3 cups	Combine in bowl and mix thoroughly. Cover and chill to hold.
Cucumbers, peeled, grated, pressed dry	1 tbsp.	⅓ cup	
Olive oil	½ tbsp.	3 tbsp.	
Lemon juice, fresh	½ tbsp.	3 tbsp.	
Parsley, fresh, minced (p. 39)	1 tsp.	2 tbsp.	
Garlic, fresh, minced	¼ tsp.	½ tbsp.	
Salt	⅛ tsp.	¾ tsp.	
Dill weed, dried	⅛ tsp.	¾ tsp.	
3 Pita bread, nonpocket, 7-inch rounds, warm	4	24	*To assemble single serving:* Place 1 pita on flat work surface. Layer ingredients across center of pita in the following order: ⅓ cup lettuce, 1 tablespoon onions, 6 chicken strips, 2 tablespoons cucumber-yogurt sauce, ¼ cup tomatoes.
Iceberg lettuce, fresh, shredded	1⅓ cups	8 cups	
Red onions, fresh, slivered	¼ cup	1½ cups	
Tomatoes, fresh, seeded, diced	1 cup	6 cups	Fold sides of pita up over filling and secure with club picks. Arrange on plate. Garnish plate with 3 olives and 1 dill sprig.
Club picks	as needed	as needed	
Kalamata olives, whole, canned, drained	12	72	
Dill sprigs, fresh	4	24	*Serve with tabbouleh.*

Portion: 10 ounces
Nutritional Data/Portion: Calories 370, Protein 28 g, Fat 8 g, Carbohydrate 47 g, Cholesterol 75 mg, Sodium 740 mg

For a **FAST FACTS VIA FAX** copy of this recipe, call 1-800-223-3755 and enter Business Tool 2516.

Yogurt is thought to have first been made by accident thousands of years ago among nomadic Balkan tribes. Balkans, particularly Bulgarians, have a remarkable number of people who live to be 100 or older. Coincidentally, their diets still consist primarily of yogurt.

Instructions for the production of yogurt were part of the first written law code established in Japan in the early 8th century.

HOW TO MAKE A GREEN ONION BRUSH
Trim off the roots of the bulb, then measure 5 to 6 inches up from the bulb and cut off the remaining greens. Slice the green part of the onion into thin strips and soak in ice water until the strips curl.

Submitted by John McKeever III
McKeever's Tavern
N. Wales, Pa.

Commercially prepared
Parmesan or Parmesan
peppercorn dressing may
be substituted for the
made-from-scratch
version featured here.

Red Pepper Parmesan Chicken Wrap

Crispy fried chicken tenderloins are accented by cool lettuce and peppery dressing for a flavorful dining experience.

INGREDIENT	QUANTITY		METHOD
	4 servings	24 servings	
1 *Roasted Red Pepper Parmesan Dressing*			
Red bell peppers, fresh, chopped	¼ cup	1 cup	Combine in food processor bowl and puree until smooth. Pour into shallow metal pan and roast in preheated conventional oven at 400°F for 7 to 8 minutes or until mixture bubbles. (Roast smaller quantity for 5 to 6 minutes.) Remove from oven. Cover and chill before using.
Onions, fresh, chopped (p. 175)	1 tbsp.	¼ cup	
Garlic, fresh, chopped	¼ tsp.	1 tsp.	
Olive oil	¼ tsp.	1 tsp.	
2 Mayonnaise	½ cup	2 cups	Combine in bowl. Add chilled red pepper mixture and mix thoroughly. Cover and chill to hold.
Milk, whole	2 tbsp.	½ cup	
Mustard, Dijon	½ tbsp.	2 tbsp.	
Parmesan cheese, grated	½ tbsp.	2 tbsp.	
Sugar, granulated	¼ tsp.	1 tsp.	
Basil, fresh, minced	½ tsp.	2 tsp.	
Salt	¹⁄₁₆ tsp.	¼ tsp.	
Black pepper, coarse	⅛ tsp.	½ tsp.	
Cayenne pepper, ground	pinch	⅛ tsp.	
3 Tyson Ready-to-Cook Original Breaded Chicken Tenderloins, frozen	12	72	Deep-fry at 350°F for 2½ minutes or until chicken is no longer pink. Remove from fryer and drain. Keep warm above 140°F.
4 Tyson Mexican Original® Herb Garlic Wraps, room temperature (p. 121)	4	24	*To assemble single serving:* Place 1 wrap on flat work surface. Layer ingredients across center of wrap in the following order: ½ cup lettuce, 2 tablespoons salsa, 2 tablespoons roasted pepper dressing, ½ cup cheese, 3 chicken tenderloins.
Iceberg lettuce, fresh, shredded	2 cups	12 cups	
Salsa, hot, commercially prepared	½ cup	3 cups	
Monterey Jack cheese, shredded	2 cups	12 cups	Fold both sides of wrap over filling. Then fold lower end of wrap over filling and roll closed, keeping ingredients tightly packed.
Club picks	8	48	
Parsley sprigs, fresh	4	24	

Secure with 2 club picks and slice in half diagonally. Arrange on plate. Garnish plate with 1 parsley sprig.

Serve with lattice-cut french fries.

Portion: 12 ounces
Nutritional Data/Portion: Calories 790, Protein 40 g, Fat 38 g, Carbohydrate 74 g, Cholesterol 95 mg, Sodium 1,830 mg

For a **FAST FACTS VIA FAX**™ copy of this recipe, call 1-800-223-3755 and enter Business Tool 2512.

Peppery Popcorn Chicken Pita

A completely new concept for pita eaters. Crispy, peppery bite-size popcorn chicken pieces are nestled among fresh vegetables with spicy mustard-mayonnaise sauce.

Line Service *Takeout*

INGREDIENT	QUANTITY 4 servings	24 servings	METHOD
1 Tyson Ready-to-Cook Homestyle Pepper Popcorn Chicken Bites™, frozen	1 lb.	6 lb.	Deep-fry at 350°F for 3 to 3½ minutes or until chicken is no longer pink. Remove from fryer and drain. Keep warm above 140°F.
2 *Mustard-Mayonnaise Sauce*			
Mayonnaise	½ cup	3 cups	Combine in bowl and mix thoroughly. Cover and chill to hold.
Mustard, Dijon	2 tbsp.	¾ cup	
Cayenne pepper sauce	1 tbsp.	⅓ cup	
Garlic, fresh, minced	1 tsp.	2 tbsp.	
3 Romaine lettuce, fresh, shredded	5 cups	30 cups	Combine in separate bowl and toss well. Cover and chill to hold.
Green bell peppers, fresh, diced (p. 88)	½ cup	3 cups	
Roma tomatoes, fresh, seeded, diced	½ cup	3 cups	
Onions, fresh, minced	1 tbsp.	⅓ cup	
4 Pita pocket bread, 6-inch rounds, warm	4	24	*To assemble single serving:* Place 1 pita on flat work surface. Slice through center of pita and separate each half to form a pocket.
Romaine lettuce leaves, fresh	8	48	
Parsley sprigs, fresh	4	24	

Combine 4 ounces chicken and 1 cup lettuce mixture with 2 rounded tablespoons mustard-mayonnaise sauce in bowl and toss well.

Line each pita half with 1 lettuce leaf. Portion filling into pockets and arrange on plate. Garnish plate with 1 parsley sprig.

Serve with french-fried potatoes.

Portion: 13 ounces
Nutritional Data/Portion: Calories 590, Protein 26 g, Fat 26 g, Carbohydrate 64 g, Cholesterol 35 mg, Sodium 1,530 mg

For a **FAST FACTS VIA FAX**™ copy of this recipe, call 1-800-223-3755 and enter Business Tool 2520.

The pita, commonly referred to as "pocket bread," is a Middle Eastern flat bread made of white or whole-wheat flour. Pita rounds are popular in this country because they split horizontally to form pockets that make them a natural for sandwiches. In their native countries, pitas are served as bread with meals, or cut into wedges and used as dippers for dishes such as baba ghanoush and hummus.

For a milder version of this recipe, use Original Popcorn Chicken Bites and omit the onions and bell peppers.

Although most people think of pita bread as a Greek specialty, historians trace it back to Turkish and other Arabic cultures that taught the Greeks how to make flat bread. ◦

To make this pita "patron friendly" for takeout, package unbaked pita and provide final baking instructions. ◦

Smoky Pesto Red Pepper Chicken Pocket

Diced chicken tenderloins are mixed with roasted red bell peppers, smoked provolone cheese, and creamy pesto mayonnaise, then heated until the flavors meld and melt together.

Speed-Scratch

Takeout

INGREDIENT	4 servings	24 servings	METHOD
❶ Tyson Fully Cooked Diced Chicken Tenderloins, ¾-inch dice, frozen	1 lb.	6 lb.	Cover tightly and slack in cooler between 32° and 36°F prior to use.
❷ Green onions, fresh, chopped	1 cup	5 cups	Combine in bowl and add chicken.
Red bell peppers, roasted, chopped (p. 66)	1 cup	5 cups	
Black olives, sliced, canned, drained	1 cup	5 cups	
Provolone cheese, smoked, shredded	1 cup	5 cups	
❸ *Pesto Mayonnaise*			
Basil pesto, commercially prepared	½ cup	3 cups	Combine in separate bowl and mix thoroughly. Add to chicken mixture and toss well.
Mayonnaise	¼ cup	1½ cups	Cover and chill below 40°F to hold.
Lemon juice, fresh	½ tbsp.	3 tbsp.	
❹ Pita pocket bread, 6-inch rounds	4	24	*To prepare single serving:* Place 1 pita on flat work surface. Slice through center of pita and separate each half to form a pocket. Portion ¾ cup chicken mixture into each half. Transfer to sheet pans.
Green leaf lettuce leaves, fresh	4	24	
Tomato slices, fresh	4	24	
Cucumber slices, fresh	4	24	Bake in preheated conventional oven† at 350°F for 7 to 10 minutes or until thoroughly heated. Remove from oven and arrange on plate.
Red onions, fresh, slivered	¼ cup	1½ cups	

Garnish plate with "salad": Layer 1 lettuce leaf with 1 tomato slice and 1 cucumber slice. Top with 1 tablespoon onions.

Portion: 12 ounces

Nutritional Data/Portion: Calories 680, Protein 46 g, Fat 33 g, Carbohydrate 51 g, Cholesterol 95 mg, Sodium 1,720 mg

†Convection oven not recommended.

For a **FAST FACTS VIA FAX** copy of this recipe, call 1-800-223-3755 and enter Business Tool 2363.

Submitted by Barbara Ball
225 Cafe
Chicago, Ill.

Pollo Spinachi Sandwich

Fresh spinach sautéed in olive oil with garlic and red pepper makes this tasty Parmesan chicken sandwich a real standout.

Line Service

INGREDIENT	QUANTITY 4 servings	24 servings	METHOD
1 Tyson Ready-to-Cook Flavor-Redi® Italian Chicken Breast Filets, 5-oz., frozen	4	24	Season chicken breast filets and dredge in flour. Shake off excess.
Salt	1 tsp.	2 tbsp.	
Black pepper, coarse	1 tsp.	2 tbsp.	
Flour, all-purpose	as needed	as needed	
2 Eggs, large, whole	2	12	Combine in bowl and whisk together until well blended. Dip chicken breast filets in egg mixture. Drain off excess.
Parmesan cheese, grated	1½ tbsp.	½ cup	
3 Olive oil	¼ cup	1½ cups	Heat in skillet or braising pan over medium-high heat. Add chicken and sauté for 3 to 4 minutes on each side or until chicken is no longer pink. Remove from heat. Keep warm above 140°F.
4 *Spinach Topping*			
Olive oil	¼ cup	1½ cups	Heat in saucepan or stockpot over medium-high heat.
5 Garlic, fresh, minced	1½ tbsp.	½ cup	Add to oil and sauté for 30 to 45 seconds or until garlic begins to brown. (Sauté smaller quantity for 15 to 30 seconds.)
Red pepper, crushed, dried	½ tsp.	1 tbsp.	
Salt	½ tsp.	1 tbsp.	
Black pepper, coarse	¼ tsp.	½ tbsp.	
6 Spinach, fresh, stemmed, packed	4 cups	24 cups	Add to garlic mixture and toss until spinach begins to wilt. Remove from heat and keep warm.
7 *Dipping Sauce*			
Chicken broth, canned	1½ cups	9 cups	Combine in saucepan and mix thoroughly. Bring to boil over high heat. Reduce heat and simmer for 20 to 30 minutes or until liquid is reduced by half. (Simmer smaller quantity for 5 to 6 minutes.) Remove from heat and keep warm.
Lemon juice, fresh	3 tbsp.	1 cup	
White wine, dry	3 tbsp.	1 cup	
Rosemary leaves, dried	1½ tsp.	3 tbsp.	
Capers, rinsed, drained	1½ tbsp.	⅓ cup	
8 Kaiser rolls, seeded, split horizontally for sandwich, grilled	4	24	*To assemble single serving:* Place 1 roll on flat work surface, grilled sides up.
Rosemary sprigs, fresh	4	24	Dip 1 chicken breast filet in sauce and place on bottom half of roll. Top chicken with ⅓ cup spinach mixture.
			Close sandwich with top half of roll. Slice in half and arrange on plate. Garnish plate with 1 rosemary sprig.
			Serve with roasted garlic mashed potatoes.

Portion: 9 ounces
Nutritional Data/Portion: Calories 590, Protein 42 g, Fat 26 g, Carbohydrate 44 g, Cholesterol 185 mg, Sodium 1,760 mg

For a **FAST FACTS VIA FAX** copy of this recipe, call 1-800-223-3755 and enter Business Tool 2551.

Thanks to a certain cartoon hero, spinach is viewed by many as a rich source of nutrition. And while it does contain large amounts of iron, vitamin A, vitamin C, and calcium, it also contains oxalic acid, which inhibits the body from absorbing most of the iron and calcium. This same acid is also responsible for the distinctive flavor of spinach.

Recipe shown on opposite page.

Submitted by Jeffrey Dunham
The Grove Grill
Memphis, Tenn.

Balsamic Chicken and Sweet Pepper Melt

Focaccia is an appropriate bread choice for this Italian-style melt made with provolone cheese, roasted bell peppers, balsamic vinegar, garlic, and basil.

Lighter Fare

INGREDIENT	QUANTITY		METHOD
	4 servings	24 servings	
Tyson Fully Cooked Flavor-Redi® Smoked Chicken Breast Filets, 3.75-oz., frozen	4	24	*To prepare single serving:* Place 1 chicken breast filet on oiled, preheated 350°F flattop griddle. Cover and heat thoroughly.
Focaccia bread rounds, 6-inch, sliced in half vertically, then sliced horizontally for sandwich	2	12	Brush outside surfaces of half of the focaccia round with oil and place on griddle, oiled side down. (Reserve other half for another sandwich.) Place 2 cheese slices on bottom half of bread and top with 3 tomato slices. Place 1 cheese slice on top half of bread. When chicken is thoroughly heated, place breast filet on tomatoes.
Olive oil	as needed	as needed	
Provolone cheese slices	12	72	
Tomato slices, fresh	12	72	
Red bell peppers, roasted, julienne (p. 66)	1 cup	6 cups	While chicken and bread are heating, add ¼ cup red bell peppers, ¼ cup yellow bell peppers, 1 tablespoon green onions, and ½ teaspoon garlic to oiled griddle and toss well to combine. Grill for 2 to 4 minutes or until tender-crisp.
Yellow bell peppers, roasted, julienne	1 cup	6 cups	
Green onions, fresh, sliced	¼ cup	1½ cups	
Garlic, fresh, minced	2 tsp.	¼ cup	
Balsamic vinegar	½ cup	3 cups	Add 2 tablespoons vinegar, 1 tablespoon basil, 1 teaspoon parsley, ⅛ teaspoon salt, and ⅛ teaspoon pepper to bell pepper mixture and mix thoroughly. Remove from grill and place on chicken.
Basil, fresh, chopped	¼ cup	1½ cups	
Parsley, flat-leaf, fresh, chopped	1½ tbsp.	½ cup	
Salt	½ tsp.	1 tbsp.	Close sandwich with top half of bread. Remove from griddle and arrange on plate. Garnish plate with 1 basil sprig.
Black pepper, coarse	½ tsp.	1 tbsp.	
Basil sprigs, fresh	4	24	

Serve with pasta salad.

Portion: 15 ounces
Nutritional Data/Portion: Calories 560, Protein 46 g, Fat 21 g, Carbohydrate 46 g, Cholesterol 105 mg, Sodium 1,520 mg

For a **FAST FACTS VIA FAX**™ copy of this recipe, call 1-800-223-3755 and enter Business Tool 2505.

This sandwich is best when made to order. It is not particularly well suited for holding or reheating.

True balsamic vinegar comes exclusively from the Modena and Reggio regions of Italy, where it has been painstakingly made from white Trebbiano grapes for a thousand years. The vinegar is aged in barrels and moved to consecutively smaller ones as evaporation reduces its volume. When available, the best examples are sold for as much as $30 per ounce. The taste of true balsamics has been compared to old port, aged Bordeaux, and classic brown sauce.

This sandwich can also be finished in a skillet as pictured on opposite page.

*"I have the simplest tastes.
I am always satisfied with the best."*
Oscar Wilde

Submitted by Daniel Pimm
Pioneer College Caterers at
Northwest College
Kirkland, Wash.

*Anaheim chiles, named
after the California city,
are among the most
commonly available chiles
in America. These long,
narrow chiles, which are
usually medium green in
color, can be stuffed (chiles
rellenos) and are also used
in salsas. Red chiles in this
family, sometimes called
Colorado chiles, are often
dried and used to make
ristras, which are hand-
strung ropes of chiles.*

*Canned green chiles may
be substituted for the
Anaheim peppers.*

RED PEPPER PICO DE GALLO

	4 servings	24 servings
Red bell peppers, fresh, diced	½ cup	3 cups
Onions, fresh, diced	½ cup	3 cups
Anaheim peppers, fresh, chopped	2 tbsp.	¾ cup
Garlic, fresh, minced	1 tbsp.	⅓ cup
Lime juice, fresh	3 tbsp.	1 cup
Salt	1 tsp.	2 tbsp.
Black pepper, coarse	½ tsp.	1 tbsp.

Combine in bowl and mix
thoroughly. Cover and chill
to hold.

Pollo Con Arroz Burrito

The translation "chicken with rice" just doesn't do it justice. Made with spicy fajita strips, Anaheim peppers, Mexican rice, and hot pepper cheese all rolled in a cheese jalapeño tortilla, this dish could only be menued by its Spanish name.

INGREDIENT	QUANTITY		METHOD
	4 servings	24 servings	
1 Tyson Ready-to-Cook Flavor-Redi® Texas-Style Chicken Breast Fajita Pieces, frozen	12 oz.	4½ lb.	Cover tightly and slack in cooler between 32° and 36°F prior to use.
			Grill on oiled, preheated flattop griddle at 350°F for 4 to 5 minutes or until chicken is no longer pink. Remove from griddle. Keep warm above 140°F.
2 Vegetable oil	1 tbsp.	⅓ cup	Heat in saucepan or stockpot over medium-high heat.
3 Onions, fresh, chopped (p. 175)	½ cup	3 cups	Add to oil and sauté for 4 to 5 minutes or until tender-crisp. (Sauté smaller quantity for 2 to 3 minutes.)
Anaheim peppers, fresh, minced	2 tbsp.	¾ cup	
Garlic, fresh, minced	1 tbsp.	⅓ cup	
4 Mexican rice blend, commercially prepared	½ cup (dry)	3 cups (dry)	Add to vegetable mixture and bring to boil over high heat. Cover and reduce heat. Simmer for 20 minutes or until rice is tender. Remove from heat. Cover and chill to hold.
Seasoning from packet enclosed in commercial rice blend	2 tbsp.	¾ cup	
Salt	1 tsp.	2 tbsp.	
Water, cold	1 cup	6 cups	
5 Tyson Mexican Original® Cheese Jalapeño Wraps, room temperature (p. 121)	4	24	*To prepare single serving:* Place 1 wrap on flat work surface. Layer ½ cup rice mixture and ¼ cup cheese across center of wrap. Top with 3 ounces chicken.
Hot pepper cheese, shredded	1 cup	6 cups	
			Fold both sides of wrap over filling. Then fold lower end of wrap over filling and roll closed, keeping ingredients tightly packed.
			Microwave on high for 30 to 45 seconds or until thoroughly heated. Slice in half diagonally and arrange on plate.
6 Sour cream	1 cup	6 cups	Portion ¼ cup each of sour cream and pico de gallo into individual containers and place on plate. Garnish plate with 3 olives and 2 cilantro sprigs.
Red Pepper Pico de Gallo (see recipe)	1 cup	6 cups	
Black olives, whole, pitted, canned, drained	12	72	
Cilantro sprigs, fresh	8	48	*Serve with refried beans.*

Portion: 12 ounces plus 2 ounces each condiment
Nutritional Data/Portion: Calories 660, Protein 39 g, Fat 28 g, Carbohydrate 65 g, Cholesterol 95 mg, Sodium 2,368 mg

For a **FAST FACTS VIA FAX** copy of this recipe, call 1-800-223-3755 and enter Business Tool 2519.

"Peppers are a rainbow of good nutrition."
Lou Seibert Pappas

*Submitted by Patricia A. Bando
and Christopher Eiseman
Boston College
Chestnut Hill, Mass.*

*Wraps cater to highly
mobile and health-conscious
people who view them as full
meals with edible wrappers.
Wraps are not bound by
ethnicity or even menu
part—Italian, Asian, Middle
Eastern, or all-American
ingredients are comfortable
in wraps. And because
wraps are often assembled to
order, a perception of health
and freshness frequently
accompanies this fun-filled
sandwich form.*

Chicken Caesar Salad Wrap

Take the country's most popular salad and turn it into a portable meal. This wrap, submitted by Boston College where it is known as the B. Caesar Wrap, is a proven winner among students. It sells at a rate of 1,250 per day across the five restaurants that serve it. Taste it and see why.

Speed-Scratch Line Service Takeout

INGREDIENT	QUANTITY		METHOD
	4 servings	24 servings	
Tyson Fully Cooked Flavor-Redi® Grilled Chicken Tenderloins, frozen	12	72	Cover tightly and slack in cooler between 32° and 36°F prior to use.
Tyson Mexican Original® White Wraps, room temperature (p. 121)	4	24	*To assemble single serving:* Place 1 wrap on flat work surface.
Romaine lettuce, fresh, chopped	6 cups	36 cups	Combine 1½ cups lettuce, ⅓ cup cheese, 3 table-
Parmesan cheese, grated	1⅓ cups	8 cups	spoons salad dressing, and ⅓ cup croutons in bowl. Toss well, then arrange across
Caesar salad dressing, commercially prepared	¾ cup	4½ cups	center of wrap. Top with 3 chicken tenderloins.
Croutons, seasoned, commercially prepared	1⅓ cups	8 cups	Fold both sides of wrap over filling. Then fold lower end of wrap over filling and roll closed, keeping ingredients tightly packed. Slice in half diagonally and arrange on plate.

Serve with chilled mixed fruit.

Portion: 10 ounces
Nutritional Data/Portion: Calories 810, Protein 55 g, Fat 40 g, Carbohydrate 58 g, Cholesterol 115 mg, Sodium 2,350 mg

For a **FAST FACTS VIA FAX** copy of this recipe, call 1-800-223-3755 and enter Business Tool 2665.

Submitted by Alfred G. Wiederwohl
Peppermills–Your Family Restaurant
Napoleon, Ohio

Hoagies—also known as submarines, grinders, and po' boys—are typically made with small loaves of Italian or French bread. They can be adapted to include almost any combination of meats, vegetables, and cheeses.

Bogie's Chicken Hoagie

Unlike a bogey in golf, this sandwich is better than par for the course. The lemon pepper mayonnaise slaw gives the sandwich an extra punch that's perfect for someone who's just come from the 18th hole.

INGREDIENT	QUANTITY 4 servings	24 servings	METHOD
1 Tyson Ready-to-Cook Tenderpressed™ Savory Chicken Breast Filets, 6-oz., frozen	4	24	Grill on oiled, preheated flattop griddle at 350°F for approximately 4½ minutes on each side or until chicken is no longer pink. Remove from griddle and season with lemon pepper.
Lemon pepper	1 tsp.	2 tbsp.	
2 Bacon slices, crisp	8	48	Top each chicken breast filet with 2 slices bacon and 1 slice cheese. Keep warm above 140°F.
White cheddar cheese slices	4	24	
3 Butter, salted	2 tbsp.	½ cup	Heat in skillet or braising pan over medium-high heat.
4 Button mushrooms, fresh, sliced	1½ cups	9 cups	Add to butter and sauté for 6 to 8 minutes or until wilted. (Sauté smaller quantity for 2 to 3 minutes.) Remove from heat and keep warm.
Garlic, fresh, minced	1 tsp.	2 tbsp.	
5 *Lemon Pepper Mayonnaise*			
Mayonnaise	¼ cup	1½ cups	Combine in bowl and mix thoroughly. Cover and chill to hold.
Lemon pepper	1 tsp.	2 tbsp.	
Lemon juice, fresh	1 tsp.	2 tbsp.	
Salt	⅛ tsp.	¾ tsp.	
6 French rolls, 6-inch, sliced horizontally for sandwich, grilled	4	24	*To assemble single serving:* Place 1 roll on flat work surface, grilled sides up.
Iceberg lettuce, fresh, shredded	2 cups	12 cups	Combine ½ cup lettuce and 1 tablespoon lemon pepper mayonnaise in bowl. Toss well and arrange on bottom half of roll.
Tomato slices, thin, fresh	8	48	
Club picks	8	48	Layer 2 tomato slices and 1 chicken breast filet over lettuce. Top with 2 tablespoons mushrooms.
Lemon slice twists, fresh	4	24	
Parsley sprigs, fresh	4	24	

Close sandwich with top half of roll. Secure with 2 club picks and slice in half diagonally. Arrange on plate. Garnish plate with 1 lemon twist and 1 parsley sprig.

Serve with crinkle-cut potato chips and a kosher dill spear.

Portion: 13 ounces
Nutritional Data/Portion: Calories 810, Protein 58 g, Fat 36 g, Carbohydrate 66 g, Cholesterol 165 mg, Sodium 1,680 mg

For a **FAST FACTS VIA FAX** copy of this recipe, call 1-800-223-3755 and enter Business Tool 2549.

"Bread is the warmest, kindest of words.
Write it always with a capital letter, like your own name."
Anonymous

Submitted by Jon DeSormeau
Salisbury State University
Salisbury, Md.

Grilled Chicken and Portobello Wrap

Here's a rich, flavorful wrap that will satisfy any appetite. Creamy ranch dressing replaces the usual mayonnaise and adds a tangy touch to this savory wrap.

INGREDIENT	QUANTITY 4 servings	24 servings	METHOD
1 Tyson Ready-to-Cook Flavor-Redi® Texas-Style Chicken Breast Fajita Pieces, frozen	8 oz.	3 lb.	Cover tightly and slack in cooler between 32° and 36°F prior to use.
			Grill on oiled, preheated flattop griddle at 350°F for 4 to 5 minutes or until chicken is no longer pink. Remove from griddle. Keep warm above 140°F.
2 Portobello mushrooms, whole, fresh	4	24	Combine in bowl and toss well. Cover and marinate for 30 minutes. Drain and grill on oiled, preheated flattop griddle at 350°F for 2 to 3 minutes on each side or until tender. Remove from griddle and slice each mushroom into 5 strips. Keep warm.
Italian vinaigrette salad dressing, commercially prepared	½ cup	3 cups	
3 Red bell pepper strips, fresh, ½-inch-wide	20	120	Grill on oiled, preheated flattop griddle at 350°F for 2 to 3 minutes or until tender-crisp. Remove from griddle and keep warm.
4 Tyson Mexican Original® Cheese Jalapeño Wraps, room temperature (p. 121)	4	24	*To assemble single serving:* Place 1 wrap on flat work surface. Spread with ¼ cup dressing.
Ranch salad dressing, commercially prepared	1 cup	6 cups	Layer ingredients across center of wrap in the following order: 1 lettuce leaf, 5 mushroom strips, 5 bell pepper strips, 2 tablespoons green onions, 2 ounces chicken.
Green leaf lettuce leaves, fresh	4	24	
Green onions, fresh, sliced	½ cup	3 cups	
Red bell pepper flowers, fresh	4	24	Fold both sides of wrap over filling. Then fold lower end of wrap over filling and roll closed, keeping ingredients tightly packed. Slice in half diagonally and arrange on plate. Garnish plate with 1 red bell pepper flower.
			Serve with vinaigrette potato salad.

Portion: 14 ounces
Nutritional Data/Portion: Calories 730, Protein 23 g, Fat 50 g, Carbohydrate 53 g, Cholesterol 75 mg, Sodium 1,540 mg

For a **FAST FACTS VIA FAX**™ copy of this recipe, call 1-800-223-3755 and enter Business Tool 2515.

Portobello mushrooms are actually a large cousin of the common white mushroom. They can easily measure 6 inches in diameter, and the rich flavor and dense, meaty texture result from the loss of moisture that occurs when the mushroom grows and reaches maturity.

The American Mushroom Institute claims there are 38,000 varieties of mushrooms.

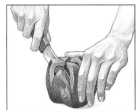

HOW TO MAKE A BELL PEPPER FLOWER

1) Trim the stem off of a firm pepper. On the tapered end of the pepper, cut out a five-pointed star.

2) Cut down from the bottom of the star points toward the stem end of the pepper, creating "petals."

3) Soak in ice water until the "petals" open, forming a "flower."

ℒegend has it that Buffalo Wings were born late one Friday night in 1964, when Teressa Bellissimo served a chicken special at her Anchor Bar & Restaurant near Buffalo, New York. When her son and a few of his college buddies came in after hours, she cooked up leftover wings, tossed them in clarified butter and cayenne pepper sauce, and served them with celery sticks and blue cheese dressing. The rest is history.⌐

BLACK BEAN, CHICKPEA, AND OLIVE SALAD

	4 servings	24 servings
Black beans, canned, rinsed, drained	1 cup	6 cups
Chickpeas, canned, rinsed, drained	1 cup	6 cups
Green olives, pimiento-stuffed, canned, drained, sliced	½ cup	3 cups
Parsley, fresh, minced	1 tbsp.	½ cup
Black pepper, coarse	½ tsp.	1 tbsp.
Salt	¼ tsp.	½ tbsp.
Olive oil	2 tbsp.	¾ cup
White wine vinegar	2 tsp.	¼ cup
Mustard, Dijon	2 tsp.	¼ cup
Honey	1 tsp.	2 tbsp.
Garlic, fresh, minced	1 tsp.	2 tbsp.

Combine first six ingredients in bowl and mix thoroughly.

In separate bowl, whisk remaining ingredients together until well blended. Pour over black bean mixture and toss well. Cover and chill to hold.

Portion ½ cup salad into individual container and serve with each wrap.

Buffalo Chicken Wrap

No bones about it. This easy-to-eat handheld item delivers all the flavors people love in a platter of Buffalo-style wings—deep-fried spicy chicken strips; cool, chunky blue cheese dressing; and celery.

Speed-Scratch ◣ *Takeout*

INGREDIENT	QUANTITY		METHOD
	4 servings	24 servings	
1 Tyson Ready-to-Cook Strips of Fire™, frozen	1 lb.	6 lb.	Deep-fry at 360°F for 3½ to 4½ minutes or until chicken is no longer pink. Remove from fryer and drain. Keep warm above 140°F.
2 Tyson Mexican Original® Cheese Jalapeño Wraps, room temperature (p. 121)	4	24	*To assemble single serving:* Place 1 wrap on flat work surface.
Mixed salad greens, fresh, commercially prepared	4 cups	24 cups	Layer ingredients across center of wrap in the following order: 1 cup salad greens, ¼ cup celery, 2 tablespoons red onions, 1 tablespoon bell peppers. Drizzle ¼ cup salad dressing over bell peppers. Top with 4 ounces chicken strips.
Celery, fresh, bias-sliced	1 cup	6 cups	
Red onions, fresh, chopped (p. 175)	½ cup	3 cups	
Green bell peppers, fresh, chopped	¼ cup	1½ cups	
Blue cheese salad dressing, chunky, commercially prepared	1 cup	6 cups	Fold both sides of wrap over filling. Then fold lower end of wrap over filling and roll closed, keeping ingredients tightly packed. Slice in half diagonally and arrange on plate.
Buffalo wing sauce, commercially prepared (optional)	1 cup	6 cups	Portion ¼ cup sauce into individual container and place on plate. Garnish plate with 1 lime wedge and 1 cilantro sprig.
Lime wedges, fresh	4	24	
Cilantro sprigs, fresh	4	24	*Serve with black bean, chickpea, and olive salad.*

Portion: 12 ounces plus 2 ounces sauce
Nutritional Data/Portion: Calories 940, Protein 32 g, Fat 59 g, Carbohydrate 73 g, Cholesterol 60 mg, Sodium 3,112 mg

For a **FAST FACTS VIA FAX**™ copy of this recipe, call 1-800-223-3755 and enter Business Tool 2359.

Submitted by Edward Carloni
Lebanon Country Club
Myerstown, Pa.

Three-Pepper Smoked Chicken Pita

Indulgent is the best word for a sandwich filled with smoked chicken, cheese, mushrooms, and red, yellow, and green bell peppers that have been sautéed in bacon and a touch of gin.

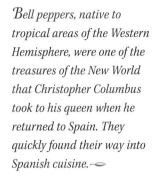

Lighter Fare *Takeout*

	INGREDIENT	QUANTITY		METHOD
		4 servings	24 servings	
1	Tyson Fully Cooked Flavor-Redi® Smoked Chicken Breast Filets, 2.75-oz., frozen	4	24	Cover tightly and slack in cooler between 32° and 36°F prior to use.
2	Bacon, smoked, ½-inch dice	1⅓ cups	8 cups	*To prepare single serving:* Sauté ⅓ cup in skillet over medium heat for 4 to 5 minutes or until crisp.
3	Button mushrooms, fresh, sliced	1⅓ cups	8 cups	Add ⅓ cup mushrooms and ⅓ cup each of peppers to bacon and drippings. Sauté over high heat for 3 to 4 minutes or until mushrooms have absorbed bacon drippings. Slice 1 chicken breast filet into thin strips and add to skillet.
	Red bell peppers, fresh, julienne (p. 88)	1⅓ cups	8 cups	
	Green bell peppers, fresh, julienne	1⅓ cups	8 cups	
	Yellow bell peppers, fresh, julienne	1⅓ cups	8 cups	
4	Gin, dry	¼ cup	1½ cups	Add 1 tablespoon to skillet and cook until evaporated.
5	Chicken broth, canned	¼ cup	1½ cups	Add 1 tablespoon broth, 1 tablespoon vinegar, and ⅛ teaspoon each of cayenne sauce, salt, and pepper to skillet. Cook until liquid has almost evaporated and chicken is thoroughly heated. Remove from heat.
	Apple cider vinegar	¼ cup	1½ cups	
	Cayenne pepper sauce	½ tsp.	1 tbsp.	
	Salt	½ tsp.	1 tbsp.	
	Black pepper, coarse	½ tsp.	1 tbsp.	
6	Swiss cheese, shredded	½ cup	3 cups	Add 2 tablespoons to chicken mixture and mix thoroughly.
7	Pita pocket bread, 6-inch rounds, warm	4	24	Place 1 pita on flat work surface. Slice through center of pita and separate each half to form a pocket.
	Green leaf lettuce leaves, fresh	8	48	
	Tomato wedges, fresh	12	72	Line each half with 1 lettuce leaf. Portion filling into pockets and arrange on plate. Garnish plate with 3 tomato wedges and 1 parsley sprig.
	Parsley sprigs, fresh	4	24	

Serve with creamy potato salad.

Portion: 12 ounces
Nutritional Data/Portion: Calories 350, Protein 24 g, Fat 11 g, Carbohydrate 34 g, Cholesterol 50 mg, Sodium 870 mg

For a **FAST FACTS VIA FAX**™ copy of this recipe, call 1-800-223-3755 and enter Business Tool 2508.

Bell peppers, native to tropical areas of the Western Hemisphere, were one of the treasures of the New World that Christopher Columbus took to his queen when he returned to Spain. They quickly found their way into Spanish cuisine.

The gin's alcohol in this recipe cooks out, leaving a wonderful depth of flavor.

Frozen mixed bell peppers may be substituted for fresh, in equal quantities.

As the popularity of takeout has grown, so have demands from patrons for interesting, good-tasting dishes that require little or no assembly—exactly what this Buffalo Chicken Wrap provides.

Submitted by Steven D. Shimmin, CEC
Fine Host Corporation
Albuquerque Convention Center
Albuquerque, N.M.

Tropical Chicken Fajita

The fajita goes Caribbean with this colorful combination of bell peppers, mangoes, and papayas, punched up with fresh mint and lime juice. The tomatillo-spiked salsa verde makes a great accompaniment.

Lighter Fare

INGREDIENT	QUANTITY 4 servings	24 servings	METHOD
1 Tyson Ready-to-Cook Flavor-Redi® Texas-Style Chicken Breast Fajita Pieces, frozen	8 oz.	3 lb.	Cover tightly and slack in cooler between 32° and 36°F prior to use.
			Grill on oiled, preheated flattop griddle at 350°F for 4 to 5 minutes or until chicken is no longer pink. Remove from grill. Keep warm above 140°F.
2 Red bell peppers, fresh, julienne (p. 88)	⅔ cup	4 cups	Combine in bowl and toss well. Cover and chill to hold.
Yellow bell peppers, fresh, julienne	⅔ cup	4 cups	
Green bell peppers, fresh, julienne	⅔ cup	4 cups	
Onions, fresh, julienne	⅔ cup	4 cups	
Jalapeño peppers, fresh, seeded, minced (p. 172)	1 tbsp.	⅓ cup	
Cilantro, fresh, minced	1 tbsp.	⅓ cup	
Mint, fresh, minced	1 tbsp.	⅓ cup	
Chili powder, dark	½ tbsp.	3 tbsp.	
Salt	1 tsp.	2 tbsp.	
Black pepper, coarse	½ tsp.	1 tbsp.	
Lime juice, fresh	¼ cup	1½ cups	
3 Pineapple, fresh, ½-inch dice	⅔ cup	4 cups	Combine in separate bowl and toss well. Cover and chill to hold.
Mangoes, fresh, ½-inch dice	⅔ cup	4 cups	
Papayas, fresh, ½-inch dice	⅔ cup	4 cups	
Salt	¼ tsp.	½ tbsp.	
Black pepper, coarse	⅛ tsp.	¾ tsp.	
4 Vegetable oil spray	as needed	as needed	*To prepare single serving:* Spray sauté pan with oil. Add ⅔ cup bell pepper mixture. Sauté over high heat for 2 to 4 minutes or until tender-crisp. Add ⅓ cup fruit mixture and heat for 30 to 60 seconds or until fruit is warm.
Tyson Mexican Original® White Flour Tortillas, 8-inch, warm	8	48	
			Place 2 tortillas on flat work surface and portion half of mixture across center of each tortilla. Add 1 ounce chicken to each tortilla and roll fajita-style. Arrange on plate.
5 Salsa Verde (see recipe)	1 cup	6 cups	Portion ¼ cup salsa into individual container and place on plate. Garnish plate with 1 mint sprig.
Mint sprigs, fresh	4	24	*Serve with banana chips.*

Portion: 8 ounces plus 2 ounces salsa
Nutritional Data/Portion: Calories 300, Protein 16 g, Fat 5 g, Carbohydrate 52 g, Cholesterol 25 mg, Sodium 1,390 mg

For a ***FAST FACTS VIA FAX*** copy of this recipe, call 1-800-223-3755 and enter Business Tool 2524.

Dicing the fruit small in this recipe makes it easier to distribute evenly with the other ingredients.

The mango tree is considered sacred in its land of origin, India. Mangoes are cultivated in temperate climates around the world, including California and Florida. When selecting mangoes, look for unblemished yellow skin with blushes of red. Also choose large fruit, because the larger the mango, the greater the fruit-to-seed ratio.

The papaya is native to North America and grows from seed into a 20-foot tree bearing fruit in just 18 months. The Solo papaya, grown in California and Florida, is the most common variety sold in the United States and averages 1 to 2 pounds in weight, but papayas can weigh as much as 20 pounds. Choose papayas that give slightly to palm pressure and have rich skin coloring.

SALSA VERDE

	4 servings	24 servings
Green salsa, commercially prepared	1 cup	6 cups
Tomatillos, fresh, chopped	2 tbsp.	¾ cup
Cilantro, fresh, minced	½ tbsp.	3 tbsp.
Lime juice, fresh	1 tsp.	2 tbsp.

Combine in bowl and mix thoroughly. Cover and chill to hold.

Submitted by Ronald Francis Lapic
Madonna Towers
Rochester, Minn.

Cordon Bleu cookery originated in the 1600s to teach the daughters of impoverished French nobility a variety of skills, including cooking. Seventeen-year-old girls at the school wore cordons bleus, "blue ribbons," to signify their status as seniors.

For a larger sandwich, use the 7-oz. Tyson Cordon Bleu product.

For an alternate plate presentation, simply place a whole cordon bleu on the bun and slice the sandwich in half as pictured.

Chicken Cordon Bleu Sandwich

Patrons will never let this sandwich be taken off the menu. Premium chicken, ham, and melted cheese, all wrapped in a crispy coating that looks like it was a lot of trouble to make, when a ready-to-cook chicken cordon bleu was simply baked off and put on a garnished bun. Voilà.

Speed-Scratch   Line Service   Takeout

INGREDIENT	QUANTITY		METHOD
	4 servings	24 servings	
Tyson Signature Specialties™ Premium Formed Breast Chicken Cordon Bleu, 5-oz., frozen	4	24	Place on parchment-lined sheet pans. Heat in preheated conventional oven at 350°F for 30 to 35 minutes or until chicken is no longer pink. Or heat in preheated convection oven at 325°F for 25 to 30 minutes. Remove from oven. Keep warm above 140°F.
Mayonnaise	¼ cup	1½ cups	Combine in bowl and mix thoroughly. Cover and chill to hold.
Mustard, Dijon	1 tsp.	2 tbsp.	
White hoagie buns, grilled	4	24	*To assemble single serving:* Place 1 bun on flat work surface, grilled sides up. Spread ½ tablespoon mayonnaise mixture on each half.
Green leaf lettuce leaves, fresh	4	24	
Tomato slices, thin, fresh	12	72	Layer bottom half of bun with 1 lettuce leaf and 3 tomato slices. Slice 1 chicken cordon bleu into 4 slices and shingle over tomatoes.
Parsley sprigs, fresh	4	24	

Close sandwich with top half of bun and slice in half diagonally. Arrange on plate. Garnish plate with 1 parsley sprig.

Serve with coleslaw.

Portion: 11 ounces
Nutritional Data/Portion: Calories 670, Protein 32 g, Fat 33 g, Carbohydrate 64 g, Cholesterol 70 mg, Sodium 960 mg

For a **FAST FACTS VIA FAX** copy of this recipe, call 1-800-223-3755 and enter Business Tool 2509.

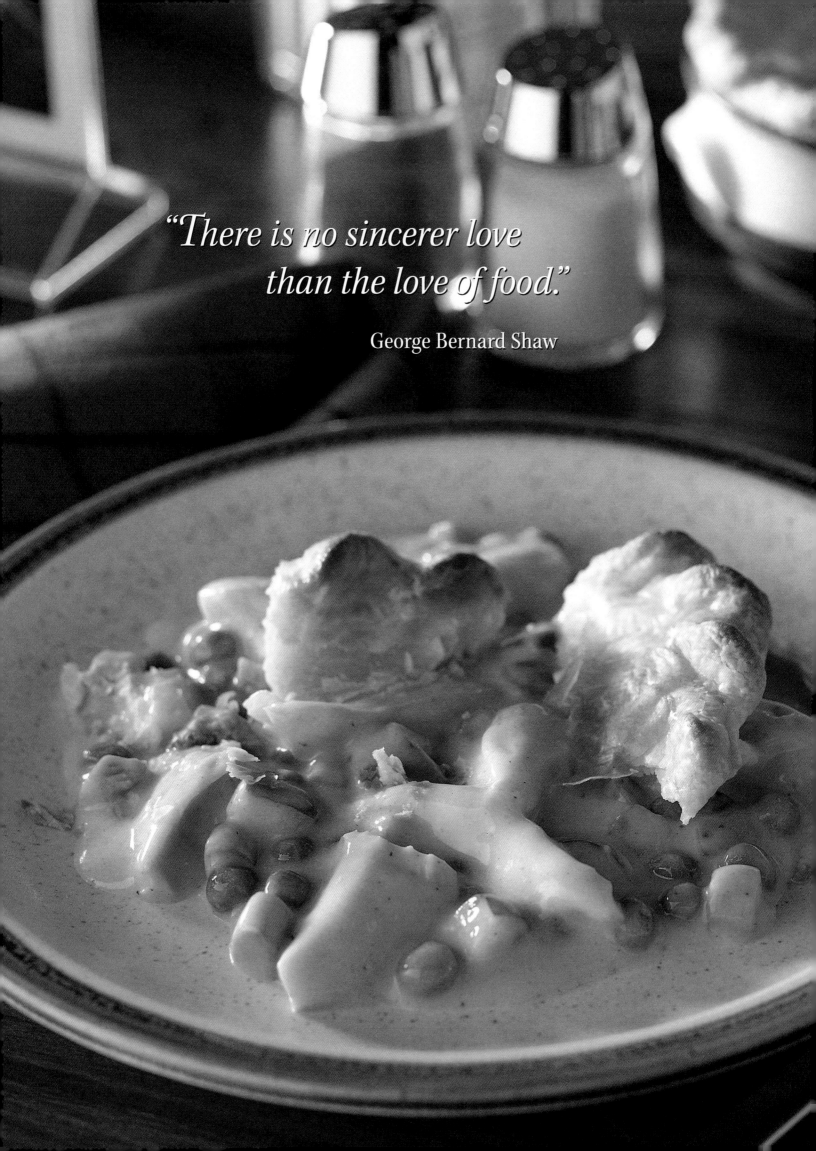

"*There is no sincerer love
than the love of food.*"

George Bernard Shaw

One-Dish Meals

Taking a singular approach to menu building

During the 18th century, the French popularized a cooking style that to some would become synonymous with one-dish meals. Although "casseroles" are fine representatives of one-dish meals, they are in no way the only ones. The quintessential chicken pot pie is another excellent, and quite popular, example. But one-dish meals have roots in cuisines around the world; and although they are always served on a single dish, they are not always prepared in a single pot or pan.

One-Dish Meals consists of a variety of chicken meals served as single courses—spaghetti, paella, quiche, stir-fry, and lasagna, as well as a variety of chicken-based casseroles. In a broader sense, with the addition of chicken, many salads, soups, and stews qualify as one-dish meals, although they are more appropriately included in other chapters of this book.

One-dish meals are typically convenient and economical to prepare, hold well, and are sometimes terrific vehicles for utilizing extra ingredients and unserved portions from previous meal periods. And since many *are* prepared in one pot or pan, one-dish meals also simplify preparation timing because everything is ready at once.

In short, one-dish meals can weave diverse and complex flavors together in one serving to provide a memorable meal experience that can be enjoyed with every bite.

Submitted by Bud Wagner
The Millheim Hotel
Millheim, Pa.

Individual casserole servings may be assembled ahead of time, held in the cooler, then baked in batches.

One of today's most popular vegetables, celery was used solely as a medicinal herb prior to the 1500s. There are two main varieties of celery, but the pale green Pascal celery is the variety with which most people are familiar.

According to carrot lore, this vegetable was originally colored purple, yellow, or white. The familiar orange hue found today was developed by the Dutch in the 1500s.

Casserole-style dishes can easily be prepared in steam table pans, but they can also be portioned into disposable oven pans for takeout as pictured.

Chicken and Sausage Bake

This simple recipe of chicken, sausage, and vegetables works just as well for carryout as it does for line service applications.

Kid Friendly   *Line Service*   *Takeout*

INGREDIENT	QUANTITY 4 servings	24 servings	METHOD
Italian sausage, mild, bulk	8 oz.	3 lb.	Sauté in skillet or braising pan over medium-high heat for 10 to 15 minutes or until brown. (Sauté smaller quantity for 5 to 8 minutes.) Crumble sausage during cooking.
Water, cold	1⅓ cups	8 cups	Add to sausage and simmer for 3 to 4 minutes to make flavored broth.
Carrots, fresh, sliced	⅓ cup	2 cups	Add to sausage and simmer for 4 to 5 minutes or until carrots are tender-crisp. (Simmer smaller quantity for 2 to 3 minutes.) Remove from heat.
Celery, fresh, sliced	⅓ cup	2 cups	
Button mushrooms, fresh, sliced	⅓ cup	2 cups	
Green peas, frozen	⅓ cup	2 cups	
Croutons, seasoned, commercially prepared	1⅓ cups	8 cups	Add to sausage mixture and mix thoroughly.
Tyson Fully Cooked Diced White Fryer Meat, ¾-inch dice, frozen	1 lb.	6 lb.	
Cream of mushroom soup, condensed, canned	1¼ cups	7½ cups	Combine in bowl and mix thoroughly. Fold into chicken mixture.
Sour cream	1¼ cups	7½ cups	Portion 1½ cups mixture into each of 24 oiled individual casserole dishes. (Use 4 dishes for smaller quantity.)
Bread crumbs, dried, buttered	¼ cup	1½ cups	Sprinkle 1 tablespoon over top of each casserole and transfer to sheet pans.
			Bake in preheated conventional oven at 375°F for 15 to 18 minutes or until bubbling. (Bake smaller quantity for 10 to 12 minutes.) Or bake in preheated convection oven at 325°F for 13 to 14 minutes. (Bake smaller quantity for 8 to 10 minutes.) Remove from oven. Keep warm above 140°F.
Parsley, fresh, minced (p. 39)	1½ tbsp.	½ cup	*To assemble single serving:* Place 1 casserole on napkin-lined plate. Sprinkle with 1 teaspoon parsley.

Portion: 14 ounces
Nutritional Data/Portion: Calories 680, Protein 50 g, Fat 41 g, Carbohydrate 27 g, Cholesterol 170 mg, Sodium 1,410 mg

For a **FAST FACTS VIA FAX**™ copy of this recipe, call 1-800-223-3755 and enter Business Tool 2617.

Frittatas and omelets have similar ingredients but different cooking methods. Frittatas are baked in the oven, while omelets are sautéed on the stovetop.

Artichoke hearts or broccoli may be substituted for the asparagus for an interesting variation.

The Germans ate spargel, *which is "white asparagus," with hollandaise sauce as early as 1732.*

Hollandaise means "in the style of Holland." It is a classic French sauce made with butter, egg yolks, and lemon juice in a double boiler to prevent overheating. It is traditionally served warm over vegetables, fish, and egg dishes. High-quality commercially prepared Hollandaise sauce is an often-used alternative.

Chicken Asparagus Frittata

This Italian specialty baked with chicken, asparagus, and red bell pepper, is much like a crustless quiche. In addition to offering patrons something different but familiar, the best part is that it can be baked ahead in quantity and easily served one piece at a time.

INGREDIENT	QUANTITY 4 servings	24 servings	METHOD
1 *Lemon-Chive Hollandaise Sauce*			
Hollandaise sauce, commercially prepared	½ cup	3 cups	Combine in saucepan and mix thoroughly. Heat over low heat for 8 to 10 minutes or until thoroughly warm. (Heat smaller quantity for 2 to 3 minutes.) Remove from heat and keep warm.
Lemon juice, fresh	½ tbsp.	3 tbsp.	
Chives, fresh, chopped	½ tsp.	1 tbsp.	
2 Olive oil	2 tbsp.	½ cup	Heat in skillet or braising pan over medium-high heat.
3 Asparagus cuts, frozen	2 cups	12 cups	Add to oil and sauté for 8 to 10 minutes or until vegetables are tender-crisp. (Sauté smaller quantity for 3 to 4 minutes.) Remove from heat.
Red bell pepper strips, fresh	½ cup	3 cups	
Onions, fresh, slivered	½ cup	3 cups	
Thyme leaves, dried	1 tsp.	2 tbsp.	
4 Tyson Fully Cooked Diced White Fryer Meat, 1-inch dice, frozen	12 oz.	4½ lb.	Combine in bowl. Add asparagus mixture and toss well.
Italian bread, parbaked, cubed	4 cups	24 cups	
Cheddar cheese, sharp, shredded	1 cup	6 cups	
5 Eggs, large, whole, lightly beaten	5	28	Combine in separate bowl and mix thoroughly. Pour over chicken mixture and mix thoroughly. Portion into two oiled full-size steam table pans. (Use third-size pan for smaller quantity.)
Heavy cream	1⅔ cups	10 cups	
Seasoned salt	1 tsp.	2 tbsp.	
Black pepper, coarse	½ tsp.	1 tbsp.	
			Bake in preheated conventional oven at 375°F for 40 to 50 minutes or until firm. (Bake smaller quantity for 30 to 40 minutes.) Or bake in preheated convection oven at 325°F for 20 to 25 minutes. (Bake smaller quantity for 15 to 20 minutes.)
6 Monterey Jack cheese, shredded	⅔ cup	4 cups	Sprinkle over casseroles and bake an additional 5 to 10 minutes or until cheese is melted. Remove from oven and cut each pan into 12 equal triangles (p. 149). (Cut smaller pan into 4 triangles.) Keep warm above 140°F.

recipe continued on next page . . .

INGREDIENT	QUANTITY		METHOD
	4 servings	24 servings	
Chive spears, fresh	12	72	*To assemble single serving:* Portion 1 frittata triangle on plate. Ladle 2 tablespoons lemon-chive hollandaise sauce over triangle. Top with 3 chive spears. Garnish plate with 1 grape cluster, 1 lemon twist, and 1 tomato half.
Red grape clusters, seedless, fresh	4	24	
Lemon slice twists, fresh	4	24	
Tomato halves, fresh, broiled (p. 231)	4	24	

7 *(section marker)*

Portion: 14 ounces
Nutritional Data/Portion: Calories 750, Protein 49 g, Fat 51 g, Carbohydrate 26 g, Cholesterol 425 mg, Sodium 780 mg

For a **FAST FACTS VIA FAX**™ copy of this recipe, call 1-800-223-3755 and enter Business Tool 2601.

This frittata can make an elegant line service presentation when served in a chafing dish.

Popcorn Chicken Bites Casserole

This recipe's genealogy can be traced back to casserole country in the Midwest. Original Popcorn Chicken Bites are a natural partner in a comforting corn-bake topped with cheddar cheese.

Speed-Scratch   Kid Friendly   Line Service   Takeout

*Submitted by Rosella Vancura
Colonial Manor Nursing Home
Lakefield, Minn.*

INGREDIENT	QUANTITY		METHOD
	4 servings	24 servings	
Eggs, large, whole, beaten	1	3	Combine in bowl and mix thoroughly. Pour into one oiled full-size steam table pan. (Use third-size pan for smaller quantity.)
Butter, salted, melted	2 tbsp.	¾ cup	
Onions, fresh, minced	1 tbsp.	⅓ cup	
Yellow corn, whole kernel, canned, drained	1 cup	6 cups	
Yellow corn, cream-style, canned	1 cup	6 cups	
Broccoli cuts, IQF	1 cup	6 cups	
Soda crackers, crushed	2 tbsp.	¾ cup	
Salt	⅛ tsp.	¾ tsp.	
Tyson Ready-to-Cook Original Popcorn Chicken Bites,™ frozen	14 oz.	5 lb.	Place chicken lightly over top of vegetable mixture. Conventional oven, preheated: Cover and bake at 375°F for 1 hour and 45 minutes or until bubbling and chicken is no longer pink. (Bake smaller quantity for 1 hour and 15 minutes.) Uncover and bake 15 minutes or until chicken is crisp. Remove from oven. Convection oven, preheated: Cover and bake at 325°F for 45 to 50 minutes or until bubbling and chicken is no longer pink. (Bake smaller quantity for 20 to 25 minutes.) Uncover and bake 10 minutes or until chicken is crisp. Remove from oven.
Cheddar cheese, mild, shredded	⅓ cup	2 cups	Sprinkle over chicken. Keep warm above 140°F.
Parsley sprigs, fresh	4	24	*To assemble single serving:* Portion 1 cup casserole on plate. Garnish plate with 1 parsley sprig.

1 **2** **3** **4** *(section markers)*

Portion: 8½ ounces
Nutritional Data/Portion: Calories 430, Protein 22 g, Fat 22 g, Carbohydrate 39 g, Cholesterol 95 mg, Sodium 1,210 mg

For a **FAST FACTS VIA FAX**™ copy of this recipe, call 1-800-223-3755 and enter Business Tool 2612.

Every part of the corn plant can be put to good use. The kernels, of course, can be eaten; the silk is used for medicinal tea; the husks are used with tamales; and the stalks are used for fodder. Country Gentleman (white corn) and Golden Bantam (yellow corn) are two popular varieties of corn.

The traditional pot pie may have landed on Plymouth Rock with the Puritans. It hails from England, where deep-dish meat pies are common. But since its arrival on this shore, chicken pot pie has become an American classic.⤜

The egg wash brushed on the top crust of the pot pie gives it a satiny finish. The egg wash can also be brushed on the inside of the pot pie before the chicken mixture is added, for a flakier and more moisture-proof bottom crust.⤜

Chicken Pot Pie

Fully cooked roasted chicken, red potatoes, cream, and prepared frozen pot pie dough refresh this classic, making it ultraconvenient and satisfying as one of the most comforting of comfort foods.

Kid Friendly *Line Service* *Takeout*

INGREDIENT	QUANTITY 4 servings	24 servings	METHOD
1 Tyson Fully Cooked Flavor-Redi® Roasted and Carved Chicken Breast Filets, frozen	2	12	Cover tightly and slack in cooler between 32° and 36°F prior to use.
2 Butter, salted	2 tbsp.	¾ cup	Heat in stockpot over medium-high heat.
3 Red potatoes, fresh, skin-on, ½-inch dice (p. 88)	1 cup	6 cups	Add to butter and sauté for 4 to 5 minutes or until onions are translucent. (Sauté smaller quantity for 2 to 3 minutes.)
Onions, fresh, slivered	1 cup	6 cups	
Poultry seasoning, dried	½ tsp.	1 tbsp.	
Black pepper, fine	¼ tsp.	½ tbsp.	
4 Flour, all-purpose	¼ cup	1½ cups	Add to vegetable mixture and mix thoroughly. Cook for 2 minutes or until flour is cooked but not brown.
5 Chicken broth, canned	2½ cups	15 cups	Gradually add to vegetable mixture and mix thoroughly. Bring to boil over high heat. Reduce heat and simmer for 3 to 5 minutes or until mixture thickens.
6 Heavy cream	½ cup	2¼ cups	Add to vegetable mixture and simmer for 3 to 5 minutes or until flavors are blended.
Diced carrots and peas blend, frozen thawed, drained	1 cup	6 cups	Pull chicken breast filets into large pieces and add to vegetable mixture. Mix thoroughly and remove from heat. Cover and chill below 40°F.
7 Pot pie crust dough, frozen, 3.5-oz. rounds, thawed (p. 147)	8	48	*To assemble single-serve pot pies:* Line twenty-four 10-ounce individual baking dishes with one crust each. (Use four baking dishes for smaller quantity.) Ladle 1¼ cups chilled chicken mixture into each crust. Top with second crust. Trim excess crust and crimp edges in decorative pattern.

recipe continued on next page . . .

INGREDIENT	QUANTITY		METHOD
	4 servings	24 servings	
Eggs, large, whole, beaten	1	2	Combine in small bowl and mix thoroughly. Brush on top crusts. Vent each crust with three ½-inch slits. Transfer to sheet pans.
Water	1 tbsp.	2 tbsp.	
			Bake in preheated conventional oven at 400°F for 35 to 40 minutes or until crust is golden brown. Or bake in preheated convection oven at 350°F for 20 to 25 minutes. Remove from oven. Keep warm above 140°F.

8

Portion: 14¾ ounces

Nutritional Data/Portion: Calories 1,200, Protein 31 g, Fat 70 g, Carbohydrate 113 g, Cholesterol 180 mg, Sodium 2,410 mg

For a **FAST FACTS VIA FAX** copy of this recipe, call 1-800-223-3755 and enter Business Tool 2357.

For line service, divide the pot pie mixture equally into two oiled full-size 2-inch-deep steam table pans. Top each pan with 12 frozen prepared biscuits. Bake in a preheated conventional oven at 375°F for 25 to 30 minutes or until the biscuits are golden brown and the pot pie mixture is bubbling. Convection oven method is not recommended.

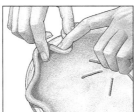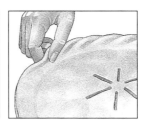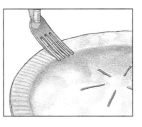

HOW TO BE CREATIVE WITH CRUST

Zigzag–Place the left index finger inside the pie's cavity and gently poke the edging crust toward the pie's outer edge between the index finger and thumb of the right hand.

Fluted–With the left index finger placed on the pie's outer edge, gently pull the edging between the right thumb and index finger toward the pie's cavity.

Pinch–Place the right thumb inside the pie's cavity and gently pinch the edging between the right thumb and right index finger.

Fork–Gently press the tines of a fork into edging crust.

Submitted by Judith Porter
Saginaw County
Commission on Aging
Saginaw, Mich.

This recipe makes a beautiful line service presentation as pictured.

Although Country Captain Chicken traditionally calls for bone-in chicken, this version was adapted to use boneless, skinless breast filets to make it easier to eat and less messy without sacrificing flavor.

A delicious accompaniment to curried dishes, "chutney" originated in India where it was called chatni. *This condiment can range from chunky to smooth and from spicy to mild, but chutneys all contain fruit, spices, sugar, and vinegar.*

Soaking raisins in hot water (macerating) rehydrates them and causes them to plump up.

Almonds are actually kernels of the fruit of the almond tree. They are packed with calcium, fiber, folic acid, magnesium, potassium, riboflavin, and vitamin E.

Country Captain Chicken

The "captain" in this recipe name is a hint that this Indian curry dish was most likely brought to Britain by a military officer. It features the classic components many Americans associate with Indian cuisine, including curry powder, rice, chutney, and raisins.

INGREDIENT	QUANTITY		METHOD
	4 servings	24 servings	
1 Tyson Ready-to-Cook Gourmet Boneless Whole Chicken Breast Filets, 8-oz., frozen	4	24	Sprinkle chicken with seasonings. Dredge in flour and shake off excess.
Salt	½ tsp.	1 tbsp.	
Black pepper, fine	¼ tsp.	½ tbsp.	
2 Flour, all-purpose	as needed	as needed	
Olive oil	¼ cup	1½ cups	Heat in skillet over medium heat. Add chicken and sauté for 4 to 5 minutes on each side or until golden brown. Remove from skillet. Keep warm above 140°F.
3 Green bell peppers, fresh, diced (p. 88)	½ cup	3 cups	Add to skillet and sauté for 7 to 8 minutes or until vegetables are wilted. (Sauté smaller quantity for 4 to 5 minutes.)
Onions, fresh, diced (p. 175)	½ cup	3 cups	
Garlic, fresh, minced	½ tsp.	1 tbsp.	
Curry powder	2 tsp.	¼ cup	
Thyme leaves, dried	½ tsp.	1 tbsp.	
4 Tomato puree, canned	¼ cup	1½ cups	Add to vegetable mixture and mix thoroughly. Bring to boil over high heat. Remove from heat and transfer to two oiled full-size steam table pans. (Use half-size pan for smaller quantity.) Arrange chicken over sauce.
Tomatoes, diced, canned, undrained	2 cups	12 cups	
Raisins, dark, macerated in hot water, drained	¼ cup	1½ cups	
Almonds, slivered, toasted	¼ cup	1½ cups	Roast in preheated conventional oven[†] at 350°F for 1 to 1½ hours or until chicken is no longer pink. (Roast smaller quantity for 50 to 60 minutes.) Remove from oven. Keep warm above 140°F.
Sugar, granulated	¼ tsp.	½ tbsp.	
Salt	¼ tsp.	½ tbsp.	
5 White rice, steamed	2 cups	12 cups	*To assemble single serving:* Portion 1 chicken breast filet on plate. Ladle ¾ cup sauce over chicken. Surround with ½ cup rice and ¼ cup chutney. Sprinkle plate with 1 tablespoon almonds and garnish with 1 thyme sprig.
Mango chutney, commercially prepared	1 cup	6 cups	
Almonds, slivered, toasted	¼ cup	1½ cups	
Thyme sprigs, fresh	4	24	

Portion: 18 ounces

Nutritional Data/Portion: Calories 780, Protein 54 g, Fat 42 g, Carbohydrate 51 g, Cholesterol 155 mg, Sodium 620 mg

[†]Convection oven not recommended.

For a **FAST FACTS VIA FAX** copy of this recipe, call 1-800-223-3755 and enter Business Tool 2616.

Submitted by Jeannie Loberg
Milwaukee Public Schools
Community Assessment and
Training Program
Milwaukee, Wis.

Baked Chicken and Rice Alfredo

Thanks to the colorful chopped vegetables and two-cheese combination, this easily prepared menu item looks good on a hot line and delivers great taste, too.

Speed-Scratch   Kid Friendly   Line Service   Takeout

	INGREDIENT	QUANTITY 4 servings	24 servings	METHOD
1	Tyson Fully Cooked Pulled White Fryer Meat, frozen	1 lb.	6 lb.	Combine in bowl and mix thoroughly. Transfer to two oiled full-size steam table pans. (Use third-size pan for smaller quantity.)
	White rice, cooked in chicken broth	2 cups	12 cups	
	Alfredo sauce, commercially prepared	2 cups	12 cups	
	Tomatoes, diced, canned, drained	1 cup	6 cups	
	Broccoli cuts, IQF	1 cup	6 cups	
	Green onions, fresh, chopped	⅓ cup	2 cups	
	Romano cheese, shredded	¼ cup	1½ cups	
	Basil leaves, dried	1 tbsp.	⅓ cup	
2	Mozzarella cheese, shredded	½ cup	3 cups	Sprinkle over top of chicken mixture.
	Parmesan cheese, grated	2 tbsp.	¾ cup	Conventional oven, preheated: Cover and bake at 375°F for 60 to 65 minutes. (Bake smaller quantity for 30 to 35 minutes.) Remove cover and bake an additional 10 to 15 minutes or until lightly browned.
				Convection oven, preheated: Cover and bake at 325°F for 40 to 45 minutes. (Bake smaller quantity for 25 to 30 minutes.) Remove cover and bake an additional 5 to 7 minutes or until lightly browned.
				Remove from oven and let rest 10 minutes. Slice each pan into 12 equal triangles. (Slice smaller pan into 4 triangles.) Keep warm above 140°F.
3	Basil sprigs, fresh	4	24	*To assemble single serving:* Portion 1 casserole triangle on plate. Garnish plate with 1 basil sprig.
				Serve with grilled garlic bread.

Portion: 13½ ounces
Nutritional Data/Portion: Calories 580, Protein 53 g, Fat 23 g, Carbohydrate 39 g, Cholesterol 145 mg, Sodium 1,540 mg

For a **FAST FACTS VIA FAX** copy of this recipe, call 1-800-223-3755 and enter Business Tool 2595.

Alfredo sauce was first created in the 1920s by a Roman restaurateur named Alfredo di Lello. His original creation was a rich sauce of butter, grated Parmesan cheese, heavy cream, and black pepper.

The pale yellow cheese of Rome—Romano—actually includes several different varieties. The sharp sheep's milk, pecorino Romano, is probably the most well known, but other varieties include caprino Romano, an extremely sharp variety made with goat's milk, and vacchino Romano, a mild cheese made with cow's milk. Most American-made Romano cheeses are cow's milk or a combination of cow's milk and goat's or sheep's milk.

HOW TO CUT TRIANGLE PORTIONS
First, cut lengthwise into two equal sections. Then, make two cuts crosswise to form six sections. Finally, cut each section diagonally to create 12 triangular servings.

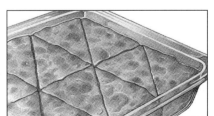

Submitted by Jane Schimpf
Bowling Green State University
Auxiliary Services
Bowling Green, Ohio

Kung Pao Chicken

Kung Pao chicken is moving beyond Chinese restaurants as it appeals to palates that love this chicken stir-fry with vegetables in spicy black bean garlic sauce.

Kung Pao chicken is arguably one of the most popular Szechuan dishes in the world, served in Chinese restaurants from New York City to Paris. According to one Chinese cooking authority, the name Kung Pao *can be loosely translated as "castle protector," a title bestowed on the person in charge of protecting the heir to the throne. Legend has it that one of the palace guards during the Qin dynasty's reign was a man from the Szechuan province whose favorite meal was spicy chicken, redolent with chiles and peanuts.*

Hot red peppers and peanuts can add an authentic touch to this American interpretation of Kung Pao.

This dish also can be served in a bowl separate from the rice to allow for family-style sharing that is popular in many Chinese restaurants.

INGREDIENT	QUANTITY 4 servings	24 servings	METHOD
1 *Kung Pao Sauce*			
Black bean garlic sauce, commercially prepared	½ cup	3 cups	Combine in bowl and mix thoroughly. Cover and reserve.
Tomato puree, canned	¼ cup	1½ cups	
Hoisin sauce, commercially prepared	¼ cup	1½ cups	
Sherry, dry	2 tbsp.	¾ cup	
Red wine vinegar	2 tbsp.	¾ cup	
Sugar, granulated	1 tbsp.	⅓ cup	
Water, cold	1 tbsp.	⅓ cup	
Garlic, fresh, minced	1 tsp.	2 tbsp.	
Red pepper, crushed, dried	½ tsp.	1 tbsp.	
Cayenne pepper, ground	½ tsp.	1 tbsp.	
2 Vegetable oil	2 tbsp.	½ cup	Heat in skillet or braising pan over medium-high heat.
3 Tyson Fully Cooked Diced Chicken Tenderloins, ¾-inch dice, frozen	1 lb.	6 lb.	Add to oil and stir-fry for 4½ to 6 minutes or until chicken is thoroughly heated. (Stir-fry smaller quantity for 3 to 4 minutes.)
4 Onions, fresh, chopped (p. 175)	2 cups	12 cups	Add to chicken and stir-fry for 3 to 4 minutes or until vegetables are tender-crisp. (Stir-fry smaller quantity for 1 to 2 minutes.)
Celery, fresh, chopped	2 cups	12 cups	
Carrots, fresh, chopped	1 cup	6 cups	Add Kung Pao sauce and mix thoroughly. Bring to simmer, then remove from heat. Keep warm above 140°F.
5 White rice, steamed, hot	2 cups	12 cups	*To assemble single serving:* Portion ½ cup rice on plate. Top with 1 cup chicken mixture. Garnish plate with 1 green onion brush.
Green onion brushes, fresh (p. 125)	4	24	

Portion: 12½ ounces

Nutritional Data/Portion: Calories 460, Protein 38 g, Fat 11 g, Carbohydrate 49 g, Cholesterol 90 mg, Sodium 1,730 mg

For a **FAST FACTS VIA FAX**™ copy of this recipe, call 1-800-223-3755 and enter Business Tool 2622.

Submitted by Jeff Trombetta
Yale University Dining Services
New Haven, Conn.

Cashew Chicken Stir-Fry

Here's a speed-scratch dish that may take more time to eat than to prepare. Tempura-battered chicken strips are stacked on top of colorful vegetables covered in duck sauce spiked with crushed red pepper and ginger.

INGREDIENT	QUANTITY 4 servings	24 servings	METHOD	
1 Tyson Ready-to-Cook Tempura Chicken Thigh Strips, frozen	1 lb.	6 lb.	Deep-fry at 350°F for 5 to 5½ minutes or until chicken is no longer pink. Remove from fryer and drain. Keep warm above 140°F.	
2 Peanut oil	as needed	as needed	Heat on preheated flattop griddle at 450°F.	
3 Stir-fry vegetable blend, fresh, commercially prepared	1½ lb.	9 lb.	Add to oil and stir-fry for 3 to 5 minutes or until vegetables are tender-crisp. Remove from griddle and transfer to steam table pan. Keep warm.	
4 *Sherried Soy Sauce*				
Soy sauce, lite	3 tbsp.	1 cup	Combine in saucepan and mix thoroughly. Bring to simmer over medium heat.	
Sherry, dry	3 tbsp.	1 cup		
Duck sauce, commercially prepared	⅓ cup	2 cups		
Red pepper, crushed, dried	¼ tsp.	½ tbsp.		
Ginger, ground	¼ tsp.	½ tbsp.		
5 Cornstarch	½ tbsp.	2 tbsp.	Combine in small bowl and mix until smooth. Gradually stir into sauce. Simmer for 1 to 2 minutes or until sauce thickens. Remove from heat and pour over vegetables.	
Water, cold	1½ tbsp.	½ cup		
6 Cashews, dry-roasted	¼ cup	1½ cups	*To assemble single serving:* Portion 1 cup vegetables with sauce on plate. Top with 4 ounces chicken. Garnish with 1 tablespoon cashews. *Serve with steamed white rice.*	

Portion: 10 ounces
Nutritional Data/Portion: Calories 480, Protein 19 g, Fat 21 g, Carbohydrate 55 g, Cholesterol 45 mg, Sodium 1,430 mg

For a **FAST FACTS VIA FAX** copy of this recipe, call 1-800-223-3755 and enter Business Tool 2627.

Jesuit missionaries introduced tempura-style cooking to the Japanese during the 16th century. The word tempura comes from the Portuguese word temporras, *which means "Friday"—the day they ate deep-fried fish.*

Keep chicken and vegetables separate until served.

For an interesting presentation, prepare the vegetables and chicken separately, then top the vegetables with the chicken in a wok as pictured. Plate tableside over rice while patrons watch in anticipation.

Submitted by Cuz Blake
The Canteen
Clarksburg, W. Va.

Quiche originated in Alsace-Lorraine in northeast France. The classic quiche Lorraine is a pastry shell baked with a custard of eggs, cream, seasonings, crisp bacon bits, and sometimes Gruyère cheese. Other popular ingredients, such as onions, mushrooms, ham, shellfish, or herbs, can also be used in the custard.~

Archaeologists uncovered pottery fragments in Switzerland that indicate the Swiss may have been making cheese—at least separating curds from whey—since about 6000 B.C. However, Swiss cheese as it is now known came some 5,000 years later when the Romans first brought cattle to the Alpine region.~

Swiss cheese is a generic term for pale yellow cheeses with large holes and slightly nutty flavor. American Swiss cheeses are patterned after Switzerland's world-famous Emmentaler and Gruyère cheeses.~

Dress up this quiche for line service with the simple addition of a tomato tulip and parsley sprigs as pictured.~

Swiss and Cheddar Chicken Quiche

Chicken, broccoli, and Swiss and cheddar cheese make this colorful quiche hearty and versatile enough to serve for breakfast, lunch, or dinner.

INGREDIENT	QUANTITY 4 servings	24 servings	METHOD
1 Pie crust, preformed, 9-inch, deep-dish, frozen	1	6	Brush pie crusts with butter and sprinkle ¼ cup cheese over bottom of each crust.
Butter, salted, melted	as needed	as needed	
Cheddar cheese, mild, shredded	¼ cup	1½ cups	
2 Tyson Fully Cooked Diced Chicken Tenderloins, ¾-inch dice, frozen	12 oz.	4½ lb.	Combine in bowl.
Broccoli, fresh, blanched, refreshed in ice water, drained, chopped	1½ cups	9 cups	
3 Eggs, large, whole, beaten	3	18	Combine in separate bowl and mix thoroughly.
Nutmeg, ground	¼ tsp.	½ tbsp.	
White pepper, fine	¼ tsp.	½ tbsp.	
4 Cornstarch	1 tbsp.	⅓ cup	Combine in small bowl and stir until smooth. Add to egg mixture and mix thoroughly.
Worcestershire sauce	1 tsp.	2 tbsp.	
5 Evaporated milk, canned	⅔ cup	4 cups	Add to egg mixture and mix thoroughly. Then add egg mixture to chicken mixture and mix thoroughly.
Heavy cream	¼ cup	1½ cups	
Swiss cheese, shredded	½ cup	3 cups	
Cheddar cheese, mild, shredded	¼ cup	1½ cups	
6 Cheddar cheese, mild, shredded	¼ cup	1½ cups	Ladle 4½ cups quiche mixture into each pie crust. Sprinkle top of each quiche with ¼ cup cheese.

Conventional oven, preheated: Bake at 375°F for 45 to 50 minutes or until filling is set. Cover quiches with foil if browning too fast. (Bake smaller quantity for 40 to 45 minutes.)

Convection oven, preheated: Bake at 325°F for 20 to 25 minutes. (Bake smaller quantity for 15 to 20 minutes.)

Remove from oven and let rest 15 minutes. Slice each quiche into quarters. Keep warm above 140°F.

recipe continued on next page . . .

INGREDIENT	QUANTITY		METHOD
	4 servings	24 servings	
Tomato tulips, fresh	4	24	*To assemble single serving:* Portion 1 quiche quarter on plate. Garnish plate with 1 tomato tulip and 1 parsley sprig.
Parsley sprigs, fresh	4	24	

7

Portion: 10 ounces
Nutritional Data/Portion: Calories 580, Protein 37 g, Fat 37 g, Carbohydrate 26 g, Cholesterol 260 mg, Sodium 810 mg

For a **FAST FACTS VIA FAX** copy of this recipe, call 1-800-223-3755 and enter Business Tool 2602.

Lemon Chicken Stir-Fry

This gently spiced stir-fry dish has a light lemon sauce that nicely complements the grilled chicken, red bell peppers, and mushrooms.

Lighter Fare *Line Service* *Takeout*

*Submitted by Geraldine Lombard
Clinton County Nursing Home
Plattsburg, N.Y.*

INGREDIENT	QUANTITY		METHOD
	4 servings	24 servings	
Vegetable oil	2 tbsp.	¾ cup	Heat in skillet or braising pan over medium-high heat.
Tyson Fully Cooked Flavor-Redi® Chicken Tenderloins with Grill Marks, frozen	16	96	Add to oil and stir-fry for 8 to 10 minutes or until vegetables are tender-crisp and chicken is thoroughly heated. (Stir-fry smaller quantity for 3 to 4 minutes.)
Red bell peppers, fresh, sliced into ¼-inch strips	1 cup	6 cups	
Button mushrooms, fresh, sliced	⅓ cup	3 cups	
Sugar, granulated	1 tbsp.	⅓ cup	Combine in bowl in order given. Mix thoroughly and add to chicken. Stir-fry for 1 to 2 minutes or until sauce thickens.
Cornstarch	1 tsp.	3 tbsp.	
Chicken broth, canned	½ cup	3 cups	
Lemon juice, fresh	3 tbsp.	1 cup	
Soy sauce	1 tbsp.	⅓ cup	
Sherry, dry	1 tbsp.	⅓ cup	
Lemon peel, fresh, ⅛-inch strips	½ tbsp.	3 tbsp.	Add to chicken mixture and stir-fry for 1 minute or until thoroughly mixed. Remove from heat. Keep warm above 140°F.
White rice, steamed, hot	2 cups	12 cups	*To assemble single serving:* Portion ½ cup rice on plate. Top with 4 chicken tenderloins and ⅓ cup vegetable/sauce mixture. Garnish plate with 1 lemon twist.
Lemon slice twists, fresh	4	24	

Portion: 11 ounces
Nutritional Data/Portion: Calories 360, Protein 37 g, Fat 10 g, Carbohydrate 31 g, Cholesterol 75 mg, Sodium 860 mg

For a **FAST FACTS VIA FAX** copy of this recipe, call 1-800-223-3755 and enter Business Tool 2623.

Garnishing plates with a little lemon zest adds to plate presentation, but a little bit goes a long way. Only the colored peel is sweet; the white pithy membrane on the peel is very bitter.

Inhabitants of the Indus River Valley, which is located in modern-day Pakistan, were among the first to cultivate lemons and other citrus fruits around 4000 B.C. Crusaders brought lemons home to Europe in the 13th century. The first lemon trees in America are thought to have been planted in Florida by Ponce de Leon in the 16th century.

Chicken Tostada

If pizza had originated in south Texas, it may have looked just like this Tex-Mex creation. This towering tostada features lettuce, onions, cheese, tomatoes, chicken fajita strips, and cilantro piled high on a crispy corn tortilla spread with spicy bean puree.

Lighter fare

INGREDIENT	QUANTITY 4 servings	24 servings	METHOD
1 Tyson Fully Cooked Flavor-Redi® Chicken Breast Fajita Strips, frozen	12 oz.	4½ lb.	Place on full-size sheet pans. (Use half-size pan for smaller quantity.) Heat in preheated conventional oven at 400°F for 15 to 18 minutes. Or heat in preheated convection oven at 400°F for 4 to 6 minutes. Remove from oven. Keep warm above 140°F.
2 *Red Kidney Bean Puree*			
Olive oil	1 tbsp.	⅓ cup	Heat in saucepan over medium heat.
3 Garlic, fresh, minced	1 tsp.	2 tbsp.	Add to oil and sauté for 30 seconds or until garlic begins to brown.
Chili powder, dark	1 tsp.	2 tbsp.	
Cumin, ground	½ tsp.	1 tbsp.	
Oregano leaves, dried	½ tsp.	1 tbsp.	
Salt	¼ tsp.	½ tbsp.	
Red pepper, crushed, dried	⅛ tsp.	¾ tsp.	
4 Red kidney beans, canned, rinsed, drained	1 cup	6 cups	Add to garlic mixture and mix thoroughly. Bring to boil over high heat. Reduce heat and simmer for 9 to 10 minutes or until flavors are blended. (Simmer smaller quantity for 7 to 8 minutes.) Remove from heat and transfer to food processor bowl. Process until pureed. Remove from processor bowl and keep warm.
Water, cold	½ cup	2 cups	
5 Tyson Mexican Original® Corn Tortillas, 6-inch, room temperature	4	24	*To prepare single serving:* Deep-fry 1 tortilla at 350°F for 30 to 60 seconds or until crisp. Remove from fryer and drain. Place on plate and spread tortilla with ¼ cup kidney bean puree.
6 Green leaf lettuce, fresh, shredded	2 cups	12 cups	Layer tortilla with ingredients in the following order: ½ cup lettuce, ½ tablespoon green onions, 1 tablespoon red onions, 3 ounces chicken, 2 tablespoons cheese, ¼ cup tomatoes, ½ tablespoon cilantro. Top with ½ tablespoon sour cream.
Green onions, fresh, chopped	2 tbsp.	¾ cup	
Red onions, fresh, chopped (p. 175)	¼ cup	1½ cups	
Mexican cheese blend, shredded	½ cup	3 cups	
Tomatoes, fresh, seeded, diced	1 cup	6 cups	
Cilantro, fresh, minced	2 tbsp.	¾ cup	
Sour cream	2 tbsp.	¾ cup	*Serve with guacamole and thick, chunky salsa.*

Portion: 9 ounces
Nutritional Data/Portion: Calories 340, Protein 27 g, Fat 13 g, Carbohydrate 31 g, Cholesterol 60 mg, Sodium 790 mg

For a **FAST FACTS VIA FAX**™ copy of this recipe, call 1-800-223-3755 and enter Business Tool 2611.

This recipe works well on a "build your own" tostada bar.

This one-dish meal can easily work across the menu when offered as a shared starter.

Popular Mexican cheese blends can include any combination of Monterey Jack, cheddar, quesadilla, and asadero cheeses.

Pinto beans or black beans may be substituted for the red kidney beans for a more Southwestern flair.

Submitted by Bill Matatall
Presbyterian Hospital of Plano
Plano, Tex.

Chicken Enchilada Casserole

The combination of melted cheese, mild green chiles, and soft corn tortillas makes
this a simple-to-prepare one-dish meal that will appeal to "children" of all ages.

*Casserole cooking
originated in France
in the early 1700s with
the invention of the
casserole dish—a deep,
round ovenproof container
with handles and a
tight-fitting lid.*

	INGREDIENT	QUANTITY 4 servings	24 servings	METHOD
1	*Enchilada Sauce*			
	Cream of chicken soup, condensed, canned	½ cup	3 cups	Combine in bowl and mix thoroughly.
	Cream of mushroom soup, condensed, canned	½ cup	3 cups	
	Milk, whole	½ cup	3 cups	
	Sour cream	½ cup	3 cups	
	Onions, fresh, diced (p. 175)	¼ cup	1½ cups	
	Garlic, fresh, minced	1 tbsp.	⅓ cup	
	Green chiles, mild, chopped, canned	2 tbsp.	¾ cup	
	Black pepper, coarse	¼ tsp.	½ tbsp.	
2	Tyson Mexican Original® Yellow Corn Tortillas, 6-inch, room temperature	6	24	*To prepare casserole:* Spread thin layer of enchilda sauce in bottom of one oiled full-size steam table pan. (Use third-size pan for smaller quantity.) Top sauce with half of tortillas, half of chicken, half of cheese, and half of sauce. Then layer remaining tortillas,
	Tyson Fully Cooked Diced White Fryer Meat, ½-inch dice, frozen	12 oz.	4½ lb.	
	Monterey Jack cheese, shredded	1 cup	6 cups	chicken, cheese, and remaining sauce in same order.
3	Cheddar cheese, mild, shredded	½ cup	3 cups	Sprinkle over casserole.
	Black olives, sliced, canned, drained	¼ cup	1 cup	Cover and bake in preheated conventional oven at 325°F for 75 to 80 minutes or until bubbling. (Cover and bake smaller quantity for 25 to 30 minutes.) Or cover and bake in preheated convection oven at 275°F for 70 to 75 minutes. (Cover and bake smaller quantity for 20 to 25 minutes.) Remove from oven and let rest 10 minutes. Keep warm above 140°F.
4	Cilantro, fresh, chopped	¼ cup	1½ cups	*To assemble single serving:* Portion 1¼ cups casserole on plate and sprinkle with 1 table-spoon cilantro.
				Serve with salsa.

Portion: 10 ounces
Nutritional Data/Portion: Calories 500, Protein 39 g, Fat 28 g, Carbohydrate 24 g, Cholesterol 130 mg, Sodium 860 mg

For a **FAST FACTS VIA FAX**™ copy of this recipe, call 1-800-223-3755 and enter Business Tool 2603.

"The best sauce in the world is hunger."
Cervantes

Recipe shown on opposite page.

Submitted by Nick Naccarato
Eagles Lodge
Spokane, Wash.

Italian Chicken and Sausage Biscuits

An Italian interpretation of biscuits and gravy, the classic breakfast or brunch meal, this easy recipe has wide appeal across all menu dayparts.

Line Service   Takeout

INGREDIENT	QUANTITY 4 servings	24 servings	METHOD
1 Tyson Ready-to-Cook Flavor-Redi® Italian Chicken Breast Filets, 5-oz., frozen	4	24	Grill on oiled, preheated flattop griddle at 350°F for 5½ to 6 minutes on each side or until chicken is no longer pink. Remove from griddle. Keep warm above 140°F.
2 Italian sausage, hot, bulk	8 oz.	3 lb.	Sauté in skillet over medium-high heat for 10 to 15 minutes or until brown. (Sauté smaller quantity for 5 to 8 minutes.) Crumble sausage during cooking. Drain drippings from skillet.
3 Button mushrooms, fresh, diced	2 cups	12 cups	Add to sausage and sauté for 5 to 10 minutes or until peppers are tender-crisp. (Sauté smaller quantity for 3 to 5 minutes.)
Green bell peppers, fresh, diced (p. 88)	½ cup	3 cups	
Red bell peppers, fresh, diced	½ cup	3 cups	
Green onions, fresh, diced	½ cup	3 cups	
Garlic, fresh, minced	1 tsp.	2 tbsp.	
4 White cream gravy, commercially prepared	2½ cups	15 cups	Add to sausage mixture and mix thoroughly. Bring to simmer, then remove from heat.
5 Parsley, fresh, minced (p. 39)	1 tbsp.	⅓ cup	Add to sausage mixture and mix thoroughly. Keep warm.
Cayenne pepper sauce	¼ tsp.	½ tbsp.	
6 Buttermilk biscuits, frozen, prepared according to package directions	4	24	To assemble single serving: Split 1 biscuit horizontally and arrange on plate, split sides up. Top with 1 chicken breast filet. Ladle ¾ cup sausage mixture across chicken. Garnish plate with 1 orange twist.
Orange slice twists	4	24	

Portion: 12 ounces
Nutritional Data/Portion: Calories 540, Protein 45 g, Fat 27 g, Carbohydrate 32 g, Cholesterol 125 mg, Sodium 1,616 mg

For a *FAST FACTS VIA FAX* copy of this recipe, call 1-800-223-3755 and enter Business Tool 2620.

A commercially prepared bell pepper and onion mixture may be substituted as a laborsaving shortcut.

What Americans call "biscuits"—light, tender quick breads made with leaveners such as baking powder—the Europeans call scones or crumpets. In the British Isles, the term biscuit refers to flat, thin cookies or crackers. In French, the word biscuit *means "twice cooked."*

During the California gold rush, '49ers depended on sourdough biscuits that used dough from the previous day's biscuits to leaven the new day's batch. It is thought that they used starter dough brought to the area by miners from Mexico.

"*All happiness depends on a leisurely breakfast.*"
John Gunther

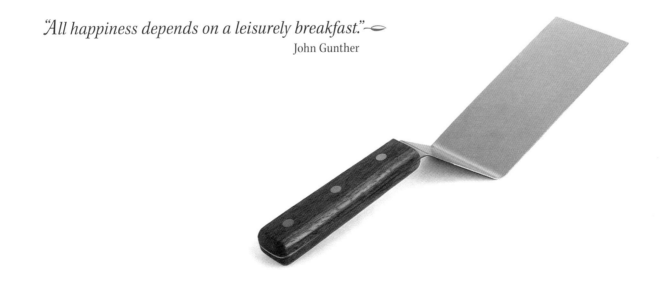

A unique line service presentation is shown in this photograph.

Confetti Chicken Hash

Hash was originally a dish of chopped leftover meat, potatoes, and vegetables heated together in a skillet, and served in homes across the country. Now hash is a popular comfort-food menu item, and it's still a great way to use leftovers.

Ancient cultures believed that the egg had greater potential as a chicken, and it wasn't until Roman times that eggs were widely used in cooking. In fact, the first custard was attributed to a pastry chef, Apicus, in 25 B.C. This, however, still does not answer the eternal question, "Which came first, the chicken or . . . ?"

INGREDIENT	QUANTITY 4 servings	24 servings	METHOD
1 Butter, salted	2 tbsp.	¾ cup	Heat in skillet or braising pan over medium heat.
2 Red potatoes, fresh, skin-on, ½-inch dice (p. 88)	1 cup	6 cups	Add to butter and sauté for 8 to 10 minutes or until potatoes are slightly tender. (Sauté smaller quantity for 5 to 6 minutes.)
3 Tyson Fully Cooked Diced White Fryer Meat, ¾-inch dice, frozen	12 oz.	4 lb.	Add to potatoes and mix thoroughly. Sauté for 4 to 5 minutes or until vegetables are tender-crisp. (Sauté smaller quantity for 1 to 2 minutes.)
Onions, fresh, chopped (p. 175)	½ cup	3 cups	
Red bell peppers, fresh, chopped	¼ cup	1½ cups	
Yellow bell peppers, fresh, chopped	¼ cup	1½ cups	
Green bell peppers, fresh, chopped	¼ cup	1½ cups	
Celery, fresh, chopped	¼ cup	1½ cups	
Carrots, fresh, shredded	2 tbsp.	¾ cup	
Garlic, fresh, minced	2 tsp.	¼ cup	
Poultry seasoning, dried	½ tsp.	1 tbsp.	
4 Stuffing croutons, seasoned	1 cup	6 cups	Add to chicken mixture and mix thoroughly. Simmer over medium heat for 4 to 5 minutes or until most of liquid is absorbed but mixture is still moist. (Simmer smaller quantity for 2 to 3 minutes.) Remove from heat. Keep warm above 140°F.
Chicken gravy, commercially prepared	2 cups	9 cups	
Salt	1 tsp.	1½ tbsp.	
Black pepper, coarse	½ tsp.	2 tsp.	
5 Eggs, large, poached	4	24	*To assemble single serving:* Portion 1 cup hash on plate. Top with 1 poached egg. Garnish plate with 1 sage sprig.
Sage sprigs, fresh	4	24	

Serve with toast points.

Portion: 10½ ounces
Nutritional Data/Portion: Calories 430, Protein 35 g, Fat 22 g, Carbohydrate 26 g, Cholesterol 300 mg, Sodium 1,640 mg

For a ***FAST FACTS VIA FAX*** copy of this recipe, call 1-800-223-3755 and enter Business Tool 2615.

Submitted by
Amy Z. and Harvey N. Kornfeld
Harvey-Ames Gourmet Catering
Katonah, N.Y.

Chicken Verdicchio

A delicious sauté of Mediterranean vegetables and chicken complemented by hearty couscous with dried apricots, cranberries, raisins, and pine nuts.

INGREDIENT	QUANTITY 4 servings	24 servings	METHOD
➊ Butter, clarified	¼ cup	1½ cups	*To prepare single serving:* Heat 1 tablespoon in sauté pan over medium heat.
➋ Tyson Ready-to-Cook Tenderpressed™ Savory Chicken Breast Filets, 4.75-oz., frozen	4	24	Add 1 chicken breast filet to butter and sauté for 2 to 3 minutes on each side or until well browned. Remove from pan.
➌ Black pepper, coarse	½ tsp.	1 tbsp.	Sprinkle ⅛ teaspoon over chicken. Keep warm above 140°F.
➍ Onions, fresh, chopped (p. 175)	½ cup	3 cups	Add 2 tablespoons to same pan. Sauté for 30 to 60 seconds or until translucent.
➎ Button mushrooms, fresh, sliced	1 cup	6 cups	Add ¼ cup mushrooms and ¼ teaspoon garlic to pan. Sauté for 30 to 60 seconds or until mushrooms are wilted.
Garlic, fresh, minced	1 tsp.	2 tbsp.	
➏ Pearl onions, whole, IQF, thawed	¼ cup	1½ cups	Add 1 tablespoon to pan and sauté for 30 to 60 seconds or until golden brown.
➐ Red bell pepper strips, roasted	16	96	Add 4 bell pepper strips, 3 each of black and green olives, and 2 artichoke halves. Mix thoroughly.
Black olives, whole, pitted, canned, drained	12	72	
Green olives, whole, pimiento-stuffed, canned, drained	12	72	
Artichoke hearts, canned, drained, halved	4	24	
➑ Chicken broth, canned	½ cup	3 cups	Add 2 tablespoons each of chicken broth and wine. Add chicken breast filet and any accumulated juices, stirring to blend. Bring to boil. Reduce heat and simmer for 1 to 1½ minutes or until chicken is no longer pink. Remove from heat and arrange on plate.
Verdicchio or other dry white wine	½ cup	3 cups	
➒ Mediterranean Couscous (see recipe)	4 cups	24 cups	Portion 1 cup couscous next to chicken. Garnish plate with 1 parsley sprig.
Parsley sprigs, fresh	4	24	

Portion: 15 ounces
Nutritional Data/Portion: Calories 748, Protein 34 g, Fat 26 g, Carbohydrate 97 g, Cholesterol 107 mg, Sodium 1,636 mg

For a **FAST FACTS VIA FAX** copy of this recipe, call 1-800-223-3755 and enter Business Tool 2613.

MEDITERRANEAN COUSCOUS

	4 servings	24 servings
Chicken broth, canned	2 cups	12 cups
Butter, salted	2 tbsp.	⅔ cup
Salt	½ tsp.	1 tbsp.
Couscous, dry	1 cup	6 cups
Cinnamon, ground	1 tsp.	2 tbsp.
Turmeric, ground	1 tsp.	2 tbsp.
Cardamom, ground	1 tsp.	2 tbsp.
Black pepper, fine	½ tsp.	1 tbsp.
Dates, dried, chopped	½ cup	3 cups
Apricots, dried, chopped	½ cup	3 cups
Cranberries, whole, dried	½ cup	3 cups
Raisins, dark	½ cup	3 cups
Water, boiling	to cover	to cover
Pine nuts, whole, toasted	1½ tbsp.	½ cup
Parsley, fresh, minced	1½ tbsp.	½ cup

Combine first three ingredients in saucepan or stockpot and bring to boil over high heat.

Combine next five ingredients in bowl and mix thoroughly. Add to broth mixture and stir well. Return to boil, then remove from heat. Cover and allow to rest undisturbed for 10 to 15 minutes or until most of liquid is absorbed.

Combine next four ingredients in separate bowl.

Pour boiling water over fruit and soak for 10 to 15 minutes or until fruit is soft and plump. Drain and add to couscous, tossing with fork to loosen any clumps. Keep warm.

Sprinkle each serving with 1 teaspoon pine nuts and 1 teaspoon parsley.

Submitted by Jonathan Mortimer
The Grove Hotel
Boise, Idaho

Smoked Chicken and Morel Mushroom Crepes

Tender crepes surround a creamy mixture of smoky chicken strips and earthy morel mushrooms. Perfect for Sunday brunches and light dinners.

Line Service

Crêpe is the French word for "pancake."

Perhaps the most famous crepes recipe, Crêpes Suzettes, is believed by some to have originated with the French chef Jean Rédoux around 1667. Others attribute the original recipe to an understudy of Auguste Escoffier who worked at the Café de Paris in Monte Carlo in 1895.

Morels are cone-shaped mushrooms with honeycomb flesh. Wild morels grow in early spring and are generally considered the most flavorful. Morel hunters tend to be very secretive about their sources, but commonly agree that morels are often found near cedar, conifer, and birch trees on warm, sunny days following rainy days.

INGREDIENT	QUANTITY 4 servings	24 servings	METHOD
1 Tyson Fully Cooked Flavor-Redi® Smoked Chicken Breast Filets, 2.75-oz., frozen	5	30	Cover tightly and slack in cooler between 32° and 36°F prior to use.
			Slice chicken breast filets in half lengthwise, then slice into strips crosswise.
2 Olive oil	1 tbsp.	⅓ cup	Heat in skillet or braising pan over medium-high heat.
3 Morel mushrooms, dried, reconstituted in hot water, drained, sliced	1 cup	6 cups	Add to oil and mix thoroughly. Add chicken and sauté for 4 to 5 minutes or until mushrooms are wilted. (Sauté smaller quantity for 2 to 3 minutes.)
Shallots, fresh, chopped	1 tbsp.	⅓ cup	
Salt	½ tsp.	1 tbsp.	
White pepper, fine	¼ tsp.	½ tbsp.	
4 Heavy cream	1½ cups	9 cups	Add to chicken mixture and mix thoroughly.
5 Cornstarch	½ tbsp.	2 tbsp.	Combine in small bowl and mix until smooth. Gradually stir into chicken mixture. Bring to simmer and simmer for 4 to 5 minutes or until mixture thickens. (Simmer smaller quantity for 1 to 2 minutes.) Remove from heat.
Water, cold	1 tbsp.	¼ cup	
			Strain and reserve cream for sauce; keep warm. Reserve solids for filling. Keep warm above 140°F.
6 Crepes, 6-inch, frozen, commercially prepared, room temperature	12	72	*To prepare single serving:* Place 3 crepes on flat work surface.
Nasturtium flowers, fresh	4	24	Spoon 2 tablespoons filling across center of each crepe. Fold lower end of each crepe over filling and roll closed, keeping filling tightly packed. Transfer to plate, seam side down. Ladle ⅓ cup cream sauce over crepes.
			Heat in preheated conventional oven‡ at 200°F for 2 to 3 minutes or until thoroughly heated. Remove from oven. Garnish plate with 1 nasturtium flower.

Portion: 10 ounces

Nutritional Data/Portion: Calories 728, Protein 41 g, Fat 47 g, Carbohydrate 35 g, Cholesterol 413 mg, Sodium 1,206 mg

‡Convection oven not recommended.

For a **FAST FACTS VIA FAX**™ copy of this recipe, call 1-800-223-3755 and enter Business Tool 2625.

"Morels are like the great love of one's life: They don't last."
Robert Courtine

Chicken Puttanesca

Decades ago, puttanesca was the meal of choice for time-pressed Italians
because it is quick and delicious. In addition to its intense flavor, the beauty
of this dish is that most of the ingredients are shelf stable or frozen, virtually
eliminating waste and greatly reducing prep labor.

INGREDIENT	QUANTITY		METHOD
	4 servings	24 servings	
1 Tyson Ready-to-Cook Tenderpressed™ Savory Chicken Breast Filets, 5-oz., frozen	4	24	Char-grill over high heat for 5 to 6 minutes on each side or until chicken is no longer pink. Or grill on oiled, preheated flattop griddle at 350°F for 6½ to 7½ minutes on each side. Remove from grill. Keep warm above 140°F.
2 *Puttanesca Sauce*			
Olive oil	2 tbsp.	½ cup	Combine in saucepan and mix thoroughly. Bring to boil over medium heat. Reduce heat and simmer for 2 to 4 minutes or until flavors are blended. (Simmer smaller quantity for 1 to 2 minutes.) Remove from heat and keep warm.
Tomatoes, crushed, in puree, canned	2 cups	9 cups	
Black olives, sliced, canned, drained	½ cup	3 cups	
Capers, rinsed, drained	1 tbsp.	⅓ cup	
Garlic, chopped, commercially prepared	½ tsp.	1 tbsp.	
Anchovy paste	¼ tsp.	½ tbsp.	
Red pepper, crushed, dried	⅛ tsp.	¾ tsp.	
3 Spaghetti, cooked al dente, drained, hot	8 oz. (dry)	3 lb. (dry)	*To assemble single serving:* Portion 1 cup spaghetti on plate. Slice 1 chicken breast filet and fan over spaghetti. Ladle ½ cup sauce over chicken and pasta. Sprinkle with 1 tablespoon cheese. Garnish plate with 1 basil sprig.
Parmesan cheese, shredded	¼ cup	1½ cups	
Basil sprigs, fresh	4	24	

Serve with focaccia bread.

Portion: 13 ounces
Nutritional Data/Portion: Calories 490, Protein 40 g, Fat 14 g, Carbohydrate 50 g, Cholesterol 90 mg, Sodium 720 mg

For a **FAST FACTS VIA FAX** copy of this recipe, call 1-800-223-3755 and enter Business Tool 2365.

Capers are actually flower buds of the caper bush, a spiny shrub native to Asia and the Mediterranean region. Sun-dried buds are usually pickled in vinegar brine and are available in two sizes: capote, or "large," and nonpareils, or "small," which are similar in size to peppercorns. The two sizes are interchangeable, according to each chef's preference.

When buying salt-packed capers, be sure the salt is white or pale yellow; dark salt is a sign of rancidity. Salt-packed capers can be stored for 2 months in an open bag. Refrigerated brine-packed capers will keep up to 3 months.

Submitted by Mike Jackson
Omni Mandalay Hotel
Irving, Tex.

Asparagus plants can live for up to 20 years. The size of the spears hints to the age of the plant. Thicker spears come from more mature plants; slender spears are from younger plants. Healthy spears can grow up to 10 inches in one day, and some spears continue growing even after they are picked!—

Hot-smoking is a method of cooking food at temperatures between 100° and 190°F. This is contrasted by the cold-smoking method, which cooks food at temperatures between 70° and 90°F and can take up to a month (depending on the food).—

If a smoke oven is not available, the same effect can still be achieved. Combine the mushrooms, olive oil, and balsamic vinegar in a bowl, then spread the mixture in a pan and place on a preheated char-grill. Cover the mixture with a metal bowl to catch the smoke. Smoke over medium heat for 4 to 5 minutes or until the mushrooms are tender.—

Chicken Rotini with Roasted Red Pepper Alfredo

Since Alfredo is synonymous with cream sauce, his name is borrowed for this recipe combining rich red bell pepper cream sauce with grilled chicken, portobello mushrooms, and asparagus. This Alfredo has been further Americanized by substituting heavy cream for butter.

INGREDIENT	QUANTITY 4 servings	24 servings	METHOD
1 Tyson Ready-to-Cook Flavor-Redi® Savory Chicken Breast Filets, 6-oz., frozen	4	24	Slack in cooler between 32° and 36°F prior to use. Char-grill over medium heat for 4 to 4½ minutes on each side or until chicken is no longer pink. Or grill on oiled, preheated flattop griddle at 350°F for 4 to 4½ minutes on each side. Remove from grill. Keep warm above 140°F.
2 *Red Pepper Alfredo Sauce* Olive oil	1 tbsp.	⅓ cup	Heat in saucepan over low heat.
3 Shallots, fresh, minced	1 tbsp.	⅓ cup	Add to oil and sauté for 1 to 2 minutes or until shallots are tender.
4 Garlic, fresh, minced	½ tbsp.	3 tbsp.	
White wine, dry	1½ cups	9 cups	Add to shallot mixture and bring to boil over high heat. Boil for 15 to 20 minutes or until liquid is reduced by half. (Boil smaller quantity for 4 to 5 minutes.)
Bay leaves, whole, dried	½	3	
5 Red bell peppers, roasted, peeled, seeded, chopped (p. 66)	1 cup	4 cups	Add to shallot mixture and simmer for 12 to 15 minutes or until flavors are blended. (Simmer smaller quantity for 5 to 6 minutes.) Discard bay leaves.
Heavy cream	3 cups	18 cups	
6 Romano cheese, grated	3 tbsp.	1 cup	Add to sauce mixture and stir until cheese is melted. Remove from heat. Transfer to food processor bowl and process until pureed. Remove from processor bowl and strain through fine mesh strainer. Cover and chill to hold.
Salt	¼ tsp.	2 tsp.	
White pepper, fine	⅛ tsp.	¾ tsp.	
7 *Smoked Mushrooms* Portobello mushrooms, fresh, sliced	1 cup	6 cups	Combine in bowl and toss well.
Olive oil	1 tbsp.	⅓ cup	Hot-smoke in smoke oven between 200° and 225°F over hickory chips for 4 to 5 minutes on each side or until mushrooms are tender. Remove from smoker. Cover and reserve.
Balsamic vinegar	1 tbsp.	⅓ cup	

recipe continued on next page . . .

INGREDIENT	QUANTITY		METHOD
	4 servings	24 servings	
8 Asparagus tips, fresh	24	144	*To prepare single serving:* Heat dry sauté pan over medium heat. Add 6 asparagus tips and pan roast for 20 seconds, stirring constantly.
Garlic rotini pasta, cooked al dente, drained, rinsed	1 lb. (dry)	6 lb. (dry)	
			Add ¼ cup smoked mushrooms, 1 cup red pepper Alfredo sauce, and 1½ cups pasta. Simmer for 2 to 3 minutes or until ingredients are hot. Transfer to plate. Slice 1 chicken breast filet and fan over pasta.
9 Red bell pepper strips, roasted	4	24	Garnish plate with 1 bell pepper strip, 1 teaspoon parsley, and 1 basil sprig.
Parsley, Italian flat-leaf, fresh, minced (p. 39)	1½ tbsp.	½ cup	
Basil sprigs, fresh	4	24	

Portion: 19 ounces
Nutritional Data/Portion: Calories 740, Protein 48 g, Fat 46 g, Carbohydrate 23 g, Cholesterol 215 mg, Sodium 720 mg

For a **FAST FACTS VIA FAX** copy of this recipe, call 1-800-223-3755 and enter Business Tool 2597.

Deep-fry the basil sprig garnish for an interesting presentation twist.

Chicken Fettuccine Carbonara

Standard carbonara starts with green peas, bacon, Parmesan cheese, and cream.
This variation adds a new twist with chicken tenderloins and pesto.

Line Service   Takeout

Submitted by Ennio Riga
Prime Hospitality
Fairfield, N.J.

INGREDIENT	QUANTITY		METHOD
	4 servings	24 servings	
1 Butter, salted	½ cup	3 cups	*To prepare single serving:* Heat 2 tablespoons in sauté pan over medium heat.
2 Onions, fresh, minced	½ cup	3 cups	Add 2 tablespoons to butter and sauté for 30 to 45 seconds or until onions begin to cook.
3 Tyson Ready-to-Cook Flavor-Redi® Savory Tenderloins, frozen	12	72	Add 3 tenderloins to onions and sauté for 2 to 3 minutes on each side or until lightly browned.
4 Chicken broth, canned	1 cup	6 cups	Add ¼ cup broth and 2 tablespoons wine. Bring to boil and boil for 1 to 2 minutes or until liquid is reduced by half.
White wine, dry	½ cup	3 cups	
5 Heavy cream	1 cup	6 cups	Add ¼ cup cream and 1 tablespoon bacon. Return to boil for 1 to 2 minutes or until chicken is no longer pink.
Bacon, crisp, minced	¼ cup	1½ cups	
6 Green peas, frozen	1 cup	6 cups	Add ¼ cup peas, 1 tablespoon Parmesan, 1 teaspoon pesto, ¼ teaspoon salt, and ⅛ teaspoon pepper. Stir until thoroughly heated. Remove from heat.
Parmesan cheese, grated	¼ cup	1½ cups	
Pesto sauce, commercially prepared	4 tsp.	½ cup	
Salt	1 tsp.	2 tbsp.	
Black pepper, fine	½ tsp.	1 tbsp.	
7 Fettuccine, cooked al dente, drained, hot	12 oz. (dry)	4½ lb. (dry)	Portion 1½ cups pasta on plate. Top with chicken and sauce. Garnish plate with 1 parsley sprig.
Parsley sprigs, Italian flat-leaf, fresh	4	24	*Serve with focaccia bread.*

Portion: 18 ounces
Nutritional Data/Portion: Calories 1,030, Protein 50 g, Fat 59 g, Carbohydrate 70 g, Cholesterol 200 mg, Sodium 1,784 mg

For a **FAST FACTS VIA FAX** copy of this recipe, call 1-800-223-3755 and enter Business Tool 2600.

Although pesto is typically made with basil, its popularity has given rise to variations made with a range of ingredients from cilantro to mint.

Chicago-Style Deep-Dish Chicken Pizza

With the introduction of this great pizza loaded with chicken, the Windy City's famous deep-dish spinach, cheese, and tomato pizzas can add a new member to their popular ranks.

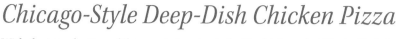

Legend has it that deep-dish pizza was created in Chicago in 1943, even though many Chicagoans will disagree about the definition of Chicago-style pizza. Some insist that it must be stuffed. For others, unstuffed deep-dish pizza like the recipe shown here is synonymous with Chicago-style pizza.

Chicago-style pizza, whether stuffed or deep-dish, is distinguished by its heartiness and by the fact that the ingredients are placed on the pizza in the opposite order of a regular pizza.

Popular Italian cheese blends can include any combination of garlic Jack, mozzarella, Asiago, Parmesan, and pecorino Romano cheeses.

INGREDIENT	QUANTITY 6 servings	METHOD
1 *Tomato Sauce*		
Tomato puree, canned	1 cup	Combine in saucepan and mix thoroughly. Bring to boil over medium-high heat. Reduce heat and simmer for 8 to 10 minutes or until flavors are blended. Remove from heat and discard basil sprigs. Cover and chill to hold.
Tomatoes, diced, canned, undrained	1½ cups	
Olive oil	1 tbsp.	
Garlic, fresh, minced	½ tsp.	
Basil sprigs, fresh	4	
Sugar, granulated	¼ tsp.	
Salt	¼ tsp.	
2 Pizza dough, presheeted, 14-inch, unbaked, frozen, slacked according to package directions	1	Fit crust into oiled 12-inch deep-dish pizza pan. Let rise at room temperature for 1½ to 2 hours or until dough springs back when touched.
3 Pizza cheese blend, shredded	4 cups	Spread evenly over crust.
4 Tyson Fully Cooked Flavor-Redi® Chicken Breast Fajita Strips, frozen	12 oz.	Arrange over cheese.
5 Spinach, fresh, chopped	1 cup	Arrange over chicken.
6 Pizza cheese blend, shredded	2 cups	Sprinkle cheese blend over spinach. Spread tomato sauce evenly over cheese. Sprinkle Romano cheese over sauce.
Romano cheese, grated	¼ cup	
		Bake in preheated conventional oven† at 450°F for 55 to 60 minutes or until crust is brown and cheese is bubbling. Remove from oven. Remove from pan and slice into wedges. Serve immediately.

Portion: One-sixth of one 12-inch pizza (12 ounces)
Nutritional Data/Portion: Calories 738, Protein 49 g, Fat 39 g, Carbohydrate 49 g, Cholesterol 136 mg, Sodium 1,758 mg

†Convection oven not recommended.

For a **FAST FACTS VIA FAX** copy of this recipe, call 1-800-223-3755 and enter Business Tool 2598.

Baked Chicken Spaghetti

Cheddar cheese, garlic, and a hint of nutmeg complement the sautéed meats and vegetables in this remarkable chicken spaghetti.

Other cuts of pasta can be substituted for a different presentation.

INGREDIENT	QUANTITY 4 servings	24 servings	METHOD
1 Butter, salted	2 tbsp.	1 cup	Combine in skillet or braising pan and heat over high heat.
Olive oil	1 tsp.	¼ cup	
2 Ground beef, lean	2 oz.	10 oz.	Add to butter and oil and sauté for 5 to 10 minutes or until brown. (Sauté smaller quantity for 2 to 3 minutes.) Crumble meat during cooking.
Ground pork, lean	2 oz.	10 oz.	
3 Onions, fresh, chopped (p. 175)	1 cup	5 cups	Add to meat mixture and sauté for 8 to 10 minutes or until liquid has evaporated. (Sauté smaller quantity for 2 to 4 minutes.)
Green bell peppers, fresh, chopped	⅔ cup	3¾ cups	
Celery, fresh, chopped	⅔ cup	3¾ cups	
Red bell peppers, fresh, chopped	½ cup	2½ cups	
Garlic, fresh, minced	1 tbsp.	3 tbsp.	
Red pepper, crushed, dried	¼ tsp.	1¼ tsp.	
Salt	¼ tsp.	1¼ tsp.	
Nutmeg, ground	⅛ tsp.	½ tsp.	
Bay leaves, whole, dried	1	3	

recipe continued on next page . . .

Baked Chicken Spaghetti continued

INGREDIENT	QUANTITY 4 servings	24 servings	METHOD
4 Flour, all-purpose	1 tbsp.	½ cup	Add to meat mixture and mix thoroughly. Cook for 2 minutes or until flour is cooked but not brown. Transfer mixture to stockpot.
5 Chicken broth, canned	3 cups	15 cups	Add to meat mixture and mix thoroughly. Bring to boil over high heat. Reduce heat and simmer for 25 to 30 minutes or until mixture thickens. (Simmer smaller quantity for 10 to 15 minutes.) Remove from heat and discard bay leaves.
Tomatoes, diced, canned, drained	⅔ cup	3¾ cups	
Heavy cream	½ cup	1½ cups	
6 Butter, salted	1 tbsp.	5 tbsp.	Combine in skillet and heat over high heat.
Olive oil	½ tsp.	1 tbsp.	
7 Button mushrooms, fresh, quartered	1⅓ cups	7½ cups	Add to butter and oil and sauté for 5 to 7 minutes or until liquid has evaporated. (Sauté smaller quantity for 2 to 3 minutes.) Add to meat mixture.
Porcini mushrooms, dried, rehydrated according to package directions, chopped	1 tbsp.	⅔ cup	
8 Tyson Fully Cooked Pulled White Fryer Meat, frozen	8 oz.	2½ lb.	Add to meat mixture and mix thoroughly.
Spaghetti, cooked al dente, drained	8 oz. (dry)	3 lb. (dry)	
9 Cheddar cheese, sharp, shredded	1 cup	6 cups	*To prepare casserole:* Layer half of chicken/spaghetti mixture in two full-size steam table pans. (Use third-size pan for smaller quantity.) Sprinkle with half of cheese. Repeat process, ending with final layer of cheese. Cover and bake in preheated conventional oven at 350°F for 1 to 1½ hours or until cheese is melted and mixture is thoroughly heated. (Bake smaller quantity for 20 to 30 minutes.) Or cover and bake in preheated convection oven at 325°F for 30 to 40 minutes. (Bake smaller quantity for 10 to 15 minutes.) Remove from oven. Keep warm above 140°F.
10 Parsley, fresh, minced (p. 39)	2 tbsp.	¾ cup	*To assemble single serving:* Portion 2 cups spaghetti mixture on plate and sprinkle with ½ tablespoon parsley. Portion 2 tablespoons cheese into individual container and serve on the side.
Parmesan cheese, grated	½ cup	3 cups	

Portion: 16½ ounces
Nutritional Data/Portion: Calories 760, Protein 48 g, Fat 37 g, Carbohydrate 59 g, Cholesterol 150 mg, Sodium 1,290 mg

For a **FAST FACTS VIA FAX** copy of this recipe, call 1-800-223-3755 and enter Business Tool 2352.

Pasta shops boomed in Naples during the 1700s, their number increasing from 60 to 280 by 1785. One could see pasta drying on balconies, rooftops, and in the streets. Street vendors prepared spaghetti over charcoal-fired stoves and sold it with grated Romano cheese.

Italy's first commercial pasta factory was opened by Paolo B. Agnese at Imperia in 1824.

Chicken Tetrazzini

Since its creation, this classic dish has combined strips of chicken and spaghetti in a rich, creamy sauce of Parmesan cheese and heavy cream. It was appropriately named in honor of an opera singer with a rich and creamy voice.

For an alternate presentation, use pulled or diced chicken; portion mixture into individual casserole dishes and bake.

During the 19th century, the fashion among chefs was to name their creations after celebrated opera singers. Luisa Tetrazzini, who was heralded as the "voice of the century," inspired this great dish.

Chef Auguste Escoffier created soufflé Tetrazzini while working at London's Savoy Hotel during the 1890s. It was one of several dishes, including Peach Melba, poularde Tosca, and poularde Belle Hélène, that he created and named to honor female patrons of the hotel.

	INGREDIENT	QUANTITY 4 servings	24 servings	METHOD
1	Spaghetti, thin, cooked al dente, drained	8 oz. (dry)	3 lb. (dry)	Arrange in two oiled full-size steam table pans. (Use third-size pan for smaller quantity.)
2	Olive oil	2 tbsp.	¾ cup	Heat in skillet or braising pan over medium-high heat.
3	Button mushrooms, fresh, sliced	4 cups	24 cups	Add to oil and sauté for 7 to 8 minutes or until mushrooms are wilted. (Sauté smaller quantity for 3 to 4 minutes.) Remove from heat and discard bay leaves. Arrange over spaghetti.
	Garlic, fresh, minced	1 tbsp.	⅓ cup	
	Parsley, fresh, minced (p. 39)	¼ cup	1½ cups	
	Bay leaves, whole, dried	2	12	
	Salt	½ tsp.	1 tbsp.	
	Black pepper, coarse	¼ tsp.	½ tbsp.	
4	Tyson Fully Cooked Flavor-Redi® Roasted and Carved Chicken Breast Filets, frozen	4	24	Shingle 12 breast filets down center of each pan. (Use 4 breasts for smaller pan.)
5	Butter, salted, melted	⅓ cup	2 cups	Combine in saucepan over medium heat and stir until smooth.
	Flour, all-purpose	¼ cup	1½ cups	
6	Chicken broth, canned	2 cups	12 cups	Gradually stir into butter/flour mixture. Bring to boil over high heat, stirring constantly. Reduce heat and simmer for 4 to 5 minutes or until sauce thickens. (Simmer smaller quantity for 1 to 2 minutes.) Remove from heat.
7	Heavy cream	1 cup	6 cups	Stir into broth mixture and pour over chicken.
	White wine, dry	½ cup	3 cups	
8	Parmesan cheese, grated	¼ cup	1½ cups	Sprinkle over chicken.
				Cover and bake in preheated conventional oven at 400°F for 60 to 70 minutes or until bubbling. (Bake smaller quantity for 35 to 40 minutes.) Or cover and bake in preheated convection oven at 350°F for 45 to 50 minutes. (Bake smaller quantity for 25 to 30 minutes.) Remove from oven. Keep warm above 140°F.
9	Parmesan cheese, grated	¼ cup	1½ cups	*To assemble single serving:* Portion 1 chicken breast filet on bed of 1¾ cups spaghetti mixture. Sprinkle with 1 tablespoon each of cheese and parsley.
	Parsley, fresh, minced	¼ cup	1½ cups	
				Serve with Italian bread.

Portion: 18 ounces
Nutritional Data/Portion: Calories 790, Protein 45 g, Fat 40 g, Carbohydrate 59 g, Cholesterol 160 mg, Sodium 1,950 mg

For a **FAST FACTS VIA FAX** copy of this recipe, call 1-800-223-3755 and enter Business Tool 2610.

Submitted by Paul S. Wilson, FMP
The Brass Pineapple Restaurant
Winchendon, Mass.

Mediterranean Chicken with Artichokes

The aroma of fresh garlic, artichoke hearts, sun-dried tomatoes, and lemon juice
is a sign that these braised chicken tenderloins are in good company.

INGREDIENT	QUANTITY		METHOD
	4 servings	24 servings	
1 New red potatoes, fresh, cut into quarters	8	48	Combine in saucepan and bring to boil over high heat. Reduce heat and simmer for 10 to 12 minutes or until potatoes are slightly tender. (Simmer smaller quantity for 8 to 10 minutes.) Remove from heat and drain. Cover and reserve.
Chicken broth, canned	1 cup	8 cups	
2 Tyson Ready-to-Cook Flavor-Redi® Savory Chicken Tenderloins, frozen	12	72	Dredge chicken in flour and shake off excess.
Flour, all-purpose	as needed	as needed	
3 Olive oil	2 tbsp.	¾ cup	Heat in skillet or braising pan over medium-high heat. Add chicken and sauté for 1 to 2 minutes on each side or until brown.
4 Button mushrooms, fresh, sliced	2 cups	12 cups	Add to chicken and mix thoroughly. Simmer for 5 to 6 minutes or until most of liquid has evaporated. (Simmer smaller quantity for 3 to 4 minutes.) Remove from heat and transfer to two full-size steam table pans. (Use half-size pan for smaller quantity.)
Sun-dried tomatoes, packed in oil, drained, minced	½ cup	3 cups	
Artichoke hearts, canned, drained, halved	2 cups	12 cups	
Garlic, fresh, minced	2 tbsp.	¾ cup	
Lemon juice, fresh	2 tbsp.	¾ cup	
White wine, dry	2 tbsp.	¾ cup	
Dill weed, dried	1 tsp.	2 tbsp.	
5 Chicken broth, canned	¼ cup	1½ cups	Pour over chicken mixture. Add potatoes and mix thoroughly.
			Cover and bake in preheated conventional oven at 400°F for 12 to 15 minutes or until chicken is no longer pink. (Cover and bake smaller quantity for 7 to 8 minutes.) Or cover and bake in preheated convection oven at 350°F for 8 to 10 minutes. (Cover and bake smaller quantity for 5 to 6 minutes.) Remove from oven.
6 Parmesan cheese, grated	¼ cup	1½ cups	Sprinkle over mixture. Keep warm above 140°F.
Parsley, fresh, minced (p. 39)	1½ tbsp.	½ cup	
7 Dill sprigs, fresh	4	24	*To assemble single serving:* Portion 1 cup vegetable mixture on plate. Top with 3 tenderloins. Garnish plate with 1 dill sprig.
			Serve with crusty French bread.

Portion: 13 ounces
Nutritional Data/Portion: Calories 350, Protein 37 g, Fat 11 g, Carbohydrate 28 g, Cholesterol 60 mg, Sodium 1,350 mg

For a **FAST FACTS VIA FAX**™ copy of this recipe, call 1-800-223-3755 and enter Business Tool 2596.

When Catherine d' Medici, the daughter of a rich Italian spice merchant, was betrothed to Henri II in 1533, her entourage introduced a wealth of new food ideas to France. One of the vegetables she introduced to French nobles was the artichoke.

"Eating an artichoke is like getting to know someone really well."
Willi Hastings

Submitted by Robert Merrifield
The Polo Grill
Tulsa, Okla.

HERB-INFUSED OIL

	1 pint
Olive oil	2 cups
Thyme, fresh, blanched, drained, chopped	½ cup
Rosemary, fresh, blanched, drained, chopped	½ cup
Basil, fresh, blanched, drained, chopped	½ cup
Garlic cloves, fresh, crushed	6

Combine in saucepan and bring to gentle simmer over low heat. Simmer for 4 to 5 minutes or until oil is flavored with herbs. Remove from heat. Cool and strain through fine mesh strainer. Cover and reserve.

MANGO CHILI SAUCE

	1 pint
Mango puree, canned	2 cups
Orange juice, made from frozen concentrate	1 cup
Sweet rice vinegar	¼ cup
Sambal chili paste	1 tsp.
Garlic clove, fresh, crushed	1
Saffron, dried	¼ tsp.
Cloves, whole	1
Gingerroot, fresh, peeled, chopped	1 tbsp.
Bay leaf, whole	1

Combine in saucepan and mix thoroughly. Bring to boil over medium heat. Reduce heat and simmer for 8 to 10 minutes or until flavors are blended. Discard bay leaf. Transfer to food processor bowl and process until pureed. Remove from processor bowl and strain through fine mesh strainer. Cool and place in squeeze bottle for service.

Barbecue Asian Chicken

For a thoroughly modern version of chow mein, chicken is marinated in sweet-and-hot cola marinade, char-grilled, added to a vegetable stir-fry with crispy noodles, and finished with mango chili sauce, banana catsup, and toasted black sesame seeds.

INGREDIENT	QUANTITY		METHOD
	4 servings	24 servings	
1 Tyson Ready-to-Cook Gourmet Boneless, Skinless Chicken Breast Filets, 6-oz., frozen	4	24	Place in full-size steam table pans. (Use half-size pan for smaller quantity.)
2 *Cola Marinade*			
Cola soft drink	½ cup	4 cups	Combine in bowl and mix thoroughly.
Lemon-lime soft drink	½ cup	4 cups	Pour over chicken and marinate below 40°F for 24 hours.
Banana catsup, hot, commercially prepared	¼ cup	2 cups	
Soy sauce	¼ cup	2 cups	
Gingerroot, fresh, peeled, chopped	2 tbsp.	¾ cup	
Garlic, fresh, minced	1 tbsp.	½ cup	
Brown sugar, dark	1 tbsp.	½ cup	
Lime juice, fresh	1 tbsp.	½ cup	
White pepper, fine	¼ tsp.	2 tsp.	
3 Napa cabbage, fresh, cut into 1-inch squares	8 cups	48 cups	Combine in bowl and mix thoroughly. Cover and chill to hold.
Snow peas, fresh, blanched, bias-sliced	1 cup	6 cups	
Green onions, fresh, bias-sliced	1 cup	6 cups	
Carrots, fresh, julienne (p. 88)	2 tbsp.	¾ cup	
4 Hoisin sauce, commercially prepared	2 tbsp.	¾ cup	Combine in separate bowl and mix thoroughly. Cover and reserve.
Asian chili sauce, hot, commercially prepared	¼ tsp.	½ tbsp.	
Rice wine vinegar	1 tbsp.	⅓ cup	*To prepare single serving:* Remove 1 chicken breast filet from marinade and char-grill over high heat for 4 to 6 minutes on each side or until chicken is no longer pink. Remove from grill. Keep warm above 140°F.
Soy sauce	1 tbsp.	⅓ cup	
5 Herb-Infused Oil (see recipe)	¼ cup	1½ cups	Heat 1 tablespoon in sauté pan over high heat.
6 Gingerroot, fresh, peeled, chopped	2 tbsp.	¾ cup	Add 2½ cups cabbage mixture, ½ tablespoon ginger, and ½ tablespoon garlic to oil. Stir-fry for 1 minute or until cabbage begins to wilt.
Garlic, fresh, minced	2 tbsp.	¾ cup	

recipe continued on next page . . .

INGREDIENT	QUANTITY 4 servings	24 servings	METHOD
7			
Rice noodles, fried, commercially prepared	1 cup	6 cups	Add ¼ cup rice noodles and ½ cup lo mein noodles to cabbage mixture and stir-fry for 1 minute or until noodles are warm.
Lo mein noodles, blanched	4 oz. (dry)	1½ lb. (dry)	
			Add 1 tablespoon hoisin mixture to noodles and stir-fry for 30 seconds or until thoroughly mixed. Remove from heat and transfer to plate. Slice chicken breast filet into strips and fan on one side of stir-fry mixture.
8			
Banana catsup, hot, commercially prepared	¼ cup	1½ cups	Pool 1 tablespoon banana catsup next to chicken. Drizzle mango chili sauce over entire plate and sprinkle with ½ teaspoon sesame seeds.
Mango Chili Sauce (see recipe)	as needed	as needed	
Black sesame seeds, whole, toasted	2 tsp.	¼ cup	

Portion: 12 ounces
Nutritional Data/Portion: Calories 700, Protein 43 g, Fat 28 g, Carbohydrate 71 g, Cholesterol 105 mg, Sodium 1,000 mg

For a **FAST FACTS VIA FAX**™ copy of this recipe, call 1-800-223-3755 and enter Business Tool 2594.

For safety reasons, it is best to keep infused oils refrigerated and use them the same day they are made. Olive oil may be substituted for the infused oil recipe.

General Tso's Chicken

A rendition of classic General Tso's Chicken, featuring vegetables and crispy tempura chicken strips tossed in a spicy sauce of chopped hot cherry peppers, orange juice, and hoisin sauce.

Line Service   Takeout

Submitted by Jeff Trombetta
Yale University Dining Services
New Haven, Conn.

INGREDIENT	QUANTITY 4 servings	24 servings	METHOD
1			
Tyson Ready-to-Cook Tempura Chicken Strips, frozen	1½ lb.	9 lb.	Deep-fry at 360°F for 3½ to 4½ minutes or until chicken is no longer pink. Remove from fryer and drain. Keep warm above 140°F.
2			
Apricot-Orange Sauce			
Apricot preserves	⅓ cup	2 cups	Combine in saucepan and mix thoroughly. Bring to boil over high heat. Reduce heat to simmer.
Orange juice concentrate, frozen	⅓ cup	2 cups	
Duck sauce, commercially prepared	3 tbsp.	1 cup	
Hot cherry peppers, canned, chopped	2 tbsp.	¾ cup	
Hot cherry pepper juice, from canned cherry peppers	3 tbsp.	1 cup	
Hoisin sauce, commercially prepared	2 tbsp.	¾ cup	
Cayenne pepper sauce	½ tsp.	1 tbsp.	
White pepper, fine	½ tsp.	1 tbsp.	
Water	½ cup	3 cups	
3			
Cornstarch	2 tbsp.	¾ cup	Combine in small bowl and mix until smooth. Gradually stir into sauce. Simmer for 1 to 2 minutes or until sauce thickens. Remove from heat and keep warm.
Water	⅔ cup	3 cups	
4			
Vegetable oil	1 tbsp.	¼ cup	Heat in skillet or braising pan over high heat.
5			
Snow peas, fresh, ½-inch bias-sliced	1 cup	5 cups	Add to oil and sauté for 8 to 10 minutes or until vegetables are tender-crisp. (Sauté smaller quantity for 1 to 2 minutes.) Remove from heat and keep warm.
Carrots, fresh, ¼-inch bias-sliced	½ cup	2 cups	
Bamboo shoots, sliced, canned, drained	½ cup	2 cups	
Salt	⅛ tsp.	½ tsp.	
White pepper, fine	⅛ tsp.	½ tsp.	
6			
Orange slice twists, fresh	4	24	*To assemble single serving:* Combine 6 ounces chicken, ¼ cup vegetable mixture, and ½ cup sauce in bowl. Gently toss to coat chicken and vegetables with sauce and arrange on plate. Garnish plate with 1 orange twist. *Serve with sticky rice.*

Portion: 11 ounces
Nutritional Data/Portion: Calories 650, Protein 21 g, Fat 30 g, Carbohydrate 75 g, Cholesterol 70 mg, Sodium 1,270 mg

For a **FAST FACTS VIA FAX**™ copy of this recipe, call 1-800-223-3755 and enter Business Tool 2619.

For a traditional Chinese presentation, serve family-size portions of the chicken and vegetables on a platter and the rice in a separate bowl. Each diner then shares and portions the chicken and rice as desired.

Duck sauce, also called plum sauce, is a thick sweet-and-sour condiment made with plums, apricots, sugar, and seasonings. It is, not surprisingly, often served with duck. But it also tastes great with chicken, pork, or spareribs.

Some historians believe that Marco Polo brought pasta to Italy from China and that the word "lasagna" originates with him.

For a colorful line service presentation, try the simple Italian colors garnish as pictured.

ITALIAN COLORS GARNISH

	4 servings	24 servings
Tomatoes, diced, canned, drained	1 cup	6 cups
Parmesan cheese, shredded	¼ cup	1½ cups
Basil sprigs, fresh	4	24

Garnish lasagna triangle with ¼ cup diced tomatoes. Sprinkle with 1 tablespoon cheese. Top with 1 basil sprig.

Pollo Lasagne Spinachi

Here is a tempting dish made with creamy Parmesan sauce and spinach layered with chicken between lasagna noodles, and topped with cheese and an Italian colors garnish.

Speed-Scratch   *Kid Friendly*   *Line Service*   *Takeout*

INGREDIENT	QUANTITY		METHOD
	4 servings	24 servings	
1 Tyson Fully Cooked Diced White Fryer Meat, ½-inch dice, frozen	12 oz.	4½ lb.	Combine in bowl and mix thoroughly.
Spinach, chopped, frozen, thawed, squeezed dry	½ cup	3 cups	
Ricotta cheese	½ cup	3 cups	
Garlic, minced, commercially prepared	1 tbsp.	¼ cup	
Italian seasoning, dried	1 tsp.	2 tbsp.	
Red pepper, crushed, dried	¼ tsp.	1 tsp.	
2 Alfredo sauce, commercially prepared	2½ cups	15 cups	Combine in separate bowl and mix thoroughly.
Parmesan cheese, grated	½ cup	3 cups	
3 Lasagna noodle sheets, precooked, frozen, thawed	2	16	*To prepare lasagna:* Spread thin layer of Alfredo sauce mixture in bottom of two oiled full-size steam table pans. (Use third-size pan for smaller quantity and cut each noodle sheet in half.) Top sauce with layers of noodles, chicken/spinach mixture, and mozzarella cheese. Repeat all layers 3 times, finishing with thin layer of Alfredo sauce mixture and sprinkling of mozzarella cheese.
Mozzarella cheese, shredded	2 cups	12 cups	

Conventional oven, preheated: Cover and bake at 350°F for 50 to 60 minutes or until bubbling. (Bake smaller quantity for 35 to 40 minutes.) Remove cover and bake an additional 8 to 10 minutes or until lightly browned.

Convection oven, preheated: Cover and bake at 300°F for 20 to 25 minutes or until bubbling. (Bake smaller quantity for 15 to 20 minutes.) Remove cover and bake an additional 8 to 10 minutes or until lightly browned.

Remove from oven and let rest 10 minutes. Cut each pan into 12 equal triangles (p. 149). (Cut smaller pan into 4 triangles.) Keep warm above 140°F.

recipe continued on next page . . .

INGREDIENT	QUANTITY		METHOD
	4 servings	24 servings	
4 Parsley, fresh, minced (p. 39)	¼ cup	1½ cups	*To assemble single serving:* Sprinkle entire surface of plate with 1 tablespoon minced parsley. Portion 1 lasagna triangle on plate. Top with Italian colors garnish.
			Serve with garlic bread.

Portion: 14 ounces
Nutritional Data/Portion: Calories 780, Protein 59 g, Fat 41g, Carbohydrate 45 g, Cholesterol 185 mg, Sodium 1,520 mg

For a **FAST FACTS VIA FAX** copy of this recipe, call 1-800-223-3755 and enter Business Tool 2373.

Sautéed Chicken with Wild Mushroom Salsa over Fettuccine

Flavorful pancetta and chicken are sautéed with a warm salsa of shiitake, cremini, and button mushrooms accented with fresh sage and rosemary.

*Submitted by Tammy Grayshock
The Peabody Orlando
Orlando, Fla.*

INGREDIENT	QUANTITY		METHOD
	4 servings	24 servings	
1 Tyson Fully Cooked Flavor-Redi® Natural Grill Chicken Breast Filets, 3-oz., frozen	4	24	Cover tightly and slack in cooler between 32° and 36°F prior to use.
2 Olive oil	¼ cup	1½ cups	*To prepare single serving:* Heat 1 tablespoon in sauté pan over medium-high heat.
3 Shallots, fresh, minced	½ cup	3 cups	Add 2 tablespoons shallots and ¼ cup pancetta. Sauté for 4 to 5 minutes or until pancetta is crisp.
Pancetta, diced	1 cup	6 cups	
4 Shiitake mushrooms, fresh, thinly sliced	1 cup	6 cups	Add ¼ cup each of mushrooms and 2 teaspoons each of sage and rosemary. Sauté for 2 to 3 minutes or until mushrooms are wilted.
Cremini mushrooms, fresh, thinly sliced	1 cup	6 cups	
Button mushrooms, fresh, thinly sliced	1 cup	6 cups	
Sage, fresh, chopped	3 tbsp.	1 cup	
Rosemary, fresh, chopped	3 tbsp.	1 cup	
5 White wine, dry	1⅓ cups	8 cups	Add ⅓ cup and deglaze pan, scraping any browned particles from bottom.
6 Chicken broth, canned	1⅓ cups	8 cups	Diagonally slice 1 chicken breast filet into strips and add to pan along with ⅓ cup chicken broth and 1½ cups fettuccine. Mix thoroughly and simmer for 1 to 2 minutes or until chicken and pasta are thoroughly heated. Remove from heat and transfer to plate. Garnish plate with 1 sage sprig.
Fettuccine, cooked al dente, drained	12 oz. (dry)	4½ lb. (dry)	
Sage sprigs, fresh	4	24	

Portion: 14 ounces
Nutritional Data/Portion: Calories 711, Protein 42 g, Fat 26 g, Carbohydrate 77 g, Cholesterol 72 mg, Sodium 1,092 mg

For a **FAST FACTS VIA FAX** copy of this recipe, call 1-800-223-3755 and enter Business Tool 2624.

Pancetta is unsmoked Italian bacon that has been cured with salt and spices. Unlike American bacon, its form is similar to that of sausage or salami.

During the 17th century, English aristocrats ate few vegetables, but they did regard mushrooms with high esteem.

Button mushrooms are immature common white mushrooms. Likewise, cremini mushrooms, which are also known as common brown or Roman mushrooms, are immature portobello mushrooms.

DIFFERENT CUTS OF PASTA
There are many interesting cuts of pasta, including (left to right) penne, orecchiette, rotini, fusilli, orzo, farfalle, ziti, and radiatore.

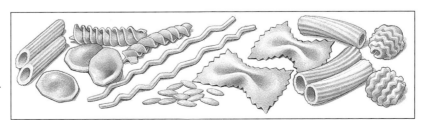

Submitted by Christopher U. Umstead
Yellow House Hotel/Bed & Breakfast
Douglasville, Pa.

Santa Fe Chicken and Corncake Stack

This architectural creation is tall with flavor. Sautéed citrus-marinated chicken breast filets are layered between jalapeño corncakes and topped with a roasted bell pepper, black olive, and onion salsa to build an impressive presentation.

Use milk to adjust the corncake batter consistency.

Corncakes can be prepared and held warm for a short time in a covered steam table pan over hot water.

This recipe can be menued as a shared starter to give patrons a sampling opportunity.

Cornbread is a simple quick bread that substitutes cornmeal for all, or part, of the flour in bread making. Some of the more popular forms of this American classic are johnnycakes, spoon bread, cornpone, and hushpuppies.

INGREDIENT	QUANTITY 4 servings	24 servings	METHOD
1 *Salsa*			
Red onions, fresh, diced (p. 175)	½ cup	3 cups	Combine in bowl and mix thoroughly. Cover and chill at least 1 hour before serving.
Black olives, sliced, canned, drained	½ cup	3 cups	
Red bell peppers, roasted, peeled, seeded, diced (p. 66)	½ cup	3 cups	
Green bell peppers, roasted, peeled, seeded, diced	⅓ cup	2 cups	
Green onions, fresh, chopped	⅓ cup	2 cups	
Jalapeño peppers, fresh, seeded, minced	2 tbsp.	¾ cup	
Garlic, fresh, minced	2 tsp.	¼ cup	
Olive oil	2 tbsp.	½ cup	
White wine vinegar	2 tbsp.	½ cup	
Salt	¼ tsp.	½ tbsp.	
2 Black pepper, coarse	⅛ tsp.	¾ tsp.	
Corncake Batter			
Mexican cornbread mix with cheese and jalapeños, commercially prepared	1 cup	5 cups	Combine in bowl and mix thoroughly. Cover and chill to hold. (Hold no longer than 1 hour.)
Sugar, granulated	½ tsp.	½ tbsp.	
Milk, whole	⅔ cup	3⅓ cups	
Eggs, large, whole, beaten	1	5	
3 Portobello mushrooms, fresh, chopped, sautéed	½ cup	3 cups	Fold into batter just before using.
4 Olive oil	¼ cup	1½ cups	*To prepare single serving:* Heat 1 tablespoon in sauté pan over medium-high heat.
5 Tyson Ready-to-Cook Tenderpressed™ Southwest Citrus Chicken Breast Filets, 5-oz., frozen	4	24	Dredge 1 chicken breast filet in flour and shake off excess. Add to oil and sauté for 3 to 4 minutes on each side or until chicken is no longer pink. Remove from heat. Slice diagonally into 3 pieces. Keep warm above 140°F.
Flour, all-purpose	as needed	as needed	
Chive sprigs, fresh	12	72	

To make 3 corncakes, ladle 2 tablespoons batter for each corncake onto oiled flattop griddle preheated to 340°F. Grill until brown on bottom side, then turn and brown on other side. Remove from griddle. Place 1 corncake on plate. Top with 1 chicken piece and repeat layers to form a tower, finishing with chicken. Mound ½ cup salsa on top and around sides of tower. Garnish top with 3 chive sprigs.

Portion: 11 ounces
Nutritional Data/Portion: Calories 490, Protein 36 g, Fat 24 g, Carbohydrate 34 g, Cholesterol 180 mg, Sodium 1,300 mg

For a **FAST FACTS VIA FAX** copy of this recipe, call 1-800-223-3755 and enter Business Tool 2607.

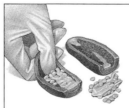

HOW TO SEED AND CORE HOT PEPPERS
1) With gloved hands, slice the stem end off the pepper to loosen the core and seeds. Slice the pepper in half lengthwise.
2) Remove the core and seeds with thumb.

Submitted by Jeff Popken
Hill and Dale Country Club
Carmel, N.Y.

Chicken Tomato Linguine

This spaghetti and meatballs for the '90s features bone-in pieces of chicken baked in a chunky tomato sauce full of mushrooms, herbs, red wine, and garlic. Because this dish actually improves as it simmers and the flavors meld together, it is a great recipe for line service and large catered events.

INGREDIENT	QUANTITY		METHOD
	4 servings	24 servings	
1 Tyson Original IQ*F Whole Bird Cuts, 6-piece cut, no wings, frozen	8 pc.	48 pc.	Cover tightly and slack in cooler between 32° and 36°F prior to use.
2 Salt	½ tsp.	1 tbsp.	Remove and discard skin from chicken. Sprinkle with seasonings and dredge in flour. Shake off excess.
Black pepper, coarse	¼ tsp.	½ tbsp.	
Flour, all-purpose	as needed	as needed	
3 Olive oil	2 tbsp.	¾ cup	Combine in skillet and heat over medium heat. Add chicken and sauté for 4 to 5 minutes on each side or until well browned. Transfer to two full-size steam table pans. (Use half-size pan for smaller quantity.)
Butter, salted	2 tbsp.	¾ cup	
4 *Tomato Sauce*			
Olive oil	1½ tbsp.	⅔ cup	Heat in saucepan or stockpot over high heat.
5 Button mushrooms, fresh, sliced	3 cups	18 cups	Add to oil and sauté for 8 to 10 minutes or until onions are translucent. (Sauté smaller quantity for 3 to 4 minutes.)
Onions, fresh, chopped (p. 175)	1 cup	6 cups	
Garlic, fresh, minced	1 tbsp.	⅓ cup	
6 Roma tomatoes, canned, undrained, chopped	4 cups	24 cups	Add to mushroom mixture and mix thoroughly. Bring to boil over high heat. Reduce heat and simmer for 18 to 20 minutes or until mixture begins to thicken, stirring occasionally. Pour over chicken.
Red wine, dry	1 cup	6 cups	
Basil leaves, dried	1 tsp.	2 tbsp.	
Oregano leaves, dried	½ tsp.	1 tbsp.	Cover and braise in preheated conventional oven at 325°F for 60 to 65 minutes or until chicken is almost falling off the bone. (Braise smaller quantity for 45 to 50 minutes.) Or cover and braise in preheated convection oven at 300°F for 45 to 50 minutes. (Braise smaller quantity for 30 to 35 minutes.) Remove from oven.
Thyme leaves, dried	½ tsp.	1 tbsp.	
Bay leaves, whole, dried	2	6	
Salt	1 tsp.	2 tbsp.	
Black pepper, coarse	½ tsp.	1 tbsp.	
			Skim off excess fat on surface of sauce if necessary. Discard bay leaves and stir sauce around chicken. Keep warm above 140°F.
7 Linguine, cooked al dente, drained, hot	12 oz. (dry)	4½ lb. (dry)	*To assemble single serving:* Portion 1½ cups pasta on plate. Top with 2 chicken pieces and 1 cup sauce from pan. Sprinkle with 1 tablespoon cheese. Garnish plate with 1 basil sprig.
Romano cheese, grated	¼ cup	1½ cups	
Basil sprigs, fresh	4	24	
			Serve with garlic bread.

Portion: 20 ounces
Nutritional Data/Portion: Calories 1,010, Protein 70 g, Fat 37 g, Carbohydrate 87 g, Cholesterol 185 mg, Sodium 1,190 mg

*Exceeds USDA standards for quick freezing.

For a **FAST FACTS VIA FAX** copy of this recipe, call 1-800-223-3755 and enter Business Tool 2599.

The bay leaf is an aromatic herb from the evergreen bay laurel tree, native to the Mediterranean. Early Greeks and Romans thought the laurel leaf possessed magical properties and even made it a symbol of triumph— thus comes the well-known adage, "Don't rest on your laurels."

Chicken, tomatoes, garlic, wine, and pasta are very common ingredients in Italian cooking. For example, many of the ingredients in this recipe are also included in the Chicken Cacciatore recipe on the following page. Yet, subtle differences in the way these ingredients are used with other ingredients give each of these recipes its own distinctive character. The use of linguine in this recipe is indicative of Tuscan-style cooking, while the "hunter-style" cacciatore is more closely related to recipes originating in the Abruzzi region.

Submitted by Anthony Seta
Perkins Family Restaurant
Memphis, Tenn.

Cacciatore *is the Italian word for"hunter." Classic cacciatore was first prepared with mushrooms, onions, tomatoes, herbs, and small game such as rabbit.*

A rondeau *is a wide, fairly shallow pot with two loop handles and is often used for chicken sautées and casseroles.*

Olive oil, *prized since it was first exported from Crete in 2475 B.C., is graded in accordance with the degree of acidity it contains. The best oils are cold-pressed, a chemical-free pressure-only process. Extra virgin olive oil—considered the finest, fruitiest, and most expensive—should be highlighted in vinaigrettes and other starring roles where its flavor can be most appreciated. Virgin grades are more practical for cooking.*

Chicken Cacciatore

A perennial favorite, this hearty "hunter-style" dish of tomato sauce with green bell peppers, onions, mushrooms, and herbs is an Italian classic. Balsamic vinegar gives this version a modern touch.

Line Service *Takeout*

INGREDIENT	QUANTITY 4 servings	QUANTITY 24 servings	METHOD
1 Tyson Tastybasted® IQ*F Breast and Leg Quarters, 9.6-oz. breast, 8.4-oz. leg, frozen	2 breast qtr. 2 leg qtr.	12 breast qtr. 12 leg qtr.	Sprinkle chicken with seasonings and dredge in flour. Shake off excess.
Salt	½ tsp.	1 tbsp.	
White pepper, fine	¼ tsp.	½ tbsp.	
2 Flour	as needed	as needed	
Olive oil	½ cup	3 cups	Heat in skillet or rondeau over medium-high heat. Add chicken and sauté for 6 to 7 minutes on each side or until golden brown. Transfer to roasting pans. Pour off excess oil, leaving browned bits in skillet.
3 Olive oil	2 tbsp.	¾ cup	Combine in same skillet and heat over medium-high heat.
Butter, salted	1 tbsp.	⅓ cup	
4 Onions, fresh, sliced	2 cups	12 cups	Add to oil and butter and mix thoroughly. Sauté for 8 to 10 minutes or until vegetables are tender-crisp. (Sauté smaller quantity for 4 to 5 minutes.)
Button mushrooms, fresh, sliced	2 cups	12 cups	
Green bell peppers, fresh, slivered	1 cup	6 cups	
5 Garlic, fresh, minced	2 tsp.	¼ cup	
White wine, dry	½ cup	3 cups	Add to onion mixture. Bring to boil and reduce by half.
6 Balsamic vinegar	2 tsp.	¼ cup	
Tomatoes, diced, canned, undrained	3 cups	18 cups	Add to onion mixture and mix thoroughly. Bring to boil over high heat. Reduce heat and simmer for 15 to 20 minutes or until sauce begins to thicken. (Simmer smaller quantity for 5 to 10 minutes.) Pour over chicken.
Tomato paste	¼ cup	1½ cups	
Basil leaves, dried	½ tbsp.	3 tbsp.	
Rosemary, fresh, chopped	1 tsp.	2 tbsp.	
Oregano leaves, dried	½ tsp.	1 tbsp.	Cover and braise in preheated conventional oven at 350°F for 1½ to 2 hours or until chicken is no longer pink. (Cover and braise smaller quantity for 50 to 55 minutes.) Or cover and braise in preheated convection oven at 300°F for 55 to 60 minutes. (Cover and braise smaller quantity for 35 to 40 minutes.) Remove from oven and discard bay leaves. Keep warm above 140°F.
Bay leaves, whole, dried	1	6	
Salt	¼ tsp.	½ tbsp.	
Black pepper, coarse	⅛ tsp.	¾ tsp.	
7 Spaghetti, cooked al dente, drained, hot	12 oz. (dry)	4½ lb. (dry)	*To assemble single serving:* Portion 1½ cups pasta on plate. Top with 1 chicken quarter (either breast or leg) and 1 cup sauce. Garnish plate with 1 basil sprig.
Basil sprigs, fresh	4	24	

Serve with Italian bread.

Portion: 20 ounces

Nutritional Data/Portion: Calories 1,022, Protein 34 g, Fat 56 g, Carbohydrate 100 g, Cholesterol 110 mg, Sodium 1,498 mg

*Exceeds USDA standards for quick freezing.

For a **FAST FACTS VIA FAX**™ copy of this recipe, call 1-800-223-3755 and enter Business Tool 2552.

Submitted by Nancy Apollo
Baywind Village Care Center
League City, Tex.

Southwestern Chicken-Stuffed Spud

Potatoes have challenged rice and pasta in recent years as the starch to be topped. This new take on potato-toppers borrows flavors from the Southwest, with chicken fajita strips, cilantro, salsa, onions, Jack cheese, sour cream, and avocado.

INGREDIENT	QUANTITY		METHOD
	4 servings	24 servings	
1 Baking potatoes, fresh, large, scrubbed	4	24	Rub potatoes with oil and place on sheet pans. Bake in preheated conventional oven at 400°F for 1 to 1½ hours or until tender. Or bake in preheated convection oven at 350°F for 45 to 50 minutes. Remove from oven and keep warm.
Vegetable oil	as needed	as needed	
2 Tyson Fully Cooked Flavor-Redi® Chicken Breast Fajita Strips, frozen	1 lb.	6 lb.	Grill on oiled, preheated flattop griddle at 350°F for 3 to 4 minutes or until chicken begins to thaw.
3 Onions, fresh, chopped	1 cup	6 cups	Add to chicken and sauté for 3 to 4 minutes or until onions are tender. Remove chicken mixture from griddle. Keep warm above 140°F.
4 Salsa, thick-and-chunky, mild, commercially prepared	½ cup	3 cups	Combine in bowl and mix thoroughly. Cover and reserve.
Orange marmalade	¼ cup	1½ cups	
Black olives, chopped, canned, drained	¼ cup	1½ cups	
Cilantro, fresh, minced	¼ cup	1½ cups	
5 Cheddar and Monterey Jack cheese blend, shredded	2 cups	12 cups	*To assemble single serving:* Place 1 baked potato on plate. Cut lengthwise and split halfway open. Top with ½ cup cheese, ½ cup chicken mixture, and ¼ cup sauce. Finish with ½ tablespoon sour cream. Garnish plate with 3 avocado slices.
Sour cream	2 tbsp.	¾ cup	
Avocado slices, fresh, tossed in lime juice	12	72	

Portion: 13 ounces
Nutritional Data/Portion: Calories 570, Protein 41 g, Fat 24 g, Carbohydrate 50 g, Cholesterol 115 mg, Sodium 1,220 mg

For a **FAST FACTS VIA FAX**™ copy of this recipe, call 1-800-223-3755 and enter Business Tool 2626.

Americans eat more potatoes than any other vegetable. In fact, the U.S. Department of Agriculture reports that per capita consumption is 124 pounds per year, and that potatoes are included in one out of every three meals we eat.

This recipe adds flair to a basic baked potato bar.

HOW TO CUT AN ONION

1) Cut the onion in half from stem to root end.

2) Place the cut side down and slice the onion vertically in desired thickness without cutting through the root.

3) Slice the onion horizontally once or twice (depending on desired width of pieces) without cutting through the root.

4) Turn the onion 90 degrees and slice vertically in desired thickness.

The dish gets its name from the wide, shallow double-handled pan in which it is traditionally prepared, but any good skillet works nicely.⁓

Fortunately, a little bit of saffron goes a long way because it is the world's most expensive spice. It takes 14,000 stigmas from crocus sativus flowers to make one ounce of saffron. The sheer number of flowers and the amount of delicate hand labor involved in harvesting and drying the stigmas contribute to its value.⁓

Christopher Columbus christened chiles as pimientos, *saying they were better and stronger than* pimientas, *"Spanish peppers."*⁓

In Greek mythology, Zeus had a bed of saffron. Throughout the Middle Ages and into the Renaissance period, it was fashionable in Italy to guild chicken with a paste of flour, egg, and saffron.⁓

Saffron is what gives this dish its yellowish color, but turmeric makes an acceptable and cost-reducing substitute.⁓

Chicken Paella

The heart of this classic Spanish one-dish meal is golden saffron rice. It is traditionally combined with a variety of meats, including chicken, shellfish, and chorizo—a spicy, coarsely ground Spanish sausage.

Line-Service

INGREDIENT	QUANTITY 4 servings	24 servings	METHOD
1 Olive oil	2 tbsp.	¾ cup	Heat in saucepan or stockpot over medium heat.
2 White rice, raw	1½ cups	9 cups	Add to oil and sauté for 5 to 6 minutes or until rice is golden. Transfer to two oiled full-size steam table pans. (Sauté smaller quantity for 1 to 1½ minutes and transfer to oiled half-size pan.)
Onions, fresh, diced (p. 175)	½ cup	3 cups	
Garlic, fresh, minced	2 tsp.	¼ cup	
3 Tyson Fully Cooked Oven Roasted Original Chicken Breasts, 8-oz., frozen	4	24	Arrange over rice mixture.
4 Chicken broth, canned	4 cups	24 cups	Combine in same saucepan or stockpot and mix thoroughly. Bring to boil over high heat. Remove from heat and pour over chicken and rice mixture.
Saffron, crushed	¼ tsp.	½ tbsp.	
			Cover tightly and bake in preheated conventional oven at 425°F for 50 to 60 minutes or until rice is almost tender. (Bake smaller quantity for 30 to 35 minutes.) Or cover tightly and bake in preheated convection oven at 375°F for 35 to 40 minutes. (Bake smaller quantity for 25 to 30 minutes.) Remove from oven and uncover.
5 Polish sausage slices, ¼-inch-thick	3 oz.	1 lb.	Add to rice mixture and mix thoroughly.
Green peas, frozen	½ cup	3 cups	
Pimientos, sliced, canned, drained	½ cup	3 cups	
6 Shrimp, large, fresh, peeled, deveined, raw	8	48	Arrange over rice mixture. Cover and return to oven.
Mussels in shells, fresh, raw	4	24	
			In conventional oven, bake for an additional 20 to 25 minutes or until rice is tender, mussel shells have opened, and chicken is thoroughly heated. (Bake smaller quantity an additional 10 to 15 minutes.) In convection oven, bake an additional 15 to 20 minutes. (Bake smaller quantity an additional 8 to 10 minutes.) Remove from oven. Keep warm above 140°F.

recipe continued on next page . . .

INGREDIENT	QUANTITY		METHOD
	4 servings	24 servings	

7

| Lemon wedges, fresh | 8 | 48 | *To assemble single serving:* Portion 1½ cups rice mixture in center of plate. Arrange 1 mussel, 2 shrimp, and 1 chicken breast over rice. Garnish plate with 2 lemon wedges and 1 parsley sprig. |
| Parsley sprigs, fresh | 4 | 24 | |

Serve with French bread.

Portion: 20 ounces
Nutritional Data/Portion: Calories 880, Protein 73 g, Fat 36 g, Carbohydrate 64 g, Cholesterol 215 mg, Sodium 2,210 mg

For a **FAST FACTS VIA FAX** copy of this recipe, call 1-800-223-3755 and enter Business Tool 2621.

Chicken Fettuccine Inferno

Warning! Contents of this pasta plate are very hot and spicy. Brandy and heavy cream can't tame the heat the habañero peppers bring to this recipe. Let customers know this is a very hot dish.

Speed-Scratch   Lighter Fare   Line Service   Takeout

*Submitted by Martin Wolf, CEC
The Chef's Gallery
Charlotte, N.C.*

INGREDIENT	QUANTITY		METHOD
	4 servings	24 servings	

1

| Tyson Ready-to-Cook Flavor-Redi® Savory Chicken Breast Filets, 5-oz., frozen | 4 | 24 | Slack in cooler between 32° and 36°F prior to use. |
| | | | Char-grill over medium heat for 4½ to 5 minutes on each side or until chicken is no longer pink. Or grill on oiled, preheated flattop griddle at 350°F for 4½ to 5 minutes on each side. Remove from grill. Keep warm above 140°F. |

2

Habañero Sauce

Red bell peppers, roasted, peeled, seeded, diced (p. 66)	1 cup	6 cups	Combine in food processor bowl and process until pureed. Transfer to saucepan and bring to boil over medium heat, stirring frequently. Reduce heat and simmer for 1 to 2 minutes or until flavors are blended. Remove from heat and keep warm.
Heavy cream	⅔ cup	4 cups	
Brandy	3 tbsp.	1 cup	
Habañero peppers, dried, chopped	¼ tsp.	½ tbsp.	
Button mushrooms, fresh, sliced, sautéed	1 cup	6 cups	
Salt	½ tsp.	1 tbsp.	
White pepper, fine	⅛ tsp.	¾ tsp.	

3

| Fettuccine, cooked al dente, drained, hot | 12 oz. (dry) | 4½ lb. (dry) | *To assemble single serving:* Portion 1½ cups pasta on plate. Top with ½ cup habañero sauce and 1 chicken breast filet. Garnish plate with 1 tablespoon cilantro. |
| Cilantro, fresh, minced | ¼ cup | 1½ cups | |

Serve with crusty sourdough rolls.

Portion: 15 ounces
Nutritional Data/Portion: Calories 530, Protein 40 g, Fat 11 g, Carbohydrate 60 g, Cholesterol 100 mg, Sodium 690 mg

For a **FAST FACTS VIA FAX** copy of this recipe, call 1-800-223-3755 and enter Business Tool 2618.

Habañeros are generally considered the hottest of the hot peppers. One particular variety, the Red Savina, tipped the Scoville heat scales at 577,000 units, making it the hottest pepper ever measured. For comparison, the hottest of jalapeños rates only about 10,000 Scoville Heat Units.

Chicken and Wild Rice Casserole

The Midwest is not only America's heartland, but also the source of many of its most treasured casseroles. Over time, the recipes brought by European homesteaders have been adapted to include local ingredients. Wisconsin-style cheddar cheese and native American marsh grass (wild rice) are the basis of this wonderful casserole.

Other varieties of cheese, such as Swiss or Monterey Jack, are great alternatives that provide interesting adaptations of this dish.

Clean wild rice thoroughly by placing it in a bowl and covering it with cold water. Stir a couple of times, then set aside. In just minutes, debris will float to the surface and can be poured off with the water.

INGREDIENT	QUANTITY		METHOD
	4 servings	24 servings	
1 Tyson Fully Cooked Diced White Fryer Meat, 1-inch dice, frozen	12 oz.	4½ lb.	Combine in bowl and mix thoroughly.
Wild rice, cooked according to package directions	½ cup (dry)	3 cups (dry)	
White rice, steamed	½ cup (dry)	3 cups (dry)	
2 Butter, salted	¼ cup	1½ cups	Heat in skillet or braising pan over medium-high heat.
3 Onions, fresh, chopped (p. 175)	1 cup	6 cups	Add to butter and sauté for 10 to 12 minutes or until vegetables are tender. (Sauté smaller quantity for 4 to 5 minutes.) Remove from heat and add to chicken mixture.
Button mushrooms, fresh, sliced	1 cup	6 cups	
Celery, fresh, sliced	½ cup	3 cups	
Green bell peppers, fresh, chopped	½ cup	3 cups	
Salt	¼ tsp.	½ tbsp.	
Black pepper, coarse	⅛ tsp.	¾ tsp.	
4 Cheddar cheese, sharp, shredded	1½ cups	9 cups	Add to chicken mixture and mix thoroughly. Transfer to two oiled full-size steam table pans. (Use half-size pan for smaller quantity.)
Heavy cream	1½ cups	9 cups	
			Bake in preheated conventional oven at 350°F for 55 to 60 minutes or until bubbling, stirring occasionally. (Bake smaller quantity for 25 to 30 minutes.) Or bake in preheated convection oven at 300°F for 25 to 30 minutes. (Bake smaller quantity for 10 to 12 minutes.) Remove from oven. Keep warm above 140°F.
5 Thyme sprigs, fresh	4	24	*To assemble single serving:* Portion 2 cups chicken mixture on plate. Garnish plate with 1 thyme sprig. *Serve with assorted whole-grain rolls.*

Portion: 15 ounces
Nutritional Data/Portion: Calories 740, Protein 41 g, Fat 45 g, Carbohydrate 44 g, Cholesterol 205 mg, Sodium 740 mg

For a **FAST FACTS VIA FAX** copy of this recipe, call 1-800-223-3755 and enter Business Tool 2614.

"Recipes are traditions, not just random wads of ingredients."

Anonymous

Submitted by Joe Sanford
Dyersburg Country Club
Dyersburg, Tenn.

*O*rzo is a small pasta whose Italian name means "barley," though in fact it resembles rice grains.~⌐

*F*or variety, add any combination of the following ingredients: broccoli, finely chopped squash, pecans, and crushed red pepper or a dash of cayenne for heat.~⌐

*O*rzo is an interesting substitute for rice in many recipes.~⌐

Chicken Orzo Provençal

Using orzo pasta instead of spaghetti lets pasta lovers dig right into this flavorful Provençal-style chicken and orzo dish and keep everything neat and tidy.

Speed-Scratch   *Line Service*   *Takeout*

INGREDIENT	QUANTITY 4 servings	QUANTITY 24 servings	METHOD
1 Tyson Ready-to-Cook Flavor-Redi® Savory Chicken Tenderloins, frozen	12	72	Place in full-size steam table pans. (Use half-size pan for smaller quantity.)
2 Sun-dried tomato and oregano salad dressing, commercially prepared	1½ cups	9 cups	Pour over chicken.

Roast in preheated conventional oven at 350°F for 50 to 55 minutes or until chicken is no longer pink. (Roast smaller quantity for 30 to 35 minutes.) Or roast in preheated convection oven at 300°F for 15 to 18 minutes. (Roast smaller quantity for 8 to 10 minutes.) Remove from oven, then remove chicken from pans, leaving sauce. Keep warm above 140°F. |
3 Orzo pasta, cooked al dente, drained	8 oz. (dry)	3 lb. (dry)	Combine in bowl and mix thoroughly. Add equal portions to sauce in pans and mix thoroughly. Arrange chicken over top of pasta mixture. Keep warm above 140°F.
Black olives, sliced, canned, drained	½ cup	3 cups	
Sun-dried tomatoes, oil-packed, drained, chopped	½ cup	3 cups	
Red bell peppers, fresh, julienne (p. 88)	½ cup	3 cups	
Yellow bell peppers, fresh, julienne	½ cup	3 cups	
4 Oregano sprigs, fresh	4	24	*To assemble single serving:* Portion 1½ cups pasta mixture on plate with 3 chicken tenderloins. Garnish plate with 1 oregano sprig.

Serve with Italian bread. |

Portion: 16 ounces
Nutritional Data/Portion: Calories 550, Protein 35 g, Fat 24 g, Carbohydrate 49 g, Cholesterol 55 mg, Sodium 1,600 mg

For a ***FAST FACTS VIA FAX*** copy of this recipe, call 1-800-223-3755 and enter Business Tool 2604.

"*Chicken for the cook is what canvas is for the painter.*"

Anthelme Brillat-Savarin

Center-of-Plate Entrees

*B*uilding menu excitement with chicken at center stage

One of the earliest examples of building meals around chicken appeared during the 14th century, when Europeans fed chickens a mixture of grains and aromatic herbs, then prepared them in seasoned broth, to enhance their flavor. At the time, however, chicken was unknown outside Europe and parts of Asia.

Early explorers were to change that. Stocking their ships with food essentials, they delivered chickens to virtually all parts of the world. For instance, after Columbus introduced chicken to the New World on his second voyage, it started showing up in cuisines from the Caribbean to Mexico.

By the turn of the 20th century, chefs—inspired by culinary masters such as Escoffier—had begun to develop chicken's potential by preparing it with flavorful sauces, herbs, spices, and varied cooking techniques.

Today, chicken's affordability, versatility, and availability have turned it into a staple menu item. As people have learned more about chicken and the many ways they can enjoy it, it has taken a place at center stage as one of the world's most popular sources of protein.

The recipes in this chapter are outstanding evidence of chicken's menu stardom. They demonstrate that it can reflect the personality of any culture, region, or individual. From the Chicken Wellington to the Chicken with Pink Peppercorn Dijon Sauce, here are 49 great ways to turn chicken into a *pièce de résistance*.

Submitted by Thomas Kovacs
Sheraton-Seattle Hotel
Seattle, Wash.

Spicy Apple-Roasted Chicken

Diced Jonathan and Granny Smith apples team nicely with chicken, hoisin sauce, sesame oil, and fresh rosemary in this East-meets-West specialty.

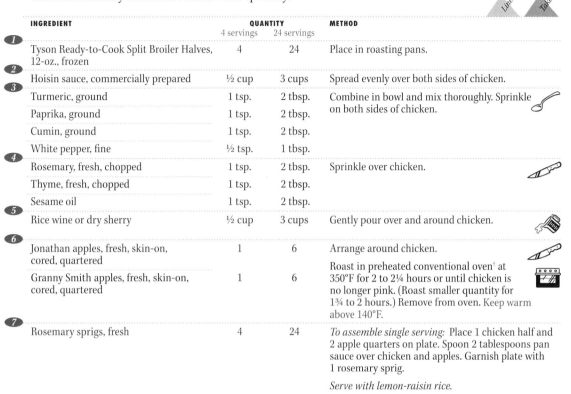

INGREDIENT	QUANTITY 4 servings	QUANTITY 24 servings	METHOD
1 Tyson Ready-to-Cook Split Broiler Halves, 12-oz., frozen	4	24	Place in roasting pans.
2 Hoisin sauce, commercially prepared	½ cup	3 cups	Spread evenly over both sides of chicken.
3 Turmeric, ground	1 tsp.	2 tbsp.	Combine in bowl and mix thoroughly. Sprinkle on both sides of chicken.
Paprika, ground	1 tsp.	2 tbsp.	
Cumin, ground	1 tsp.	2 tbsp.	
White pepper, fine	½ tsp.	1 tbsp.	
4 Rosemary, fresh, chopped	1 tsp.	2 tbsp.	Sprinkle over chicken.
Thyme, fresh, chopped	1 tsp.	2 tbsp.	
Sesame oil	1 tsp.	2 tbsp.	
5 Rice wine or dry sherry	½ cup	3 cups	Gently pour over and around chicken.
6 Jonathan apples, fresh, skin-on, cored, quartered	1	6	Arrange around chicken.
Granny Smith apples, fresh, skin-on, cored, quartered	1	6	Roast in preheated conventional oven† at 350°F for 2 to 2¼ hours or until chicken is no longer pink. (Roast smaller quantity for 1¾ to 2 hours.) Remove from oven. Keep warm above 140°F.
7 Rosemary sprigs, fresh	4	24	*To assemble single serving:* Place 1 chicken half and 2 apple quarters on plate. Spoon 2 tablespoons pan sauce over chicken and apples. Garnish plate with 1 rosemary sprig.
			Serve with lemon-raisin rice.

Portion: 14 ounces
Nutritional Data/Portion: Calories 650, Protein 44 g, Fat 37 g, Carbohydrate 26 g, Cholesterol 170 mg, Sodium 680 mg

†Convection oven not recommended.

For a **FAST FACTS VIA FAX**™ copy of this recipe, call 1-800-223-3755 and enter Business Tool 2585.

Hoisin sauce, also known as Peking sauce, is a thick, sweet-and-spicy, reddish-brown sauce widely used in Chinese cooking. This mixture of soybeans, garlic, chile peppers, and spices is used as a table condiment in China as commonly as we use salt and pepper.

Turmeric, also known as curcuma and Indian saffron, comes from the rhizomes of a plant related to ginger. It has been used in cooking since around 600 B.C., and was also used to dye fabrics and mustard yellow.

Although Granny Smith apples are grown in America, they are still imported from New Zealand and Australia where the variety originated. Because of the timing of seasons between the northern and southern hemispheres, these firm, tart cooking apples are readily available year-round.

Submitted by Stephen VanEgmond
The Peabody Orlando
Orlando, Fla.

Although the season for cultivated fresh blueberries is from June until early October, fresh New Zealand blueberries can be purchased in winter months at premium prices. Blueberries should be firm, uniform in size, and indigo blue with a silvery frost. They should not be washed until ready for use.

Sage is a native Mediterranean herb prized for its culinary and medicinal value for centuries. Its name is a derivative of the Latin salvus, *which means "safe." According to one source, the Chinese valued sage so highly that they would trade two crates of their best tea for one crate of sage. And a Provençal proverb assures that, "he who has sage in his garden needs no doctor."*

Cranberry-Citrus Chicken with Fruit Dressing

Those who crave Thanksgiving dinner year-round will be attracted to this special chicken dish, served with breadcrumb dressing made with dried blueberries and cherries, raisins, and brandy.

Lighter Fare   Line Service   Takeout

	INGREDIENT	QUANTITY		METHOD
		4 servings	24 servings	
1	Cranberry sauce, whole berry, canned	½ cup	3 cups	Combine in saucepan and mix thoroughly. Heat over low heat until cranberry sauce is dissolved. Keep warm.
	White wine, dry	2 tbsp.	⅓ cup	
2	Tyson Ready-to-Cook Tenderpressed™ Southwest Citrus Chicken Breast Filets, 5-oz., frozen	4	24	Grill on oiled, preheated flattop griddle at 350°F for 6½ to 7½ minutes on each side or until chicken is no longer pink. Remove from griddle and dip chicken in cranberry mixture to thoroughly coat each side. Keep warm above 140°F.
3	*Sun-dried Fruit Dressing*			
	Butter, salted	1 tbsp.	⅓ cup	Heat in skillet over medium-high heat.
4	Onions, fresh, ¼-inch dice (p. 175)	½ cup	3 cups	Add to butter and sauté for 4 to 5 minutes or until tender. (Sauté smaller quantity for 2 to 3 minutes.)
	Celery, fresh, ¼-inch dice (p. 88)	¼ cup	1½ cups	
5	Raisins, dark	1 tbsp.	½ cup	Add to onion mixture and mix thoroughly.
	Raisins, golden	1 tbsp.	½ cup	
	Blueberries, whole, dried	1 tbsp.	½ cup	
	Cherries, whole, dried	1 tbsp.	½ cup	
6	Brandy	⅓ cup	2 cups	Add to onion mixture and flambé. Boil for 5 to 6 minutes or until most of liquid has evaporated. (Boil smaller quantity for 1½ to 2 minutes.) Remove from heat and cool.
7	White bread, fresh, ½-inch cube	4 cups	24 cups	Combine in bowl and toss well.
	Sage, rubbed, dried	1 tbsp.	⅓ cup	
	Salt	½ tsp.	1 tbsp.	
	Black pepper, coarse	¼ tsp.	1½ tsp.	

recipe continued on next page . . .

	INGREDIENT	QUANTITY 4 servings	24 servings	METHOD
8	Eggs, large, whole, well-beaten	1	6	Add to bread cubes. Add cooled fruit mixture to bread and mix thoroughly. Transfer to buttered half-size steam table pan. (Use third-size pan for smaller quantity.)
				Bake in preheated conventional oven at 400°F for 30 to 35 minutes or until golden brown. (Bake smaller quantity for 15 to 20 minutes.) Or bake in preheated convection oven at 325°F for 12 to 13 minutes. (Bake smaller quantity for 6 to 10 minutes.) Remove from oven and keep warm.
9	Cranberry sauce, whole berry, canned	½ cup	3 cups	*To assemble single serving:* Portion ⅔ cup dressing on plate. Top with 1 glazed chicken breast filet. Garnish plate with 2 tablespoons cranberry sauce and 1 sage sprig.
	Sage sprigs, fresh	4	24	
				Serve with baked acorn squash and steamed fresh green beans.

Insert a toothpick to test the doneness of the dressing, just as if testing a cake. If it comes out clean, the dressing is done.

Portion: 9 ounces
Nutritional Data/Portion: Calories 393, Protein 25 g, Fat 8 g, Carbohydrate 58 g, Cholesterol 116 mg, Sodium 897 mg

For a **FAST FACTS VIA FAX**™ copy of this recipe, call 1-800-223-3755 and enter Business Tool 2572.

Sautéed Chicken with Four-Berries Sauce

This dish stands out because of the temptingly sweet reduction of blueberries, strawberries, blackberries, raspberries, white wine, onions, and mushrooms.

Speed-Scratch   Lighter Fare   Line Service   Takeout

*Submitted by Edward Sullivan
Dot's Restaurant
Wilmington, Vt.*

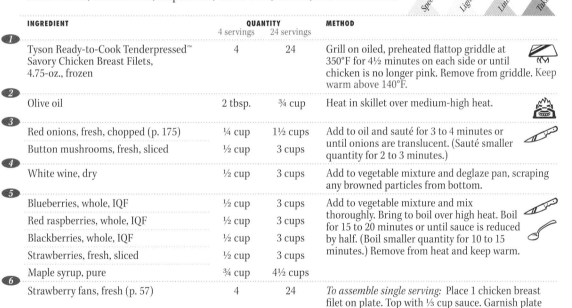

	INGREDIENT	QUANTITY 4 servings	24 servings	METHOD
1	Tyson Ready-to-Cook Tenderpressed™ Savory Chicken Breast Filets, 4.75-oz., frozen	4	24	Grill on oiled, preheated flattop griddle at 350°F for 4½ minutes on each side or until chicken is no longer pink. Remove from griddle. Keep warm above 140°F.
2	Olive oil	2 tbsp.	¾ cup	Heat in skillet over medium-high heat.
3	Red onions, fresh, chopped (p. 175)	¼ cup	1½ cups	Add to oil and sauté for 3 to 4 minutes or until onions are translucent. (Sauté smaller quantity for 2 to 3 minutes.)
	Button mushrooms, fresh, sliced	½ cup	3 cups	
4	White wine, dry	½ cup	3 cups	Add to vegetable mixture and deglaze pan, scraping any browned particles from bottom.
5	Blueberries, whole, IQF	½ cup	3 cups	Add to vegetable mixture and mix thoroughly. Bring to boil over high heat. Boil for 15 to 20 minutes or until sauce is reduced by half. (Boil smaller quantity for 10 to 15 minutes.) Remove from heat and keep warm.
	Red raspberries, whole, IQF	½ cup	3 cups	
	Blackberries, whole, IQF	½ cup	3 cups	
	Strawberries, fresh, sliced	½ cup	3 cups	
	Maple syrup, pure	¾ cup	4½ cups	
6	Strawberry fans, fresh (p. 57)	4	24	*To assemble single serving:* Place 1 chicken breast filet on plate. Top with ⅓ cup sauce. Garnish plate with 1 strawberry fan.
				Serve with lemon rice.

Raspberries were introduced to Roman orchards in 65 B.C. after being brought from Mount Ida near the ancient city of Troy. Today, they are considered to be the most flavorful member of the berry family.

Blackberries are the largest of the wild berries and are called brambles in the United Kingdom.

Native Americans taught colonial settlers in New York and Vermont how to tap maple trees for their sap and boil it into syrup. It takes between 20 and 50 gallons of sap to make 1 gallon of pure maple syrup, or sweetwater as the Indians called it.

Portion: 7 ounces
Nutritional Data/Portion: Calories 366, Protein 22 g, Fat 10 g, Carbohydrate 51 g, Cholesterol 60 mg, Sodium 250 mg

For a **FAST FACTS VIA FAX**™ copy of this recipe, call 1-800-223-3755 and enter Business Tool 2629.

Submitted by Louis Johns DiGiovanni
Giovanni's Ristorante
Bethlehem, Pa.

*Parsley, which has come
to be the great American
garnish, has ancient roots on
the island of Sardinia, where
it was featured on early
coinage. Parsley is particularly rich in vitamins A
and C, calcium, iron, and
manganese—just a spoonful
of fresh chopped parsley will
provide the daily allowance
of these nutrients. It is also a
worthy breath freshener.*

Chicken Fontina with Red Peppers and Spinach

Fontina cheese, roasted red bell peppers, and spinach prepared with white balsamic vinegar make this chicken entree especially flavorful and beautiful. Large quantities can be made ahead and baked off at once for banquets and catering.

INGREDIENT	QUANTITY 4 servings	24 servings	METHOD
1 Tyson Ready-to-Cook Tenderpressed™ Savory Whole Butterfly Chicken Breast Filets, 8-oz., frozen	4	24	Dredge chicken breast filets in flour and shake off excess.
2 Flour, all-purpose	as needed	as needed	
Olive oil	2 tbsp.	¾ cup	Heat oil in skillet over medium heat. Add chicken and sauté for 3 to 4 minutes on one side. Sprinkle each chicken breast filet with ½ teaspoon garlic. Turn and sauté an additional 2 to 3 minutes or until chicken is no longer pink. Transfer to roasting pans.
Garlic, fresh, minced	2 tsp.	¼ cup	
3 Butter, salted	2 tbsp.	¾ cup	Heat in saucepan or stockpot over medium-low heat.
4 Spinach, fresh, washed, tightly packed	8 cups	48 cups	Add to butter and sauté for 2 to 3 minutes or until wilted, stirring occasionally. (Sauté smaller quantity for 1 to 2 minutes.) Remove from heat. Drain and transfer to bowl.
5 White balsamic vinegar	¼ cup	1 cup	Add to spinach and mix thoroughly. Top each chicken breast filet with ½ cup spinach.
Salt	1 tsp.	2 tbsp.	
Black pepper, coarse	1 tsp.	2 tbsp.	
6 Fontina cheese slices	8	48	Top spinach with 1 cheese slice, ¼ cup bell peppers, and finish with second slice of cheese.
Red bell peppers, roasted, peeled, seeded, julienne (p. 66)	1 cup	6 cups	
			Bake in preheated conventional oven at 350°F for 7 to 8 minutes or until cheese is melted. Or bake in preheated convection oven at 300°F for 4 to 5 minutes. Remove from oven. Keep warm above 140°F.
7 Parsley sprigs, Italian flat-leaf, fresh	4	24	*To assemble single serving:* Place 1 chicken breast filet on plate. Garnish plate with 1 parsley sprig.
			Serve with spaghetti topped with marinara sauce.

Portion: 11 ounces
Nutritional Data/Portion: Calories 497, Protein 38 g, Fat 33 g, Carbohydrate 14 g, Cholesterol 130 mg, Sodium 1,293 mg

For a **FAST FACTS VIA FAX** copy of this recipe, call 1-800-223-3755 and enter Business Tool 2557.

Submitted by John McKeever III
McKeever's Tavern
North Wales, Pa.

Chicken Chesterfield

The namesake of this dish is an English city with Roman history. The recipe features an Italian-seasoned chicken breast filet topped with crispy bacon and smothered in a bubbly mixture of horseradish-mustard sauce and white cheddar cheese.

INGREDIENT	QUANTITY 4 servings	24 servings	METHOD
1 Tyson Ready-to-Cook Flavor-Redi® Italian Chicken Breast Filets, 4-oz., frozen	8	48	Grill on oiled, preheated flattop griddle at 350°F for 6 to 7 minutes on each side or until chicken is no longer pink. Remove from griddle. Keep warm above 140°F.
2 *Horseradish-Mustard Sauce*			
Mayonnaise	½ cup	3 cups	Combine in bowl and mix thoroughly. Cover and chill to hold.
Horseradish, prepared	¼ cup	1½ cups	
Mustard, spicy brown	¼ cup	1½ cups	
Worcestershire sauce	½ tbsp.	3 tbsp.	
Cayenne pepper sauce	⅛ tsp.	¾ tsp.	
3 Bacon, crisp, coarsely chopped	½ cup	3 cups	*To prepare single serving:* Top 2 chicken breast filets with 2 tablespoons bacon, ¼ cup horseradish-mustard sauce, and ½ cup cheese.
White cheddar cheese, shredded	2 cups	12 cups	
			Broil for 1 to 1½ minutes or until cheese blends with sauce and lightly browns.
4 Green beans, French-cut, frozen, steamed, seasoned	4 cups	24 cups	Portion 1 cup green beans on plate. Top with 2 chicken breast filets. Sprinkle chicken with ⅛ teaspoon paprika.
Paprika, ground	½ tsp.	1 tbsp.	
			Serve with crusty French bread.

Portion: 14 ounces
Nutritional Data/Portion: Calories 820, Protein 67 g, Fat 56 g, Carbohydrate 16 g, Cholesterol 210 mg, Sodium 1,660 mg

For a ***FAST FACTS VIA FAX*** copy of this recipe, call 1-800-223-3755 and enter Business Tool 2555.

The term "green beans" generally refers to any bean variety of which the entire pod is edible. The common green bean is also called the string bean (after the string that has all but been eliminated through genetic engineering) and the snap bean (for the characteristic sound the bean makes when broken in two).

Haricots vert, *French for "green string beans," taste great and make an attractive plate presentation.*

Asparagus may be substituted for the green beans.

Submitted by Michele Duval
Cape Neddick Inn Restaurant
York, Me.

*Fennel is an aromatic
vegetable with pale-green
celerylike stalks and bright-
green feathery foliage. The
base and stems of finocchio,
"Florence fennel," can be
eaten raw in salads or
cooked in a variety of ways.
Common fennel is the source
of the greenish-brown seeds
used in both sweet and
savory foods, as well as to
flavor many liqueurs.*⌒

Grilled Chicken with Roasted Vegetables on Polenta

Tender roasted leeks, fennel bulbs, and bell peppers surround a large French-cut,
oregano-rubbed, grilled chicken breast on a pillow of warm Parmesan polenta.

Line Service *Takeout*

INGREDIENT	QUANTITY		METHOD
	4 servings	24 servings	
1 Tyson Signature Specialties™ French Cut Whole Chicken Breasts, wing joints attached, 10-oz., frozen	4	24	Cover tightly and slack in cooler between 32° and 36°F prior to use.
2 *Oregano Marinade*			
Lemon juice, fresh	¼ cup	1½ cups	Combine in bowl and mix thoroughly. Rub over chicken breasts. Char-grill over medium heat for 8 to 10 minutes on each side or until chicken is no longer pink. Remove from grill. Keep warm above 140°F.
Olive oil	¼ cup	1½ cups	
Oregano, fresh, chopped	2 tbsp.	¾ cup	
Garlic, fresh, minced	2 tsp.	¼ cup	
Salt, kosher	½ tsp.	1 tbsp.	
Black pepper, coarse	½ tsp.	1 tbsp.	
3 *Roasted Vegetables*			
Leeks, fresh, cleaned, sliced lengthwise into quarters (p. 189)	2	12	Place vegetables in shallow roasting pans and drizzle with butter.
Fennel bulbs, fresh, cut into 8 wedges leaving core attached	1	6	Roast in preheated conventional oven at 350°F for 35 to 40 minutes or until tender. (Roast smaller quantity for 20 to 30 minutes.) Or roast in preheated convection oven at 300°F for 10 to 12 minutes. (Roast smaller quantity for 6 to 8 minutes.) Remove from oven and keep warm.
Butter, salted, melted	¼ cup	1 cup	
4 Red bell peppers, whole, fresh (p. 66)	1	6	Quickly char skins over high open flame or under broiler until evenly blackened. Transfer to plastic bag for approximately 10 minutes. Remove from bag. Peel, seed and slice each pepper into 8 strips. Add to roasted vegetables and keep warm.
Yellow bell peppers, whole, fresh	1	6	
Green bell peppers, whole, fresh	1	6	

recipe continued on next page . . .

INGREDIENT	QUANTITY		METHOD
	4 servings	24 servings	
5 *Polenta*			
Chicken broth, canned	4 cups	24 cups	Bring to boil in saucepan or stockpot over high heat.
6 Yellow cornmeal, fine	¾ cup	4½ cups	Reduce heat to medium and gradually whisk in cornmeal. Stir until mixture is creamy. Cook for 20 minutes, stirring frequently. If mixture becomes too thick, add water ¼ cup at a time. Remove from heat.
Water, warm	as needed	as needed	
7 Parmesan cheese, grated	½ cup	3 cups	Add to cornmeal mixture and mix thoroughly. Keep warm.
Black pepper, fine	¼ tsp.	½ tbsp.	
8 Oregano sprigs, fresh	4	24	*To assemble single serving:* Portion 1 cup polenta in center of plate. Top with 1 chicken breast. Surround chicken with roasted vegetables: 2 each of red, yellow, and green bell pepper strips, 2 leek quarters, and 2 fennel wedges. Garnish plate with 1 oregano sprig.

Portion: 24 ounces
Nutritional Data/Portion: Calories 920, Protein 53 g, Fat 64 g, Carbohydrate 36 g, Cholesterol 160 mg, Sodium 2,088 mg

For a ***FAST FACTS VIA FAX*** copy of this recipe, call 1-800-223-3755 and enter Business Tool 2587.

Cornmeal was introduced to Italian cuisine in 1650, and within 100 years, polenta was a dietary staple in many areas. This cornmeal mush is traditionally eaten hot with a little butter, or cooked until firm then cooled, cut into squares, and fried or grilled.

HOW TO CLEAN LEEKS

Trim leaves to remove the tough green portion. Trim root end but leave enough of the root to hold the layers together. Rinse under cold running water, separating each layer to wash out all grit and sand between the layers.

Submitted by Anthony Danna, CEC
Kernville Steak & Seafood
Lincoln City, Ore.

Kosher salt is coarse-grained salt that is also additive-free. ⌐

ZUCCHINI, BELL PEPPER, AND CORN SAUTÉ

	4 servings	24 servings
Butter, salted	1½ tbsp.	½ cup
Yellow corn, whole kernel, frozen	1 cup	7 cups
Zucchini, fresh, sliced in half lengthwise, seeded, ¼-inch slice	1 cup	7 cups
Red bell peppers, fresh, chopped	½ cup	4 cups
Red onions, fresh, slivered	½ cup	4 cups
Garlic, fresh, minced	1 tbsp.	⅓ cup
Salt	½ tsp.	1 tbsp.
Black pepper, coarse	¼ tsp.	½ tbsp.

Heat butter in skillet over medium-high heat.

Add corn to butter and sauté for 2 to 3 minutes or until lightly browned. (Sauté smaller quantity for 1 to 1½ minutes.)

Add remaining ingredients to corn and sauté for 4 to 5 minutes or until vegetables are tender-crisp. (Sauté smaller quantity for 1 to 3 minutes.) Remove from heat and keep warm.

Grilled Cilantro Chicken with Vegetable Sauté

Aromatic cilantro butter melts when put on the hot grilled chicken breast that's been marinated in tequila and mustard. Sautéed zucchini, corn, and red bell peppers serve as a colorful side dish.

INGREDIENT	QUANTITY		METHOD
	4 servings	24 servings	
1 Tyson Ready-to-Cook Gourmet Boneless, Skinless Whole Chicken Breast Filets, 6-oz., frozen	4	24	Place in full-size steam table pans. (Use half-size pan for smaller quantity.)
2 *Tequila-Mustard Marinade*			
Tequila	½ cup	3 cups	Combine in bowl and mix thoroughly. Pour over chicken. Cover and marinate below 40°F for 12 hours.
Mustard, Dijon	½ cup	3 cups	
Garlic, fresh, minced	1 tbsp.	⅓ cup	
Cilantro, fresh, chopped	1 tbsp.	⅓ cup	
Black pepper, coarse	2 tsp.	¼ cup	
3 *Cilantro Butter*			
Butter, unsalted, softened	½ cup	3 cups	Combine in bowl and mix thoroughly. Cover and reserve at room temperature for no more than 2 hours.
Lemon juice, fresh	1 tbsp.	⅓ cup	
Worcestershire sauce	2 tsp.	¼ cup	
Cilantro, fresh, blanched, chopped	1 tbsp.	⅓ cup	
Salt	¼ tsp.	½ tbsp.	
White pepper, fine	⅛ tsp.	¾ tsp.	
4 Vegetable oil spray	as needed	as needed	Remove chicken from marinade and spray with oil. Char-grill over high heat for 4 to 5 minutes on each side or until chicken is no longer pink. Remove from grill. Keep warm above 140°F.
5 Salt, kosher	as needed	as needed	*To assemble single serving:* Place 1 chicken breast filet on plate. Sprinkle lightly with salt and top with 2 tablespoons cilantro butter. Portion ½ cup vegetables on plate. Garnish plate with 1 cilantro sprig.
Zucchini, Bell Pepper, and Corn Sauté (see recipe)	2 cups	12 cups	
Cilantro sprigs, fresh	4	24	*Serve with onion rolls.*

Portion: 9 ounces
Nutritional Data/Portion: Calories 245, Protein 24 g, Fat 13 g, Carbohydrate 9 g, Cholesterol 83 mg, Sodium 513 mg

For a **FAST FACTS VIA FAX** copy of this recipe, call 1-800-223-3755 and enter Business Tool 2578.

Submitted by Jonathan Mortimer
The Grove Hotel
Boise, Idaho

Chicken Piccata

Tart lemon and salty capers harmonize in a rich reduction of white wine, butter, and shallots.
Truly an elegant Italian classic.

Speed-Scratch *Takeout*

INGREDIENT	QUANTITY		METHOD
	4 servings	24 servings	
1 Tyson Ready-to-Cook Tenderpressed™ Lemon Herb Chicken Breast Filets, 6-oz., frozen	4	24	*To prepare single serving:* Season 1 chicken breast filet with ¼ teaspoon salt and ⅛ teaspoon pepper. Dredge in flour and shake off excess.
Salt	1 tsp.	2 tbsp.	
White pepper, fine	½ tsp.	1 tbsp.	
Flour, all-purpose	as needed	as needed	
2 Olive oil	¼ cup	1½ cups	Heat 1 tablespoon in sauté pan over medium-high heat. Add chicken and sauté for 7 to 8 minutes on each side or until chicken is no longer pink. Transfer to plate. Keep warm above 140°F.
3 White wine, dry	¼ cup	1½ cups	Add 1 tablespoon wine, ½ tablespoon lemon juice, and ¾ teaspoon shallots to pan. Deglaze pan, scraping any browned particles from bottom. Reduce liquid by half.
Lemon juice, fresh	2 tbsp.	¾ cup	
Shallots, fresh, minced	1 tbsp.	⅓ cup	
4 Butter, salted	½ cup	3 cups	Reduce heat to low. Whisk 2 tablespoons into sauce, 1 teaspoon at a time, allowing to melt between additions.
5 Capers, rinsed, drained	1 tbsp.	⅓ cup	Add ¾ teaspoon capers to sauce and mix thoroughly. Pour over chicken. Garnish plate with 1 lemon twist.
Lemon slice twists, fresh	4	24	
			Serve with rice pilaf and fresh asparagus.

Portion: 6 ounces
Nutritional Data/Portion: Calories 468, Protein 16 g, Fat 40 g, Carbohydrate 14 g, Cholesterol 113 mg, Sodium 1,129 mg

For a **FAST FACTS VIA FAX**™ copy of this recipe, call 1-800-223-3755 and enter Business Tool 2560.

Piccata *is a Northern Italian term that actually refers to the thin cutlet of meat (most often veal) traditionally accompanied by a light sauce based on white wine and lemon, and sometimes capers and parsley.*

Chicken *easily stands in for veal and is increasingly doing just that in many menu classics. Here, its adaptability shows that the lighter flavor and great economy of chicken actually enhance the dish.*

An Indian legend claims that the ingenious wife of an Iroquois chief is responsible for making the first maple syrup. As the legend goes, the chief had hurled his tomahawk into a maple tree one evening, where it remained all night. After he retrieved it the following morning, the weather turned warm and sap started flowing from the gash in the tree. It dripped and collected in a vessel that happened to be sitting at the base of the tree. Later in the day, his wife set out to retrieve water for the evening meal and discovered her container already full. Not wanting to waste anything, she tasted the sap and decided to cook with it. When the chief returned from his day of hunting he could smell the sweet aroma wafting from their campsite. And so the story goes . . . ⌐

Fried Chicken with Spring Vegetables

Putting more pizzazz into picnic baskets is easy with this flavorful combo of fried chicken and gourmet-to-go dishes, including maple corn and cabbage cole slaw, Mediterranean tomato-red pepper salad, and spicy garlic-glazed green beans.

Lighter Fare *Line Service* *Takeout*

INGREDIENT	QUANTITY 4 servings	24 servings	METHOD
1 *Maple Corn and Cabbage Cole Slaw*			
Yellow corn, whole kernel, frozen	¾ cup	4½ cups	Combine in bowl and mix thoroughly.
Green cabbage, fresh, ¼-inch dice	¾ cup	4½ cups	
Onions, fresh, ¼-inch dice (p. 175)	¼ cup	1½ cups	
Red bell peppers, fresh, ¼-inch dice (p. 88)	¼ cup	1½ cups	
Green bell peppers, fresh, ¼-inch dice	¼ cup	1½ cups	
2 Apple cider vinegar	2 tbsp.	¾ cup	Combine in separate bowl and mix thoroughly. Pour over corn mixture and toss well. Cover and chill to hold.
Maple syrup, pure	1 tbsp.	⅓ cup	
Mustard, Dijon	½ tbsp.	3 tbsp.	
Dry mustard powder	½ tsp.	1 tbsp.	
Salt, kosher	¼ tsp.	½ tbsp.	
Red pepper, crushed, dried	⅛ tsp.	¾ tsp.	
Gingerroot, fresh, peeled, grated	½ tsp.	1 tbsp.	
Garlic, fresh, minced	½ tsp.	1 tbsp.	
3 *Mediterranean Red Salad*			
Red bell peppers, fresh, sliced in half, seeded	1	6	Place cut side down on sheet pan. Broil for 4 to 5 minutes or until skins are charred. Remove from broiler and cool. Peel and slice into ½-inch-wide strips. Place in bowl.
4 Red onions, fresh, slivered	½	3	Place on oiled sheet pan. Roast in preheated conventional oven at 500°F for 13 to 15 minutes or until edges begin to char. Remove from oven and add to peppers.
5 Roma tomatoes, fresh	3	18	Slice lengthwise into 8 wedges. Seed and add to peppers.
6 Olive oil	2 tbsp.	¾ cup	Combine in separate bowl and whisk together until blended.
Red wine vinegar	½ tbsp.	3 tbsp.	
Lemon juice, fresh	½ tbsp.	3 tbsp.	

recipe continued on next page . . .

INGREDIENT	QUANTITY		METHOD
	4 servings	24 servings	
7			
Capers, rinsed, drained	½ tsp.	1 tbsp.	Add to oil mixture and mix thoroughly. Pour over pepper mixture and toss well. Cover and chill to hold.
Basil, fresh, chopped	2 tsp.	3 tbsp.	
Mint, fresh, chopped	2 tsp.	3 tbsp.	
8			
Szechuan Green Beans			
Vegetable oil	1 tbsp.	⅓ cup	Heat in skillet or braising pan over medium heat.
9			
Green onions, fresh, minced	⅓ cup	2 cups	Add to oil and stir-fry for 1 to 2 minutes or until soft but not brown.
Garlic, fresh, minced	1 tsp.	2 tbsp.	
10			
Green beans, fresh, trimmed	1 lb.	6 lb.	Add to onion mixture and stir-fry for 4 to 5 minutes or until color turns bright green.
Salt	⅛ tsp.	½ tsp.	
11			
Soy sauce	1 tbsp.	⅓ cup	Combine in bowl and add to bean mixture. Stir-fry for 1 to 2 minutes or until green beans are tender-crisp. Remove from heat and cool. Cover and chill or hold at room temperature.
Rice wine vinegar	1 tbsp.	⅓ cup	
Red pepper, crushed, dried	⅛ tsp.	¾ tsp.	
12			
Tyson Deli-Style Breaded Tastybasted® Deli-Lightful, 6-piece cut, frozen	12 pc. (4 breasts, 4 thighs, 4 drums)	72 pc. (24 breasts, 24 thighs, 24 drums)	Pressure-fry at 325°F for 19 to 22 minutes or until chicken is no longer pink. (Place thighs and breasts in open pressure fryer for 3 to 4 minutes. Add drums and pressure-fry an additional 16 to 18 minutes.)
			Or deep-fry at 350°F for 21 to 24 minutes or until chicken is no longer pink. (Place thighs and breasts in fryer for 3 to 4 minutes. Add drums and deep-fry an additional 18 to 20 minutes.)
			Remove from fryer and drain. Keep warm above 140°F.
13			
Basil sprigs, fresh	4	24	*To assemble single serving:* Arrange 3 pieces chicken (1 breast, 1 thigh, and 1 drum) on one side of plate. Arrange ½ cup corn and cabbage slaw, ½ cup Mediterranean salad, and 1 scant cup Szechuan green beans around chicken. Garnish plate with 1 basil sprig.

Portion: 21 ounces
Nutritional Data/Portion: Calories 357, Protein 11 g, Fat 24 g, Carbohydrate 30 g, Cholesterol 30 mg, Sodium 736 mg

For a **FAST FACTS VIA FAX**℠ copy of this recipe, call 1-800-223-3755 and enter Business Tool 2567.

According to Greek mythology, Pluto found the beautiful nymph Mentha irresistible, especially her aroma. Out of jealousy, Pluto's wife, Persephone, turned Mentha into greenery. Ironically, mint is often considered a symbol of hospitality.

Turnips, which have white skin and a purplish top, have been part of the Greek diet since the 4th century B.C. Small young turnips have a delicate texture and flavor, bordering on sweet. With age, they get woodier and have a much stronger flavor. Turnips should be heavy for their size.

Rutabagas, which resemble large turnips, are thought to be a cross between cabbage and turnips. They are sometimes called Swedes, or Swedish turnips, because the name stems from the Swedish word rotabagge.

Beets range in color from dark red to white. One variety, the Chioggia, has the red and white striped pattern of candy canes.

Honey-Stung Fried Chicken and Harvest Vegetables

Fried chicken makes perfect sense when served with a colorful platter of fall vegetables, including sweet potatoes, acorn squash, rutabagas, and turnips, all roasted with fresh rosemary.

Line Service *Takeout*

INGREDIENT	QUANTITY		METHOD
	4 servings	24 servings	
1 *Roasted Vegetables*			
Carrot slices, fresh, ¼-inch bias	12	72	Combine in bowl.
New red potatoes, fresh, skin-on, blanched 5 minutes, drained, halved	4	24	
Acorn squash rings, fresh, ¼-inch-thick, seeded	4	24	
Turnip slices, fresh, ¼-inch-thick	4	24	
Rutabaga slices, fresh, ¼-inch-thick	4	24	
Sweet potato slices, fresh, ¼-inch-thick, skin-on	4	24	
Leeks, fresh, cleaned, sliced lengthwise into quarters (p. 189)	1	6	
2 Beet slices, fresh, ¼-inch-thick	4	24	Place in separate bowl from other vegetables.
3 Olive oil	2 tbsp.	¾ cup	Combine in separate bowl and mix thoroughly. Pour over vegetable mixture and beet slices and toss well. Arrange in single layer on parchment-lined sheet pans, keeping beets separated from other vegetables.
Rosemary, fresh, minced	1 tbsp.	⅓ cup	
Salt, kosher	½ tsp.	1 tbsp.	
			Roast in preheated conventional oven at 450°F for 18 to 20 minutes or until tender. (Roast smaller quantity for 15 to 18 minutes.) Or roast in preheated convection oven at 400°F for 18 to 20 minutes. (Roast smaller quantity for 13 to 15 minutes.) Remove from oven and keep warm.
4 Tyson Fully Cooked Honey Stung® Fried Chicken, 3-piece portions, 10-oz., frozen	4 packs	24 packs	*To prepare single serving:* Deep-fry 1 pack at 350°F for 6 to 9 minutes. Remove from fryer and drain. Arrange chicken on one side of plate. Arrange 3 roasted carrot slices and 1 each of all other vegetables on opposite side of plate. Garnish plate with 1 rosemary sprig.
Rosemary sprigs, fresh	4	24	

Portion: 17 ounces

Nutritional Data/Portion: Calories 550, Protein 22 g, Fat 30 g, Carbohydrate 50 g, Cholesterol 95 mg, Sodium 1,120 mg

For a **FAST FACTS VIA FAX**℠ copy of this recipe, call 1-800-223-3755 and enter Business Tool 2566.

Submitted by Harry Honer
Marriott Management Services
Trenton, N.J.

Blackened Blue Cheese Chicken with Mango-Pepper Salsa

The rich filling of blue cheese, bacon, and garlic is balanced by a fresh salsa of bell peppers, mangoes, and lime in these delicious stuffed chicken medallions.

INGREDIENT	QUANTITY 4 servings	24 servings	METHOD
1 Tyson Ready-to-Cook Flavor-Redi® Hot Spiced Chicken Breast Filets, 5-oz., frozen	4	24	Slack in cooler between 32° and 36°F prior to use.
2 *Mango-Pepper Salsa*			
Mangoes, fresh, ¼-inch dice	½ cup	3 cups	Combine in bowl and mix thoroughly. Cover and chill to hold.
Red bell peppers, fresh, ¼-inch dice (p. 88)	2 tbsp.	¾ cup	
Yellow bell peppers, fresh, ¼-inch dice	2 tbsp.	¾ cup	
Lime juice, fresh	1 tbsp.	⅓ cup	
Green onions, fresh, chopped	½ tbsp.	3 tbsp.	
Parsley, fresh, minced (p. 39)	¼ tsp.	½ tbsp.	
Cumin, ground	⅛ tsp.	¾ tsp.	
Coriander, ground	⅛ tsp.	¾ tsp.	
Cayenne pepper, ground	⅛ tsp.	¾ tsp.	
Salt	⅛ tsp.	¾ tsp.	
3 Blue cheese crumbles, softened	½ cup	3 cups	Combine in bowl and mix thoroughly. Lightly pound each chicken breast filet to even thickness. Spread 2 tablespoons cheese mixture over each chicken breast filet.
Butter, unsalted, softened	¼ cup	1½ cups	
Garlic, fresh, minced	½ tsp.	1 tbsp.	
4 Peppered bacon, crisp, crumbled	¼ cup	1½ cups	Sprinkle 1 tablespoon over cheese. Roll chicken breast filets into cylinder shape and secure with wooden pick.
5 Cajun spice blend, dried	as needed	as needed	Roll each chicken breast filet in spice blend until well coated. Heat oiled iron skillet over high heat until very hot. Add chicken breast filets and cook for 2 to 3 minutes or until entire outside surface is blackened. Transfer to oiled roasting pans.
			Roast in preheated conventional oven at 400°F for 10 to 12 minutes or until chicken is no longer pink. (Roast smaller quantity for 6 to 8 minutes.) Or roast in preheated convection oven at 350°F for 8 to 10 minutes. (Roast smaller quantity for 4 to 6 minutes.) Remove from oven. Keep warm above 140°F.
6 Cilantro sprigs, fresh	4	24	*To assemble single serving:* Remove wooden pick from 1 chicken breast filet. Slice chicken into 4 medallions and fan on plate. Spoon ½ tablespoon pan juices over top of chicken. Portion 2 tablespoons mango salsa on the side. Garnish plate with 1 cilantro sprig.
			Serve with steamed white rice.

Portion: 8 ounces
Nutritional Data/Portion: Calories 390, Protein 36 g, Fat 24 g, Carbohydrate 8 g, Cholesterol 130 mg, Sodium 1,670 mg

For a **FAST FACTS VIA FAX**™ copy of this recipe, call 1-800-223-3755 and enter Business Tool 2630.

Cheese curds are injected with various molds to form the blue or green veins that give blue cheeses their characteristic flavors and appearances. Among the most popular forms produced in America are Roquefort, Gorgonzola, Danablu, and Stilton, which originated in France, Italy, Denmark, and England, respectively. Although they are all blue cheeses, they are not interchangeable in all recipes.

For line service and takeout, the chicken breast filet should not be sliced.

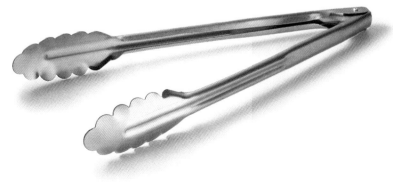

Submitted by Michael A. Jerez
Cafe Madrid–Bella Pasta
Mesa, Ariz.

Kebabs have been popular in Turkey since the 14th century.

Eggplants should be stored in a cool, dry place for no more than 2 days after purchase because they are very perishable and become bitter with age.

Chicken and Vegetable Kebabs with Tomato-Caper Coulis

Two kebabs, each with chicken and its own assortment of grilled vegetables, are complemented with a luscious coulis of Roma tomatoes, capers, and white balsamic vinegar. Paired with vegetable salad, including artichoke hearts and avocado slices, it makes a particularly impressive plate presentation.

Line Service   *Takeout*

INGREDIENT	QUANTITY		METHOD
	4 servings	24 servings	
1 Tyson Ready-to-Cook Tenderpressed™ Savory Chicken Breast Filets, 4-oz., frozen	4	24	Cover tightly and slack in cooler between 32° and 36°F prior to use.
2 Thin wooden skewers, 6-inch, soaked in water	8	48	Slice each chicken breast filet in half lengthwise, then slice in half crosswise to make 4 pieces.
Red onion wedges, fresh	4	24	Thread half of skewers with 1 chicken piece, 1 onion wedge, 1 chicken piece, and 1 eggplant chunk.
Eggplant chunks, fresh, 1-inch	4	24	
Zucchini chunks, fresh, 1-inch	4	24	Thread remaining half of skewers with 1 chicken piece, 1 zucchini chunk, 1 chicken piece, and 1 tomato half. Arrange in steam table pans.
Roma tomato halves, fresh	4	24	
3 *Kebab Marinade*			
Olive oil	⅓ cup	2 cups	Combine in bowl and mix thoroughly. Spread over skewers, turning to coat chicken and vegetables. Cover and marinate below 40°F at least 4 hours.
Rosemary, fresh, minced	2 tbsp.	¾ cup	
Parsley, fresh, minced (p. 39)	1 tbsp.	⅓ cup	
Oregano, fresh, minced	1 tbsp.	⅓ cup	
Basil, fresh, minced	1 tbsp.	⅓ cup	
Thyme, fresh, minced	1 tbsp.	⅓ cup	
Salt	¼ tsp.	2 tsp.	
Black pepper, coarse	⅛ tsp.	1 tsp.	
4 *Vegetable Salad*			
Carrots, fresh, julienne (p. 88)	1 cup	6 cups	Combine in bowl.
Artichoke quarters, canned, drained	12	72	
Avocado slices, fresh	8	48	

recipe continued on next page . . .

Chicken and Vegetable Kebabs with Tomato-Caper Coulis continued

INGREDIENT	QUANTITY 4 servings	24 servings	METHOD
5 Olive oil	⅓ cup	2 cups	Combine in separate bowl and mix thoroughly. Pour over vegetables and toss well. Cover and chill to hold.
Lemon juice, fresh	2 tbsp.	¾ cup	
Sugar, granulated	1 tsp.	2 tbsp.	
Salt	¼ tsp.	½ tbsp.	
Black pepper, coarse	¼ tsp.	½ tbsp.	
6 *Tomato-Caper Coulis*			
Olive oil	½ tbsp.	3 tbsp.	Heat in skillet over medium heat.
7 Onions, fresh, diced (p. 175)	2 tbsp.	¾ cup	Add to oil and sauté for 4 to 5 minutes or until translucent. (Sauté smaller quantity for 1 to 2 minutes.)
8 White wine, dry	2 tbsp.	¾ cup	Add to onions and reduce by three-fourths.
9 White balsamic vinegar	2 tbsp.	¾ cup	Add to onions and bring to boil over high heat. Reduce heat and simmer for 25 to 30 minutes or until flavors are concentrated. (Simmer smaller quantity for 5 to 7 minutes.) Remove from heat and cool slightly. Transfer to food processor bowl and process until pureed. Strain through fine mesh strainer.
Roma tomatoes, fresh, sliced	1 cup	6 cups	
Chicken broth, canned	½ cup	3 cups	
10 Roma tomatoes, fresh, minced	¾ cup	4½ cups	Add to pureed mixture and mix thoroughly. Keep warm.
Capers, rinsed, drained	1 tbsp.	⅓ cup	
Basil, fresh, chopped	½ tbsp.	3 tbsp.	
Salt	⅛ tsp.	¾ tsp.	
Black pepper, coarse	⅛ tsp.	¾ tsp.	
11 Mixed salad greens, fresh, commercially prepared	8 cups	48 cups	*To prepare single serving:* Remove 2 skewers (1 onion/eggplant and 1 zucchini/tomato) from marinade.
Red cherry peppers, canned, drained	4	24	Char-grill over medium heat for 12 to 14 minutes, turning frequently, or until chicken is no longer pink. Remove from grill and arrange on plate.
Green grape clusters, seedless, fresh	4	24	Portion 2 cups greens on plate. Top with vegetable salad. Garnish plate with 1 cherry pepper and 1 grape cluster. Drizzle ⅓ cup coulis over plate.

Portion: 14 ounces
Nutritional Data/Portion: Calories 413, Protein 25 g, Fat 28 g, Carbohydrate 19 g, Cholesterol 61 mg, Sodium 1,020 mg

For a **FAST FACTS VIA FAX** copy of this recipe, call 1-800-223-3755 and enter Business Tool 2570.

For added flavor and presentation appeal, use trimmed rosemary branches as skewers.

Coulis generally refers to a thick puree or sauce. It was originally used to describe the juices from cooked meat.

Submitted by Matt Swingos
Swingos On The Lake
Lakewood, Ohio

Feta cheese is traditionally made of sheep's or goat's milk. It is sometimes referred to as pickled cheese because it is cured and stored in its own whey brine.

In Greek, oregano means "joy of the mountain." It is an important herb in Greek cooking, especially in conjunction with lemon. Oregano is closely related to marjoram, but has a cleaner, fresher flavor, especially when used fresh.

Greco Chicken

Save your patrons a trip to the Mediterranean. This dish offers the wonderful fresh flavors we associate with Greece, including tangy feta cheese, oregano, tomatoes, lemons, and broiled chicken.

INGREDIENT	QUANTITY 4 servings	QUANTITY 24 servings	METHOD
1 Tyson Ready-to-Cook Flavor-Redi® Savory Chicken Breast Filets, 6-oz., frozen	4	24	Slack in cooler between 32° and 36°F prior to use.
2 Oregano, fresh, minced	1½ tbsp.	½ cup	*To prepare single serving:* Season 1 chicken breast filet with 1 teaspoon oregano, ⅛ teaspoon salt, and ⅛ teaspoon pepper.
Seasoned salt	½ tsp.	1 tbsp.	
Black pepper, coarse	½ tsp.	1 tbsp.	
3 Butter, salted	¼ cup	1½ cups	Heat 1 tablespoon in sauté pan over medium heat. Add chicken and sauté for 1 to 2 minutes on each side or until browned.
4 Plum tomato wedges, fresh	2 cups	12 cups	Add ½ cup tomatoes, ⅓ cup onions, and ½ teaspoon oregano to chicken. Sauté for 2 to 3 minutes or until onions are translucent.
Red onions, fresh, slivered	1⅓ cups	8 cups	
Oregano, fresh, minced	2 tsp.	¼ cup	
5 Lemon juice, fresh	½ cup	3 cups	Add 2 tablespoons lemon juice and 1½ tablespoons wine to chicken. Simmer for 1 to 2 minutes or until chicken is no longer pink. Remove from heat and arrange on plate.
Sauvignon Blanc wine	6 tbsp.	2¼ cups	
6 Feta cheese, crumbled	½ cup	3 cups	Sprinkle 2 tablespoons cheese over chicken and sauce. Garnish plate with 1 teaspoon lemon zest and 1 oregano sprig.
Lemon zest, fresh	1½ tbsp.	½ cup	
Oregano sprigs, fresh	4	24	*Serve with chilled spinach salad.*

Portion: 10 ounces

Nutritional Data/Portion: Calories 302, Protein 25 g, Fat 17 g, Carbohydrate 14 g, Cholesterol 97 mg, Sodium 815 mg

For a **FAST FACTS VIA FAX**™ copy of this recipe, call 1-800-223-3755 and enter Business Tool 2588.

Submitted by Jim Phillip
ARAMARK
Hoffman Estates, Ill.

Chicken Medallions with Red Onions and Mushrooms

A confiture-style mixture of red wine, caramelized red onions, and mushrooms transforms thigh filets into marvelous chicken medallions.

Confiture *is French for "preserves." The term is also used to describe a mixture of vegetables that is slow-cooked for a long period of time to bring out the natural sweetness of the ingredients.*

INGREDIENT	QUANTITY 4 servings	24 servings	METHOD
1 *Red Onion and Mushroom Mixture*			
Butter, salted	2 tsp.	¼ cup	Heat in skillet or braising pan over high heat.
2 Red onions, fresh, julienne (p. 88)	1½ cups	9 cups	Add to butter and sauté for 5 to 6 minutes or until onions are translucent. (Sauté smaller quantity for 2 to 3 minutes.)
Button mushrooms, fresh, thinly sliced	1½ cups	9 cups	
3 Sugar, granulated	2 tbsp.	¾ cup	Add to onion/mushroom mixture and sauté for 6 to 8 minutes, stirring constantly, or until onions are caramelized. (Sauté smaller quantity for 3 to 4 minutes.)
4 Red wine, dry	½ cup	3 cups	Add to onion/mushroom mixture and simmer for 8 to 10 minutes or until most of liquid has evaporated. (Simmer smaller quantity for 3 to 4 minutes.) Remove from heat and keep warm.
Red wine vinegar	¼ cup	1½ cups	
Salt	¼ tsp.	1 tsp.	
Black pepper, coarse	¼ tsp.	1 tsp.	
5 Tyson Ready-to-Cook Gourmet Boneless, Skinless Chicken Thigh Filets, 3.5-oz., frozen	8	48	*To prepare single serving:* Season 2 chicken thigh filets with ¼ teaspoon salt and ⅛ teaspoon pepper. Dredge in flour and shake off excess.
Salt	1 tsp.	2 tbsp.	
Black pepper, coarse	½ tsp.	1 tbsp.	
Flour, all-purpose	as needed	as needed	
6 Olive oil	¼ cup	1½ cups	Heat 1 tablespoon oil in sauté pan over medium heat. Add chicken and sauté for 3 to 4 minutes on each side or until chicken is no longer pink. Transfer to plate. Top with ¼ cup red onion and mushroom mixture. Garnish plate with 1 parsley sprig.
Parsley sprigs, fresh	4	24	

Serve with roasted new potatoes.

Portion: 9½ ounces
Nutritional Data/Portion: Calories 522, Protein 36 g, Fat 34 g, Carbohydrate 21 g, Cholesterol 162 mg, Sodium 890 mg

For a **FAST FACTS VIA FAX** copy of this recipe, call 1-800-223-3755 and enter Business Tool 2558.

"Onions can make even heirs and widows weep."
Benjamin Franklin

Recipes on pages 201 and 202.

Submitted by Anthony Danna, CEC
Kernville Steak & Seafood
Lincoln City, Ore.

Sicilian-Style Chicken

Artichokes, sun-dried tomatoes, capers, white wine, and balsamic vinegar impart the flavors of the sunny Mediterranean to this great chicken dish.

INGREDIENT	QUANTITY		METHOD
	4 servings	24 servings	
1 Tyson Ready-to-Cook Flavor-Redi® Savory Chicken Breast Filets, 6-oz., frozen	4	24	Slack in cooler between 32° and 36°F prior to use.
2 Flour, all-purpose	as needed	as needed	Dredge chicken breast filets in flour and shake off excess.
3 Butter, clarified	¼ cup	1½ cups	Heat in skillet over medium heat. Add chicken and sauté for 2 to 3 minutes on each side or until browned. Transfer to roasting pans. Remove excess butter from skillet.
4 White wine, dry	⅓ cup	2 cups	Add to skillet and deglaze pan, scraping any browned particles from bottom.
5 Button mushrooms, fresh, quartered	1 cup	6 cups	Add to wine and mix thoroughly. Transfer to roasting pans with chicken.
Red bell peppers, fresh, julienne (p. 88)	1 cup	6 cups	
Artichoke hearts, marinated, drained, quartered	½ cup	3 cups	
Sun-dried tomatoes, oil-packed, drained, julienne	¼ cup	1½ cups	
Capers, rinsed, drained	1 tbsp.	⅓ cup	
Balsamic vinegar	1 tbsp.	⅓ cup	
Salt	½ tsp.	1 tbsp.	
6 Chicken broth, canned	1 cup	6 cups	Whisk together until smooth and add to chicken and vegetables.
Cornstarch	1 tsp.	2 tbsp.	
			Roast in preheated conventional oven at 350°F for 25 to 30 minutes or until chicken is no longer pink. (Roast smaller quantity for 10 to 15 minutes.) Or roast in preheated convection oven at 300°F for 18 to 20 minutes. (Roast smaller quantity for 8 to 10 minutes.) Remove from oven. Keep warm above 140°F.
7 Parsley, fresh, chopped	¼ cup	1½ cups	*To assemble single serving:* Place 1 chicken breast filet on plate. Ladle ½ cup vegetables and sauce over chicken. Garnish plate with 1 tablespoon parsley.
			Serve with buttered orzo.

Portion: 9 ounces
Nutritional Data/Portion: Calories 272, Protein 25 g, Fat 15 g, Carbohydrate 11 g, Cholesterol 83 mg, Sodium 1,180 mg

For a **FAST FACTS VIA FAX**™ copy of this recipe, call 1-800-223-3755 and enter Business Tool 2633.

Artichoke is a name that's shared by three unrelated plants: the globe artichoke, the Jerusalem artichoke, and the Chinese, or Japanese, artichoke. The edible bud of the globe artichoke, a close relative of the thistle plant, will bloom into 6-inch bluish flower heads if left to mature. The Jerusalem artichoke is a tuber that derives its name not from the well-known city but from the Italian word for "sunflower," girasole, to which the plant is closely related. Chinese artichokes are tubers from flowers belonging to the mint family.

Globe artichokes should be deep green in color and heavy for their size. Tight leaf formations should "squeak" when pressed together. Slight discoloration, which may result on leaf edges due to frost damage, is okay, but heavy browning indicates that an artichoke is past its prime. Spring is artichoke season, and the midcoastal region of California is where most of America's supply is grown.

This recipe is pictured on opposite page.

Submitted by Ennio Riga
Prime Hospitality
Fairfield, N.J.

GOLDEN RAISIN COUSCOUS

	4 servings	24 servings
Chicken broth, canned	2 cups	12 cups
Butter, salted	2 tbsp.	⅔ cup
Salt	½ tsp.	1 tbsp.
Couscous, dry	1 cup	6 cups
Raisins, golden	½ cup	3 cups
Almonds, slivered, toasted	1½ tbsp.	½ cup
Parsley, fresh, minced	1½ tbsp.	½ cup

Combine first three ingredients in saucepan or stockpot. Bring to boil over high heat.

Add couscous and raisins to broth mixture and mix thoroughly. Return to boil, then remove from heat. Cover and allow to rest undisturbed for 10 to 15 minutes or until most of liquid is absorbed.

Add almonds and parsley to couscous and toss well. Keep warm.

Portion: 6 ounces

This recipe is pictured on page 200.

Spicy Orange Chicken

This beautifully glazed breast filet of citrus-marinated chicken has a triple treat of orange flavor, with zest, juice, and liqueur.

	INGREDIENT	QUANTITY 4 servings	24 servings	METHOD
1	Butter, clarified	¼ cup	1½ cups	*To prepare single serving:* Heat 1 tablespoon in sauté pan over medium heat.
2	Tyson Ready-to-Cook Tenderpressed™ Southwest Citrus Chicken Breast Filets, 5-oz., frozen	4	24	Dredge 1 chicken breast filet in flour and shake off excess. Add to butter and sauté for 2 to 3 minutes on each side or until golden brown.
	Flour, all-purpose	as needed	as needed	
3	Shallots, fresh, chopped	1½ tbsp.	½ cup	Add 1 teaspoon shallots and 1 teaspoon garlic to chicken. Sauté for 10 to 15 seconds or until shallots begin to cook.
	Garlic, fresh, chopped	1½ tbsp.	½ cup	
4	Orange juice, fresh	2 cups	12 cups	Add ½ cup orange juice, 2 tablespoons chicken broth, 1 tablespoon liqueur, and ⅛ teaspoon cayenne pepper to chicken and mix thoroughly.
	Chicken broth, canned	½ cup	3 cups	
	Orange-flavored liqueur	¼ cup	1½ cups	
	Cayenne pepper, ground	½ tsp.	1 tbsp.	Bring to boil over high heat. Reduce heat and simmer for 3 to 4 minutes or until sauce is reduced by half and chicken is no longer pink.
5	Salt	1 tsp.	2 tbsp.	Season mixture with ¼ teaspoon salt and ⅛ teaspoon pepper. Remove from heat and transfer to plate.
6	Black pepper, fine	½ tsp.	1 tbsp.	
	Orange slices, seedless, fresh, peeled	8	48	Top chicken breast filet with 2 orange slices and sprinkle with 1 teaspoon orange zest. Garnish plate with 1 basil sprig.
	Orange zest, fresh	1½ tbsp.	½ cup	
	Basil sprigs, fresh	4	24	*Serve with golden raisin couscous.*

Portion: 7 ounces

Nutritional Data/Portion: Calories 370, Protein 37 g, Fat 15 g, Carbohydrate 27 g, Cholesterol 105 mg, Sodium 1,310 mg

For a **FAST FACTS VIA FAX**™ copy of this recipe, call 1-800-223-3755 and enter Business Tool 2586.

Queen's Chicken with Sherried Honey Sauce

English walnuts crown this refined chicken entree seasoned with shallots, thyme, and a reduction of chicken stock, brown sugar, and honey. It's fit for a queen's palate.

Submitted by Enzo Russo
Bernie Little's Riverhouse
Evansville, Ind.

Commercially produced brown sugar is white sugar with molasses, which gives it its soft texture. The ratio of molasses to sugar determines whether the brown sugar is marketed as light or dark. Though similar in color and flavor, brown sugar should not be confused with raw sugar.

	INGREDIENT	QUANTITY 4 servings	24 servings	METHOD
1	Tyson Ready-to-Cook Flavor-Redi® Savory Chicken Breast Filets, 5-oz., frozen	4	24	Slack in cooler between 32° and 36°F prior to use.
2	Butter, clarified	½ cup	3 cups	*To prepare single serving:* Heat 2 tablespoons in sauté pan over medium-high heat. Add 1 chicken breast filet and sauté for 3 to 4 minutes on each side or until golden brown. Pour off all but 1 tablespoon of butter.
3	Shallots, fresh, minced	2 tsp.	¼ cup	Add ½ teaspoon shallots and ½ teaspoon thyme to chicken and sauté for 30 seconds or until shallots begin to cook.
	Thyme, fresh, chopped	2 tsp.	¼ cup	
4	Sherry, dry	¼ cup	1½ cups	Add 1 tablespoon to chicken and flambé.
5	Chicken broth, canned	½ cup	3 cups	Add 2 tablespoons chicken broth, 1 tablespoon brown sugar, ½ tablespoon honey, and ⅛ teaspoon pepper to chicken and mix thoroughly. Simmer for 1 to 2 minutes or until sauce is reduced by half and chicken is no longer pink. Remove from heat.
	Brown sugar, golden	¼ cup	1½ cups	
	Honey	2 tbsp.	¾ cup	
	Black pepper, fine	½ tsp.	1 tbsp.	
6	Green grapes, seedless, fresh, quartered lengthwise	¼ cup	1½ cups	Add 1 tablespoon to chicken and mix thoroughly. Transfer chicken to plate and pour sauce over chicken.

recipe continued on next page . . .

INGREDIENT	QUANTITY		METHOD
	4 servings	24 servings	
English walnuts, chopped	¼ cup	1½ cups	Sprinkle chicken with 1 tablespoon walnuts and 1 teaspoon parsley. Garnish plate with 1 thyme sprig.
Parsley, fresh, minced (p. 39)	1½ tbsp.	½ cup	
Thyme sprigs, fresh	4	24	*Serve with asparagus.*

Portion: 7 ounces
Nutritional Data/Portion: Calories 354, Protein 24 g, Fat 18 g, Carbohydrate 26 g, Cholesterol 83 mg, Sodium 596 mg

For a **FAST FACTS VIA FAX**™ copy of this recipe, call 1-800-223-3755 and enter Business Tool 2581.

One cup of firmly packed brown sugar is an equivalent substitute for a cup of granulated sugar, but they aren't always interchangeable.

This recipe is pictured on page 200.

Chicken with Pink Peppercorn Dijon Sauce

Beautiful pink peppercorns add a hint of sweetness and color to the pungent, creamy Dijon mustard sauce in this recipe.

*Submitted by Ennio Riga
Prime Hospitality
Fairfield, N.J.*

INGREDIENT	QUANTITY		METHOD
	4 servings	24 servings	
Tyson Ready-to-Cook Flavor-Redi® Savory Chicken Breast Filets, 3-oz., frozen	8	48	Slack in cooler between 32° and 36°F prior to use.
Salt	1 tsp.	2 tbsp.	*To prepare single serving:* Season 2 chicken breast filets with ¼ teaspoon salt and ¼ teaspoon pepper. Dredge in flour and shake off excess.
Black pepper, coarse	1 tsp.	2 tbsp.	
Flour, all-purpose	as needed	as needed	
Butter, salted	¼ cup	1½ cups	Heat 1 tablespoon in sauté pan over medium-high heat. Add chicken breast filets and sauté for 2 to 3 minutes on each side or until lightly browned.
White wine, dry	½ cup	3 cups	Add 2 tablespoons wine, 2 tablespoons broth, and 1 tablespoon mustard to chicken and mix thoroughly. Simmer for 30 to 60 seconds or until liquid is reduced by half.
Chicken broth, canned	½ cup	3 cups	
Mustard, Dijon, extra strong	¼ cup	1½ cups	
Heavy cream	1 cup	6 cups	Add ¼ cup cream and ½ teaspoon peppercorns to chicken mixture and mix thoroughly. Simmer for 1 to 2 minutes or until chicken is no longer pink. Remove from heat and arrange on plate.
Peppercorns, pink, crushed	2 tsp.	¼ cup	
Tomato halves, fresh, broiled (p. 231)	4	24	Garnish plate with 1 broiled tomato half and ½ tablespoon parsley.
Parsley, fresh, minced (p. 39)	2 tbsp.	¾ cup	
			Serve with pasta, crisp green salad, and crusty bread.

Portion: 8 ounces
Nutritional Data/Portion: Calories 550, Protein 36 g, Fat 40 g, Carbohydrate 9 g, Cholesterol 200 mg, Sodium 1,770 mg

For a **FAST FACTS VIA FAX**™ copy of this recipe, call 1-800-223-3755 and enter Business Tool 2556.

Pink peppercorns are not true peppercorns. They are the dried berries from the Baies rose plant, which is cultivated in Madagascar and imported through French connections. They have a strong scent and a slightly sweet flavor.

True Dijon mustard is often considered extra strong because it is made with black mustard seeds, which are the most pungent variety. Mustard's potency is heightened by the addition of water to the dried, ground seeds, or lessened by the addition of vinegar and salt. Tamer Dijon-style mustards are made with brown seeds and a higher percentage of vinegar.

Submitted by Jutta S. Johnson
Presbyterian Hospital
Albuquerque, N.M.

The piñon, *also known as*
Indian nut, pine nut, pignoli,
and pignolia, *is a high-fat*
nut harvested from several
varieties of pine trees. The
labor-intensive process
of extracting the nuts from
pinecones is what makes
them expensive. Pine
nuts are probably best
known as an ingredient
in classic pesto.

Toast pine nuts in a dry
heavy skillet over medium-
high heat. Or place on a
dry sheet pan in a 300°F
conventional oven for 10
minutes. Stir frequently
to prevent burning.

Chicken Piñon

Pine nuts give a toasty nut crunch to the chicken coating, then show up again to demonstrate their distinctive rich and buttery flavor in the tequila cream sauce.

INGREDIENT	QUANTITY 4 servings	24 servings	METHOD
1 Tyson Ready-to-Cook Flavor-Redi® Savory Chicken Breast Filets, 5-oz., frozen	4	24	Slack in cooler between 32° and 36°F prior to use.
2 Heavy cream	1 cup	6 cups	Combine in saucepan and bring to boil over high heat. Reduce heat and simmer for 5 to 6 minutes or until flavors are blended. (Simmer smaller quantity for 4 to 5 minutes.)
White wine, dry	¼ cup	1½ cups	
Tequila	1½ tbsp.	½ cup	
3 Pine nuts, whole, toasted	¼ cup	1½ cups	Add to cream mixture and simmer for 15 to 20 minutes or until flavors are concentrated. (Simmer smaller quantity for 8 to 10 minutes.)
Tomatoes, fresh, seeded, minced	¼ cup	1½ cups	
Jalapeño peppers, fresh, seeded, minced (p. 172)	2 tbsp.	½ cup	
Garlic, fresh, minced	½ tsp.	1 tbsp.	
Chicken base concentrate**	½ tsp.	1 tbsp.	
Cilantro, fresh, chopped	2 tbsp.	¾ cup	
Salt	½ tsp.	2 tsp.	
Cumin, ground	¼ tsp.	½ tbsp.	
White pepper, fine	¼ tsp.	1 tsp.	
4 Flour, all-purpose	½ tsp.	1 tbsp.	Combine in bowl and blend well. Add to sauce and mix thoroughly. Simmer for 1 to 2 minutes or until sauce thickens. Remove from heat and keep warm.
Butter, salted, softened	½ tsp.	1 tbsp.	
5 Pine nuts, finely chopped	1 cup	6 cups	*To prepare single serving:* Dredge 1 chicken breast filet in pine nuts. Press to coat nuts evenly over chicken.
6 Olive oil	¼ cup	1½ cups	Heat 1 tablespoon in sauté pan over medium heat. Add chicken and sauté for 4 to 5 minutes on each side or until chicken is no longer pink. Remove from heat and transfer to plate.
7 Red and green bell peppers, fresh, slivered	¼ cup	2 cups	Top chicken breast filet with ⅓ cup sauce. Garnish chicken with 1 tablespoon bell pepper mixture.

Serve with mixed green salad and crunchy crostini.

Portion: 8 ounces
Nutritional Data/Portion: Calories 840, Protein 31 g, Fat 81 g, Carbohydrate 18 g, Cholesterol 134 mg, Sodium 666 mg

**This recipe uses a base with the reconstitution ratio of 1 teaspoon per cup.

For a *FAST FACTS VIA FAX*™ copy of this recipe, call 1-800-223-3755 and enter Business Tool 2561.

Submitted by Gerald Bonsey, CEC, AAC
The York Harbor Inn
York Harbor, Me.

Lobster-Stuffed Chicken with Boursin Cheese Sauce

In addition to the rich lobster filling, this indulgent chicken dish is completed with an extra-rich Boursin-style cream sauce. It is indeed worthy of special occasions.

INGREDIENT	QUANTITY 4 servings	24 servings	METHOD
1 Tyson Ready-to-Cook Tenderpressed™ Savory Whole Butterfly Chicken Breast Filets, 8-oz., frozen	4	24	Cover tightly and slack in cooler between 32° and 36°F prior to use.
2 *Lobster Stuffing*			
Lobster meat, steamed, ½-inch dice	8 oz.	3 lb.	Combine in bowl and mix thoroughly.
Snack crackers, butter-flavored, crushed	1 cup	6 cups	
Sherry, dry	2 tbsp.	¾ cup	
Green onions, fresh, sliced	½ tbsp.	3 tbsp.	
Parsley, fresh, chopped	½ tbsp.	3 tbsp.	
Garlic, fresh, minced	1 tsp.	2 tbsp.	
Worcestershire sauce	1 tsp.	2 tbsp.	
Salt	½ tsp.	1 tbsp.	
White pepper, fine	½ tsp.	1 tbsp.	
3 Butter, clarified	2 tbsp.	½ cup	Heat in skillet over medium-high heat.
4 Onions, fresh, minced	¼ cup	1½ cups	Add to butter and sauté for 3 to 4 minutes or until tender. (Sauté smaller quantity for 1 to 2 minutes.) Remove from heat. Add to stuffing mixture and mix thoroughly.
Celery, fresh, minced	¼ cup	1½ cups	
			Portion ½ cup stuffing in center of each chicken breast filet. Wrap chicken around stuffing and secure with wooden pick. Place in oiled roasting pans, seam side down.
			Roast in preheated conventional oven at 375°F for 45 to 50 minutes or until chicken is no longer pink. (Roast smaller quantity for 20 to 25 minutes.) Or roast in preheated convection oven at 325°F for 20 to 25 minutes. (Roast smaller quantity for 12 to 15 minutes.) Remove from oven. Keep warm above 140°F.
5 *Boursin Sauce*			
Heavy cream	1 cup	6 cups	Bring to boil in saucepan over medium heat.
6 Boursin-style cheese, garlic-and-herb-flavored	5 oz.	30 oz.	Whisk into cream. Reduce heat to low and gently simmer sauce for 10 to 12 minutes or until slightly thickened. Stir frequently with rubber spatula so cheese does not burn on bottom of pan. (Simmer smaller quantity for 5 to 7 minutes.) Remove from heat and keep warm in water bath.
7 Chive blossoms, fresh	4	24	*To assemble single serving:* Remove wooden pick from 1 chicken breast filet and place chicken on plate. Ladle ⅓ cup Boursin sauce over chicken. Garnish with 1 chive blossom.
			Serve with steamed asparagus and roasted new red potatoes.

Portion: 11 ounces

Nutritional Data/Portion: Calories 687, Protein 38 g, Fat 52 g, Carbohydrate 21 g, Cholesterol 238 mg, Sodium 1,138 mg

For a **FAST FACTS VIA FAX** copy of this recipe, call 1-800-223-3755 and enter Business Tool 2577.

Boursin is a triple-cream, smooth white French cheese with a buttery texture. It is often flavored with herbs, garlic, or cracked pepper.

Lobsters were so common along the New England coastline in the 17th century that the meat was generally held in low esteem. For centuries, it was food for the poor.

The name "Sloppy Joe" was bestowed on a Key West barkeeper named Joe Russell by his patron and friend Ernest Hemingway. Whether the popular sandwich that goes by the same name originated there or not cannot be determined. Most likely, both were named for their sloppy nature. ⌐

Mesquite is a spiny deep-rooted tree or shrub that grows in thickets in the southwestern United States and throughout Mexico. Its seed pods are common grazing material for livestock, but it is best known in barbecue for the sweet, smoky flavor the wood smoke lends to meats. ⌐

Also known as Tuscan peppers, pepperoncini are thin 2- to 3-inch-long chiles with wrinkled skin. Their flavor is slightly sweet, and their heat ranges from medium to medium-hot. ⌐

Messy Mike Barbecue Chicken

Sloppy Joe has a cowboy cousin, and his spicy personality makes him the family favorite. Mesquite chicken strips are simmered in barbecue sauce with lime juice, black beans, and spices, then piled on Texas toast with cheese and bacon to make a hearty meal.

INGREDIENT	QUANTITY 4 servings	24 servings	METHOD
Tyson Fully Cooked Mesquite Chicken Pizza Toppings, Natural Proportion Strips, frozen	1 lb.	6 lb.	Combine in saucepan or stockpot and mix thoroughly. Cover and bring to boil over medium heat. Reduce heat and simmer for 2 to 4 minutes or until flavors are blended. (Simmer smaller quantity for 1 to 2 minutes.) Remove from heat. Keep warm above 140°F.
Barbecue sauce, mesquite flavor, commercially prepared	¾ cup	4½ cups	
Chili sauce, commercially prepared	¾ cup	4½ cups	
Lime juice, fresh	½ cup	3 cups	
Green chiles, mild, chopped, canned	½ cup	3 cups	
Black beans, canned, rinsed, drained	½ cup	3 cups	
Chili powder, dark	1 tbsp.	¼ cup	
Cumin, ground	½ tsp.	1 tbsp.	
Texas toast slices, toasted	8	48	*To assemble single serving:* Shingle 2 slices toast on plate. Top with 2 slices bacon and 1 cup chicken mixture. Sprinkle with 1 tablespoon onions and top with 2 cheese triangles. Garnish plate with 2 pepperoncini and 1 parsley sprig.
Bacon slices, thick, crisp	8	48	
Onions, fresh, chopped (p. 175)	¼ cup	1½ cups	
American process cheese slices, each cut into 2 triangles	4	24	
Pepperoncini, canned, drained	8	48	
Parsley sprigs, fresh	4	24	*Serve with slaw and buttered corn on the cob.*

Portion: 12 ounces

Nutritional Data/Portion: Calories 620, Protein 45 g, Fat 25 g, Carbohydrate 56 g, Cholesterol 147 mg, Sodium 3,006 mg

For a **FAST FACTS VIA FAX** copy of this recipe, call 1-800-223-3755 and enter Business Tool 2579.

Submitted by Miles James
James at the Mill
Johnson, Ark.

Wild Mushroom-Crusted Chicken with Asparagus Risotto

Aromatic coriander, with its hints of sage, fennel, and lemon, seasons this chicken breast filet that is crusted with a nutty, buttery blend of exotic black trumpet and golden chanterelle mushrooms.

INGREDIENT	QUANTITY		METHOD
	4 servings	24 servings	
① Tyson Ready-to-Cook Tenderpressed™ Savory Chicken Breast Filets, 5-oz., frozen	4	24	Place in full-size steam table pans. (Use third-size pan for smaller quantity.)
② *Coriander Marinade*			
Corn oil	2 cups	12 cups	Combine in bowl and mix thoroughly. Pour over chicken breast filets. Marinate below 40°F for 24 hours.
Coriander seeds, cracked, toasted	¼ cup	1½ cups	
Salt	½ tbsp.	3 tbsp.	
Black pepper, cracked	½ tbsp.	3 tbsp.	
③ *Mushroom Bread Crumbs*			
Bread crumbs, unseasoned, dried	1¼ cups	6¼ cups	Combine in shallow container and mix thoroughly.
Black trumpet mushrooms, dried, coarse-ground	½ oz.	2½ oz.	
Golden chanterelle mushrooms, dried, coarse-ground	½ oz.	2½ oz.	
④ Corn oil	¼ cup	1½ cups	*To prepare single serving:* Heat 1 tablespoon in sauté pan over medium-high heat. Remove 1 chicken breast filet from marinade and liberally coat both sides with mushroom bread crumbs. Add chicken to oil and sauté for 1 to 2 minutes on each side or until golden brown.
			Remove from heat and finish in preheated conventional oven at 350°F for 7 to 8 minutes or until chicken is no longer pink. Or finish in preheated convection oven at 300°F for 3 to 4 minutes. Remove from oven and place on plate.
⑤ Asparagus Risotto (see recipe)	6 cups	36 cups	Portion 1½ cups risotto on plate and garnish with 1 teaspoon cheese.
Parmesan cheese, grated	1½ tbsp.	½ cup	

Portion: 17 ounces

Nutritional Data/Portion: Calories 1,080, Protein 45 g, Fat 55 g, Carbohydrate 102 g, Cholesterol 140 mg, Sodium 1,090 mg

For a **FAST FACTS VIA FAX**™ copy of this recipe, call 1-800-223-3755 and enter Business Tool 2668.

"Asparagus inspires gentle thoughts."
Charles Lamb

ASPARAGUS RISOTTO

	4 servings	24 servings
Asparagus, pencil-size, fresh	10 oz.	3¾ lb.
Olive oil	1 tbsp.	⅓ cup
Onions, fresh, finely chopped	½ cup	3 cups
Spinach, fresh, washed, drained, stems removed	5 oz.	2 lb.
Butter, salted	⅓ cup	2 cups
Water, cold	2 tbsp.	½ cup
Salt	¼ tsp.	½ tbsp.
Black pepper, fine	⅛ tsp.	¾ tsp.
Butter, salted	2 tbsp.	¾ cup
Onions, fresh, finely chopped	½ cup	3 cups
Arborio rice, dry	1⅔ cups	10 cups
White wine, dry	⅓ cup	2 cups
Chicken broth, canned, hot	3⅓ cups	20 cups
Parmesan cheese, grated	⅓ cup	2 cups
Salt	¼ tsp.	½ tbsp.
Black pepper, fine	⅛ tsp.	¾ tsp.

Wash asparagus and cut spears in half. Cover and reserve top halves. Coarsely chop bottom halves.

Heat oil in saucepan or stockpot over medium-high heat. Add onions and chopped asparagus. Sauté for 3 to 6 minutes or until onions are translucent.

Add next five ingredients to onion mixture and bring to simmer. Cover and simmer for 2 to 7 minutes or until spinach is wilted. Remove from heat and transfer to food processor bowl. Process until pureed. Remove from processor bowl and press through a fine mesh strainer. Keep warm.

Heat butter in saucepan or stock-pot over medium heat. Add onions to butter and sauté for 3 to 6 minutes or until translucent. Add rice to onions and mix thoroughly to coat rice with butter.

Add wine to rice mixture and mix thoroughly. Simmer for 1 to 2 minutes or until wine has evaporated. Add broth to rice 4 cups at a time. Stir constantly, letting rice absorb broth after each addition. (Add ⅔ cup of broth at a time to smaller quantity.) Total cooking time should be 20 to 30 minutes. Rice should be tender but firm.

Add asparagus tips, asparagus/spinach puree, cheese, and seasoning. Mix thoroughly until cheese is melted. Remove from heat and keep warm.

This recipe is pictured on the inside cover.

Submitted by Domenic Cocchia
Cobbs Mill Inn
Weston, Conn.

Apples and molasses were often used in recipes during colonial times, and English walnuts were a favorite in Williamsburg cooking. ◡

If diced apples are held in water, they will add too much moisture to the stuffing. Slightly browned apples are fine for this stuffing since it is dark with molasses and cinnamon. ◡

Molasses is the syrupy mixture that remains after sugar cane or sugar beets are refined. Light molasses is the product of the first boiling of sugar syrup and is lighter in both flavor and color than dark molasses, the byproduct of a second boiling. Blackstrap molasses is very thick, dark, and almost bitter, and comes from the third boiling. As a rule, the dark syrups are used in cooking, while the light ones are more often used as table syrups. ◡

For line service and takeout, the chicken breast filet should not be sliced. ◡

Chicken Williamsburg

In this Williamsburg-style dish, a sweet apple-mustard glaze coats a roasted chicken breast filet stuffed with tart apples, English walnuts, cinnamon, and brown sugar.

INGREDIENT	QUANTITY 4 servings	24 servings	METHOD
1 Tyson Ready-to-Cook Gourmet Boneless Whole Chicken Breast Filets, 8-oz., frozen	4	24	Cover tightly and slack in cooler between 32° and 36°F prior to use.
2 *Glaze*			
Apple jelly	¼ cup	1½ cups	Combine in saucepan and mix thoroughly. Heat over low heat for 5 to 7 minutes or until jelly is dissolved. (Heat smaller quantity for 2 to 4 minutes.) Remove from heat and keep warm.
Mustard, honey-Dijon	2 tbsp.	¾ cup	
Applejack liqueur	1 tbsp.	⅓ cup	
3 *Stuffing*			
Granny Smith apples, fresh, peeled, cored, diced	2 cups	12 cups	Combine in skillet or braising pan and sauté over high heat for 4 to 5 minutes or until liquid thickens. (Sauté smaller quantity for 2 to 3 minutes.) Remove from heat and cool to room temperature before using.
Raisins, dark	⅔ cup	4 cups	
English walnuts, chopped	⅓ cup	2 cups	
Honey	⅓ cup	2 cups	Lightly pound each chicken breast filet to even thickness. Portion ½ cup stuffing in center of each breast filet. Wrap chicken around stuffing and secure with wooden pick. Place in oiled roasting pans, seam side down, and brush with glaze.
Molasses, dark	2 tbsp.	¾ cup	
Cinnamon, ground	1 tbsp.	⅓ cup	
Brown sugar, dark	1 tbsp.	⅓ cup	
			Roast in preheated conventional oven at 350°F for 50 to 55 minutes or until chicken is no longer pink. (Roast smaller quantity for 35 to 40 minutes.) Or roast in preheated convection oven at 300°F for 20 to 25 minutes. (Roast smaller quantity for 15 to 20 minutes.)
			Brush once with glaze halfway through roasting time. Remove from oven and brush with remaining glaze. Keep warm above 140°F.
4 Sage sprigs, fresh	4	24	*To assemble single serving:* Remove wooden pick from 1 chicken breast filet. Slice chicken into 5 medallions and fan on plate. Garnish plate with 1 sage sprig.
			Serve with braised leeks.

Portion: 9 ounces
Nutritional Data/Portion: Calories 600, Protein 39 g, Fat 21 g, Carbohydrate 64 g, Cholesterol 125 mg, Sodium 260 mg

For a **FAST FACTS VIA FAX**™ copy of this recipe, call 1-800-223-3755 and enter Business Tool 2631.

"Dining is and always was a great artistic opportunity." ◡
Frank Lloyd Wright

Submitted by Rosa Randolph
Grace Hospital
Detroit, Mich.

Frangelico liqueur was created three centuries ago by an Italian monk named Frangelico, who distilled wild hazelnuts and other natural flavorings. Today, the unique Frangelico liqueur is a distillation of toasted hazelnuts, alcohol, and water. Toasted cocoa, toasted coffee, vanilla berries, rhubarb root, and sweet orange flowers are added, and the liqueur is matured in oak casks.

The United States is the world's leading producer of English walnuts, which also are called Persian walnuts. They also are grown commercially in China, France, India, Iran, Turkey, and Yugoslavia.

Monk's Cherry Chicken with Wild Rice

Many great things were invented in monasteries—clocks, champagne, and cappuccino. Another monastic creation, hazelnut liqueur, flavors the sinful "monk-style" sauce of heavy cream, dried cherries, mushrooms, and walnuts in this sweet, surprising dish.

INGREDIENT	QUANTITY		METHOD
	4 servings	24 servings	
1 Tyson Ready-to-Cook Tenderpressed™ Savory Whole Butterfly Chicken Breast Filets, 6-oz., frozen	4	24	*To prepare single serving:* Dredge 1 chicken breast filet in flour and shake off excess.
Flour, all-purpose	as needed	as needed	
2 Olive oil	½ cup	3 cups	Heat 2 tablespoons in sauté pan over high heat. Add chicken and sauté for 1½ to 2 minutes on each side or until lightly browned.
3 Garlic, fresh, minced	1½ tbsp.	½ cup	Add 1 teaspoon garlic and ¼ cup mushrooms to chicken and mix thoroughly. Sauté for 2 to 3 minutes or until mushrooms are tender.
Shiitake mushrooms, fresh, sliced	1 cup	6 cups	
4 Hazelnut liqueur	¾ cup	4½ cups	Add 3 tablespoons liqueur, 2 tablespoons walnuts, and 2 tablespoons cherries to chicken and mix thoroughly.
English walnuts, chopped	2 tbsp.	¾ cup	
Sour cherries, dried	2 tbsp.	¾ cup	
5 Heavy cream	2 cups	12 cups	Add ½ cup cream, ⅛ teaspoon salt, and ⅛ teaspoon lemon pepper to chicken and mix thoroughly. Bring to boil and boil for 8 to 10 minutes or until cream is reduced by half and chicken is no longer pink. Remove from heat.
Salt	½ tsp.	1 tbsp.	
Lemon pepper, coarse	½ tsp.	1 tbsp.	
6 Long-grain and wild rice, prepared according to package directions	2 cups	12 cups	Portion ½ cup rice on plate. Top with chicken and pan sauce. Garnish plate with 2 chive spears.
Chive spears, fresh	8	48	*Serve with asparagus spears.*

Portion: 13 ounces
Nutritional Data/Portion: Calories 1,039, Protein 28 g, Fat 76 g, Carbohydrate 65 g, Cholesterol 223 mg, Sodium 1,156 mg

For a **FAST FACTS VIA FAX** copy of this recipe, call 1-800-223-3755 and enter Business Tool 2580.

Submitted by Robert Brumfield
Seaway Hotels/The Biltmore Hotel
Coral Gables, Fla.

Chicken with Wild Mushrooms on Celeriac Puree

The richly colored and flavored three-mushroom duxelles makes an upscale presentation that's enhanced by the subtle flavor and texture of the celeriac puree.

This recipe includes a contemporary version of the classic duxelles, which is a mixture of finely chopped mushrooms, shallots, and herbs, slowly cooked in butter until it forms a thick paste.

Before refrigerating, cover the celeriac puree with plastic wrap or pour a thin layer of cream over it to keep it from drying out. Reheat prior to serving.

Celeriac, also known as celery root and celery knob, is the root of a special celery cultivated just for its root. This brown vegetable tastes like a cross between strong celery and parsley. Choose relatively small, firm roots with as few rootlets and knobs as possible.

INGREDIENT	QUANTITY 4 servings	24 servings	METHOD
1 Shiitake mushrooms, fresh, julienne	1 cup	6 cups	Combine in bowl and mix thoroughly. Cover and chill to hold.
Oyster mushrooms, fresh, julienne	1 cup	6 cups	
Button mushrooms, fresh, thinly sliced	1 cup	6 cups	
2 *Celeriac Puree*			
Water, cold	4 cups	16 cups	Combine in saucepan or stockpot and bring to boil over high heat.
Lemon juice, fresh	2 tbsp.	6 tbsp.	
3 Celeriac, fresh, peeled, cut into 2-inch chunks	¾ lb.	4½ lb.	Add to boiling water. Return to boil and boil, uncovered, for 40 minutes or until celeriac is tender. (Boil smaller quantity for 30 minutes.) Remove from heat and drain. Transfer to food processor bowl and process until pureed. Transfer to mixing bowl.
4 Heavy cream	½ cup	1½ cups	Whisk into puree ¼ cup at a time.
5 Butter, unsalted	1 tbsp.	¼ cup	Add to puree and whisk until thoroughly blended. Keep warm.
Salt	½ tsp.	2 tsp.	
White pepper, fine	¼ tsp.	½ tsp.	
6 Butter, clarified	¼ cup	1½ cups	*To prepare single serving:* Heat ½ tablespoon in sauté pan over medium-high heat.
7 Tyson Ready-to-Cook Tenderpressed™ Savory Chicken Breast Filets, 6-oz., frozen	4	24	Add 1 chicken breast filet to butter and sauté for 4 to 5 minutes on each side or until chicken is no longer pink. Remove chicken from pan. Keep warm above 140°F.
8 Butter, salted	2 tbsp.	¾ cup	To same sauté pan, add ½ tablespoon butter and ½ tablespoon shallots. Mix thoroughly and sauté for 20 to 30 seconds or until shallots begin to cook. Add generous ½ cup mushroom mixture and sauté for 2 to 3 minutes or until tender.
Shallots, fresh, minced	2 tbsp.	¾ cup	
9 Chicken broth, canned	¼ cup	1½ cups	Add 1 tablespoon and deglaze pan, scraping any browned particles from bottom.
10 Port wine	1 cup	6 cups	Add ¼ cup port, 1 teaspoon balsamic vinegar, ⅛ teaspoon salt, and ⅛ teaspoon pepper and mix thoroughly. Return chicken to pan and boil for 1 to 2 minutes or until liquid has reduced by half. Remove from heat.
Balsamic vinegar	1½ tbsp.	½ cup	
Salt	½ tsp.	1 tbsp.	
Black pepper, coarse	½ tsp.	1 tbsp.	
11 Chives, fresh, chopped	2 tsp.	¼ cup	*To assemble single serving:* Portion ⅓ cup celeriac puree on plate. Top with 1 chicken breast filet and pan sauce. Garnish plate with ½ teaspoon chives.

Serve with chilled salad of fresh spring greens.

Portion: 9½ ounces
Nutritional Data/Portion: Calories 454, Protein 25 g, Fat 34 g, Carbohydrate 16 g, Cholesterol 156 mg, Sodium 1,205 mg

For a ***FAST FACTS VIA FAX*** copy of this recipe, call 1-800-223-3755 and enter Business Tool 2634.

Submitted by Michael D. Francis
and Diane Hanson
Friendship Village
Waterloo, Iowa

Three-Mushroom Chicken Fricassee

Oyster, cremini, and shiitake mushrooms with heavy cream add new relevance to this rich and hearty dish prepared in a classic style.

INGREDIENT	QUANTITY		METHOD
	4 servings	24 servings	
1 Tyson Ready-to-Cook Flavor-Redi® Savory Chicken Breast Filets, 5-oz., frozen	4	24	Slack in cooler between 32° and 36°F prior to use.
2 Oyster mushrooms, fresh, diced	¾ cup	4½ cups	Combine in bowl. Cover and reserve.
Cremini mushrooms, fresh, diced	¾ cup	4½ cups	
Shiitake mushrooms, fresh, diced	¾ cup	4½ cups	
3 Butter, clarified	¼ cup	1½ cups	*To prepare single serving:* Heat 1 tablespoon in sauté pan over medium heat.
4 Flour, all-purpose	as needed	as needed	Dredge 1 chicken breast filet in flour and shake off excess. Add to butter and sauté for 3 to 4 minutes on each side or until browned.
5 Shallots, fresh, minced	3 tbsp.	1 cup	Add 2 teaspoons to chicken and sauté for 10 to 20 seconds or until shallots begin to cook.
6 White wine, dry	1⅓ cups	8 cups	Add ⅓ cup wine and 3 tablespoons broth to chicken. Simmer for 4 to 5 minutes or until liquid is reduced by half and chicken is no longer pink. Add ¼ cup mushroom mixture to chicken and mix thoroughly.
Chicken broth, canned	¾ cup	4½ cups	
7 Heavy cream	½ cup	3 cups	Add 2 tablespoons cream, ⅛ teaspoon salt, ⅛ teaspoon pepper, and a pinch of nutmeg to chicken. Mix thoroughly. Transfer mushroom sauce to plate and top with chicken breast filet.
Salt	½ tsp.	1 tbsp.	
Black pepper, coarse	½ tsp.	1 tbsp.	
Nutmeg, ground	as needed	as needed	
8 Butter, salted	2 tbsp.	¾ cup	Heat ½ tablespoon butter in separate sauté pan over high heat. Add an additional ¼ cup mushroom mixture and sauté for 30 to 40 seconds or until thoroughly heated. Remove from heat and arrange over chicken. Garnish plate with 1 sage sprig.
Sage sprigs, fresh	4	24	

Serve with stuffed baked potato and fresh garden peas.

Portion: 8½ ounces
Nutritional Data/Portion: Calories 510, Protein 33 g, Fat 31 g, Carbohydrate 12 g, Cholesterol 160 mg, Sodium 1,020 mg

For a ***FAST FACTS VIA FAX*** copy of this recipe, call 1-800-223-3755 and enter Business Tool 2591.

Fricassees are hearty stews in which the meat has been first sautéed in butter, then stewed with vegetables. Wine is a common ingredient.

The oyster mushroom, also known as oyster cap, tree mushroom, pleurotte, and shimeji, is fan-shaped and grows in close clusters, often on rotting tree trunks. It has a robust, somewhat peppery flavor when eaten raw, but is milder when cooked.

The cremino mushroom (cremini is plural) is a dark brown, slightly firmer relative of the common white mushroom. When mature, it is better known as a portobello mushroom. This variety is also referred to as the common brown mushroom or Roman mushroom.

Any variety of edible mushroom will work well in this recipe.

Submitted by Tom Clarke
University of California–San Diego
LaJolla, Calif.

*G*reen olives are usually picked young, soaked in lye, and fermented in brine for 6 to 12 months. The common black olive, also known as the Mission olive, is a ripe green olive.—⌒

*F*or line service presentation, transfer vegetable mixture to two full-size steam table pans. Arrange 36 slices of chicken over the vegetables in each pan. (Transfer smaller quantity to one half-size pan and arrange 12 slices of chicken over the vegetables.)—⌒

Chicken Romagna Roulade over Sautéed Vegetables

A gourmet-quality roulade makes a unique and exciting dish requiring little more than sautéing some bell peppers, onions, olives, and endive.

Lighter Fare Line Service Takeout

INGREDIENT	QUANTITY		METHOD
	4 servings	24 servings	
1 Tyson Signature Specialties™ Poletti de Romagna Roulade, frozen	1	6	Brush each roulade with oil and place on parchment-lined sheet pan.
Vegetable oil	as needed	as needed	Roast in preheated conventional oven at 350°F for 65 to 75 minutes or until chicken is no longer pink. Or roast in preheated convection oven at 325°F for 55 to 65 minutes. Remove from oven and cool slightly.
			Remove and discard netting. Cut each roulade into twelve ½-inch slices (approximately 2½ ounces each). Keep warm above 140°F.
2 Olive oil	3 tbsp.	1 cup	Heat in skillet or braising pan over medium-high heat.
3 Onions, fresh, chopped (p. 175)	1 cup	6 cups	Add to oil and sauté for 6 to 7 minutes or until tender. (Sauté smaller quantity for 4 to 5 minutes.)
Garlic, fresh, minced	1 tsp.	2 tbsp.	
4 Tomatoes, diced, canned, drained	1½ cups	9 cups	Add to onion mixture and sauté for 8 to 10 minutes or until peppers are tender. (Sauté smaller quantity for 4 to 5 minutes.)
Yellow bell peppers, fresh, ½-inch dice (p. 88)	1 cup	6 cups	
Red bell peppers, fresh, ½-inch dice	1 cup	6 cups	
5 Green olives, whole, pimiento-stuffed, canned, drained	¼ cup	1½ cups	Add to vegetable mixture and mix thoroughly.
Black olives, whole, oil-cured, pitted	¼ cup	1½ cups	
Oregano leaves, dried	½ tbsp.	3 tbsp.	
Red pepper, crushed, dried	½ tsp.	½ tbsp.	
6 Curly endive, fresh, coarsely chopped	4 cups	24 cups	Add to vegetable mixture and sauté for 5 to 7 minutes or until wilted. (Sauté smaller quantity for 2 to 3 minutes.) Remove from heat and keep warm.
Salt	¼ tsp.	½ tbsp.	
Black pepper, coarse	⅛ tsp.	¾ tsp.	

recipe continued on next page . . .

INGREDIENT	QUANTITY		METHOD
	4 servings	24 servings	
7 Romano cheese, fancy shred	¼ cup	1½ cups	*To assemble single serving:* Portion ¾ cup vegetables on plate. Top with 3 slices chicken. Garnish with 1 tablespoon cheese, 1 teaspoon capers, and 1 tablespoon basil.
Capers, rinsed, drained	1½ tbsp.	½ cup	
Basil, fresh, chiffonade (p. 28)	¼ cup	1½ cups	

Serve with Caesar salad and Italian garlic bread.

Portion: 14 ounces
Nutritional Data/Portion: Calories 242, Protein 9 g, Fat 16 g, Carbohydrate 18 g, Cholesterol 22 mg, Sodium 842 mg

For a **FAST FACTS VIA FAX**™ copy of this recipe, call 1-800-223-3755 and enter Business Tool 2562.

Pecan Chicken

A wonderful honey-pecan butter defines this light-tasting dish whose elegant flavor belies just how easy it is to prepare.

Submitted by James R. Brand, CCM
Bradenton Country Club
Bradenton, Fla.

INGREDIENT	QUANTITY		METHOD
	4 servings	24 servings	
1 *Harvest Butter*			
Butter, unsalted, softened	¾ cup	4½ cups	Combine in bowl and whisk until well blended. Cover and reserve at room temperature no more than 2 hours.
Pecans, toasted, finely chopped	½ cup	3 cups	
Honey	3 tbsp.	1 cup	
2 Tyson Ready-to-Cook Tenderpressed™ Savory Chicken Breast Filets, 6-oz., frozen	4	24	Season chicken and dredge in flour. Shake off excess.
Salt	¼ tsp.	½ tbsp.	
White pepper, fine	¼ tsp.	½ tbsp.	
Flour, all-purpose	as needed	as needed	
3 Eggs, large, whole	2	12	Combine in bowl and whisk thoroughly. Dip chicken breast filets in egg mixture and drain off excess.
Water, cold	1 tbsp.	6 tbsp.	
4 Butter, clarified	¼ cup	1½ cups	Heat in skillet over medium-low heat. Add chicken and sauté for 3 to 4 minutes on each side or until golden brown. Transfer to parchment-lined sheet pans. Spread ¼ cup harvest butter over top of each chicken breast filet.
			Roast in preheated conventional oven at 350°F for 12 to 14 minutes or until chicken is no longer pink. (Roast smaller quantity for 8 to 10 minutes.) Or roast in preheated convection oven at 300°F for 6 to 8 minutes. (Roast smaller quantity for 3 to 5 minutes.) Remove from oven. Keep warm above 140°F.
5 Sage sprigs, fresh	4	24	*To assemble single serving:* Place 1 chicken breast filet on plate. Spoon 1 tablespoon pan juices over chicken. Garnish plate with 1 sage sprig.

Serve with sweet potatoes.

Portion: 6½ ounces
Nutritional Data/Portion: Calories 725, Protein 26 g, Fat 61 g, Carbohydrate 23 g, Cholesterol 295 mg, Sodium 542 mg

For a **FAST FACTS VIA FAX**™ copy of this recipe, call 1-800-223-3755 and enter Business Tool 2573.

Clarified butter, also known as drawn butter, is unsalted butter that's been melted slowly to separate milk solids and evaporate most of the water. Any foam is skimmed off the top, and the clear butter is poured or skimmed off the milky residue at the bottom. Because the milk solids tend to burn in cooking, clarified butter has a higher smoke point and can be used to cook at higher temperatures.

Submitted by James Martine
Pedros Mexican Restaurante
Madison, Wis.

Yucatan Chicken Platter

This is the king of Mexican dinner platters. Roasted citrus-marinated chicken halves with hearty sides of Yucatan potatoes, black beans, Mexicali corn, and refreshing melon salsa share the stage on one large platter.

Line Service *Takeout*

INGREDIENT	QUANTITY 4 servings	24 servings	METHOD
1 Tyson Tastybasted® Marinated IQ*F Chicken Halves, 22-oz., frozen	4	24	Place in full-size steam table pans.
2 *Citrus Marinade*			
Vegetable oil	1 cup	6 cups	Combine in bowl and mix thoroughly.
White vinegar	½ cup	3 cups	
Water, cold	¼ cup	1½ cups	
Garlic, fresh, chopped	1 tbsp.	⅓ cup	
Salt	½ tsp.	1 tbsp.	
Black pepper, coarse	½ tsp.	1 tbsp.	
3 Limes, whole, fresh, cut in half	3	18	Squeeze juice from fruit and add to bowl along with fruit halves. Mix thoroughly and pour over chicken. Cover and marinate below 40°F for 24 hours.
Oranges, whole, fresh, cut in half	3	18	
			Remove chicken from marinade and transfer to roasting pans.
			Roast in preheated conventional oven at 425°F for 55 to 60 minutes or until chicken is no longer pink. (Roast smaller quantity for 45 to 50 minutes.) Or roast in preheated convection oven at 375°F for 25 to 30 minutes. (Roast smaller quantity for 20 to 25 minutes.) Remove from oven. Keep warm above 140°F.
4 *Yucatan Potatoes*			
Green bell peppers, whole, fresh, seeded	1	6	Cut each pepper into 12 equal strips. Cut each onion into 12 equal wedges.
Red bell peppers, whole, fresh, seeded	1	6	
Onions, fresh, medium-size	1	6	
5 Olive oil	2 tbsp.	½ cup	Heat in skillet or braising pan over medium-high heat. Add peppers and onions and sauté for 8 to 10 minutes or until tender-crisp. (Sauté smaller quantity for 4 to 5 minutes.) Remove from heat and keep warm.
6 Russet potatoes, whole, fresh	4	24	Cut each potato into 8 wedges. Deep-fry at 350°F for 8 to 10 minutes or until golden brown. Remove from fryer and drain. Keep warm.
7 *Black Beans*			
Black beans, canned, undrained	5 cups	30 cups	Combine in saucepan and mix thoroughly. Bring to boil over high heat. Reduce heat and simmer for 25 to 30 minutes or until flavors are blended. (Simmer smaller quantity for 10 to 15 minutes.) Remove from heat and keep warm.
Garlic, fresh, minced	2 tbsp.	½ cup	
Onions, fresh, fine dice (p. 175)	2 cups	12 cups	
Salt	½ tsp.	1 tbsp.	
Black pepper, coarse	¼ tsp.	½ tbsp.	

recipe continued on next page . . .

Sidebar

*T*he Yucatan peninsula is the nexus of the Maya, one of the world's greatest ancient civilizations. As early as 250 B.C., it is believed that the Mayan people had developed a thriving network of cities and agricultural systems. Yucatecan food has several distinctive features. The use of black beans is more commonplace, as is the use of lime juice. Seasoning pastes such as chile- and achiote-spiked adobo, and marinades such as escabeche *(based on lime juice or vinegar, herbs and oil)* are also regional favorites.

MELON SALSA

	4 servings	24 servings
Cantaloupe, fresh, peeled, ¼-inch dice	1½ cups	9 cups
Honeydew melon, fresh, peeled, ¼-inch dice	1½ cups	9 cups
Red bell peppers, fresh, ¼-inch dice	¼ cup	1½ cups
Green onions, fresh, diced	¼ cup	1½ cups
Jalapeño peppers, fresh, seeded, minced	1 tbsp.	⅓ cup
Cilantro, fresh, chopped	¼ cup	1½ cups
Lime juice, sweetened, bottled	1½ tbsp.	½ cup
White vinegar	½ tbsp.	3 tbsp.

Combine in bowl and mix thoroughly. Cover and chill to hold. (Salsa must be prepared 24 hours before serving.)

Yucatan Chicken Platter continued

INGREDIENT	QUANTITY		METHOD
	4 servings	24 servings	
Mexicali Corn			
Butter, salted	¼ cup	1½ cups	Heat in skillet over medium-high heat.
Yellow corn, whole kernel, frozen	1 lb.	6 lb.	Add to butter and sauté for 1 to 2 minutes or until corn is no longer frozen.
Salt	¼ tsp.	½ tbsp.	
Black pepper, coarse	⅛ tsp.	¾ tsp.	
Red bell peppers, fresh, diced to size of corn kernels (p. 88)	½ cup	3 cups	Add to corn and mix thoroughly. Remove from heat and keep warm.
Jalapeño peppers, fresh, seeded, minced (p. 172)	1 tsp.	2 tbsp.	
Melon Salsa (see recipe)	3 cups	18 cups	*To assemble single serving:* Place 1 chicken half in center of platter. Surround chicken with vegetables: 3 each of green and red bell pepper strips, 3 onion wedges, and 8 fried potato wedges.

To assemble single serving: Place 1 chicken half in center of platter. Surround chicken with vegetables: 3 each of green and red bell pepper strips, 3 onion wedges, and 8 fried potato wedges.

Portion 1 cup black beans and 1 cup corn around chicken. Portion ⅔ cup salsa into individual container and place on platter.

Serve with enchiladas.

Portion: 45 ounces

Nutritional Data/Portion: Calories 1,069, Protein 38 g, Fat 50 g, Carbohydrate 124 g, Cholesterol 117 mg, Sodium 1,399 mg

*Exceeds USDA standards for quick freezing.

For a **FAST FACTS VIA FAX** copy of this recipe, call 1-800-223-3755 and enter Business Tool 2593.

This complete meal is great for catering.

Although this recipe is technically lighter fare, its large serving size keeps it from being included in the category.

"What I say is, if a man really likes potatoes, he must be a pretty decent sort of fellow."
A.A. Milne

Submitted by John R. Gorman
Catering by John
Redmond, Wash.

Fresh poblano chiles may be substituted for the Anaheim peppers.

Arizona Chicken

Roasting tomatoes and peppers to enhance and concentrate their flavors is a favorite cooking method throughout the Southwest. Roasted Anaheim peppers, heavy cream, and taco seasoning are the essence of this simple yet enticing recipe.

Line Service　　Takeout

	INGREDIENT	QUANTITY		METHOD
		4 servings	24 servings	
1	Tyson Ready-to-Cook Tenderpressed™ Savory Whole Butterfly Chicken Breast Filets, 6-oz., frozen	4	24	Lightly season chicken breast filets.
2	Taco seasoning, dried	2 tbsp.	¾ cup	
	Olive oil	2 tbsp.	¾ cup	Heat in skillet over medium-high heat. Add chicken and sauté for 2 to 3 minutes on each side or until golden brown. Transfer to roasting pans.
3	Anaheim peppers, whole, fresh	2	12	Spear peppers with long fork. Quickly char skins over high open flame until evenly blackened. Transfer to plastic bag for approximately 10 minutes. Remove from bag. Peel, slice each pepper in half lengthwise, and seed. Place 1 pepper half over each chicken breast filet.
4	Heavy cream	⅓ cup	2 cups	Combine in saucepan and mix thoroughly until cornstarch is dissolved.
	Cornstarch	1 tsp.	2 tbsp.	
5	Green onions, fresh, minced	1½ tbsp.	½ cup	Add to cream and mix thoroughly. Bring to boil over medium-high heat, stirring constantly. Remove from heat and pour over chicken and peppers.
	Parsley, fresh, minced (p. 39)	2 tsp.	¼ cup	
	Black pepper, fine	⅛ tsp.	¾ tsp.	
6	Mexican cheese blend, shredded	1½ cups	9 cups	Sprinkle over chicken and peppers.
				Roast in preheated conventional oven at 350°F for 25 to 30 minutes or until chicken is no longer pink. (Roast smaller quantity for 20 to 25 minutes.) Or roast in preheated convection oven at 300°F for 12 to 14 minutes. (Roast smaller quantity for 6 to 8 minutes.) Remove from oven. Keep warm above 140°F.

recipe continued on next page . . .

INGREDIENT	QUANTITY		METHOD
	4 servings	24 servings	
7 Tomato slices, fresh, ¼-inch-thick, roasted	20	120	*To assemble single serving:* Arrange 5 roasted tomato slices on plate. Top with 1 chicken breast filet and 1 tablespoon sauce from pan.
			Serve with black beans and rice.

Portion: 7 ounces
Nutritional Data/Portion: Calories 422, Protein 32 g, Fat 30 g, Carbohydrate 8 g, Cholesterol 127 mg, Sodium 633 mg

For a **FAST FACTS VIA FAX** copy of this recipe, call 1-800-223-3755 and enter Business Tool 2583.

Hazelnut Chicken with Shiitake Cream Sauce

American tastes are turning to ingredients such as hazelnuts and shiitake mushrooms, which Europeans and the Japanese have long considered culinary staples. It will only take one bite of this exotic creamy mushroom sauce on hazelnut-coated chicken to create a new fan.

Submitted by Cathy Brown
One-One-One Main Street
Greenwich, N.Y.

Line Service   *Takeout*

INGREDIENT	QUANTITY		METHOD
	4 servings	24 servings	
1 Tyson Ready-to-Cook Flavor-Redi® Savory Chicken Breast Filets, 4-oz., frozen	4	24	Slack in cooler between 32° and 36°F prior to use.
2 *Shiitake Cream Sauce*			
Shiitake mushrooms, fresh, sliced	1 cup	6 cups	Heat saucepan or stockpot over medium heat. Add ingredients to heated pan and cook until most of sherry has evaporated.
Sherry, dry	2 tbsp.	¾ cup	
3 Heavy cream	2 cups	12 cups	Add to mushrooms and simmer for 1 hour 20 minutes to 1 hour 30 minutes or until liquid is reduced by half. (Simmer smaller quantity for 30 to 40 minutes.) Remove from heat and keep warm.
Salt	½ tsp.	1 tbsp.	
White pepper, fine	¼ tsp.	½ tbsp.	
4 *Hazelnut Crust*			
Hazelnuts, toasted, skinned	½ cup	3 cups	Place in food processor bowl and process until nuts and bread crumbs are of similar size. Transfer to shallow pan.
Bread crumbs, unseasoned, dried	½ cup	3 cups	
5 Eggs, large, whole	2	12	Combine in bowl and whisk thoroughly.
Water, cold	1 tbsp.	⅓ cup	
6 Flour, all-purpose	as needed	as needed	Dredge chicken breast filets in flour and shake off excess. Dip in egg mixture and drain excess. Dredge in hazelnut mixture, coating well on all sides.
7 Butter, salted	2 tbsp.	¾ cup	Heat in skillet over medium-high heat. Add chicken and sauté for 3 to 4 minutes on each side or until crust is brown. Transfer to roasting pans.
			Roast in preheated conventional oven at 350°F for 12 to 14 minutes or until chicken is no longer pink. (Roast smaller quantity for 8 to 10 minutes.) Or roast in preheated convection oven at 300°F for 6 to 8 minutes. (Roast smaller quantity for 3 to 4 minutes.) Remove from oven. Keep warm above 140°F.
8 Sage sprigs, fresh	4	24	*To assemble single serving:* Place 1 chicken breast filet on plate. Top with ¼ cup shiitake cream sauce. Garnish plate with 1 sage sprig.

Portion: 7½ ounces
Nutritional Data/Portion: Calories 779, Protein 31 g, Fat 62 g, Carbohydrate 23 g, Cholesterol 340 mg, Sodium 822 mg

For a **FAST FACTS VIA FAX** copy of this recipe, call 1-800-223-3755 and enter Business Tool 2574.

To toast and skin hazelnuts, place them in a single layer on a sheet pan. Bake in a preheated conventional oven at 300°F for 15 minutes. Remove from the oven and transfer to a cloth towel. Cover with a second towel and rub vigorously to remove skins. ⌐

America's first hazelnut tree was planted at a Hudson's Bay outpost in the Oregon Territory in 1858. However, until the late 1940s, the U.S. imported most of its hazelnuts from Italy, Spain, Turkey, and France. ⌐

Hazelnuts are also called filberts and cobnuts. ⌐

Submitted by Janine Disparte Pace
Our Class Act Restaurant
Bothell, Wash.

Chicken Wellington

Golden puff pastry encases chicken, herbed cheese, walnuts, mushrooms, and spinach to create a flavorful dish that is amazingly easy to prepare.

Fortunately, excellent laborsaving puff pastries are readily available. Pâte feuilletée, *the classic French "puff pastry," is made by placing pats of chilled butter between layers of pastry dough, then rolling it out, folding it in thirds, letting it rest, then repeating the time-consuming process seven or eight times.*

	INGREDIENT	QUANTITY 4 servings	24 servings	METHOD
1	Tyson Ready-to-Cook Tenderpressed™ Savory Chicken Breast Filets, 4-oz., frozen	4	24	Cover tightly and slack in cooler between 32° and 36°F prior to use.
2	Butter, salted	1 tbsp.	⅓ cup	Heat in skillet or braising pan over high heat.
3	Garlic, fresh, minced	1 tbsp.	⅓ cup	Add to butter and sauté for 8 to 10 minutes or until tender. (Sauté smaller quantity for 4 to 5 minutes.) Transfer to bowl. Reserve ⅓ cup mushrooms for use in gravy. (Reserve 1 tablespoon mushrooms for smaller quantity.)
	Button mushrooms, fresh, sliced	3 cups	18 cups	
4	Spinach, leaf, IQF, thawed, pressed dry	1 cup	6 cups	Add to same pan and sauté over high heat for 3 to 4 minutes or until moisture has evaporated. Remove from heat. Reserve ⅓ cup spinach for use in gravy. (Reserve 1 tablespoon spinach for smaller quantity.) Add remaining spinach to mushrooms.
5	Boursin-style cheese, garlic-and-herb-flavored	⅔ cup	4 cups	Add to mushroom/spinach mixture and mix thoroughly.
	English walnuts, minced	½ cup	3 cups	
	Parsley, fresh, minced (p. 39)	2 tbsp.	¾ cup	
6	Puff pastry, commercially prepared, cut into 7-inch squares (p. 219)	4	24	Place pastry squares on floured work surface. Place 1 chicken breast filet on each pastry and tuck narrow end of chicken under itself to form a square. Top each chicken breast filet with ½ cup mushroom/spinach mixture. Fold opposite corners of each pastry square over the filling to meet at the center and pinch together to seal. Pinch remaining edges to seal. Transfer to parchment-lined sheet pans.
7	Eggs, large, whole, slightly beaten	1	2	Brush each pastry square with egg.
				Bake in preheated conventional oven at 400°F for 40 to 45 minutes or until pastry is golden and chicken is no longer pink. (Bake smaller quantity for 35 to 40 minutes.) Or bake in preheated convection oven at 350°F for 18 to 20 minutes. (Bake smaller quantity for 15 to 18 minutes.) Remove from oven. Keep warm above 140°F.
8	Chicken gravy, commercially prepared, hot	1⅓ cups	8 cups	Add reserved mushrooms and spinach to gravy. Mix thoroughly and keep warm.
	Parsley, fresh, minced	3 tbsp.	1 cup	*To assemble single serving:* Spread ⅓ cup gravy on plate and top with 1 pastry square. Garnish with 2 teaspoons parsley.

Portion: 9 ounces
Nutritional Data/Portion: Calories 795, Protein 46 g, Fat 56 g, Carbohydrate 33 g, Cholesterol 171 mg, Sodium 648 mg

For a **FAST FACTS VIA FAX**™ copy of this recipe, call 1-800-223-3755 and enter Business Tool 2554.

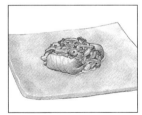
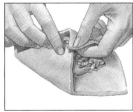

HOW TO WRAP CHICKEN BREAST FILET IN PUFF PASTRY

1) *Working on a floured surface, place a chicken breast filet on the pastry square. Tuck the narrow end of the breast filet under itself to form a square.*

2) *Fold opposite corners of each pastry square over the filling to meet at the center and pinch together to seal.*

3) *Repeat the procedure with the remaining corners. Then pinch the remaining open edges to seal.*

Submitted by Steven Tokarz
Southgate at Shrewsbury
Shrewsbury, Me.

Margarita Grilled Chicken

You can taste the tequila and lime in every juicy bite. The secret is to pour the lime juice and tequila on the frozen breast while it's grilling. Easy technique with masterful results.

Speed-Scratch · Lighter Fare · Line Service · Takeout

	INGREDIENT	QUANTITY 4 servings	24 servings	METHOD
1	Limes, fresh, cut in half	2	12	Preheat flattop griddle to 450°F and generously rub with cut surface of limes.
2	Tyson Fully Cooked Flavor-Redi® Natural Grill Chicken Breast Filets, 3-oz., frozen	4	24	Place on griddle and squeeze juice from lime halves over chicken.
3	Tequila	¼ cup	1½ cups	Grill chicken breast filets for 2½ to 3 minutes on each side or until lightly browned and caramelized. Baste with tequila to keep moist. Remove from griddle and cover. Keep warm above 140°F.
4	Green onions, fresh, chopped	¼ cup	1½ cups	*To assemble single serving:* Place 1 chicken breast filet on plate and sprinkle with 1 tablespoon green onion. Garnish plate with 1 lime twist.
	Lime slice twists, fresh	4	24	*Serve with a medley of steamed vegetables.*

Portion: 3 ounces
Nutritional Data/Portion: Calories 138, Protein 22 g, Fat 4 g, Carbohydrate 3 g, Cholesterol 62 mg, Sodium 384 mg

For a **FAST FACTS VIA FAX**™ copy of this recipe, call 1-800-223-3755 and enter Business Tool 2590.

Spearing a fork into the uncut end of a lime makes it easier to rub down the griddle.

In early sailing days, limes were fed to British sailors to prevent scurvy. Some think this is the root of the irreverent nickname "limey."

Mango-Pepper Salsa is a terrific accompaniment to this recipe (see recipe on page 195).

"The greatest dishes are very simple dishes."
Auguste Escoffier

Submitted by Jonathan Mortimer
The Grove Hotel
Boise, Idaho

Flavored crusts can be based on bread crumbs, panko, nuts, herbs, and even seeds. This version transforms plain chicken into a journey to the tropics, where limes are commonly used to sharpen flavor and provide acidic balance to the richness and spicy heat sometimes associated with Nuevo Latino, Caribbean, and Pan-Asian cuisines.

The two most common varieties of avocado in America are the Haas, which has a pebbly textured, almost black skin, and the Fuerte, which is smooth-skinned and green in color.

Lime-Crusted Avocado Chicken with Summer Tomato Sauce

Creamy avocado filling is the perfect complement to the chicken crusted with tangy lime and bread crumbs in this upscale dish.

Line Service   *Takeout*

INGREDIENT	QUANTITY		METHOD
	4 servings	24 servings	
1 Tyson Ready-to-Cook Tenderpressed™ Savory Whole Butterfly Chicken Breast Filets, 8-oz., frozen	4	24	Cover tightly and slack in cooler between 32° and 36°F prior to use.
2 *Summer Tomato Sauce*			
Olive oil	1 tbsp.	⅓ cup	Heat in saucepan over medium heat.
3 Garlic, fresh, minced	½ tsp.	1 tbsp.	Add to oil and sauté for 10 to 15 seconds or until garlic begins to cook.
4 Tomatoes, fresh, quartered	2 cups	12 cups	Add to garlic and sauté for 1 to 2 minutes or until tomatoes begin to cook.
5 White wine, dry	3 tbsp.	1 cup	Add to tomato mixture and bring to boil over high heat. Reduce heat and simmer for 10 to 12 minutes or until reduced by half. (Simmer smaller quantity for 4 to 5 minutes.) Transfer to food processor bowl.
Salt	½ tsp.	1 tbsp.	
Black pepper, coarse	¼ tsp.	½ tbsp.	
6 Basil leaves, fresh, julienne	1 tbsp.	⅓ cup	Add to tomato mixture and process until smooth. Remove from processor bowl and keep warm.
7 *Avocado Stuffing*			
Cream cheese, softened	4 oz.	24 oz.	Combine in mixer bowl and blend on medium-high speed for 5 to 6 minutes or until smooth. (Blend smaller quantity for 2 to 3 minutes.) Transfer to bowl. Cover and chill for 20 minutes.
Avocado, fresh, chopped	⅔ cup	4 cups	
Cumin, ground	1 tsp.	2 tbsp.	
Salt	1 tsp.	2 tbsp.	
Chili powder, dark	½ tsp.	1 tbsp.	
Black pepper, coarse	½ tsp.	1 tbsp.	
8 Salt	2 tsp.	¼ cup	Portion ¼ cup stuffing in center of each chicken breast filet. Wrap chicken around stuffing and secure with wooden pick. Season and lightly dust with flour. Shake off excess.
White pepper, fine	1 tsp.	1½ tbsp.	
Flour, all-purpose	as needed	as needed	

recipe continued on next page . . .

INGREDIENT	QUANTITY		METHOD
	4 servings	24 servings	
9 Eggs, large, whole	2	12	Combine in bowl and whisk thoroughly.
Half-and-half	1 tbsp.	⅓ cup	
10 *Lime Crust*			
Bread crumbs, unseasoned, dried	2½ cups	15 cups	Combine in separate bowl and mix thoroughly.
Lime zest, fresh	1 tbsp.	⅓ cup	Dip floured chicken breast filets in egg mixture, then coat in lime breading.
Thyme leaves, dried	1 tsp.	2 tbsp.	
11 Canola oil	½ cup	3 cups	Heat in skillet over high heat. Add chicken and sauté for 2½ to 3½ minutes on each side or until golden brown. Transfer to parchment-lined sheet pans.
			Roast in preheated conventional oven at 400°F for 35 to 40 minutes or until chicken is no longer pink. (Roast smaller quantity for 25 to 30 minutes.) Or roast in preheated convection oven at 350°F for 20 to 25 minutes. (Roast smaller quantity for 15 to 17 minutes.) Remove from oven. Keep warm above 140°F.
12 Thyme sprigs, fresh	4	24	*To assemble single serving:* Portion ¼ cup tomato sauce on plate. Remove wooden pick from 1 chicken breast filet and place chicken in sauce. Garnish plate with 1 thyme sprig.
			Serve with steamed vegetable medley on the side.

Portion: 12 ounces
Nutritional Data/Portion: Calories 884, Protein 37 g, Fat 54 g, Carbohydrate 64 g, Cholesterol 203 mg, Sodium 3,007 mg

For a ***FAST FACTS VIA FAX*** copy of this recipe, call 1-800-223-3755 and enter Business Tool 2628.

To ripen avocados, place them in a paper bag or a confined area at room temperature for 2 to 4 days.

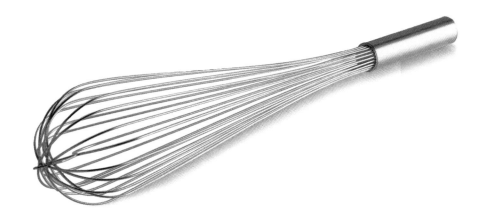

Submitted by Nick J. Naccarato
Eagles Lodge
Spokane, Wash.

For the alternative presentation shown in the photograph, criss-cross two strips of bread dough over each chicken breast filet. Sprinkle with as many poppy seeds, or sesame seeds, as desired.

Honey-Dijon Chicken Cheese Twists

This fun and delicious dish is made by surrounding a crusted chicken breast filet with herbed-cheese bread dough and honey-Dijon sauce.

Kid Friendly   Line Service   Takeout

INGREDIENT	QUANTITY 4 servings	24 servings	METHOD
1 Frozen bread dough, commercially prepared, slacked according to package directions	3 oz.	1 lb.	Place dough on floured work surface and roll into 12-inch square. (Roll smaller quantity into 4-inch square.)
2 Butter, salted, softened	½ tbsp.	3 tbsp.	Combine in bowl and mix thoroughly. Spread evenly over dough.
Garlic powder	1/16 tsp.	¼ tsp.	
Oregano leaves, dried	1/16 tsp.	¼ tsp.	
Basil leaves, dried	pinch	⅛ tsp.	
3 Mozzarella cheese, shredded	1½ tbsp.	½ cup	Sprinkle over dough. Then fold dough into thirds to form rectangle, 4 inches wide x 12 inches long. Slice widthwise into 24 strips, ½ inch wide x 4 inches long. (Fold smaller square in half to form rectangle, 2 inches wide x 4 inches long. Slice widthwise into 4 strips, ½ inch wide x 4 inches long.)
4 Tyson Ready-to-Cook Homestyle Crusted Chicken Breast Filets, 4-oz., frozen	4	24	Gently pull and twist 1 dough strip diagonally across each chicken breast filet and pinch together at center back to seal ends. Place each chicken breast filet 2 inches apart on oiled sheet pans. Cover lightly and let dough rise in warm place (140°F), free from draft, for 30 minutes.
5 Egg whites	2 tbsp.	¼ cup	Combine in small bowl and whisk thoroughly. Brush dough twists with egg wash.
Water, cold	1 tsp.	2 tsp.	
6 Poppy seeds, whole	as needed	as needed	Sprinkle over dough twists.
			Bake in preheated conventional oven at 400°F for 20 to 23 minutes or until chicken is no longer pink. (Bake smaller quantity for 18 to 20 minutes.) Or bake in preheated convection oven at 350°F for 15 to 18 minutes. (Bake smaller quantity for 12 to 14 minutes.) Remove from oven. Keep warm above 140°F.

recipe continued on next page . . .

INGREDIENT	QUANTITY		METHOD
	4 servings	24 servings	
7 Honey-Dijon salad dressing, commercially prepared	½ cup	3 cups	*To assemble single serving:* Ladle 2 tablespoons dressing on plate and microwave on high for 10 to 15 seconds or until warm. Top with 1 chicken breast filet. Garnish plate with 1 oregano sprig.
Oregano sprigs, fresh	4	24	
			Serve with fresh green beans.

Portion: 6 ounces
Nutritional Data/Portion: Calories 380, Protein 22 g, Fat 18 g, Carbohydrate 40 g, Cholesterol 35 mg, Sodium 720 mg

For a **FAST FACTS VIA FAX**™ copy of this recipe, call 1-800-223-3755 and enter Business Tool 2553.

Pecan-Crusted Cranberry Chicken

This pecan-crusted chicken entree with a cranberry-wine reduction is a delicious tribute to two native American fruits: the pecan and the cranberry.

Submitted by Mary Ryan
Glen Haven Hotel
Homer, N.Y.

INGREDIENT	QUANTITY		METHOD
	4 servings	24 servings	
1 Tyson Ready-to-Cook Flavor-Redi® Savory Chicken Breast Filets, 6-oz., frozen	4	24	Slack in cooler between 32° and 36°F prior to use.
2 Pecan crumbs, fine	1 cup	6 cups	Combine in bowl and mix thoroughly. Cover and reserve.
Flour, all-purpose	½ cup	3 cups	
			To prepare single serving: Dredge 1 chicken breast filet in pecan mixture. Press to coat crumbs evenly over chicken.
3 Butter, salted	¼ cup	1½ cups	Heat 1 tablespoon in sauté pan over medium-low heat. Sauté chicken for 5 to 6 minutes on each side or until chicken is no longer pink. Transfer to plate. Keep warm above 140°F.
4 Dried cranberries, reconstituted in cranberry juice	1 cup	6 cups	To same sauté pan, add ¼ cup reconstituted cranberries, 2 tablespoons wine, and 1 tablespoon green onions and mix thoroughly.
White wine, dry	½ cup	3 cups	
Green onions, fresh, minced	¼ cup	1 cup	
5 Cranberry juice, canned	1 cup	6 cups	Add ¼ cup to cranberry mixture and simmer for 1½ to 2 minutes or until reduced by half.
6 Pecan halves	½ cup	3 cups	Add 2 tablespoons pecans to cranberry mixture and mix thoroughly. Remove from heat and spoon over chicken breast filet. Garnish plate with 1 sage sprig.
Sage sprigs, fresh	4	24	
			Serve with baked butternut squash.

Portion: 10½ ounces
Nutritional Data/Portion: Calories 653, Protein 26 g, Fat 43 g, Carbohydrate 46 g, Cholesterol 82 mg, Sodium 400 mg

For a **FAST FACTS VIA FAX**™ copy of this recipe, call 1-800-223-3755 and enter Business Tool 2565.

While visiting London to plead the case for the colonies, Benjamin Franklin wrote to his daughter and asked her to send him a care package of his favorite foods to help him overcome his homesickness. Cranberries were among the foods he requested.

Cranberries are also called bounceberries because ripe ones bounce.

For takeout, put the cranberry-wine sauce in a separate container.

Submitted by David Cook
Valley Lo Sports Club
Glenview, Ill.

Hickory-Bourbon Smoked Chicken Breast

Grilled portobello mushrooms and artichoke-red bell pepper salsa finish off a cider- and bourbon-marinated hickory-smoked chicken breast for a hearty meal of complementary flavors.

In the times before refrigeration systems were common, cold-smoking and salting were used to prevent the fats in foods from turning rancid. Today, cold-smoking techniques are usually used to flavor rather than preserve foods. Cold-smoking is preferred for delicate foods, such as cheeses and vegetables, and is also frequently used to smoke quick-cooking meats such as seafood, poultry and bacon.

The subtle use of liquid smoke in the marinade will substitute for cold-smoking. Use 2 tablespoons for 24 servings, or 1 teaspoon for 4 servings.

BASIL OIL

	1 pint
Olive oil	2 cups
Basil leaves, fresh, blanched, drained	4 cups
Salt	½ tsp.
White pepper	¼ tsp.

Combine olive oil and basil leaves in saucepan and bring to very gentle simmer over low heat. Simmer for 4 to 5 minutes or until oil is flavored with basil. Remove from heat. Cool and strain through fine mesh strainer.

Add salt and pepper to oil and mix thoroughly. Cover and reserve.

For safety reasons, it is best to keep infused oils refrigerated and use them the same day they are made.

INGREDIENT	QUANTITY 4 servings	24 servings	METHOD
1 Tyson Ready-to-Cook Gourmet Boneless, Skinless Whole Chicken Breast Filets, 10-oz., frozen	4	24	Place in full-size steam table pans. (Use half-size pan for smaller quantity.)
2 *Cider-Bourbon Marinade*			
Apple cider	½ cup	3 cups	Combine in bowl and mix thoroughly. Pour over chicken. Cover and marinate below 40°F for 8 to 12 hours.
Bourbon	⅓ cup	2 cups	
Olive oil	⅓ cup	2 cups	
Shallots, fresh, minced	1 tbsp.	⅓ cup	
Thyme, fresh, chopped	1 tbsp.	⅓ cup	
Parsley, fresh, chopped	1 tbsp.	⅓ cup	
Garlic, fresh, minced	½ tsp.	1 tbsp.	
Five-spice powder	½ tsp.	1 tbsp.	
Salt	½ tsp.	1 tbsp.	
Black pepper, coarse	½ tsp.	1 tbsp.	
3 *Portobello Mushroom Marinade*			
Balsamic vinegar	½ cup	3 cups	Combine in bowl and mix thoroughly.
Olive oil	¼ cup	1½ cups	
Garlic, fresh, minced	½ tsp.	1 tbsp.	
Thyme, fresh, minced	1 tbsp.	⅓ cup	
4 Portobello mushrooms, whole, fresh	4	24	Add to vinegar mixture and toss well. Marinate for 15 minutes. Char-grill over medium heat for 3 minutes on each side or until tender. Remove from grill and keep warm.
5 *Artichoke Salsa*			
Artichoke hearts, canned, drained	1 cup	5 cups	Combine in food processor bowl and pulse until finely chopped. Remove from processor bowl. Cover and reserve.
Red bell peppers, fresh, diced (p. 88)	½ cup	1½ cups	
Red onions, fresh, diced	2 tbsp.	⅔ cup	
Garlic, fresh, minced	1 tsp.	2 tbsp.	
Parsley, fresh, chopped	1 cup	4 cups	
Thyme, fresh, chopped	1 tbsp.	⅓ cup	
6 Hickory chips	3 cups	6 cups	Combine in bowl and soak for 45 minutes. Remove chicken from marinade and cold-smoke in smoke oven at 85°F over hickory chips for 20 minutes. Remove from smoker.
Bourbon	¾ cup	1½ cups	
Water	¾ cup	1½ cups	
			To finish chicken, char-grill over high heat for 6 to 8 minutes on each side or until chicken is no longer pink. Remove from grill. Keep warm above 140°F.
7 Basil Oil (see recipe)	as needed	as needed	*To assemble single serving:* Slice 1 mushroom into 5 strips. Place on plate to form star pattern. Quickly sauté ⅓ cup artichoke salsa just enough to heat and place in center of mushroom star. Top with 1 chicken breast filet. Drizzle basil oil around plate and garnish with 1 tablespoon tomatoes and 1 tablespoon basil.
Roma tomatoes, fresh, seeded, diced	¼ cup	1½ cups	
Basil, fresh, julienne	¼ cup	1½ cups	

Serve with house salad and Italian bread.

Portion: 12 ounces
Nutritional Data/Portion: Calories 680, Protein 64 g, Fat 40 g, Carbohydrate 13 g, Cholesterol 165 mg, Sodium 320 mg

For a **FAST FACTS VIA FAX** copy of this recipe, call 1-800-223-3755 and enter Business Tool 2575.

Jamaican Jerk Chicken

Spicy jerk-style chicken is a snap to make with the help of commercially prepared jerk seasoning. Add an inventive touch with sweet Jamaican salsa and jicama carrot cole slaw.

INGREDIENT	QUANTITY 4 servings	24 servings	METHOD
1 Tyson Tastybasted® IQ*F Marinated Chicken Breast Halves, 8.7-oz., frozen	4	24	Place in full-size steam table pans. (Use half-size pan for smaller quantity.)
2 Onions, fresh, chopped (p. 175)	1 cup	6 cups	Combine in food processor bowl and process until mixture becomes paste.
Green onions, fresh, chopped	1 cup	6 cups	
Garlic, fresh, chopped	2 tbsp.	¾ cup	Spread mixture over all surfaces of chicken. Cover and marinate below 40°F for 24 hours.
Jalapeño peppers, fresh, seeded, chopped (p. 172)	2 tsp.	¼ cup	
Jerk seasoning, commercially prepared	6 tbsp.	2¼ cups	Char-grill chicken over medium-high heat for 30 to 40 minutes or until chicken is no longer pink, turning frequently. Remove from grill. Keep warm above 140°F.
Soy sauce	2 tbsp.	¾ cup	
Vegetable oil	1 tbsp.	⅓ cup	
3 Jicama Carrot Cole Slaw (see recipe)	2 cups	12 cups	*To assemble single serving:* Place 1 chicken breast half on plate. Arrange ½ cup cole slaw and ⅓ cup salsa around chicken. Garnish plate with 1 jalapeño pepper flower.
Jamaican Salsa (see recipe)	1⅓ cups	8 cups	
Green jalapeño pepper flowers, fresh	4	24	

Portion: 14 ounces

Nutritional Data/Portion: Calories 550, Protein 36 g, Fat 27 g, Carbohydrate 42 g, Cholesterol 110 mg, Sodium 1,710 mg

*Exceeds USDA standards for quick freezing.

For a **FAST FACTS VIA FAX** copy of this recipe, call 1-800-223-3755 and enter Business Tool 2355.

Jicama, also known as Mexican yam bean, old cocoyan, or yam bean root, is cousin to the sweet potato and native to Mexico and South America. Crisp like a potato yet slightly sweet, jicama can be prepared a variety of ways: fried, baked, boiled, steamed, stir-fried, and is often served raw.

JAMAICAN SALSA

	4 servings	24 servings
Bananas, firm, ¼-inch dice	1 cup	6 cups
Red bell peppers, fresh, ¼-inch dice	½ cup	3 cups
Green onions, fresh, thinly sliced	½ cup	3 cups
Jalapeño peppers, fresh, seeded, minced	1 tsp.	2 tbsp.
Lime juice, fresh	2 tbsp.	½ cup
Brown sugar, golden	1 tbsp.	¼ cup
Cilantro, fresh, minced	1 tbsp.	¼ cup
Salt	¼ tsp.	½ tbsp.

Combine in bowl and mix thoroughly until sugar is dissolved. Cover and chill 10 minutes before serving.

JICAMA CARROT COLE SLAW

	4 servings	24 servings
Jicama, fresh, peeled, shredded	2 cups	12 cups
Carrots, fresh, shredded	1 cup	6 cups
Jalapeño peppers, fresh, seeded, minced	2 tsp.	¼ cup
Cilantro, fresh, minced	2 tbsp.	¾ cup
Mint, fresh, minced	1 tbsp.	⅓ cup
Vegetable oil	2 tbsp.	¾ cup
Orange juice, fresh	2 tbsp.	¾ cup
White wine vinegar	2 tbsp.	¾ cup
Gingerroot, fresh, peeled, grated	1 tsp.	2 tbsp.
Garlic, fresh, minced	½ tsp.	1 tbsp.
Sugar, granulated	½ tsp.	1 tbsp.
Salt	½ tsp.	1 tbsp.
Peanuts, dry-roasted, salted, chopped	2 tbsp.	¾ cup

Combine first five ingredients in bowl.

Combine next seven ingredients in separate bowl and mix thoroughly. Pour over jicama mixture and toss well. Cover and chill before serving.

Garnish each serving with ½ tablespoon peanuts.

See sidebar on page 19 for how to make a chile pepper flower.

Submitted by Glenn Zamet
Founder's Hill Brewing Company
Downers Grove, Ill.

Stout is strong dark beer that originated in the British Isles. It is fragrant with hops and brewed with dark-roasted barley. The German practice of hopping beer was introduced to England during the reign of Henry VIII in the 16th century.

Stout and Brown Sugar Roasted Chicken

This brewer's feast features chicken infused with rich hoppy flavor, and served with creamy wild mushroom and bacon mashed potatoes for patrons with stout appetites.

INGREDIENT	QUANTITY 4 servings	24 servings	METHOD
1 Tyson Original IQ*F Chicken Halves, 17.5-oz., frozen	4	24	Place in full-size steam table pans.
2 *Stout and Brown Sugar Marinade*			
Stout	2 cups	12 cups	Combine in bowl and mix thoroughly. Pour over chicken. Cover and marinate below 40°F for 24 hours.
Brown sugar, golden	½ cup	3 cups	
Mustard, Dijon	¼ cup	1½ cups	Remove chicken from marinade and transfer to roasting pans.
Worcestershire sauce	2 tsp.	¼ cup	
Salt	½ tbsp.	3 tbsp.	Roast in preheated conventional oven at 375°F for 55 to 60 minutes or until chicken is no longer pink. (Roast smaller quantity for 45 to 50 minutes.) Or roast in preheated convection oven at 325°F for 40 to 45 minutes. (Roast smaller quantity for 30 to 35 minutes.) Remove from oven and skim grease from roasting pans. Keep warm above 140°F.
Black pepper, coarse	1½ tbsp.	½ cup	
3 *Mushroom and Bacon Mashed Potatoes*			
Milk, whole	⅔ cup	4 cups	Heat in saucepan over medium heat for 6 to 8 minutes or until steaming. (Heat smaller quantity for 3 to 4 minutes.)
Heavy cream	⅔ cup	4 cups	
Butter, salted	2 tbsp.	¾ cup	
4 Mashed potatoes, frozen, commercially prepared	2⅔ cups	16 cups	Add to milk mixture and cook over medium heat for 20 to 25 minutes, stirring constantly to prevent scorching. (Cook smaller quantity for 5 to 7 minutes.) Remove from heat and keep warm.
5 Bacon, smoked, diced	¼ cup	1½ cups	Sauté in skillet over medium heat for 6 to 7 minutes or until crisp. (Sauté smaller quantity for 2 to 4 minutes.) Discard most of bacon drippings.

recipe continued on next page . . .

INGREDIENT	QUANTITY 4 servings	24 servings	METHOD
6 Cremini mushrooms, fresh, sliced	½ cup	3 cups	Add to bacon and sauté for 4 to 5 minutes or until tender. (Sauté smaller quantity for 2 to 3 minutes.) Remove from heat. Add to mashed potatoes and mix thoroughly. Keep warm.
Oyster mushrooms, fresh, sliced	½ cup	3 cups	
Shiitake mushrooms, fresh, sliced	½ cup	3 cups	
Garlic, fresh, minced	½ tsp.	1 tbsp.	
Salt	¼ tsp.	2 tsp.	
7 Plum tomatoes, fresh, halved lengthwise, grilled	4	24	*To assemble single serving:* Portion ⅔ cup potatoes in center of plate. Top with 1 chicken half and spoon 2 tablespoons pan juices over chicken. Garnish plate with 2 grilled tomato halves.

Serve with sautéed fresh spinach.

Portion: 17 ounces
Nutritional Data/Portion: Calories 780, Protein 21 g, Fat 51 g, Carbohydrate 56 g, Cholesterol 140 mg, Sodium 1,450 mg

*Exceeds USDA standards for quick freezing.

For a **FAST FACTS VIA FAX**™ copy of this recipe, call 1-800-223-3755 and enter Business Tool 2582.

The first written reference to the potato appeared in the mid-1500s. The author called a potato "battata" or "papa."

Roasted Adobo Chicken

A basic adobo seasoning of vinegar, chiles, and herbs enhanced with sazon, oregano, and garlic provides an exotic Latin American flair to this simple chicken dish.

Line Service *Takeout*

*Submitted by Jeff Trombetta
Yale University Dining Services
New Haven, Conn.*

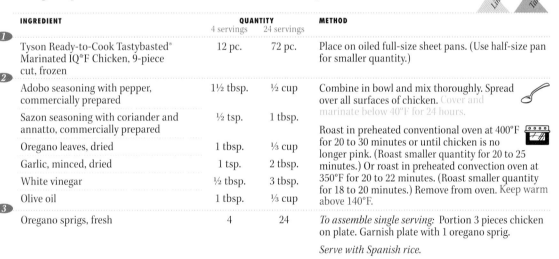

INGREDIENT	QUANTITY 4 servings	24 servings	METHOD
1 Tyson Ready-to-Cook Tastybasted® Marinated IQ*F Chicken, 9-piece cut, frozen	12 pc.	72 pc.	Place on oiled full-size sheet pans. (Use half-size pan for smaller quantity.)
2 Adobo seasoning with pepper, commercially prepared	1½ tbsp.	½ cup	Combine in bowl and mix thoroughly. Spread over all surfaces of chicken. Cover and marinate below 40°F for 24 hours.
Sazon seasoning with coriander and annatto, commercially prepared	½ tsp.	1 tbsp.	Roast in preheated conventional oven at 400°F for 20 to 30 minutes or until chicken is no longer pink. (Roast smaller quantity for 20 to 25 minutes.) Or roast in preheated convection oven at 350°F for 20 to 22 minutes. (Roast smaller quantity for 18 to 20 minutes.) Remove from oven. Keep warm above 140°F.
Oregano leaves, dried	1 tbsp.	⅓ cup	
Garlic, minced, dried	1 tsp.	2 tbsp.	
White vinegar	½ tbsp.	3 tbsp.	
Olive oil	1 tbsp.	⅓ cup	
3 Oregano sprigs, fresh	4	24	*To assemble single serving:* Portion 3 pieces chicken on plate. Garnish plate with 1 oregano sprig.

Serve with Spanish rice.

Portion: 8 ounces
Nutritional Data/Portion: Calories 580, Protein 45 g, Fat 43 g, Carbohydrate 3 g, Cholesterol 245 mg, Sodium 740 mg

*Exceeds USDA standards for quick freezing.

For a **FAST FACTS VIA FAX**™ copy of this recipe, call 1-800-223-3755 and enter Business Tool 2632.

Adobo is a common seasoning used widely throughout Hispanic-influenced countries. It is closely affiliated with cultures that evolved from Spanish settlements in areas that are now Mexico, the Caribbean, and the Philippines, although it is not associated with Spanish cuisine. Adobo dishes typically consist of fish or meat marinated in a sauce that contains vinegar and garlic.

Broccoli was first cultivated 2,500 years ago on the island of Cyprus. It has been on banquet tables since ancient Roman times, when it was sautéed in oil and seasoned with onion, cumin, and coriander.

Broccoli is a member of the Crucifer family, which also includes Brussels sprouts, cauliflower, and many leafy greens such as kale, mustard greens, and turnips. This entire plant family is known to contain antioxidants, which research has suggested may provide protection against certain forms of cancer.

Comforting Chicken Divan

Alfredo sauce, blended with vermouth and Swiss cheese, distinguishes this comfortable rendition of the classic '50s Chicken Divan invented at the Divan Parisien restaurant in New York.

Speed-Scratch *Line Service*

INGREDIENT	QUANTITY		METHOD
	4 servings	24 servings	
1 Tyson Fully Cooked Flavor-Redi® Natural Grill Chicken Breast Filets, 4.5-oz., frozen	4	24	Place on foil-lined sheet pans. Bake in preheated conventional oven at 400°F for 17 to 22 minutes. Or bake in preheated convection oven at 375°F for 10 to 12 minutes. Remove from oven. Keep warm above 140°F.
2 Alfredo sauce, commercially prepared	1 cup	4 cups	Combine in saucepan and mix thoroughly. Heat over medium-low heat for 5 to 6 minutes or until cheese is thoroughly melted, stirring frequently. (Heat smaller quantity for 1 to 2 minutes.) Remove from heat and keep warm.
Swiss cheese, shredded	½ cup	2 cups	
Vermouth, dry	1 tbsp.	¼ cup	
3 Homestyle white bread slices, toasted, cut in half diagonally	4	24	*To assemble single serving:* Arrange 2 toast halves on plate. Top with 1 chicken breast filet. Ladle ¼ cup sauce over chicken. Garnish with 5 small broccoli florets.
Broccoli florets, fresh, steamed	20	120	*Serve with crisp green salad.*

Portion: 8 ounces
Nutritional Data/Portion: Calories 364, Protein 32 g, Fat 18 g, Carbohydrate 19, Cholesterol 101 mg, Sodium 1,007 mg

For a **FAST FACTS VIA FAX**™ copy of this recipe, call 1-800-223-3755 and enter Business Tool 2371.

Submitted by Scott Terle
American Retirement Corporation
Brentwood, Tenn.

Ginger-Peanut Crusted Chicken

Ginger lovers will enjoy these chicken breast filets flavored with a double hit of ginger from the crunchy ginger-peanut breading and creamy ginger-spiked white wine sauce.

INGREDIENT	QUANTITY 4 servings	24 servings	METHOD
1 *Ginger-Peanut Breading*			
White bread, fresh, crusts removed	2 oz.	12 oz.	Place in food processor bowl and process until finely ground.
2 Peanuts, roasted	¼ cup	1½ cups	Add to bread crumbs and process until finely chopped.
3 Garlic, fresh, chopped	2½ tsp.	⅓ cup	Add to bread crumb mixture and process until thoroughly mixed. Transfer to shallow container.
Cilantro, fresh, chopped	2½ tsp.	⅓ cup	
Cumin, ground	1 tsp.	2 tbsp.	
Peanut oil	1 tbsp.	⅓ cup	
4 Gingerroot, fresh, peeled, grated	1 tbsp.	⅓ cup	Add to bread crumb mixture and mix thoroughly. Cover and reserve.
5 *White Wine Sauce*			
Chicken broth, canned	1 cup	6 cups	Combine in saucepan and mix thoroughly. Bring to boil over medium-high heat, stirring constantly. Reduce heat and simmer for 1 to 2 minutes or until flavors are blended. Remove from heat and keep warm.
White sauce mix, dried, commercially prepared	2 tbsp.	¾ cup	
Vermouth, dry	1 tbsp.	⅓ cup	
Gingerroot, fresh, peeled, grated	1 tsp.	2 tbsp.	
Cayenne pepper, ground	⅛ tsp.	¾ tsp.	
6 Tyson Ready-to-Cook Tenderpressed™ Savory Chicken Breast Filets, 6-oz., frozen	4	24	Season chicken breast filets.
Salt	½ tsp.	1 tbsp.	
Cayenne pepper, ground	¼ tsp.	½ tbsp.	
7 Vegetable oil	¼ cup	1½ cups	Heat in skillet over medium-high heat. Add chicken and sauté for 2 to 3 minutes on each side or until golden brown. Transfer to parchment-lined sheet pans. Coat top of each breast filet with 2 rounded tablespoons ginger-peanut breading.
			Roast in preheated conventional oven at 400°F for 18 to 20 minutes or until chicken is no longer pink. (Roast smaller quantity for 15 to 18 minutes.) Or roast in preheated convection oven at 350°F for 10 to 12 minutes. (Roast smaller quantity for 8 to 10 minutes.) Remove from oven. Keep warm above 140°F.
8 Lime slice twists, fresh	4	24	*To assemble single serving:* Ladle ¼ cup white wine sauce on plate and top with 1 chicken breast filet. Garnish plate with 1 lime twist and 1 cilantro sprig.
Cilantro sprigs, fresh	4	24	

Portion: 8 ounces
Nutritional Data/Portion: Calories 398, Protein 28 g, Fat 26 g, Carbohydrate 15 g, Cholesterol 61 mg, Sodium 1,115 mg

For a **FAST FACTS VIA FAX** copy of this recipe, call 1-800-223-3755 and enter Business Tool 2568.

Most gingerroot used in America grows in Jamaica, although it thrives in tropical regions around the world and is integral to cuisines everywhere it grows. The name comes from a Sanskrit word for "horn root."

Fresh unpeeled gingerroot can be tightly wrapped and refrigerated for up to 3 weeks or frozen for up to 6 months.

For line service, the white wine sauce should be put in the steam table pan first; then the chicken should be placed on top of it.

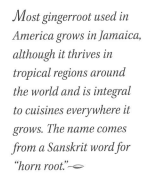

Submitted by Bruce Ahart
The Biltmore Hotel
Coral Gables, Fla.

Salmon may be substituted for the white fish and will provide a nice color contrast.

Classic beurre blanc sauce is made by adding cold butter to a wine, shallot, and vinegar reduction. The name means "white butter."

Chicken with Seafood Stuffing in Chive Beurre Blanc

A delicate seafood stuffing is a lovely filling for chicken breast filets, and creamy chive butter sauce makes this dish a satisfying choice.

INGREDIENT	QUANTITY 4 servings	24 servings	METHOD
① Tyson Ready-to-Cook Tenderpressed™ Savory Chicken Breast Filets, 6-oz., frozen	4	24	Cover tightly and slack in cooler between 32° and 36°F prior to use.
② *Seafood Stuffing*			
White fish fillets, fresh (flounder, sole, or pike)	3 oz.	1 lb.	Combine in food processor bowl and process until well blended. Transfer to mixing bowl.
Egg whites	2 to 3 tbsp.	¾ to 1 cup	
Cayenne pepper, ground	¼ tsp.	½ tbsp.	
Salt	⅛ tsp.	¾ tsp.	
White pepper, fine	¹⁄₁₆ tsp.	¼ tsp.	
③ White bread crumbs, fresh	1 cup	6 cups	Fold into fish mixture. Add more bread crumbs or cream if needed to adjust to a firm consistency.
Heavy cream	2 tbsp.	¾ cup	
④ Crabmeat, fresh	3 tbsp.	1 cup	Add to fish mixture and mix thoroughly. Cover and chill before shaping.
Shrimp, fresh, coarsely chopped	2 tbsp.	¾ cup	
Bay scallops, fresh, coarsely chopped	2 tbsp.	¾ cup	Form ¼ cup seafood stuffing into an oval and place in center of each chicken breast filet. Wrap chicken around filling and secure with wooden pick.
Parsley, Italian flat-leaf, fresh, chopped	½ tbsp.	3 tbsp.	
Tarragon, fresh, chopped	½ tbsp.	3 tbsp.	
⑤ Butter, unsalted	½ cup	3 cups	Heat in skillet over medium heat. Add chicken breast filets and sauté for 4 to 5 minutes or until lightly browned on all sides. Transfer to full-size sheet pans, seam side down. (Use half-size pan for smaller quantity.)
			Roast in preheated conventional oven at 350°F for 35 to 40 minutes or until chicken is no longer pink. (Roast smaller quantity for 10 to 15 minutes.) Or roast in preheated convection oven at 300°F for 25 to 30 minutes. (Roast smaller quantity for 5 to 7 minutes.) Remove from oven. Keep warm above 140°F.
⑥ *Chive Beurre Blanc*			
White wine, dry	2 cups	6 cups	Combine in saucepan and bring to boil over high heat. Reduce heat and simmer for 15 to 20 minutes or until reduced by half. (Simmer smaller quantity for 5 to 7 minutes.)
Shallots, fresh, minced	2 tbsp.	⅓ cup	
Garlic, fresh, minced	½ tsp.	1 tbsp.	
⑦ Heavy cream	⅓ cup	2 cups	Add to shallot mixture and simmer an additional 15 to 20 minutes. (Simmer smaller quantity for 4 to 5 minutes.) Remove from heat and strain through fine mesh strainer. Keep warm.
⑧ Butter, salted, cut into pieces	¼ cup	1½ cups	Gradually fold into sauce just before serving. (This sauce will hold for only a short time.)
Chives, fresh, chopped	1 tbsp.	⅓ cup	
⑨ Leeks, fresh, ½-inch bias-sliced, steamed, buttered (p. 189)	2 cups	12 cups	*To assemble single serving:* Portion ½ cup leeks on plate. Remove wooden pick from 1 chicken breast filet. Slice chicken diagonally into thin slices and fan over leeks. Ladle ¼ cup sauce over chicken.
			Serve with a broiled tomato half (p. 231).

Portion: 11 ounces
Nutritional Data/Portion: Calories 596, Protein 33 g, Fat 39 g, Carbohydrate 30 g, Cholesterol 180 mg, Sodium 906 mg

For a **FAST FACTS VIA FAX**™ copy of this recipe, call 1-800-223-3755 and enter Business Tool 2584.

Submitted by June M. Dowling
Littles at the Beach Restaurant
Myrtle Beach, S.C.

Chicken Florentina Cordon Bleu

Melted Swiss cheese hides a treasure of spinach and bacon cooked in an herbed garlic-tomato sauce and layered with sliced ham over sautéed chicken.

Anisette adds nice character to this dish. If the sweet licorice-flavored liqueur is not on hand, the recipe is excellent without it.

INGREDIENT	QUANTITY 4 servings	24 servings	METHOD
1 Tyson Ready-to-Cook Flavor-Redi® Italian Chicken Breast Filets, 5-oz., frozen	4	24	Slack in cooler between 32° and 36°F prior to use.
2 *Garlic-Tomato Sauce*			
Tomato sauce, canned	1 cup	6 cups	Combine in saucepan and bring to boil over medium heat. Reduce heat and simmer for 2 to 3 minutes or until flavors are blended. Remove from heat and keep warm.
Water, cold	¼ cup	1½ cups	
Olive oil	¼ cup	1½ cups	
Basil leaves, dried	½ tsp.	1 tbsp.	
Oregano leaves, dried	½ tsp.	1 tbsp.	
Garlic, fresh, minced	½ tsp.	1 tbsp.	
Salt	½ tsp.	1 tbsp.	
Black pepper, coarse	¼ tsp.	½ tbsp.	
3 *Spinach Topping*			
Butter, salted	2 tbsp.	¾ cup	Heat in skillet over medium heat.
4 Onions, fresh, chopped (p. 175)	2 tsp.	¼ cup	Add to butter and sauté for 1 to 1½ minutes or until translucent.
5 Bacon, crisp, crumbled	2 tbsp.	¾ cup	Add to onions along with 3 cups garlic sauce. (Use ½ cup for smaller quantity.) Mix thoroughly and remove from heat.
Anisette liqueur (optional)	2 tsp.	¼ cup	
6 Spinach, chopped, frozen, thawed, pressed dry	1 cup	6 cups	Add to onion mixture and mix thoroughly. Keep warm.
7 Flour, all-purpose	as needed	as needed	*To prepare single serving:* Dredge 1 chicken breast filet in flour and shake off excess.
8 Butter, salted	2 tbsp.	¾ cup	Heat ½ tablespoon in sauté pan over medium heat. Add chicken and sauté for 1 to 1½ minutes on each side or until browned. Reduce heat and sauté for 1½ to 2½ minutes on each side or until chicken is no longer pink. Remove from heat and transfer to plate.
9 Ham slices, thin	4	24	Layer 1 chicken breast filet with ¼ cup spinach topping, 1 ham slice, 1 cheese slice, and ¼ cup garlic sauce. Broil under salamander for 2 to 3 minutes or until top is golden. Remove from broiler. Garnish plate with 1 basil sprig.
Swiss cheese slices, thin	4	24	
Basil sprigs, fresh	4	24	

Serve with orzo tossed in garlic and olive oil.

Portion: 8½ ounces
Nutritional Data/Portion: Calories 506, Protein 32 g, Fat 39 g, Carbohydrate 9 g, Cholesterol 118 mg, Sodium 1,256 mg

For a **FAST FACTS VIA FAX**℠ copy of this recipe, call 1-800-223-3755 and enter Business Tool 2563.

HOW TO CUT AND BROIL A TOMATO

1) *Around the middle (widest part), insert a V-knife into the center of the tomato. Repeat this process to obtain a sawtooth cut resembling a crown.*
2) *Gently separate the tomato halves. Spray with oil and broil under a salamander until golden brown.*

Submitted by C. Dennis Pierce
University of Connecticut
Storrs, Conn.

Apricot Mustard-Glazed Cornish Hen

Not only do Cornish hens add elegant menu variety, they require minimal labor and hold up well for large banquets. The tangy, sweet apricot-mustard glaze gives the Cornish a beautiful burnished color and sophisticated flavor.

Apricots have been grown in China for over 4,000 years. Today, California produces about 90 percent of the American crop, although the trees will thrive in any temperate climate. A relative of the peach, the skin and flesh color of apricots can range from pale yellow to deep orange.

The Rock Cornish game hen is actually a tender young chicken, brought to market in 28 days rather than the 42-day period that is standard for broilers. The breed was developed in 1965 by Don Tyson, who crossed the White Rock and Cornish breeds.

INGREDIENT	QUANTITY 4 servings	24 servings	METHOD
1 Tyson Ready-to-Cook Split Cornish Hens, 9-oz., frozen	4	24	Place in full-size steam table pans. (Use half-size pan for smaller quantity.)
2 *Marinade*			
White wine, dry	1 cup	6 cups	Combine in bowl and mix thoroughly. Pour over Cornish hens. Cover and marinate below 40°F for 24 hours.
Olive oil	2 tbsp.	¾ cup	
Garlic, fresh, minced	1 tbsp.	⅓ cup	
Salt	½ tsp.	1 tbsp.	
Black pepper, coarse	½ tsp.	1 tbsp.	
3 *Apricot-Mustard Glaze*			
Apricots, dried	4 oz.	1½ lb.	Combine in saucepan and bring to boil over high heat. Reduce heat and simmer for 15 to 18 minutes or until liquid is reduced by half. (Simmer smaller quantity for 8 to 10 minutes.) Remove from heat. Transfer to food processor bowl and process until pureed. Transfer to mixing bowl.
Water, cold	1½ cups	9 cups	
4 Butter, salted	2 tbsp.	½ cup	Heat in skillet over low heat.
5 Shallots, fresh, minced	¼ cup	1½ cups	Add to butter and sauté for 4 to 5 minutes or until tender. (Sauté smaller quantity for 2 to 3 minutes.) Add to apricots.
6 White wine vinegar	⅓ cup	2 cups	Add to apricot mixture and mix thoroughly. Cover and reserve two-thirds of mixture at room temperature for serving. Use remaining mixture for glazing.
Rice wine vinegar	⅓ cup	2 cups	
Honey	1 cup	6 cups	
Mustard, hot	2 tbsp.	¾ cup	Remove hens from marinade and transfer to roasting pans. Brush with apricot-mustard glaze.
Salt	¾ tsp.	1½ tbsp.	
White pepper, fine	¼ tsp.	½ tbsp.	
			Roast in preheated conventional oven‡ at 425°F for 55 to 60 minutes or until hens are no longer pink. (Roast smaller quantity for 45 to 50 minutes.)
			Brush hens with glaze twice during final 20 minutes of roasting time. Remove from oven. Keep warm above 140°F.
7 Rosemary sprigs, fresh	4	24	*To assemble single serving:* Place 1 Cornish hen half on plate. Spoon 2 tablespoons glaze into individual container and place on plate. Garnish plate with 1 rosemary sprig.
			Serve with rosemary roasted potatoes and sautéed spinach.

Portion: 8½ ounces

Nutritional Data/Portion: Calories 570, Protein 18 g, Fat 19 g, Carbohydrate 89 g, Cholesterol 132 mg, Sodium 759 mg

‡Convection oven not recommended.

For a **FAST FACTS VIA FAX** copy of this recipe, call 1-800-223-3755 and enter Business Tool 2571.

Submitted by Ennio Riga
Prime Hospitality
Fairfield, N.J.

Italian Country Chicken

This recipe is based on an Italian specialty called Chicken Paesano or "countryman's chicken," but has a few distinctive twists, notably the additions of toasted pine nuts and sherry. Serving it with garlic, potato, and parsnip puree makes it a truly rustic country dish with robust flavors.

Line Service | *Takeout*

	INGREDIENT	QUANTITY 4 servings	24 servings	METHOD
1	Tyson Tastybird® Original IQ*F Chicken Breast Halves, 6.5-oz., frozen	4	24	Cover tightly and slack in cooler between 32° and 36°F prior to use.
2	Salt	1 tsp.	2 tbsp.	Season chicken breast halves.
	Black pepper, coarse	½ tsp.	1 tbsp.	
3	Olive oil	1 tbsp.	¼ cup	Heat in skillet over medium-high heat. Add chicken and sauté for 8 to 10 minutes or until skin is golden and crispy. Transfer to roasting pans.
4	Garlic, fresh, chopped	1 tbsp.	2 tbsp.	Add to same skillet and sauté for 8 to 10 seconds or until golden.
5	White wine, dry	½ cup	2 cups	Add to garlic and bring to boil. Boil for 8 to 10 minutes or until mixture is reduced by half. (Boil smaller quantity for 2 to 3 minutes.) Remove from heat.
	Balsamic vinegar	1 tbsp.	3 tbsp.	
6	Sherry, dry	¼ cup	1 cup	Add to garlic/wine mixture and mix thoroughly. Pour over chicken.
				Cover and roast in preheated conventional oven at 350°F for 40 to 45 minutes or until chicken is no longer pink. (Roast smaller quantity for 20 to 25 minutes.) Or cover and roast in preheated convection oven at 325°F for 18 to 20 minutes. (Roast smaller quantity for 12 to 18 minutes.) Remove from oven.
7	Button mushrooms, fresh, sliced	2 cups	12 cups	Add to chicken and mix thoroughly. Keep warm above 140°F.
	Brown sauce with mushrooms, commercially prepared, hot	½ cup	3 cups	
	Basil leaves, fresh, chopped	¼ cup	1½ cups	
8	Tomatoes, fresh, seeded, ¼-inch dice	2 tbsp.	¾ cup	*To assemble single serving:* Place 1 chicken breast half on plate. Ladle ⅓ cup pan sauce over chicken. Sprinkle with ½ tablespoon tomatoes, 1 teaspoon pine nuts, and 1 teaspoon parsley. Garnish plate with 1 basil sprig.
	Pine nuts, whole, toasted	1½ tbsp.	½ cup	
	Parsley, fresh, minced (p. 39)	1½ tbsp.	½ cup	
	Basil sprigs, fresh	4	24	

Serve with garlic, potato and parsnip puree.

Portion: 9½ ounces
Nutritional Data/Portion: Calories 375, Protein 29 g, Fat 26 g, Carbohydrate 8 g, Cholesterol 92 mg, Sodium 662 mg

*Exceeds USDA standards for quick freezing.

For a **FAST FACTS VIA FAX**™ copy of this recipe, call 1-800-223-3755 and enter Business Tool 2559.

Most Paesano recipes call for tomatoes, garlic, and olive oil—the "holy trinity" of Sicilian ingredients. This simple, rustic Italian cooking style likely came to the United States with the mass wave of Southern Italian and Sicilian immigration that occurred during the 1920s.

Sherry is a fortified Spanish wine originally produced around 1100 B.C. in the town of Jerez (Scheres) where it was called Xeres wine. Xeres wine was quite popular among the English, who were the first to call it sherry.

Espagnole, or "brown sauce," is one of the seven moterh *("mother") sauces in French cooking. It consists of a rich meat stock, a* mirepoix *of browned vegetables, a brown roux, herbs, and occasionally tomato paste. It is used as the base for dozens of other sauces.*

*For a zesty flavor
alternative, lemon pepper
seasoning may be
substituted for the salt
and pepper.*

*Avoid storing carrots near
apples, as the ethylene gas in
apples can give carrots a
bitter taste.*

*Carrots were introduced
to England during the 1500s
by Flemish weavers who
were fleeing persecution in
Spain. They were in turn
introduced to the Virginia
Colony at Jamestown
around 1608.*

*The Red Bell Pepper Coulis
can be made with drained,
canned roasted red
bell peppers.*

*For line service and takeout,
the chicken breast filet
should not be sliced.*

Spa-Style Vegetable-Stuffed Chicken Rolls

Colorful circles of tender-crisp julienned vegetables are revealed when this
chicken roll is roasted, sliced, and fanned on a bed of bright red bell pepper coulis.

INGREDIENT	QUANTITY		METHOD
	4 servings	24 servings	
1 Tyson Ready-to-Cook Tenderpressed™ Savory Chicken Breast Filets, 6-oz., frozen	4	24	Cover tightly and slack in cooler between 32° and 36°F prior to use.
2 *Red Bell Pepper Coulis*			
Red bell peppers, whole, fresh, cut in half, seeded	4 or 5 (2 cups purée)	25 or 26 (12 cups purée)	Char-grill over high heat for 4 to 5 minutes or until skin is blistered and charred. Remove from grill. Cool and remove skin. Process in food processor until pureed, then transfer to saucepan.
3 Chicken broth, canned	1 cup	6 cups	Add to purée and bring to boil over medium-high heat. Reduce heat and simmer for 50 to 60 minutes or until mixture is reduced by one-third. (Simmer smaller quantity for 18 to 20 minutes.) Stir frequently to avoid scorching. Remove from heat and keep warm.
Basil leaves, fresh, minced	1½ tbsp.	½ cup	
Oregano leaves, fresh, minced	1½ tbsp.	½ cup	
Garlic, fresh, minced	½ tsp.	1 tbsp.	
4 Spinach leaves, large, fresh	8	48	Lightly pound chicken breast filets to even thickness. Line each breast filet with 2 spinach leaves. Arrange ⅓ cup each of julienned vegetables over spinach. Roll each breast into cylinder shape and tie with string to secure. Transfer to oiled roasting pans.
Carrots, fresh, julienne (p. 88)	1⅓ cups	8 cups	
Zucchini, fresh, julienne	1⅓ cups	8 cups	
Onions, fresh, julienne	1⅓ cups	8 cups	
5 Vegetable oil	as needed	as needed	Brush each chicken breast filet with oil and season with salt and pepper.
Salt	1 tsp.	2 tbsp.	
Black pepper, coarse	½ tsp.	1 tbsp.	Cover and roast in preheated conventional oven at 375°F for 40 to 45 minutes or until chicken is no longer pink. (Cover and roast smaller quantity for 30 to 35 minutes.) Or cover and roast in preheated convection oven at 325°F for 30 to 35 minutes. (Cover and roast smaller quantity for 20 to 25 minutes.) Remove from oven. Keep warm above 140°F.

recipe continued on next page . . .

INGREDIENT	QUANTITY		METHOD
	4 servings	24 servings	
6 Basil sprigs, fresh	4	24	*To assemble single serving:* Ladle ½ cup red bell pepper coulis onto plate. Remove string from 1 chicken breast filet and slice into 4 medallions. Fan over coulis. Garnish plate with 1 basil sprig.

Serve with angel hair pasta.

Portion: 13 ounces

Nutritional Data/Portion: Calories 176, Protein 25 g, Fat 3 g, Carbohydrate 14 g, Cholesterol 52 mg, Sodium 1,128 mg

For a **FAST FACTS VIA FAX** copy of this recipe, call 1-800-223-3755 and enter Business Tool 2592.

Tandoori-Style Chicken

A simple method combining yogurt, lemon, garlic, and toasted aromatic spices makes it easy to impart the characteristic tandoori-style flavor and color to chicken with no need for special equipment.

*Submitted by Jeff Trombetta
Yale University Dining Services
New Haven, Conn.*

INGREDIENT	QUANTITY		METHOD
	4 servings	24 servings	
1 Tyson Ready-to-Cook Original IQ*F Breast Quarters, 9.25-oz., frozen	4	24	Place in full-size steam table pans. (Use half-size pan for smaller quantity.)
2 Yogurt, low-fat	1 cup	6 cups	Combine in bowl and mix thoroughly.
Lemon juice, fresh	¼ cup	1½ cups	
Garlic, fresh, minced	1 tbsp.	⅓ cup	
3 Salt, kosher	½ tbsp.	3 tbsp.	Combine in sauté pan and toast over medium heat, stirring constantly, until spices turn dark and start to smoke. Immediately add to yogurt mixture and mix thoroughly.
Coriander, ground	1 tsp.	2 tbsp.	
Cumin, ground	1 tsp.	2 tbsp.	
Chili powder, light	1 tsp.	2 tbsp.	Pour yogurt mixture over chicken, coating thoroughly. Cover and marinate below 40°F for 24 hours. Remove chicken from marinade and transfer to oiled full-size sheet pans. (Use half-size pan for smaller quantity.)
Cayenne pepper, ground	½ tsp.	1 tbsp.	
4 Butter, clarified	½ cup	3 cups	Roast in preheated conventional oven at 375°F for 60 to 75 minutes or until chicken is no longer pink. Baste frequently with butter. (Roast smaller quantity for 50 to 60 minutes.) Or roast in preheated convection oven at 325°F for 30 to 35 minutes. (Roast smaller quantity for 25 to 30 minutes.) Remove from oven. Keep warm above 140°F.
5 Lemon wedges, fresh	4	24	*To assemble single serving:* Place 1 chicken breast quarter on plate. Garnish plate with 1 lemon wedge and 1 parsley sprig.
Parsley sprigs, fresh	4	24	

Serve with fresh carrot salad and rice pilaf.

Portion: 7¼ ounces

Nutritional Data/Portion: Calories 419, Protein 18 g, Fat 38 g, Carbohydrate 2 g, Cholesterol 157 mg, Sodium 515 mg

*Exceeds USDA standards for quick freezing.

For a **FAST FACTS VIA FAX** copy of this recipe, call 1-800-223-3755 and enter Business Tool 2589.

The traditional tandoor oven is a round-top oven made of brick and clay that is used to bake foods directly over a smoky fire. It is used in India and at Indian restaurants throughout the world. Meats cooked tandoori-style are usually skewered to better utilize the tall cylindrical shape of the oven. The average operating temperature of a tandoor oven is about 500°F, which will cook half a chicken in just 5 minutes.

Cornish hens may be substituted for the breast quarters in this recipe.

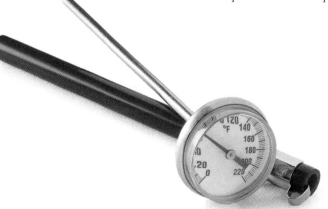

Submitted by Michael A. Jerez
Cafe Madrid–Bella Pasta
Mesa, Ariz.

TOMATILLO SAUCE

	4 servings	24 servings
Tomatillos, fresh, chopped	1 cup	6 cups
Sun-dried tomatoes, dry	½ cup	3 cups
Chicken broth, canned	1 cup	6 cups
Onions, fresh, chopped	½ cup	3 cups
Garlic, fresh, chopped	½ tbsp.	3 tbsp.
Cilantro, fresh, chopped	¼ cup	1½ cups
Black pepper, coarse	⅛ tsp.	¾ tsp.

Combine first three ingredients in saucepan. Bring to boil over high heat. Reduce heat and simmer for 5 to 10 minutes or until tomatoes are tender. Transfer to food processor bowl.

Add remaining ingredients to tomatillo mixture and process until mixture is slightly coarse. Remove from processor bowl and keep warm.

RISOTTO

	4 servings	24 servings
Butter, salted	2 tbsp.	¾ cup
Shallots, fresh, minced	2 tbsp.	¾ cup
Garlic, fresh, minced	1 tbsp.	⅓ cup
Arborio rice, dry	¾ cup	4½ cups
White wine, dry	½ cup	3 cups
Chicken broth, canned	2½ cups	15 cups
Parmesan cheese, grated	¼ cup	1½ cups
Fennel seed, whole	⅛ tsp.	¾ tbsp.

Heat butter in saucepan or stockpot over medium heat. Add shallots and garlic and sauté for 1 to 3 minutes or until tender.

Add rice to shallot mixture and stir until well coated with butter.

Add wine to rice ½ cup at a time. Stir constantly, letting rice absorb wine after each addition.

Add chicken broth to rice ½ cup at a time. Stir constantly, letting rice absorb broth after each addition. Total cooking time should be 20 to 25 minutes.

Add cheese and fennel seed to rice and stir until cheese is melted. Remove from heat and keep warm.

This recipe is pictured on the front cover.

Grilled Chicken and Vegetables with Tomatillo Sauce

The clever fusion of Southwestern and Mediterranean ingredients makes for tantalizing taste and a showy presentation featuring grilled chicken, zucchini, and eggplant; creamy risotto; and a tomatillo sauce made with sun-dried tomatoes.

INGREDIENT	QUANTITY		METHOD
	4 servings	24 servings	
1 Tyson Ready-to-Cook Tenderpressed™ Savory Chicken Breast Filets, 6-oz., frozen	4	24	Brush chicken breast filets with oil and char-grill over medium heat for 7 to 8 minutes on each side or until chicken is no longer pink. Remove from grill and sprinkle with herbs. Keep warm above 140°F.
Olive oil	as needed	as needed	
Fines herbes, dried	2 tsp.	¼ cup	
2 Eggplant slices, fresh, ½-inch-thick	4	24	Lightly salt and allow to stand 10 to 15 minutes. Pat dry.
Salt	as needed	as needed	
3 Olive oil	as needed	as needed	Brush all vegetables, including eggplant, with oil. Char-grill over medium heat for 8 to 12 minutes or until tender. Season vegetables with salt and pepper and keep warm.
Zucchini slices, fresh, ¼-inch-thick, bias-sliced	4	24	
Red onion slices, fresh, ⅓-inch-thick	4	24	
Button mushrooms, fresh, whole	4	24	
Roma tomatoes, fresh, halved lengthwise	2	12	
Fennel bulb, fresh, peeled, quartered	1	6	
Salt	½ tsp.	1 tbsp.	
Black pepper, coarse	¼ tsp.	½ tbsp.	
4 Risotto (see recipe)	2 cups	12 cups	*To assemble single serving:* Place 1 chicken breast filet on plate. Arrange 1 slice each of eggplant, zucchini, and onion, 1 whole mushroom, 1 tomato half, and 1 fennel quarter around chicken. Portion ½ cup risotto and ¼ cup sauce on plate. Sprinkle ½ tablespoon each of tarragon and parsley over entire plate.
Tomatillo Sauce (see recipe)	1⅓ cups	8 cups	
Tarragon, fresh, minced	2 tbsp.	¾ cup	
Parsley, fresh, minced (p. 39)	2 tbsp.	¾ cup	

Portion: 18 ounces
Nutritional Data/Portion: Calories 374, Protein 37 g, Fat 14 g, Carbohydrate 29 g, Cholesterol 82 mg, Sodium 2,319 mg

For a **FAST FACTS VIA FAX** copy of this recipe, call 1-800-223-3755 and enter Business Tool 2569.

Contributors

Our sincere thanks to the following foodservice professionals for sharing their ideas, and their time, in an effort to make each user of *Tastes of the Times* more successful in the pursuit of menuing chicken.

Todd Adelman
Bruce Ahart
MeLissa Alkinburgh
A. William Allen, CEC, DTR
Andina Cafe & Coffee Roastery
Nancy Apollo
Ann Atkins, CHA
Greg Babcock
Barbara Ball
Patricia A. Bando
Noah S. Barton
Ralph Binder
Stephen Blackler
Cuz Blake
Gerald Bonsey, CEC, AAC
James R. Brand, CCM
Sue Brinkhaus
Kirk Brooks
Cathy Brown
Robert Brumfield
Edward Carloni
Charles Carter
Cristo Christu
Tom Clarke
Domenic Cocchia
David Cook
William Cordo
Harry Crane
Gail Cunningham
Anthony Danna, CEC
Susan Dearborn
Jon DeSormeau
Bennie E. Dewberry, Jr., CEC
Louis Johns DiGiovanni
Disneyland
Helen Doherty, RD
June M. Dowling
Sherri Driscoll
Jeffrey Dunham
Michele Duval
Christopher Eiseman
Rob S. Enniss
Michael D. Francis

John B. Franke
Marlin Freyholtz, Jr.
John Gonzales
John R. Gorman
Tammy Grayshock
Doug Hammond
Diane Hanson
Harry Honer
Camp Howard
Mike Jackson
Miles James
Michael A. Jerez
Jutta S. Johnson
Nancy Joseph
Bill Kellermeyer
Lucille Kingsbury, RD
Robert Knudson
Amy Z. Kornfeld
Harvey N. Kornfeld
Thomas Kovacs
Joseph A. Kunst
Robert J. Kurchin
Ronald Francis Lapic
Jim Lassiter, CCC
Francisco Lira
Jeannie Loberg
Geraldine Lombard
Brian Martin
James Martine
Bill Matatall
Brenda McGahagin, RD
John McKeever III
Robert Merrifield
Audrey Mitchell
Michael J. Monti
Jonathan Mortimer
Nick J. Naccarato
Cary Neff
Neiman Marcus, The Zodiac
Eric C. Nielsen, CFM
Janine Disparte Pace
Michael A. Pelillo
Jim Phillip

C. Dennis Pierce
Daniel Pimm
Jeff Popken
Judith Porter
John Randolph
Rosa Randolph
Ennio Riga
Frank J. Roudis
Ma. Emelita G. Rudolph
Enzo Russo
Mary Ryan
Joe Sanford
Jane Schimpf
Anthony Seta
Bonnie B. Severance
Michael Shane
Steven D. Shimmin, CEC
Prescott Slee
Glen A. Smith
Mark R. Smith
Ella Mae Stutz
Edward Sullivan
Matt Swingos
Scott Terle
Steven Tokarz
Jeff Trombetta
Christopher U. Umstead
George Upton
Lee Valentine, Jr.
Rosella Vancura
Stephen VanEgmond
Darren Victory
Tom Vissers
Bud Wagner
Lillian Walsh
Michael D. Ward
D.L. Webster and Staff
Alfred G. Wiederwohl
Paul S. Wilson, FMP
Martin Wolf, CEC
Bob Wright
Glenn Zamet

Index